China and Iran

CHINA AND IRAN

Ancient Partners in a Post-Imperial World

JOHN W. GARVER

UNIVERSITY OF WASHINGTON PRESS Seattle and London

This publication is supported in part by the Donald R. Ellegood International
Publications Endowment.

University of Washington Press
PO Box 50096, Seattle, WA 98145
www.washington.edu/uwpress

Library of Congress Cataloging-in-Publication Data

Garver, John W.
   China and Iran : ancient partners in a post-imperial world / John W. Garver.
      p.   cm.
   Includes bibliographical references and index.
   ISBN 978-0-295-98631-9 (pbk. : alk. paper)
      1. China—Foreign relations—Iran.   2. Iran—Foreign relations—China.
   3. China—Foreign relations—20th century.   I. Title.
   DS740.5.I63G27   2006
   327.51055—dc22   2006004913

The paper used in this publication is acid-free and 90 percent recycled from at least
50 percent post-consumer waste. It meets the minimum requirements of American
National Standard for Information Sciences—Permanence of Paper for Printed Library
Materials, ANSI Z39.48–1984.

Cover:
Chinese stamp: PRC postage stamp issued in 1985 commemorating the 580th anniversary of Cheng He's voyages across the Indian Ocean. Between 1414 and 1432 Chinese
fleets under the command of imperial official Cheng He called three times at Persian
Gulf ports, undertaking the "friendly exchange of gifts" and expanding China-Persia
contacts. Cheng He's missions represented a brief period of Chinese naval supremacy
in the Indian Ocean before being superseded by Portuguese power.

Iranian stamp: Stamp of the Islamic Republic of Iran issued in 1983 showing the sword
of Allah cutting off the evil-doing hand of the Five Permanent members of the U.N.
Security Council extending from the U.N. headquarters building in New York City. The
little finger on the left marked "CHK" represents China. Tehran was then upset by the
United Nations' failure to punish Iraq for its attack on Iran and deemed China a junior
partner in nefarious U.S. schemes.

Contents

List of Illustrations

Preface and Acknowledgments

A study of Sino-Iranian relations is timely because those countries play important roles in two of the most important regions of the world—the energy-rich Persian Gulf and the economic dynamo of East Asia. China is a rising global power and Iran is perhaps the strongest state in the Persian Gulf. The growing global demand for oil, and China's role in generating that demand and Iran's and the Persian Gulf's role in supplying that demand, adds further importance to the relationship. Moreover, there is a long tradition of cooperation between these two important countries. Since the early 1970s Iran and China have cooperated in important areas, and each has deemed that cooperation valuable. This relationship may become even more important as the energy equation between the two intensifies. Added importance derives from the fact that the United States has had great difficulty engaging both China and Iran. Even more, many U.S. conflicts with China involve China's ties with Iran: China's cooperation with Iran's missile, nuclear, chemical, and advanced conventional weapons programs. Dealing with the Iranian nuclear issue in the U.N. Security Council, the International Atomic Energy Agency, or elsewhere will require China's cooperation. The United States' involvement in Iraq and Afghanistan, both bordering on Iran, requires an understanding of Iran's foreign relations, including its relations with a major power and permanent Security Council member like China. In short, the China-Iran relation is an important one for the United States to understand.

The fact that there has been very little scholarship on the Sino-Iranian relation also makes this study timely. In the past forty or so years, only two books on the Sino-Iranian relationship have been published, one in English and one in Chinese. The English book, authored by Indian diplomat A. H. H. Abidi and published in 1982, was an excellent work but was written just after Iran's 1979 revolution and just after Deng Xiaoping's consolidation of power in China. There has been much water under the bridge since then. The Chinese study, written by Zhu Jiejin and published in 1988, deals with the ancient and medieval periods, with only the book's politically correct introduction and conclusion, from the "twenty-centuries of cooperation" reviewed in the body of the book, pointing to implications for contemporary Sino-Iranian relations. The volume you are holding is, I believe, only the second in-depth, book-length, English-language study of the Sino-Iranian relationship and the first that extensively considers the post-1979 period of the Islamic Republic of Iran and post-Mao China.

Another justification for this book is that it touches on the relation between Western countries (which I take the United States to be) and non-Western ones (i.e., both Iran and China). The contemporary clash between radical Islam and Western secularism is one of the main elements of early twenty-first-century world politics, with the Islamic Republic of Iran being one of the leading exponents of Islamic fundamentalism (though not Osama Bin Laden's Wahhabi-inspired terrorism). Understanding the relation between the People's Republic of China and the Islamic Republic of Iran illuminates one aspect of China's relation to this important global political dynamic.

An additional reason for this book is more existential. Since I left the American Midwest where I was born and raised and began roving Eurasia, I have been intrigued by the great, magnificent non-Western civilizations arrayed about that region: China, India, and Persia. Understanding the interactions of those nations and civilizations with one another, with the West, with Europe and its outlying daughters, has been a life-long quest. A previous study, *Protracted Contest: Sino-Indian Rivalry in the Twentieth Century*, dealt with the China-India relationship. This book is a continuation of the quest to fathom the relations among these ancient, great, non-Western civilizations. Perhaps in an era in which modern technology is shrinking the globe and bringing the West and these ancient non-Western nations together with phenomenal speed, such understanding will be useful. Even failing that, it is an intriguing problem. As a scholar I have tried to set aside my American perceptual-normative lenses and understand the relation between China and Iran as the leaders of those two countries have understood it.

Thanks are due to a number of people who assisted the creation of this book. Robert Sutter of Georgetown University, Gilbert Rozman of Princeton

University, Ahmad Faruqui of the American Institute of International Studies, Evan Medeiros of RAND Corporation, Penelope Prime of Kennesaw State University, and Mark Gorwitz of WMD Proliferation critiqued various chapters. Special thanks are due to Steven I. Levine, who criticized the entire manuscript and challenged me on more tendentious propositions. Rouhollah K. Ramazani, professor emeritus at the University of Virginia, served as a guide and critic on Iranian issues. At various points my research was assisted by Greg Knight, Tom King, and Elizabeth Frisa at the U.S. Department of State; Judith Japhe, Fred Mokhtari, Phil Saunders, Jack Gill, and Ray Takeyh at the National Defense University; and Henry Sokolski of the Nonproliferation Policy Education Center. The Stockholm International Peace Research Institute in Sweden made available to me its large clippings file on international arms transfers. Special thanks are due to Alyson J. K. Bailes, director of SIPRI, for arranging that visit, and to Dr. Seimon Wezeman, who graciously provided aggregate statistical data on Iran's arms purchases. Professor Jing-dong Yuan at the Monterey Institute of International Studies assisted in achieving access to the rich online database on nuclear proliferation issues maintained by MIIS and the Nuclear Threat Initiative. Mikkal Herberg with the National Bureau of Asia Research advised on various energy-related matters. Bao Shuming, director of the China Economic Data Project at the University of Michigan, assisted with Chinese statistical data. Golam Reza Afkhami of the Foundation for Iranian Studies in Bethesda, Maryland, opened to me his personal library. The resources and staff of the Library of Congress in Washington, D.C., were also invaluable. The wide array of databases available via LOC computers were especially useful; I found there many articles from obscure publications not available elsewhere.

In Atlanta, Martha Saghini and Mary Axford in the interlibrary-loan department and Barbara Walker of the government documents department of the Georgia Institute of Technology library provided crucial support. Ms. Walker's assistance in utilizing effectively Tech's large collection of documents on microfiche from the Federal Broadcast Information Service was especially important. Nikil Kulkarni, a master's student from India in Tech's Sam Nunn School of International Affairs, served as a reliable and innovative research assistant during the 2004–5 academic year. Emory University's library was also extremely useful. The Nunn School's director, William J. Long, made the usual efficient and prompt arrangements permitting externally funded faculty research.

Internationally, I thank Professor Han Hua of Beijing University's School of International Affairs for hosting and arranging a research visit to Beijing in fall 2004. Professor Yitzhak Shichor of Haifa University and Hebrew

University in Israel arranged a similar research visit to Israel, and Uday Bhaskar, deputy director of the Institute for Defense Studies and Analysis, arranged a research visit to New Delhi early in 2005. Special thanks are due to Dr. Mustafa Zahrani, first with the permanent mission of the Islamic Republic of Iran to the United Nations in New York City and later the director of the Institute for Political and International Studies in Tehran, for arranging a research visit to Tehran in fall 2004. This study benefited immensely from that visit. In Beijing, Tehran, New Delhi, and Tel Aviv numerous scholars and diplomats, including several former high-ranking diplomats with first-hand knowledge of Sino-Iranian ties, shared their experiences and views with me. Although these sources must remain anonymous, this book was crafted with the visages of these honest servants of their nations very much in mind and in an effort to represent in a fair fashion their countries' policies.

Finally, the Smith Richardson Foundation generously provided financial support releasing me from two semesters' teaching duties in which to write this book and making possible several international and domestic research trips.

China and Iran

1 / The Spirit of Sino–Iranian Relations:
Civilization and Power

When delving into Sino-Iranian relations, one quickly encounters an abundance of rhetoric about ancient civilizations, millennia of friendly interactions, common oppression at Western hands, and so on. One also encounters expressions of esteem for the other's influence. What is one to make of this rhetoric? Should it be set aside, and relations explained entirely in terms of concrete interests? It is clear there existed such interests underpinning Sino-Iranian cooperation in various periods: containing the Soviet Union in the 1970s, countering U.S. hegemonism in the 1990s, developing the economies and military forces in their own countries, supplying and consuming energy, and so on. It also quickly becomes apparent that it was these interests, and not free-floating civilizational solidarities, that primarily motivated Beijing and Tehran to cooperate. And yet the two sides fell back repeatedly to this civilizational rhetoric, as though it reflected a basic meeting of the minds, a deep kinship. The more prominent the interaction, or the more difficult the situation facing the two powers, the greater the use of this civilizational rhetoric. At critical junctures—opening or repairing relations, initiating new areas of cooperation, and addressing questions of war and peace—the two sides typically resorted to this rhetoric. Rhetoric of civilizational solidarity seemed to be a sort of emotional bonding that played a significant role in the relationship. The rhetoric seemed to be useful. It seemed to lubricate the process of Sino-Iranian cooperation.

In thinking through this problem, I concluded that this civilizational solidarity constitutes a sort of spirit of Sino-Iranian relations, a worldview and state of mind used to frame relationships. Civilizational rhetoric functions as symbols used to evoke underlying value-laden beliefs related to the modern histories of the two nations. The spirit of Sino-Iranian relations arises, I believe, from the fact that both were among the most accomplished, powerful, and durable kingdoms created by humankind since the beginning of urban settlement—and that these rich and proud kingdoms were brought low and stripped of their earlier high status by Western powers during the modern era. At least, this is the belief shared by Iranian and Chinese nationalist narratives.

There is a tendency to dismiss Chinese and Iranian civilizational rhetoric as unimportant boilerplate, opening lines, gong clanging, or atmospheric music. I take a different view. I believe this rhetoric provides symbols reflecting and linked to belief systems that in turn trigger certain emotional and normative responses. For both China and Iran this rhetoric is linked to beliefs about what happened over the past several centuries, along with corollary resentments, hatreds, and sympathies for others. What is involved is the construction of self and group identity—beliefs about who one is, what one aspires to, and about whom others are and their aspirations.

Reference to a similar American civilizational spirit may clarify my argument. A sense that America has a mission to advance liberty in the world has run like a red line throughout its history. That idea has taken many different forms, from a "city on the hill" in colonial Massachusetts, to an "empire of liberty" in the early nineteenth century, to the anti-Communist crusade of the Cold War, to the neoconservative argument for intervention in Iraq in 2003. That American self-identity of mission of liberty did not translate always and everywhere into u.s. foreign policy; when it did, that translation was not necessarily direct or simple. Nor does reference to this American civilizational spirit rule out reference to self-interest or self-aggrandizement. United States foreign policy was often a complex mix of idealistic mission and crass self-interest. Chinese relations with Iran are similar, I have concluded. Proper understanding requires appreciation of both beliefs and interests.

I do not mean to suggest that Iran looms as large in the Chinese spirit as "freedom" does in the American. Few Chinese know or think much about Iran.[1] The Chinese spiritual equivalent of "liberty" in American civilization is the deep sense of victimization and grievance associated with China's "century of national humiliation." But when the Chinese foreign policy elite does think about Iran, they tend to do so in terms of China's fall via national humiliation from ancient greatness. They tend to see in Iran's modern fall from greatness confirmation of their beliefs about China's national humiliation, and China's modern relation with Iran is seen as part of China's struggle to blot out and overcome its putative national humiliation.

There are several discrete propositions that Chinese analysts and the leaders they advise about Sino-Iranian relations use to frame "Iran" as part of China's national humiliation narrative. These are

1. Iran, like China, is a brilliant, accomplished non-Western nation every bit the equal of Western nations over the sweep of human history and with no reason to feel inferior to, or act deferentially toward, Western nations.
2. Iran, like China, was aggressed against and humiliated by Western powers, and both nations understand the bitterness of that experience.
3. The same Western nations that humiliated China and Iran in the modern era still aspire today to keep them weak and for this reason are unhappy about close cooperation between them.
4. A world free from Western hegemonism will include a strong and rich cooperative relation between China and Iran.
5. In a world free from the aftermath of China's and Iran's national humiliation, the status of each in its respective region would be much greater than it is at present, and the role of arrogant Western powers in those regions would be correspondingly reduced.

These shared civilizational beliefs lead to the conclusion that the existing world order, created and still dominated by Western powers, is profoundly unjust and must be replaced by a new, more just order—the post-imperial world of the subtitle of this book. This is a sentiment shared, in different forms, by diverse Chinese and Iranian leaders: Shah Mohammad Reza Pahlavi and Mao Zedong, Deng Xiaoping and Ayatollah Ruhollah Khomeini, Jiang Zemin and Ayatollah Seyed Mohammad Ali Hoseyn Khamenei. (Khomeini should not be confused with his successor, Khamenei.) Again, I stress: these sentiments do not seem to determine policy. That is done by practical interests. Certain policy statements do seem to be primarily symbolic affirmations of these civilizational beliefs, for example, Beijing's bedrock affirmation of the handling of Persian Gulf affairs by the Persian Gulf states themselves. But it is difficult to identify practical consequences of even this statement, which seems, rather, to be essentially a symbolic affirmation of deep, shared beliefs.

Ann-Marie Brady has pointed out that a common Chinese diplomatic method is to seek "common points" in dealing with foreigners and then use those commonalties, along with positive incentives in the form of pleasant and useful interactions with Chinese officials, to develop "positive sentiment" (*ganqing*) toward China. This *ganqing* is, in turn, used to develop "friendship" (*youyi*) toward China, which is in turn operationalized to mean support for the policy goals elucidated by the Chinese Communist Party (CCP) at that particular time.[2] Brady's formulation captures very well one function of Beijing's stress on civilizational commonalties in Sino-Iranian relations. Use of rhetorical symbols of civilizational solidarity creates *ganqing* between Chinese and Iranian leaders.

CIVILIZATION, NATIONAL TRAUMA, AND POWER

The concepts of *civilization* and *power* are useful for analyzing the two components of the spirit of Sino-Iranian ties. *Civilization* refers to a way of viewing the world, the self and others, in terms of supranational groupings differentiated by distinctive clusters of values and lifestyles. *Power* refers to the relative coercive capabilities of centralized political organizations known as states. Ideas of civilization and power have deeply influenced the thinking of both China and Iran about their mutual relationship. Perceived interests of state and nation that constitute the substance of each country's foreign policy toward the other *cannot* be derived directly from considerations of either civilization or state power. Yet the complex of ideas associated with each of these overarching concepts forms the *context* of each side's consideration of interests and derivative policies toward the other.

Regarding civilization, people today live at the end of a five-century-long period of Western domination of world affairs. The European countries began acquiring a decisive technological lead over other regions of the world circa 1500 CE and combined this growing technological advantage with a peculiarly dynamic form of society. This combination soon pushed Europeans into neighborhoods of Iran and China. The Portuguese led the way, combining revolutionary technologies of seafaring and gunpowder firearms to produce a revolution in military affairs. A Portuguese emissary first arrived on the Island of Hormuz at the mouth of the Persian Gulf in 1489 to collect intelligence on the main spice-trading centers in that region. In 1507 a Portuguese armada of six ships under the command of Afonso de Albuquerque, one of Portugal's main empire builders in Asia, arrived in the Gulf to begin the process of Portuguese expansion there.[3] After demanding that Hormuz pay tribute to Portugal, Albuquerque pushed farther east, crossing the eastern Indian Ocean and reaching the East Indies and seizing Malacca in 1511. In 1514 Portuguese empire builders reached southern China, and in 1517 the king of Portugal dispatched a mission to the "king of China"—an appellation of egregious lèse-majesté from the perspective of the Chinese *imperial* court. Within a few years the Portuguese had ensconced themselves at Macao. In 1515 Albuquerque set sail from Goa, India (which had also become part of Portugal's new Indian Ocean empire), and returned with a more powerful fleet to Hormuz. This time Albuquerque brought that rich spice-trade center under firm Portuguese control. Lisbon, the new terminus of the seaborne spice route, quickly grew rich and became the capital of one of the leading empires in the world. Deprived of its previous monopoly on Europe's spice supply, the Islamic Middle East began its long economic decline.

Other European empire builders soon followed the Portuguese example: Spanish, Dutch, English, and French. By 1700 English commercial and naval power dominated the Gulf. Russian expansion across Siberia (a process that began in 1581 and reached the Sea of Okhotsk by 1639) was part of the same wave of European expansion. While over land, rather than over water as with the more westerly European states, Russia's conquest of Siberia was premised on the same advantage of a decisive lead in gunpowder technology that enabled tiny Portugal to impose its will on vast kingdoms around the Indian Ocean littoral. Russian expansion would soon abut Russian-ruled territories against both the Chinese and the Persian empires. The Treaty of Nerchinsk in 1689 delineated Russian and Chinese boundaries in the Far East, establishing a status quo that endured until Chinese power declined over a century and a half later. Between 1803 and 1828 Russia expanded into what are now the countries of Georgia, Armenia, and Azerbaijan, making Russian power contiguous with northwestern Iran. In 1858 and 1860 Russia seized further large swaths of Siberia from China, including what is today the Russian Maritime Province. During the 1870s and 1880s Russia conquered the khanates constituting today's Uzbekistan and Turkmenistan, thereby establishing Russian power on Iran's northeastern border. Meanwhile, maritime powers Britain, the United States, France, and Germany expanded their presence in China's and Iran's coastal areas.

While the European eruption that began in the late fifteenth century was extremely complex, the aspect germane to this study was this: Europeans began investing and pressing upon Asia; Asians did not invest and press upon Europe. By 1900 most of Asia was under European rule. And in areas where Europeans did not rule directly—including both Persia and China—they exercised extraordinary influence.

The European, Western empires did not initially have the capacity to impose their will on such powerful states as the Safavid empire of Persia (1502–1722) or the Ming and Qing empires of China (1368–1644 and 1644–1911, respectively). (The territorial expanse of several of these empires is depicted in figure 1.1, presented later in this chapter.) Nor was it immediately apparent that traditional forms of social organization would prove inadequate and that Asian societies would have to abandon many ancient ways if their polities were to escape European domination. By the middle of the nineteenth century, however, both Persia and China confronted rapidly deepening crises in the face of Western power and the social, economic, and political forms that generated that superior Western power.

The crises of Persia and China in confronting Western power were remarkably similar—at least as constructed by the nationalist narratives of the two countries. Speaking broadly, Western powers penetrated ever more deeply into Persian and Chinese empires, especially following the opening of the Suez Canal in 1869 and the development of steam-powered, propeller-driven, iron-built ships about the same time. In Persia, the northern part of the country became a Russian sphere of economic and political influence, while the southern part was a British sphere. In China, efforts by China's government to keep out or limit the foreign presence were defeated by repeated Western military blows. China was forced to accept Western-dictated relations embodied in a system of treaties between China and the Western powers. By 1900 China had been transformed into spheres of influence of a half-dozen Western powers— and Japan, an aspiring and adept student of Western ways. In both Persia and China corrupt officials were often willing to facilitate for personal gain the penetration of Western interests. Fringe lands of both the Persian and Chinese empires were stripped away. Iran lost Azerbaijan, Armenia, and Dagestan to Russia. China lost Hong Kong to Britain, Taiwan to Japan, and the northern watershed of the Amur River to Russia, while the tributaries of Vietnam and Korea were lost respectively to France and Japan.

In both Persia and China deepening foreign penetration stirred popular resistance—again, according to the dominant nationalist narratives of the two countries. In both countries traditional political institutions lost legitimacy and finally collapsed about the same time. Persia experienced a series of aborted attempts at parliamentary and constitutional government, rebellions, martial law, and dictatorships between 1906 and 1921. That process finally culminated in the establishment of a new dynasty by Reza Khan Pahlavi in 1925 dedicated to authoritarian, secular, military-backed Westernization along the lines laid out by Mustafa Kemal Ataturk of Turkey. In China an attempt at constitutional monarchy collapsed in 1898 to be followed by republican revolution in 1911. This in turn was followed by a period of fragmentation before a modernizing, military-dominated government led by Chiang Kai-shek began recentralizing power in 1927.

There is not, of course, an exact parallel between the Chinese and the Iranian experience. China reached the nadir of its national degradation not at European but at Japanese hands in the 1930s and 1940s. Iran's tormenters were entirely European (at least since the 1790s). Moreover, Iran reached its nadir considerably later than China—at least in the orthodox, Islamicist narrative upheld in Iran since that country's Islamic revolution in 1979. According to that narrative, the 1941–79 rule of Mohammad Reza Pahlavi (the son of Reza Khan) constituted Iran's nadir, nothing less than an enslavement of Iran by the United States.

From the standpoint of the dominant Iranian and Chinese historical narratives, the encounter with Western power adumbrated above constituted a deeply painful national humiliation. Great, powerful nations that had created empires controlling vast regions of West and East Asia for many centuries, spanning three millennia, were destroyed by aggressive Western powers intruding into regions of Asia distant from those Western nations. Moreover, the Persian and Chinese empires were veritable treasure-houses of civilizational achievements. In areas of art, architecture, philosophy, technology, religion, and government, the great Persian and Chinese empires were in no way inferior to the small and frequently warring principalities of Europe. Only in the modern era had China and Persia fallen into a position of inferior capacity that allowed them to be humiliated by the West.

This deeply felt awareness of this national humiliation by the West typically finds expression in rhetorical symbols accompanying high-profile or important Sino-Iranian interactions. The first step toward establishment of the modern Sino-Iranian relation, for example, was a visit by Princess Ashraf Pahlavi, the shah's younger sister, to China in April 1971, shortly after the u.s. Ping-Pong team visited China. In his speech welcoming Princess Ashraf Premier Zhou Enlai stressed the ancient ties between the two countries and the bringing low of both great countries by "foreign aggression." "Long standing historical contacts and traditional friendship have existed between China and Iran," Zhou said, dating back "more than two thousand years." In modern times, however, "both China and Iran have been subjected to foreign aggression and oppression and have gone through similar sufferings."[4] Five months later a *Renmin ribao* (People's Daily—the newspaper of the Central Committee of the Chinese Communist Party) editorial greeting the establishment of ambassadorial relations between China and Iran sounded the same theme: "Friendly contacts between [China and Iran] date back more than two thousand years through the famous 'silk road.'" Those friendly contacts were interrupted by "imperialist obstructions and sabotage," and "both the Chinese and Iranian peoples were subjected to imperialist ravage and are now still confronted with the common task of opposing imperialist aggression and safeguarding state sovereignty and national independence."[5] When Empress Farah

and Prime Minister Amir Abbas Hoveyda visited Beijing a year after normalization, Zhou returned to the same theme in his banquet speech: "Iran
is a country with a long history and an ancient civilization. The industrious,
courageous and talented Iranian people created the splendid Persian culture,
which remains a rich legacy for mankind and adds luster to the treasury of
world civilization." "Friendly contacts and traditional friendship between the
Chinese and Iranian peoples date back to ancient times."[6] In her reply-speech,
Empress Farah played the same themes. When China's paramount leader Hua
Guofeng visited Iran in August 1978, he too stressed that both China and
Iran were ancient civilizations humiliated in modern times by "imperialist
aggression and oppression." Both peoples had waged heroic and ultimately
victorious struggles against that oppression. These commonalties, plus
"twenty centuries" of friendship between the Chinese and Iranian peoples,
provided a solid basis for continuing cooperation, Hua said.[7]

The same themes of ancient civilizations continued after Iran's Islamic revolution. For example, during the first visit to China by a top-level Islamic
Republic of Iran (IRI) leader, Ali Akbar Hashemi Rafsanjani, in 1985, the chairman of the Standing Committee of China's National People's Congress
(China's parliament), Peng Zhen, noted that both China and Iran "had had
similar experiences as victims of imperialism and colonialism and were subjected to hegemonic threat today."[8] Premier Zhao Ziyang and Rafsanjani
agreed that China and Iran were both "Third World countries with similar
histories" and shared many views on international issues. Rafsanjani noted
that both countries had "shared experience of the colonialist scourge," and
this convinced him that China would not encroach on the interests of Iran
while developing relations with it.[9] When IRI president Seyed Ali Khamenei
visited China in 1989, his counterpart People's Republic of China (PRC) president Yang Shangkun stressed that because the two countries shared a "common history" they had common duties in the world today. Both countries
had been engaged in a constant struggle against imperialism and had both
succeeded in their campaigns, Yang told Khamenei.[10]

When President Yang Shangkun made in 1991 the first visit by a Chinese
head of state to Iran since the establishment of the IRI, he traced the "two-
thousand years of friendly exchanges" between two peoples.[11] A decade later
IRI president Mohammad Khatami visited Beijing as part of an effort to repair
a major downturn in Sino-Iranian relations. Khatami was fulsome in resort
to rhetoric of civilizational solidarity. Iran and China were "cradles of two
great civilizations," Khatami said, and both had to "reconstruct their futures
by relying on their own indigenous culture."[12] The June 2000 joint communiqué issued by presidents Khatami and Jiang Zemin referred to China and

Iran as "two great civilizations in Asia," endorsed the Iranian call for making 2001 the United Nations' "year of dialogue among civilizations," and "stressed the necessity of respect for human rights and for the history, culture, and religions of each country in defending and developing [those] human rights and fundamental freedoms."[13] "Dialogue among civilizations" was Khatami's counter to the "clash of civilizations" thesis that Washington was supposedly pursuing, while the endorsement of country-specific standards of human rights was a rebuttal of the Western notion of universal rights. When PRC State Council member Wu Yi visited Tehran a bit later, she too noted that, "as countries with ancient civilizations, both China and Iran have made great contributions to mankind."[14]

A corollary of common pride in ancient accomplishments and resentment of treatment by the West is determination by both Iran and China to restore their well-deserved high international status destroyed by putative humiliation at Western hands. Both China and Iran are inspired by a sense that their outstanding civilizational achievements over long stretches of history entitle them to an esteemed rank in the community of states, and a sense that the current international order, dominated as it is by the West, that does not accord them such a status is profoundly unjust. This drive for restored national/civilizational greatness has existed, I believe, under both Mao Zedong and Deng Xiaoping and under both Iran's pre-1979 Kingdom of Iran and the IRI, although manifest in different ways during each of these periods. Regarding foreign policies of Shah Mohammad Pahlavi, for example, R. K. Ramazani, the doyen of Iran foreign policy studies, concluded, "Memories of a glorious ancient civilization and an imperial past have a significant bearing on the foreign policy of the Kingdom of Iran. Contemporary policy makers . . . like . . . earlier rulers . . . in one way or another reveal the abiding influence of past memories on foreign policy behavior."[15] After 1979 the leader of Iran's Islamic revolution, Ayatollah Ruhollah Khomeini, put religious purposes ahead of national interests, according to Ramazani. Khomeini viewed Iran as a servant of a greater, transnational Islamic revolution, although the largely Shiite Iranian nation would perforce be the leading force and guiding center of that revolution. Since Khomeini's death in 1989, Iran's leaders have become increasingly pragmatic in their approach to the Persian Gulf, dropping their earlier efforts to foster Islamic revolution in the Gulf countries. Yet "Iran's long-term goal in the Persian Gulf" remains, according to Ramazani, "regional security *maintained by the littoral powers*."[16] Since Iran is the most powerful of those littoral states, it would play a leading role in a post-Western Persian Gulf regional security system.

After supreme leader Khomeini's passing, IRI president Rafsanjani laid out the new, more secular vision of pax Iranica in the Gulf. Turbulence in the Gulf had historically been due, Rafsanjani argued, to the intervention of external great powers in that region. Because of its rich energy resources and strategic location, "it is impossible for there to be a world power that does not look toward the Persian Gulf with some degree of interest." Thus, "World history has been the ceaseless effort of the great powers to establish their hegemony over the Persian Gulf, and their fears that their rivals might gain control of the region." "The expansionist countries of the world have opted in the past to create some sort of policeman and arm one power in order to serve as the guardian of the region" or to establish their own direct, military presence in the region. Both approaches were "absolutely unacceptable" to the IRI:

> From our viewpoint, this method of "fomenting trouble between neighbors so that the masters will be requested to establish a presence in the region" is reprehensible. This completely violates the great humanitarian and Islamic traditions and principles of the region. To seek protection from others out of fear of one's own neighbors or brothers or co-religionists is not in accordance with the spirit of Islam and freedom loving people. Why should humans put themselves in a position where they fear their neighbors and invite foreigners by saying "come and protect us" or "why don't you settle the dispute between us here." This is despicable. It demonstrates one's immaturity, one's ignorance and is a sign of human barbarism. These solutions are only for the extremely ignorant individuals who fight on the street with knives until a policeman intervenes and breaks them up.[17]

The countries of the Persian Gulf littoral should work together in a spirit of friendship, mutual respect, and compromise to make the region secure, according to Rafsanjani. Differences should be settled among the countries involved and via sincere dialogue and in a peaceful manner. Countries of the region should conciliate and not provoke each other. It was true, Rafsanjani acknowledged, that Iran was among the most influential countries of the Gulf. Yet this would have no influence on friendly regional cooperation: "Although we are the largest country in the region, although we have the longest coastline, and although we are one of the oldest nations in the region, we are willing to cooperate with the smaller nations of the region—even if others are reluctant to do so."[18] Again, implicit in the withdrawal of extraregional big powers from the Persian Gulf was the de facto domination by the more powerful littoral states of that region.

As for China, Mao Zedong's vision of China as the center of first the Asian and then (after the split with Moscow circa 1960) the world revolution had certain similarities to Khomeini's vision of Iran as the center of the global Islamic revolution. Both Mao and Khomeini envisioned their nations as providing the model, correct guidance, and support for a revolution against the unjust, Western-dominated, and Western-created international order. After Mao's death, as after Khomeini's in Iran, China's leaders downgraded transnational revolutionary objectives, giving primary emphasis to national interests. But post-Mao China remains inspired by the notion that China should be recognized as the leading country of Asia and one of the leading countries of the world—a position China once enjoyed but unjustly lost through the process of national humiliation—and that China is now engaged in restoring itself to its rightful position of high status and power.

It must once again be emphasized that these vague civilizational urges are not necessarily translated into policy—no more than the American civilizational impulse to spread freedom and democracy around the world is necessarily translated into u.s. policy. Prior to 1971, civilizational commonalties between China and Iran were not sufficient to bring the two countries together. Only changes in the international environment in the 1960s creating common Chinese and Iranian national interests sufficed to do that. Even after 1979, when Iran's Islamic revolution maximized convergence of the anti-Western perspectives of Tehran and Beijing, civilizational sentiments frequently clashed with other practical and important interests. In 1997 civilizational impulses did not suffice to prevent substantial Chinese disengagement from Iran. And when policy application of civilizational impulses does occur, methods of expression may be circuitous. Yet this sense of Sino-Iranian civilizational solidarity did infuse China-Iran relations. It provided, to repeat, the spirit of Sino-Iranian relations.

TWENTY CENTURIES OF FRIENDLY COOPERATION: THE NARRATIVE OF SINO-IRANIAN FRIENDSHIP

The narrative of Sino-Iranian relations extolled by Beijing and Tehran stresses the long, friendly, mutually beneficial, cooperative interactions between the two countries. Contact between Han China and the Parthian empire of Persia began in 139 BCE, when a Chinese envoy named Zhang Qian traveled west to the northern bank of the Oxus River (today known as the Amu Darya River and roughly on the border between Turkmenistan and Uzbekistan) to contact the Yuezhi tribes who were then posed to destroy the Hellenistic kingdom of Bactria. The Han court had sent Zhang Qian to contact the Yuezhi in search of allies against the powerful horse-riding people, the Xiongnu, then bedeviling China. Zhang Qian did not reach Parthia, but acquired detailed knowledge of that powerful kingdom, which he conveyed back to the Han capital at Changan.[19] A period of intense diplomatic activity and development of trade relations between the Han and Parthian empires began via what came to be called the Silk Road (actually a dozen or so caravan routes). During the pre-Islamic period Persians played a major role in organizing trade between China and the regions to its west. Large numbers of Persians, and later Arabs, settled in Guangzhou and Hanoi (then a part of the Chinese empire). The highly Persianized kingdom of Kushan (a post-Bactrian, post-Yuezhi state established in the Oxus region) became the main center for transmission of Buddhism to China in the second through the fourth centuries CE. The first translator of the Buddhist sutras into Chinese was a Parthian (Persian) prince from Kushan. Other Persian and Indian Buddhist missionaries arrived in China via Kushan. Zoroastrianism, Nestorian Christianity, and Manichaeism were additional Persian influences on China during the sixth and seventh centuries. Persian influences on Tang China were extensive. Magic routines from Persia were highly appreciated in China.[20] Persian poetry influenced China's great Tang dynasty poetry. The game of polo came from Persia and found great favor in Chinese imperial courts. The ritual dances performed in Zoroastrian "fire temples" roused Chinese interest. Persian cuisine found favor in China and greatly influenced Chinese cooking. In the words of one authority, "There was [in Tang China] a great vogue especially in the first half of the eighth century for Iranian objects and customs of all kinds: food stuffs, clothing, furniture, music, and dancing."[21]

Trade between China and the pre-Islamic Sassanian Persian empire was substantial. Large quantities of Sassanian coins have been discovered in China. By the early ninth century Chinese porcelain was being exported to the Near East, mostly by sea, creating a flow that would become for several centuries a major element of the emerging global economic system. Chinese celedons, *san cai* (three-color) ware, and white ware were highly sought after. So great was that demand that Chinese supply was inadequate, leading to the development of a large Persian porcelain industry to supply unmet demand.

Contact between Persia and China grew even closer after the Mongol conquest of both countries in the thirteenth century. Persian officers and officials served the Yuan Mongol imperium in China, and Chinese personnel served the Il-Khanate Mongol imperium in Persia. Chinese and Persian knowledge of one another became much deeper. There were nearly annual diplomatic missions between Yuan China and Il-Khanate Persia. Chinese astronomical instruments and knowledge, printing, and paper money were transmitted to Persia and the Arab Near East during this period, while Arabic and Persian alchemy, mathematics, Euclidean geometry, medicine, and pharmacology were transmitted to China. Artistic exchanges were also vital. The cobalt blue pigment that became the basis for the blue color in China's famous blue and white porcelain was introduced to China as "Mohammedan blue" from the Near East, possibly Persia. By the time of China's Ming dynasty in the fourteenth century, large quantities of Chinese blue and white ware were being exported to Persia and the Arab Near East. Once again Chinese products appealed to Persian tastes. So popular did blue and white ware become that, as with the first wave of Chinese porcelains in the ninth century, the Persian ceramics industry expanded to copy Chinese products and supply unmet demand. For several centuries Persian blue and white ware was a mainstay of world trade—until overwhelmed by revived Chinese, Japanese, and Dutch competition in the seventeenth century.[22]

Contemporary Sino-Iranian interactions are decorated with references to this rich history of earlier cooperation. It is indisputable that China and Persia have a long and rich relationship. Factual accuracy is not, however, the crux. The factual elements constituting a narrative may be accurate, without addressing the meaning conveyed by that narrative. One set of facts can be used to convey to a group of people one sense of who they are, while another set of facts can be used to convey a very different sense of group identity. The crucial question (at least for the purposes here) is not whether the facts so arranged are accurate, but what meaning does a particular arrangement of facts convey. Simply put, why do Chinese and Iranians constantly invoke these particular facts, and what is signified by that invocation? In this sense the "facts" of ancient exchanges between China and Iran, and contemporary references to those facts, are, I believe, symbols evoking the civilizational commonalties outlined earlier.

Recounting the rich record of mutually beneficial, peaceful, premodern interaction does several things within the framework of state-sponsored nationalist ideologies of the two countries. First, such references underline the civilizational accomplishments of China and Persia and the fact that neither was inferior to the West. If the West has served during the post-1979 period as the "other" for both the PRC and the IRI—that is, what each was not, at least at the level of state-supported ideologies—China and Iran served for each other as part of the in-group, the group of which one was a part, and that stood in contradistinction to the Western "other." Ancient China and Iran each provides the other a mirror in which each sees a reflection of its own ancient glory and affirmation of self-worth against the putatively arrogant and condescending attitudes of the Western nations. Second, narrating the facts of ancient Chinese-Iranian cooperation suggests that that relationship is natural, nonobjectionable, and positive. Destruction of this natural,

positive relationship was part of the Western "humiliation" of both countries, just as contemporary Western objection to Sino-Iranian relations
reflects lingering Western attitudes of superiority toward both countries.
Third, stress on the peaceful nonmilitary nature of Sino-Iranian intercourse
conveys implicit moral superiority over the violent, imperialist Western powers. It also demonstrates that there is no fundamental conflict of interest
between China and Iran and therefore no barrier to cooperation.

The politically correct introduction and conclusion to an authoritative 1988
Chinese history of Sino-Iranian relations illustrates the contemporary political utility of the record of Sino-Iranian cooperation. The author of that study
confessed to having been "assigned" (*weituo*) to write the volume in order to
"promote Sino-Iranian mutual understanding and friendship, and strengthen
the unity of the people of the two countries in the antihegemonist struggle."[23]
The bulk of the book documented ancient and medieval friendly exchanges
between China and Persia. The conclusion to the book made the point that
those relations were "interrupted by imperialist sabotage and disruption" and
that "China and Iran both suffered from aggression and oppression by imperialism and colonialism." Today they face the "need to unite and oppose hegemonism." "This is the objective of the common struggle," the book concluded.[24]

Another example of the use of ancient civilizational accomplishments and
modern oppression by Western imperialists to foster *ganqing*, and thus
friendship, was an eighty-one-page booklet published in Iran in 1973, just as
Beijing was pushing for closer antihegemony cooperation with Tehran.[25] The
booklet was written by Iranian parliamentary senator Abbas Massoudi, who
was then the publisher of one of Iran's largest newspapers, *Ettela'at*, and had
been invited to tour Cultural Revolution–era China. While on tour Massoudi
was instructed by high-ranking Chinese officials, including China's leading
establishment intellectual Guo Morou and China's perennial Iran-hand He
Ying, on China's view of the world. The booklet chronicled both the ancient
interactions between Chinese and Persian civilizations and the oppression of
China by Western and Japanese imperialism in the nineteenth and twentieth centuries. The booklet began: "Iran and China boast of very ancient relations. There is evidence that their historic and cultural contacts date back to
several centuries before Christ. The two countries talk of relations, which
might well be over 2,500 years or 3,000 years old."[26]

Massoudi explained that "in every society and gathering of the Chinese I
entered I found them speaking highly of their proud historical background
and the regeneration of ties with Iran." His "Chinese friends," Massoudi found,
paid "great attention to and [showed] interest in Iran."[27] His Chinese friends
also regaled Massoudi with tales of abuse by Westerners. At one banquet,

Massoudi was told the legendary but apocryphal story of a "no dogs or Chinese allowed" sign at a park on the foreign-dominated Shanghai waterfront. "One Chinese told me," Massoudi recounted, "that at one of the large parks near the beach in Shanghai [the foreigners] had installed a sign: 'Dogs permitted, Chinese prohibited.' After the change in regime, this sign was replaced by another that read: 'Dogs permitted, imperialists prohibited.' Many indignities were inflicted on the Chinese by the foreigners, be they the Japanese, or the Americans or the Europeans."[28] Thus it was that "the whole country rose in revolt under the banner of Mao Tse-tung."[29]

The director of Asian and African Affairs at China's Ministry of Foreign Affairs, He Ying opened talks with Senator Massoudi by stressing the common role the two countries had played "since ancient times using their respective influence to nullify foreign domination in their respective countries." He Ying "recalled that for several centuries China had been fighting against foreign influences." Thus, China "greatly admired Iran's wise and well-thought out foreign policy which coincides with that of the People's Republic. Both countries [seek] to cut down foreign influence," He Ying told Massoudi.[30] (As shown in a later discussion, He Ying would later play a key role in overcoming early suspicions of IRI leaders about Communist-ruled China.) The bulk of Massoudi's eighty-one-page booklet described the ancient and medieval exchanges and cultural influences between China and Persia. Between the lines one could read the message that before the European eruption arrived to oppress both China and Persia, those two countries interacted thickly, peacefully, and to mutual benefit. Those interactions had been cut off by the period of Western imperialism, but now that that period was at an end, the two countries would resume their earlier, traditional, and well-founded cooperation aimed at putting the world to right by upholding the interests of the "Third World" against imperialists.

THE PRACTICE OF POWER

A second primal fact coloring relations between China and Iran is that each possesses, and each recognizes that the other possesses, capabilities superior to those of most of the other states in their respective regions. Table 1.1 illustrates this reality of relatively superior Iranian power by comparing the national capabilities of Iran to its neighbors. Among that set of countries, only Turkey, Saudi Arabia, and Pakistan have capabilities approximating those of Iran. Turkey and Pakistan are, however, remote from the Persian Gulf, while Saudi Arabia, though wealthy from its vast oil resources, has a small population and a small non-oil industrial manufacturing base. Iran alone in the immediate Gulf combines a large and fairly well-educated population, strong industry, and rich petroleum resources. Iran possessed in 2004 the twentieth largest economy in the world, 7 percent of the world's oil reserves, and 15 percent of the world's natural gas reserves.[31] The Persian Gulf contains about 50 percent of the world's oil supply.

Chinese representatives have frankly and routinely acknowledged Iran's strong national power. When receiving the first IRI foreign ministerial visit to China in September 1983, for example, President Li Xiannian noted that Iran is a country of "strategic importance."[32] Meeting with IRI prime minister Hoseyn Musavi in Tehran several years later, Chinese foreign ministry advisor Gong Dafei noted that "both China and Iran are big Asian states."[33] Meeting with Majlis speaker Rafsanjani in Beijing in June 1985, Foreign Minister Wu Xueqian said China considered Iran to be "strategically important." Wu added that "we are therefore serious about our ties" with Iran and did not consider those relations to be "transient."[34] In other words, China viewed Iran as important because it was powerful. Arriving in Tehran for an official goodwill visit in July 1991, blunt-spoken Premier Li Peng said in his written statement to reporters: "As a big country in Asia, Iran plays an important role in both regional and international affairs."[35] Arriving for a state visit several months later, President Yang Shangkun made the same point: Iran "is a large country in the Gulf region."[36] A Beijing Review article on Jiang Zemin's 2002 visit to Iran used the same words to describe Iran.[37] Receiving Iranian vice president Mohammad Sattarifar in Beijing in April 2004, China's paramount leader Hu Jintao said that China considered Iran as a developing regional power and attached great significance to cooperation with it.[38]

Chinese analysts have been equally frank in appraising the significance of Iran's geographic position: dominating the oil-rich Persian Gulf, separating Russia or the Union of Soviet Socialist Republics (USSR) from that Gulf, and offering convenient overland transit between Central Asia and the Indian Ocean. A Beijing radio broadcast announcing the formation of the IRI in March 1979, for example, elucidated Iran's "important strategic position." Sharing a 1,740-kilometer border with the Soviet Union, Iran constituted, along with Turkey and Pakistan, "a shield against the southward expansion of Soviet hegemony." Iran also dominated the "bottleneck of the Strait of Hormuz . . . thus controlling the West's major petroleum passageway."[39]

Iranian commentators are well aware of the role played by Iran's relatively superior power capabilities in *Chinese* calculations. "Because of its strategic position in the Persian Gulf," the chairman of the national security and foreign policy committee of the Majlis, Mohsen Mirdamadi, explained in February 2001, Iran plays "a significant role in Chinese foreign policy."[40]

TABLE 1.1

Indicators of National Capabilities, 2001: Iran's Relative Standing in the Region

Country	Population (millions)	GDP current US$ billions	GDP (per capita, PPP US$)	Industry, value added (US$ billions)	Electricity output (gwh)	Growth rate 1991–2001	Military expenditure (US$ billions)	Literacy rate, adults 15 and over	School enrollment (%)
Iran	64.5	117.06	6,099	42.85	130,100	4.3	5.62	77	19
Turkey	68.5	145.24	5,932	32.58	122,725	0.0	7.12	—	25
Saudi Arabia	21.3	183.26	12,967	93.88	137,388	2.7	20.71	77	22
Pakistan	141.5	58.77	1,957	12.39	72,430	3.8	2.64	—	—
Afghanistan	27.3	—	—	—	—	0.0	—	—	—
Armenia	3.1	2.12	2,732	0.63	5,745	-1.3	0.07	99	26
Azerbaijan	8.1	5.71	2,877	2.62	18,969	-0.8	0.15	—	23
Bahrain	0.7	7.94	16,200	—	6,779	5.1	0.33	88	—
Georgia	5.2	3.20	2,087	0.66	6,937	-6.3	0.02	—	36
Iraq	23.7	—	—	—	34,932	-4.6	—	—	14
Kuwait	2.3	34.22	15,977	—	33,500	4.6	3.87	82	—
Oman	2.5	19.94	13,553	—	9,737	5.1	2.43	73	7
Qatar	0.6	17.13	—	—	9,856	2.6	0.00	—	23
Turkmenistan	4.7	3.44	4,241	1.43	10,825	4.0	0.00	—	—
UAE	3.5	69.22	—	—	40,155	—	1.73	77	—

SOURCE: *World Bank, World Development Indicators.*

Perhaps it is obvious that cooperation with more capable states is desirable because it confers a greater ability to achieve mutually sought goals. But appreciation of China's understanding of Iran's relatively great capabilities is an important starting point. As subsequent chapters show, Beijing's overtures to Tehran in the 1970s and again in the 1990s were inspired by a realization that Iran could play an important role in blocking Soviet "expansionism" and u.s. "unipolarity," respectively. Moreover, the impulse to make friends with more powerful states is especially strong for China since it sees itself as an emerging global power. China is more likely to achieve this ambition if other relatively powerful countries in Asia, like Iran, are well inclined toward it and view Chinese power as benign. Formation of a friendly, multidimensional, cooperative partnership between China and Iran based on mutual trust and understanding would be a significant element of Chinese influence in Asia in the twenty-first century. Formation of such a relationship is, I believe, the overarching goal of Chinese policy toward Iran, a goal independent of specific policy objectives of this or that period of time. A cooperative relation with Iran multiplies China's own influence in an important region of the world. For Iran, cooperation with China is attractive for similar reasons: Tehran hopes China's power may be adequate to check, or at least resist, aggressive u.s. actions. In both capitals there is a sense that, as significant regional powers, Iran and China will be more able to achieve their common purposes if they cooperate.

TRADITION OF STRATEGIC CONTRACT AND COOPERATION

Another level of Chinese-Iranian mutual appreciation is a historical analysis of the exercise of Chinese and Persian state power over several millennia. There is a rich history of strategic consultation and occasional strategic cooperation between Chinese and Persian empires, and an equally important absence of conflict between those imperial states. This too forms a basis for contemporary cooperation between the two countries. As PRC diplomat Gong Dafei noted to IRI prime minister Musavi in February 1986, there have always been friendly interactions between Chinese and Persian states with no conflicts between them.[41] The politically correct introduction to the authoritative 1988 Chinese study of Sino-Iranian relations made the same point: "Historically, China and Iran have only had friendship and have never experienced unpleasantness, have only engaged in the friendly exchange of gifts and never had armed conflict."[42]

Geographic realities underlay the peaceful, cooperative relations between the great Persian and Chinese empires. These two empires were far apart— at least in the premodern era when a galloping horse was the fastest available means of overland transportation. Moreover, the terrain separating Chinese and Persian realms was very difficult when the most advanced transportation technology was a camel carrying several hundred kilograms and able to walk for several days between oases. The virtually impassable Tibetan plateau blocked southerly movement and channeled communications to the north where the Kunlun, Tian Shan, Pamirs, Karakoram, and Hindu Kush mountains made transportation difficult in the premodern era. Much of Inner Asia separating China and Persia was arid or semiarid, with only oases or relatively small river valleys amenable to agriculture. This made supporting large armies difficult, requiring long, vulnerable, and expensive logistic columns. Largely because of these factors, the two imperial systems came in direct contact only for brief periods in the seventh and eighth centuries. Figure 1.1 depicts the physical relation between the great empires of China and Persia.

The far western holdings of Jin and Tang China depicted in figure 1.1 did not last long. The Western Jin dynasty, although it succeeded in reunifying China after several hundred years of fragmentation, lasted only fifty years. As Jin power collapsed and China again fragmented for another three hundred years, Chinese power in the far west receded. Then in the 640s and 650s Tang Chinese power again expanded to the west, reaching its historic westernmost limit. In 650 Tang forces decisively defeated the Western Turks and extended Tang rule into what is today Kyrgyzstan and eastern Kazakhstan. Principalities farther west that had previously recognized the suzerainty of the Western Turks shifted fealty to the Tang throne, thereby extending Tang authority as far west as the Oxus River valley and today's northern and western Afghanistan. To the east in today's Xinjiang, the Tarim basin was organized as a Chinese protectorate named "Persian government general" and ruled by a former Sassanian noble. Tang rule in the Oxus valley was brief, however. In 665 rebellion led to the independence of Tang's westerly principalities.[43]

Again in the 740s Tang power pressed into Central Asia, this time turning Tashkent and Ferghana into Tang tributaries. Those principalities had sought Tang support against advancing Arab armies, and Tang accepted and dispatched an army of thirty thousand commanded by a Korean general. This led to the famous clash of Arab and Chinese armies on the Talas River in 751 CE in today's northwestern Kyrgyzstan. Tang forces were defeated, Chinese rule withdrew east into today's Xinjiang, and Central Asia was drawn into the Islamic rather than the Confucian cultural sphere. Tang rule over even Xinjiang soon evaporated under the impact of the rise of Tibetan power and major rebellion in China beginning in 755. Chinese artisans captured by Arab forces at Talas carried the secrets of papermaking to the Islamic world.

The centers of strategic interest of each empire also oriented them in

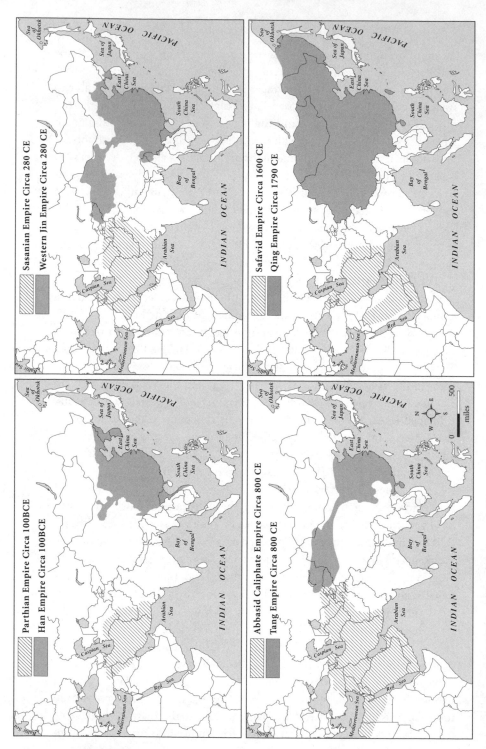

FIGURE 1.1 Spatial Relation of the Persian and Chinese Empires

directions away from one another. Chinese empires typically sought first of all to reconquer Chinese-populated lands "lost" during earlier periods of fragmentation. This meant that the main direction of Chinese expansion was to the south since being "Chinese" was largely defined by a way of life based on settled and highly productive agriculture, and since Chinese who migrated to the arid lands north and west of the Chinese agricultural heartland typically adopted non-Chinese lifestyles to survive and thus ceased to be "Chinese" within a generation or two. Chinese attempts to conquer and Sinicize the non-farming, herding peoples to the north and west tended to be ephemeral—at least prior to modern transportation technology. The most tempting direction of expansion for Persian empires was to the west and south. The rich lands of Mesopotamia and the trade centers of the Persian Gulf, and occasionally India, were the typical targets of Persian empire builders.

A desire to control the lucrative trade routes between them did draw the two imperial systems into Inner Asia and thus geographically toward one another. Moreover, both China and Persia were chronically threatened by horse-riding herding peoples to their north, and countering threats from those peoples sometimes prompted Chinese and/or Persian strategists to look toward the other. The pivotal mission of Zhang Qian to the trans-Oxus in the second century BCE, for example, was inspired by a Chinese search for allies against the Xiongnu. The Yuezhi sought by Zhang Qian had been defeated by the Xiongnu and migrated westward in response. According to the Chinese ambassador to Iran in the 1990s, Hua Liming, the earliest recorded agreement between Iran and China came in 115 BCE when Parthian emperor Mehrdad II and Han emperor Wu Di agreed to cooperate against the Xiongnu.[44]

Several centuries later when the Arab onslaught against the Sassanian empire began in 634, the last Sassanian emperor, Yazdgard III, looked to Tang China for help. Yazdgard sent a mission to the Tang capital, Changan, requesting support against the invader. Tang emperor Gao-tsung declined the request but permitted the emperor's son, Prince Firuz, who had led the Sassanian mission, to remain in Changan and build a Zoroastrian temple there. According to one account, in 677 Gao-tsung dispatched a Chinese army to restore Prince Firuz and the Sassanian throne. The army advanced as far west as Kucha, on the northern route of the Tarim caravan route in Xinjiang and then the capital of the Tang protectorate named "Persian government-general," before turning back.[45] The Arab Islamic conquest of Zoroastrian Persia in the seventh century was a war of foreign conquest.[46] Chinese support for Sassanian at this juncture can be viewed as support for the Persian people's struggle for national independence and against foreign invasion. This too is an element of the psychology of contemporary Sino-Iranian relations.

The fact that both China and Persia were rich, settled, agricultural, and urban societies chronically confronting more primitive and poorer but war-like herding societies to their north shaped their relations with each other in another way as well; it imbued in both civilizations the notion of cultural superiority, which made their "fall" at Western hands in the modern era more painful. This strong and long similarity of superior, more civilized Chinese and Persian peoples chronically fending off barbarians facilitates the contemporary use of the other as a mirror validating each society's own self-worth.

OIL AND POWER IN THE TWENTIETH AND TWENTY-FIRST CENTURIES

Power in the modern era operates differently than in ancient and medieval periods. Modern technologies of transportation have profoundly altered the impact of geography on interactions among states. Previously impassable terrain can now be easily flown over or penetrated by sturdy transportation machines nearly oblivious to difficulties of terrain. In the premodern era, state power was roughly proportional to territory: the more territory and population a state controlled, the more wealth and soldiers it had, and the more powerful it consequently was. Modern industry and technology profoundly alter this relationship too. After the industrial and scientific revolutions, smaller but more industrially and technologically advanced nations could easily be more powerful than bigger, more populous states. This brings the discussion to oil, the use of oil in relation to modern technology, and to the role of Iran and the Persian Gulf in the production of oil. China's appreciation of modern Iran's relative influence, as well as the political significance of the Central Asian land separating Iran and China, is premised on an understanding of the role of oil in the modern world.

Chinese analysts have long recognized the role of oil in the determination of state power in the modern era. A Chinese study titled *The Third World's Oil Struggle* published in 1981 stressed the key role of oil in determination of economic and military power in the twentieth century.[47] The development of the internal combustion engine, including the diesel engine, had profoundly altered industry, transportation, and military affairs, the book explained. Trucks, airplanes, and diesel locomotives began quickly moving cargoes over great distances. Industries were frequently powered by diesel engines or by electricity produced by burning oil. Prior to the twentieth century petroleum had been used basically for home lighting and lubrication. During the twentieth century it was used increasingly as a fuel, powering the motions of industrial-age machines. This produced a "revolution in the energy structure" of human society.[48] Oil increasingly replaced other forms of energy to become the main source of motion in human-built machines.

Oil had distinct advantages over the other major fossil fuel, coal, the Chinese study pointed out. Oil had nearly twice the per-unit caloric value of coal. Its liquid state made oil easy to load and to burn. Consequently, as capitalist countries developed, they shifted progressively from coal to oil. In 1910 only 5 percent of global energy came from oil. By 1970 oil's share had risen to 45 percent, superseding coal's 31 percent. For the industrialized capitalist countries, oil was even more important. In 1970, 68 percent of Western Europe's and 70 percent of Japan's energy came from oil. Not only had oil become the "life blood of industry" and the motive force of the "mobility revolution," it was vital to the conduct of modern warfare with its numerous tanks, trucks, airplanes, submarines, and warships. "Without oil there is no modern national defense or modernized warfare," the Chinese study asserted. The role of oil in modern warfare was illustrated by U.S. oil exports during World War II. During one year of that conflict U.S. oil exports were more than eighty times U.S. oil exports throughout World War I. The study quoted Joseph Stalin to summarize the vital importance of oil in the twentieth century:

In conclusion, it is just as Stalin pointed out: the oil problem is a matter of life and death for imperialism, because whoever controls more oil will hold a commanding position in future wars. Whoever controls more oil will be able to command world industry and commerce. Since the shift of the ships of advanced countries to engines, oil has become an ever more important factor in the struggle of the great powers in wartime and in peacetime.[49]

It was also the situation, the Chinese study continued, that most of the world's oil lay in the "Third World"—the name adopted by Mao Zedong circa 1970 for the Asian, African, and Latin American countries that had borne the brunt of the European eruption in the modern period. The poverty and economic backwardness of those Third World countries was largely a function of a long period of Western, capitalist imperialist domination, according to Mao's "Three Worlds theory" (in common, of course, with all Marxist economic theory). A central dynamic of the twentieth century was the struggle of the peoples of the Third World for emancipation from imperialist domination and exploitation. The Bolshevik revolution, the Soviet Union's victory over Nazi Germany and Japan, the establishment of the socialist camp in the late 1940s, the formation of the People's Republic of China in 1949, the rapid industrial and military development of the socialist camp, and the collapse of the European colonial empires after 1945 had given tremendous impetus to the struggle of

the Third World for emancipation from capitalist imperialism. Yet that struggle continued, and a key manifestation of it was the fight by Third World countries to win control over their own natural resources, for example, oil.

The Chinese 1981 study calculated that 75 percent of the world's oil reserves
lay in Third World countries. Another 6 percent lay in countries of the Second
World—Mao's name for the industrialized capitalist countries other than the
United States and which adroit diplomacy could possibly draw into the antihegemony camp. The two superpowers, the United States and the Soviet Union,
the "First World" in Mao's nomenclature, held within their territories 16 percent of world oil reserves. This geographic distribution of oil resources combined with the logic of power—mechanical, political, and military—dictated
that the two hegemony-seeking superpowers strive to control the Third
World's oil. The system of oil control existing after World War II had been set
up during the period of unfettered Western colonialism early in the twentieth century and was a cartel of seven giant Western oil firms each backed by
their government, according to the Chinese study. During the course of the
twentieth century, u.s. imperialism had become dominant within that cartel, while British, Dutch, French, and Italian firms remained participants in
the system of imperialist oil exploitation upheld by u.s. power. From the standpoint of these Western capitalist firms and governments, control over the rich
oil resources of Third World countries was a source of monopoly profits and
cheap fuel. From the standpoint of u.s. imperialism, domination of world
oil was a key mechanism for retaining the loyalty of its European and Japanese
allies, controlling the Third World, containing the Soviet Union, and through
all of this, achieving world hegemony. From the standpoint of the Third World
countries, control over their oil resources was a vital pathway to economic
development, independent national power, and genuine (as opposed to
bogus neocolonial) sovereignty. This contradiction between exploitation and
liberation constituted the "Third World's oil struggle."

Globally, two areas contained the richest oil and gas resources in the 1970s:
the littoral of the Gulf of Mexico, stretching from the Louisiana coast
through Mexico's Campeche Bay to Venezuela, and the Middle East. Of these
two regions, the Middle East was by far the richest. In the Middle East, Saudi
Arabia and Iran obtained the highest production, while Iran fell in ranking,
well below Saudi Arabia, in terms of reserves. This is illustrated by table 1.2,
taken from the 1981 Chinese study. The Gulf of Mexico was, of course, a region
remote from China and in which China had historically played no role. With
Persia, however, China had a long and rich tradition of cooperation. And as
seen earlier, Iran had relative national capabilities potentially adequate to dominate the broader Persian Gulf region.

TABLE 1.2

Distribution of Global and Middle Eastern Oil Resources, 1975

	% Total world production	Crude oil reserves (million tons)	Crude oil production (million tons)
First World	36.5		
Second World	5.0		
Third World	58.5		
Middle East	36.8		
Saudi Arabia		20,547.0	451.0
Kuwait*		10,027.0	107.0
UAE**		8,893.0	94.0
Iran		8,293.0	283.0
Iraq		4,726.0	111.0
Oman		773.0	17.0
Qatar		767.0	22.0
Syria		204.0	10.0
Turkey		51.0	2.5
Bahrain		37.0	2.8
Africa	9.2		
Latin America	8.4		
Southeast Asia	3.0		
Other	1.1		

* Includes the "neutral zone."
** Includes Abu Dhari, Dubayy, and Shariqah in addition to UAE as constituted in 1975.
SOURCE: Di san shijie shiyou duozheng [The Third World's Oil Struggle] (Beijing: San lian shudian, 1981), 14–15, 24.

This confluence of factors meant that contemporary Chinese calculations regarding Iran touched on the global correlation of forces. Through relations with Iran, China might be able to influence the global allocation of oil and hence the global balance of power. Within the framework of Mao's Three Worlds theory, for example, the two superpowers sought to control Persian Gulf oil as a step to global domination. China could hinder the superpower drive for world domination by supporting Iran's struggle against superpower hegemony—that is, by supporting Iran's efforts to deny the superpowers control over Gulf oil. Via influence with Tehran and Iranian control over Persian Gulf oil, Beijing might be able to influence to a significant degree the evolution of the structure of state power in the world. By helping deny to one or another hostile power a significant portion of the world's oil supply, Beijing could foster a configuration of power favorable to China. A variant of the same theme would emerge in the 1990s: by strengthening Iran's position in the Gulf, Beijing would hobble the u.s. drive for unipolar hegemony and make it more likely that that oil would be available to China under special conditions.

SPIRIT VERSUS INTERESTS

Civilizational solidarity and mutual appreciation of the other's national power formed the spirit of Sino-Iranian relations, the framework within which Sino-Iranian interactions occurred. Writ large, the spirit of Sino-Iranian ties means that Beijing seeks cooperation with Iran as a way of making the world whole after the humiliation of ancient non-Western nations at Western hands in the modern era. But such sentiments say little about the specific interests sought by cooperation during various periods or about interests that argued *against* such cooperation. In fact, Beijing would have to continually balance its impulse toward cooperation with Iran against other important interests. Those interests frequently trumped spiritual impulses.

Several sets of Chinese interests have from time to time contradicted PRC-IRI cooperation. These interests will be explicated in later chapters, but it is well to introduce them here. They are: protection of Sino-u.s. comity on which China's remarkably successful post-1978 development drive depends; protection of China's international reputation as a responsible, sober power; fear of war and other instability in the Middle East arising, in part, from IRI militancy and which might disrupt China's economic development effort; and fear of militant Islamic ideology of the IRI influencing China's Muslim community and Central Asia. Civilizational solidarity and calculations of the role Iran can play in the global correlation of forces are always present and color China's relations with Iran. Combined with powerful common interests, these frequently bring the two countries together. Yet China's leaders have continually had to balance the gains achieved via cooperation with Iran against the costs. Not infrequently these calculations have led Beijing to keep considerable distance from Tehran and even, occasionally, to suspend certain types of cooperation with Iran. But when Beijing has made such choices, it has done so with great reluctance and frequently only under great pressure. There seems to be a strong Chinese preference for cooperation with a civilizational comrade, which is also a major power in a major region of the world.

2 / The PRC–Kingdom of Iran
Relationship, 1971–78

THE SHAH'S "GREAT CIVILIZATION"
AND MAO'S UNITED FRONT PENCHANT

Mohammad Reza Pahlavi, the shah or king of Iran from 1941 to 1979, was inspired by a vision of restored Iranian greatness. In this vision, Iran was to be a prosperous, industrialized, welfare state with formidable economic and military power. Iran's enhanced power would enable it to deal effectively with challenges to Iranian interests in the Persian Gulf and northwest Indian Ocean region and to conduct relations with Iran's neighbors from a position of strength. Iran would be the paramount power in the Persian Gulf–Arabian Sea region, dealing confidently and proactively with challenges to Iran's interests in that region. Iran's achievement of a "great civilization" was the term the shah sometimes used to refer to the realization of this vision.[1]

The shah, like his father, Reza Khan, was a modernizer in the mold of Japan's Meiji emperor or Turkey's Mustafa Kemal Ataturk. Like Meiji and Ataturk, the shah saw Western society as the model for modernization and pushed through extremely ambitious programs designed to tear his nation away from traditional ways and propel it along the path of modernization. The shah was determined to override the inevitable opposition to such an ambitious effort, although his ultimate flight into exile in 1979 indicated he lacked the iron resolve necessary for this task.[2]

The shah recognized internal economic development as the crucial basis for such a "great civilization," and from the early 1960s he presided over ambitious modernization programs financed by oil revenues. In 1963 the shah launched a wide-ranging land reform program dubbed the "white revolution," giving land to 1.6 million farming families and thereby greatly alleviating the problem of tenant farming. Land reform also deepened tensions between the shah's government and Iran's Islamic clerics since mosques or clerics were often landlords. Other of the shah's modernizing reforms also had the effect of reducing the clergy's influence in the villages: the establishment of state-run schools, the extension of political rights to women and the enforcement of a minimum age of eighteen years for females at marriage, the development of modern electronic mass communication, and the embrace of Western fashions by much of Iran's elite. Female wearing of the chador was banned from universities and government offices. Industrialization and urbanization proceeded at a rapid pace.[3]

Realization of state control over Iran's oil and gas resources was a key component of the shah's vision of restored Iranian greatness. According to R. K. Ramazani, Iran under the shah waged a twenty-year struggle to overthrow what Iranians universally viewed as a humiliating agreement imposed on Iran by Western oil companies after the u.s.-sponsored 1953 coup ousting reformist leader Muhammad Musaddiq. Within three years of the unsatisfactory 1954 oil agreement, the shah was building up the National Iran Oil Company (NIOC) into a full-range international oil company capable of someday assuming operation of Iran's oil industry. By the late 1960s that objective had been realized; NIOC was involved in a wide range of exploration, production, and "downstream" operations, domestically and internationally, in cooperation with nonmajor Western oil companies outside the geographic scope of the 1954 agreement. By 1968 the shah began challenging the big Western oil companies *within* the geographic area of the 1954 agreement. Through a series of tough negotiations and confrontations between 1968 and 1973, Iran forced the big Western companies to accept, first, increases in production levels and then increased taxes and per-barrel sales prices. By 1970 the shah had established the principle that Iran's oil resources constituted its national wealth, and that the government had the right to take whatever measures it found necessary to use that wealth for the benefit of the nation's development. The culmination of this two-decade-long struggle came in 1973 with the nationalization of Iran's oil resources. On the tenth anniversary of the launching of the white revolution, the shah confronted the Western oil majors' signatory to the 1954 agreement with an ultimatum. Either they could sign a new agreement recognizing Iran's full sovereignty over its oil, or they could insist on continuing the 1954 agreement. In the former case, the companies could continue cooperating with Iran on friendly terms. In the latter case, the Western firms would suffer a number of penalties. The companies saw the wisdom of continued cooperation with the shah's government, and a new agreement was signed in February establishing Iran's full sovereignty over all oil, including that within the geographic area of the 1954 agreement. Henceforth the relation between Iran and the Western oil companies was to be that between a seller (Iran) and buyers (the Western companies). The final act came in July when Iran nationalized all oil resources and operations.[4]

The shah's capture of control over Iran's oil resources in the early 1970s (along with major price increases won by the Organization of Petroleum Exporting Countries [OPEC]) greatly increased the revenues available to the state for industrialization. As urbanization accelerated, large numbers of former village dwellers moved to ballooning cities, where they confronted strange ways and economic insecurity. In both villages and cities the Islamic clergy—one of the most important of Iran's traditional elites—found their social status and influence undercut by secularism and state economic policies. Iran's political elite, plus a substantial portion of the urban middle classes, favored Western education and adopted Western manners. Western ways offensive to more traditional Iranians included consumption of alcohol, immodest women's dress, and 1960s-style youth culture. Nightclubs and cinemas showing Hollywood movies multiplied. Prostitution became more widespread—or at least more open. Drug use spread. Lush state development budgets combined with pervasive state guidance to produce corruption. A cultural gulf increasingly opened between the Westernized elite and middle classes and the far more traditional lower classes. The ways of the Westernized elites were offensive to villagers and recently urbanized villagers. The extremely rapid pace of social change under the shah's ambitious Western-supported and oil-financed development programs of the 1970s generated high levels of growth and tension. Unfortunately the shah did not build political institutions to channel and give voice to these tensions, but moved, instead, toward ever more authoritarian forms of government—a sure receipt for rebellion. In 1975 the shah dissolved all political parties, replacing them with a single, state-dominated political organization. This move pushed middle-class people into opposition to the regime. The shah's political police, SAVAK, became notorious for their arbitrary arrests and use of torture.[5]

The shah's pursuit of Iran's "great civilization" had a deep influence on Iran's relations with China by making the shah desirous of China's support for realization of Iran's regional preeminence. The shah's goal was for Iran to create and preserve in the broader Persian Gulf region an environment favorable to achievement of Iranian interests, and then to use Iran's enhanced position in the Gulf as a stepping-stone to global political status. This broad objective translated into Iranian efforts to safeguard the Persian Gulf monarchies against subversion by radical Arab nationalists and the Soviet Union. These weak monarchies, most of them just emerging from British tutelage and moving toward independence, were friendly to the West and looked to Western-aligned Iran for succor against security threats from radical, republican, Arab nationalist governments in Baghdad and Cairo. By serving as guardian of the Gulf monarchies, Iran would maintain stability, exclude hostile radical Arab (especially Iraqi and Egyptian) or Soviet presence, and expand Iran's influence. The shah also wanted Iran to assume the role of ensuring free transit of Gulf energy resources via the Strait of Hormuz. Those energy exports were vital to Iran's own economic health and central to the overriding interests of the Western powers in the region. With Britain abandoning its traditional role of safeguarding Gulf sea-lanes, the shah envisioned Iran assuming that task.[6]

Britain's early 1969 announcement that it would withdraw its military forces from east of Suez by the end of 1971 offered the shah an opportunity for Iran to secure Western support for Iran to play a larger regional role.[7] By early 1969, virtually as soon as London announced its east of Suez withdrawal decision, the shah announced a "hands-off policy" toward the Gulf (the term is Ramazani's), according to which the security affairs of the Gulf should be determined by the littoral countries of that body of water. Extraregional big powers—be they the Soviet Union, the United States, Britain, or China— should not establish military bases in the Gulf region.[8] This was part of the shah's effort to establish Iran in a greater regional role. If military bases of nonlittoral powers such as the United States and the Soviet Union were excluded from the Gulf and perhaps even the Indian Ocean, Iran's relative position would be much enhanced. The shah's ambitious military expansion programs were designed to give Iran the strongest armed forces in the region. Iranian military power would be underpinned, in the shah's conception, by the strongest, most technologically advanced economy in the region.

To realize this ambitious goal of regional preeminence, the shah needed to secure the support of as many great powers as possible. In this the shah's diplomacy was very successful. By the late 1970s he had secured u.s., Chinese, European, Japanese, and even a significant degree of Soviet recognition of Iran's new role. China's role in the construction of Iran's "great civilization" was not economic. The shah saw economic development as the basis of Iran's rise and looked to the West, and to a far less extent the Soviet Union and Moscow's East European allies, for the essential supports for that development: economic assistance, investment, technology, education and technical advice, and markets for Iranian goods including petroleum. China was itself an exporter of petroleum in the late 1960s and 1970s. Nor was Chinese technology attractive to Iran, being far behind the Western technology readily available to Iran. Iran and China also produced basically the same set of export goods in the 1960s and 1970s—agricultural goods, cheap manufactured goods, and raw materials—and sold them to essentially the same countries, the developed capitalist countries of the West. China did not have much to offer Iran economically in the 1960s and 1970s.

It was in the *political* area that China's support was important for the realization of the shah's "great civilization." China was a great power that understood military force. During the 1965 India–Pakistan War, for example, China had threatened to intervene in support of Pakistan, a threat that contributed significantly to the Indian, Soviet, and u.s. efforts to swiftly end the fighting. In the aftermath of China's 1962 defeat of India, China's military reputation in South Asia carried considerable weight. Moreover, Tehran and Beijing shared common interests in protecting Pakistan against Indian subjugation. As the shah told a reporter in 1967, China was a nation with nuclear weapons and more than seven hundred million people. As such it was a power that simply had to be recognized.[9]

Because of China's power, Iranian links with China gave the shah leverage with Moscow and, to a lesser extent, with Washington. Via links with China, the shah could play on Soviet fears by raising in Soviet minds a possible China-Iran anti-Soviet bloc backed by the United States. The u s s r had long been the shah's nemesis, largely because of Russia's history of military intervention in northern Iran, plus the Soviet Union's support for anti-shah, antimonarchy groups, especially the Communist-led Tudeh party. A diplomatic opening to Moscow in the early 1960s led to a dramatic shift in Soviet policy in 1963, with Moscow dropping support for anti-shah forces and instead starting to laud the shah's "progressive" nature. Several factors were behind Moscow's decision to conciliate the shah's Iran. One factor was the serious deterioration of Soviet-Chinese relations that began in 1960. Confronted with spiraling conflict with China in the east, Moscow needed to reduce tension in the west. However, should China and Iran join hands against the Soviet Union, possibly with u.s. support and connivance, Moscow's situation would be much worse. The shah was deeply concerned throughout the 1970s about growing Soviet presence in regions around Iran, in Iraq, Yemen, and so on. Fundamentally the shah feared that the Soviet Union's traditional presence on Iran's northern land borders would be joined with a Soviet naval presence to Iran's south, effectively encircling Iran with Soviet military power. From 1969 on, Tehran's opening to Beijing signaled Moscow that if Soviet ties with Iraq, especially, went too far, the Soviet Union might find itself confronting the specter of a China-Iran-United States bloc.

Iraq was Iran's major regional rival in the Gulf. For centuries under Ottoman and Safavid rule, Persian rulers had exploited religious divisions in

Ottoman-ruled Iraq, while Ottoman rulers of Iraq reciprocated by exploiting ethnic divisions within the Safavid realm. On top of this reciprocal subversion was laid modern rivalries.[10] After Iraq's 1958 republican revolution overthrew that country's monarchy, Iraq emerged as a radical state with aspirations to regional leadership. Iraq's new rulers saw themselves as pan-Arab nationalist revolutionaries, fighting to expel Western imperialist presence from the Gulf region. These aspirations clashed with those of the shah. Republican Iraq also looked to the Soviet Union for support in this anti-Western struggle. By the 1970s the USSR was increasing its support for Iraq, confronting Iran with an increased challenge. To repeat, from the shah's point of view, links with China acted as a brake on Soviet-Iraqi relations. Tehran's China card could easily be overplayed, however, resulting not in greater Soviet restraint but in hostility. Finally, if Chinese support could be secured, this would go some way toward institutionalizing Iran's dominant position in the Gulf—just as would Soviet or American recognition.

The shah's confidant minister of court Asadollah Alam had an interesting exchange regarding Soviet apprehensions of China during a discussion with the Soviet ambassador during a March 1970 visit by USSR president Nikolai Podgorny to Tehran. An expression of interest by Alam in increased Soviet economic assistance to Iran led the Soviet ambassador to point to financial constraints on Moscow's abilities. When Alam pressed further, the ambassador explained: "We are heavily committed to our defense budget" because "the Chinese . . . have laid claim to our far eastern territories, claiming that we acquired them by extortion." "They seem to have a point, I said smiling," replied Alam. The Iranian minister continued provocatively: "At least some of this land was taken from China back in the days of the Tsars. China is overpopulated and needs space into which she may expand. Naturally she looks to the relatively deserted territories beyond her northern frontier, the only space available which happens at the same time to form part of Russia." The Soviet ambassador signaled his agreement, according to Alam. A month later and in the context of persuading the United States to increase credits supporting Iranian arms purchases, Alam suggested to the shah that "there may be benefits for us in selling oil to Red China." The shah ordered Alam to investigate the matter further.[11] In other words, if Washington was afraid of Sino-Iranian rapprochement, the United States was more likely to sell the advanced weapons Iran wanted and otherwise conciliate Tehran.

Leverage with Washington provided by Iranian links with Beijing was far less important in Iranian thinking that achieving leverage with Moscow. But Iranian development of ties with "Red China" would demonstrate a degree of Iranian independence of the United States. This was useful domestically and in such venues as the nonaligned movement or the U.N. General Assembly—as well as in negotiations with Washington over such issues as arms sales. Yet the shah never intended to break with the United States. Indeed the shah's pursuit of Iran's "great civilization" was predicated on U.S. backing and support.[12]

Turning to Mao Zedong, the red thread of Mao's thinking about international affairs from the 1930s until his death in 1976 was the notion of a united front of non-Western peoples and governments against the various imperialist powers. The notion of a united front in which relatively small groups of Communist revolutionaries merged with larger non-Communist forces was, of course, one of V. I. Lenin's main contributions to world history. Iran figured prominently in Lenin's proposed united front. He placed Iran among a small set of big countries offering good revolutionary prospects. (The others were China, India, Turkey, Egypt, and Java and the Arab-speaking lands.) In one of the more famous debates within the Communist movement—at the 1920 Second Congress of the Communist International between Lenin and Indian revolutionary M. N. Roy—Lenin argued in favor of alliance with non-Communist but "anti-imperialist" movements such as those led by Reza Khan in Iran, Ataturk in Turkey, and Sun Yat-sen in China. Achieving such alliances was a key thrust of Soviet foreign policy during the 1920s.[13]

Mao spent a lifetime developing Lenin's theory of the united front. Mao's thinking about the united front changed as China's international situation changed and as he struggled to apply the united front to that ever-changing situation. Consequently the targets to be attacked by that united front and the potential members of the united front (the crucial question of "enemies and friends" in Mao's lexicon) and the forms of struggle deemed most efficacious, varied in Mao's thinking from period to period. But the central idea that the non-Western nations oppressed by Western imperialism in the modern era should unite to end that oppression, was a constant. For Mao as for Lenin, Persia's strong national consciousness—manifested in both its long history and in its revolutionary struggles of the twentieth century—plus its large size and population, gave Iran a potentially important role in each phase of his united front thinking.

During the period of close PRC alignment with the USSR in the early 1950s, Beijing's propaganda attitude toward Iran followed Moscow's lead, but took a distinctly more moderate, less vitriolic tone. While Soviet propaganda damned the Pahlavi regime as reactionary and an imperialist lackey, Beijing criticized only specific moves of the Iranian government and with much more moderate tones. United States imperialism, not the Iranian government, was the main target of Beijing's criticism. In October 1955, for example, when Iran joined the Western-leaning Baghdad pact, *Renmin ribao* found that move "dangerous and regrettable" and "in conflict with the Bandung Afro-Asian spirit," but not reflecting a dubious class character of Iran's regime. (The conference in Bandung, Indonesia, in April 1955 was the first meeting of the post-colonial African and Asian countries.) *Renmin ribao* recognized Iran's need to pursue a policy of "peace and independence," but concluded it had chosen the "wrong path" by "tying itself to the u.s. war chariot." In March 1959, when Iran signed a security alliance with the United States, Beijing again criticized it as a breach of the Bandung principle. But criticism of Iran's decision to ally with the United States was overshadowed by criticism *of the United States* for its sinister moves and plans for Iran.[14] Again the implication was that Iran could and should move away from alignment with the United States and join the anti-imperialist united front where it properly belonged.

The Sino-Soviet split of the early 1960s led Mao to expel the Soviet Union, its allies, and pro-Soviet Communist parties from the united front, while simultaneously giving primacy to armed rural insurrection as the road to revolutionary victory. This new revolutionary orientation brought China into conflict with Iran when Beijing began supporting revolutionary anti-regime movements in South Yemen and Oman.[15] Of course, one practical problem for Beijing's revolutionary line at this juncture was that Iran's main anti-regime movement, the Tudeh party, was closely aligned with the Soviet Union. Success for the Tudeh party could well have meant a major setback for China's efforts to check Soviet expansionism, as well as vindication of Soviet leadership over the world Communist movement.

By the early 1970s Mao conceived of the united front not primarily in terms of insurrectionary armed struggle by farmers but in terms of united action by Third World governments against both u.s. "imperialism" and Soviet "social imperialism," these being identified as two forms of "superpower hegemony." In this new formulation of Mao's united front, Iran was assigned a major role.

Iran's role in challenging Western oil companies in the early 1970s was one factor winning Iran a prominent role in Mao's Third World united front against superpower hegemony. Beijing saw the increasing assertiveness of the oil-producing countries as a major manifestation of the Third World's united antihegemony struggle. From Beijing's perspective, the struggle of Third World oil producers was the cutting edge of the revolutionary struggle to create a new international order. By seizing control of oil and taking it out of the hands of the imperialists, the governments of the Third World oil-producing countries were leading the way in creation of a new world order. The old, exploitative, imperialist order established through centuries of Western domination could be overthrown and a new, just, equitable, post-imperialist order established. No longer was the industrial proletariat or the armed peasantry the primary revolutionary force.

Iran under the shah was, in fact, one of the more militant countries leading the drive of OPEC to redefine the relationship between oil-producing countries and international oil firms. One of the first major assertions of power by OPEC came in February 1971 during a meeting in Tehran, when the oil-producing countries forced the Western oil companies to raise the posted price of oil by 3 percent and the oil tax rate by 5 percent. The month after the Tehran OPEC conference Premier Zhou Enlai lauded it during Pahlavi princess Ashraf's pathbreaking visit to Beijing: "In order to safeguard state sovereignty and protect their natural resources, Iran together with other members of the Organization of Petroleum Exporting Countries have recently waged effective struggles against the Western imperialist oil monopoly consortium and won victory. We express support for your just struggle and sincere congratulations on your victory."[16]

A *Renmin ribao* editorial marking the establishment of Sino-Iranian relations in August 1971 expressed China's "resolute support" for the "effective struggles" and "positive results" secured by the "Iranian government and people" in the struggle against "Western petroleum monopoly groups."[17] Again in July 1973 when Iran passed the law establishing Iranian ownership of all oil resources in Iran, China weighed in with support. *Peking Review* proclaimed the new Iranian move "a resounding victory" ending seventy-two years in which Iran's "oil resources have been in the hands of the big monopoly groups of the West." The Iranian move was "another victory chalked up by the people of Iran in their protracted struggle to protect their oil rights and interests."[18] Beijing saw OPEC's efforts to raise oil prices as part of the Third World's struggle against superpower hegemony. A 1974 year-end roundup by Xinhua proclaimed:

> The Third World's anti-imperialist and anti-hegemonist struggles in the past year have brought to the surface a number of fundamental problems [in the imperialist system] . . . once distorted or covered up. . . . The Arab people achieved great successes through the use of the oil weapon. In doing so they revealed one of the secrets of how the imperialists and superpowers amassed their wealth: making super-profits by forcing down the price of Third World raw materials. . . . The Third World's conscious application of their raw materials as a weapon against imperialism and hegemonism is a new thing, a formidable weapon which strikes panic in the hearts of the imperialists and superpowers, threatening to deprive them of the means by which to batten onto the Third World. . . . The

Third World fight against economic plunder has cut down the imperialist and superpower world market aggravating the capitalist world crisis.[19]

Beijing rejected the proposition that OPEC price increases were responsible for the global recession that began circa 1973. Following the onset of severe global economic recession, the heads of OPEC countries met at Algiers, Algeria, in March 1975 with one key purpose of this first-ever OPEC summit meeting being to rebut Western charges that OPEC's actions had precipitated the global recession. Again Beijing weighed in with support. *Peking Review* pointed out that the declaration issued by the Algiers conference "resolutely refuted the fallacy used by the imperialists and the superpowers to ascribe the economic crisis confronting the capitalist world to adjusted oil prices." That crisis was due to "the profit mad monopoly capitalists" who had pushed oil prices up, not to the actions of the oil-producing countries. "The Third World oil producing countries have simply adjusted the extremely unfair oil prices and got back some of their legitimate rights," *Peking Review* opined. "Yet U.S. imperialism is so furious that it resorts to open intimidation and even the threat of force."[20] When Vice Premier Li Xiannian visited Tehran shortly after the Algiers conference, he conveyed Beijing's endorsement of the shah's leading role in it. The shah had "personally attended" and "made an admirable contribution" to the conference, Li said. China "warmly hails the great achievements of the conference" and "firmly supports the just position of the developing countries on their right to enjoy and exercise permanent sovereignty over their own natural resources and on the establishment of a new and equitable international economic order."[21] Some commentary in *Peking Review* went so far as to hint at Iranian use of military force to counter U.S. military threats against militant oil-producing countries. Reporting on U.S. speculations about possible military action against militant OPEC countries, *Peking Review* quoted Iranian commentary to the effect that "the Shah has said that nobody could dictate to us or shake his fists at us because we could do the same."[22]

There was a strong element of Sino-Soviet rivalry in China's relations with Iran in the 1970s. Beijing courted Tehran in order to advise, educate, and urge Iran toward greater vigilance and activism in countering Soviet advances. Third World countries should not allow the Soviet bear to come in the back door, while driving the American wolf out the front door, China urged Tehran. Moscow courted Tehran in order to limit Iranian movement toward China. Moscow seemed during the 1970s to be achieving its long-sought-after breakout of the Western anti-Soviet containment system. From Moscow's perspective, Beijing had added its voice to the ultrareactionaries urging reinvigoration

of that containment, and Maoist hysteria needed to be countered by demonstrations of Soviet friendship toward Tehran. The shah was able to exploit
this Sino-Soviet rivalry to Iran's advantage and secure a remarkable degree
of both Chinese and Soviet recognition of Iran's "great civilization" role in
the Persian Gulf.

TRENDS IN THE INTERNATIONAL
SYSTEM AND SINO-IRANIAN RAPPROCHEMENT

Several international trends helped bring Tehran and Beijing together in the
1970s. By the end of that decade there existed an extraordinarily broad convergence of national interests between China and Iran. One trend was the
recession of British military power from the Persian Gulf region. Britain had
been the dominant military power in the Persian Gulf–Arabian Sea region
since the eighteenth century. London's decision to withdraw British military
forces from east of Suez created a vacuum that deeply influenced the policies of other powers. From the shah's perspective, the British move created
the opportunity for Iran to fill the power vacuum created by London's decision. As the shah said in his final testament, "Who but Iran could fulfill this
function?"[23] The shah's early 1969 declaration that the security of the Persian
Gulf should be guaranteed by the littoral states themselves, and China's subsequent endorsement of that claim, must be viewed in the context of the historic ebbing of British power.

The United States had accepted British primacy in the Gulf region since
1940. It was in that year—with German and Italian armies pushing across
North Africa toward the Middle East—that u.s. strategists recognized the
role petroleum resources of the Middle East played in the global balance of
power. United States leaders concluded that keeping those resources out of
the hands of hostile powers and available to friendly powers played a major,
perhaps even decisive, role in the global balance. As the Cold War developed
after 1945, this principle still applied, with the primary u.s. concern now being
the ussr. Washington concluded that Soviet control over Middle East oil
would give Moscow considerable leverage over the West European and Japanese economies dependent on that oil. In the event of an East-West war, Soviet
control over Middle East oil could well make a decisive difference in the outcome. Washington was loath, however, to assume direct u.s. responsibility
for securing Persian Gulf oil and preferred to support Britain in that role. By
the time Britain was moving toward its east of Suez decision, u.s. resources
were stretched very thin. Demand for additional military forces in Vietnam
had already dangerously siphoned u.s. forces from the North Atlantic Treaty

Organization (NATO) theater and the strategic reserve in the continental United States. Few U.S. forces were available to fill the vacuum created by London's withdrawal decision. Thus, rather than scrap the tried-and-proven policy of relying on some other friendly power to guard Gulf oil, Washington looked for a friendly power to perform that task. The shah volunteered Iran, seeing this as a way of securing top-of-the-line U.S. military equipment long denied him by the United States, and of securing U.S. support for the more prominent Iranian position in the region that he, the shah, had long sought.[24] China shared Washington's desire to keep Persian Gulf oil resources out of Soviet hands. Iran's increasing role in accomplishing that task made Iran important to China.

Chinese apprehension over growing Soviet position in Asia deepened throughout the late 1960s and 1970s and was another trend bringing Beijing and Tehran together. As China slid into chaos and internal strife during the Cultural Revolution, Soviet military forces concentrated on China's borders while Moscow hinted it might intervene in support of China's "healthy Marxist-Leninists," that is, anti-Mao, forces. By 1968 the border conflict between China and the Soviet Union had become militarized, with tensions escalating along that long frontier. Clashes on the Ussuri River in February and March 1969 brought the two countries to the brink of war, with Moscow contemplating all-out nuclear attack to "solve the China problem" for several generations. Sino-Soviet war was avoided, of course, but Beijing became deeply fearful of the growth of Soviet power in areas around China. Soviet influence in countries to China's south would further encircle China with Soviet military power and diminish China's security. Were Moscow to achieve primacy in the vast swath of land and waters between Vietnam and the Red Sea, China would be in a Soviet vise. Beijing's hopes for developing friendly, cooperative relations with countries of that region would also be doomed. Even more dangerous was the possibility that Moscow might succeed in winning control over Middle East oil and gain the leverage over West Europe and Japan that such control implied. Were Moscow to achieve a preponderant position in Eurasia, China's security environment would be severely diminished. Equally dangerous—to both China and Iran—would be a sphere of influence agreement between Moscow and Washington. Moscow might agree to ease its pressure in Europe in exchange for U.S. recognition of Soviet primacy in Southwest or continental East Asia. By the early 1970s Tehran and Beijing were both strongly critical of U.S. policies of détente with the Soviet Union, fearing that those policies would lead to such a sphere of influence arrangement, leaving them to confront increased Soviet pressure with lessened U.S. support.

TABLE 2.1

Presence of Soviet and u.s. Warships in the Indian Ocean, 1968–73

Number of ship days, surface combatants, and auxiliaries						
	1968	*1969*	*1970*	*1971*	*1972*	*1973*
Soviet Union	1,760	3,668	3,579	3,804	8,007	8,543
United States	1,688	1,315	1,246	1,337	1,435	2,154

u.s. and Soviet port calls in the Indian Ocean		
	Soviet Union	*United States*
1968	42	71
1969	68	71
1970	65	65
1971	47	97
1972	110	74
1973	153	115

SOURCE: Michael A. Palmer, *Guardians of the Gulf: A History of America's Expanding Role in the Persian Gulf, 1832–1992* (New York: Macmillan, 1992), 281.

One element of Moscow's growing position in the region was a steadily expanding naval presence in the Indian Ocean. Soviet warships first entered that ocean in 1968—and did so in a big way. Already in that year the presence of Soviet surface warships exceeded that of the United States, a situation illustrated by table 2.1. Thereafter the Soviet naval presence expanded rapidly. By 1973 the Soviet naval presence was three times that of the United States. Soviet warships called with increasing frequency at ports of Moscow's friends India, Iraq, the People's Democratic Republic of Yemen, and, after 1975, united Vietnam.

Friendship treaties with Egypt and India in 1971 and with Iraq in 1972 further strengthened Moscow's position in that region. India, Egypt, and Iraq were all leading regional powers. The Soviet Union was the major arms supplier of all three. Regarding India, the essential purpose of that treaty with Moscow was to isolate Pakistan in the face of forthcoming Indian intervention in eastern Pakistan. Long-simmering conflicts between the Bengalis of East Pakistan and the Punjabis that dominated the national institutions of Pakistan had reached crisis by 1971. In the middle of that year Indian leaders decided to use Indian military force to liberate the Bengali people of East Pakistan, creating a new nation of Bangladesh and partitioning Pakistan. The success of this Soviet-supported Indian move greatly reduced the capabilities of Pakistan, China's quasi-ally relied on by Beijing to maintain a South Asian balance of power that constrained India.

Common opposition to India was another basis of Sino-Iranian entente of the 1970s. The shah shared Beijing's skepticism about India's growing regional role and efforts to emasculate Pakistan. The shah believed that the Soviets were behind the campaign to break up Pakistan and elevate India to the dominant position in South Asia and the Indian Ocean, while supporting subversion of the pro-Iranian monarchies in the Persian Gulf. Were Soviet-Indian efforts to prevail, Iran's hopes of preeminence in the Gulf would be doomed. To a significant degree, Beijing's drive to improve relations with Iran in the 1970s was a counter to Soviet efforts to advance India and Iraq. In effect a China-Iran–United States combination was emerging to counter an India-Iraq-Soviet Union coalition, with Pakistan being a key arena of rivalry between those two blocs. In a broader sense, Iran under the shah and India under Indira Gandhi were rivals for regional status in the 1970s. Both drew on support of major powers to enhance their regional status—Iran looked to the United States and China, and India to the Soviet Union. Beijing saw India as Moscow's proxy in the South Asian region and sought to limit Indian influence. Support for Iran limited Indian as well as Soviet influence.

Iran and China had convergent interests in supporting Pakistan. Iran and Pakistan were allies in the Central Treaty Organization (CENTO) (along with Turkey and Britain). From Iran's perspective, alliance with Pakistan allowed Tehran to keep Iran's eastern frontier relatively trouble free, allowing Tehran to concentrate on Iraq and the Persian Gulf. A strong Pakistan also served as a buffer with India. Tehran had characterized the 1965 India-Pakistan war as Indian aggression, and given Pakistan considerable assistance. The shah launched an effort at rapprochement with India circa 1969 as part of his effort to secure international support for a larger Iranian role in the Persian Gulf, but that effort unraveled with New Delhi's August 1971 alliance with the USSR and subsequent dismemberment of Pakistan.[25] Following the Indian intervention and breakup of Pakistan in late 1971, the shah was very much concerned with preventing the further unraveling of Pakistan under the impact of multiple challenges: secessionist movements in Baluchistan and the Northwest Frontier Province, with both movements being supported from outside. The Baluch insurgency gained strength following East Pakistan's successful secession in December 1971. Iraq supported the Baluchistan insurgency, with the Baluch Liberation Front being based in Baghdad. Suspicions of Iraqi support for the insurgents were confirmed in February 1973 when a Pakistani raid on the Iraqi embassy produced three hundred machine guns and sixty thousand rounds of ammunition destined for the Baluch rebels. Iran feared further dismemberment of Pakistan would eliminate a buffer between itself and India. In January 1973 the shah quietly visited Pakistan's Zulfikar Ali Bhutto in the latter's hometown in the Sind province of Pakistan, to discuss the situation along the Baluchistan border.[26] Three months later the Iranian ambassador to Pakistan stated that Iran considered the security of Pakistan "vital" to Iran's own security. And the next month, May, Bhutto visited Iran to discuss "bilateral relations and the situation in the region." During Bhutto's visit the shah guaranteed Pakistan's security, proclaiming,

> Once again I repeat that we will always be on your side: we are compelled to mention that what happens to our neighbor in the east, that is, the State of Pakistan, is vitally important to us; and should another event befall that country we would not tolerate it. The reason for this is not only our fraternal affection for you as a Muslim nation, but because of Iranian interests we would not be able to tolerate other changes or difficulties in Pakistan. It is quite natural that we strongly affirm that we will not close our eyes to any secessionist movement— God forbid—in your country.[27]

Shortly after Bhutto's visit to Iran, the shah deployed Iranian counterinsurgency forces to Pakistan's Baluchistan province to combat the separatist rebellion there. Operating with helicopters, the Iranian forces were capable of swift movement and were quite effective in suppressing the insurgency.[28]

Pakistan was one of China's closest allies. Mao had actually decided to strike against India in support of Pakistan during the 1965 war, although Pakistan agreed to a cease-fire before that could happen.[29] Following Pakistan's catastrophic 1971 defeat by India, China moved swiftly to rebuild Pakistan's shattered military capabilities. It was at this juncture (ca. 1974–76) that China began assisting Pakistan's nuclear weapons program—another strong sign of China's commitment to Pakistan's security. In the words of A. H. H. Abidi, both Iran and China were "anxious to preserve whatever was left of Pakistan."[30] Thus, when Chinese foreign minister Ji Pengfei visited Tehran in June 1973, he expressed Beijing's "appreciation" for the agreements recently reached by the shah and Bhutto.[31]

The Soviet Union–Iraq treaty of friendship signed in April 1972 was even more threatening to Tehran. That treaty pledged Iraq and the USSR to cooperation and mutual support in combating "imperialism, Zionism, and other threats to peace."[32] Under the treaty the Soviet Union began large-scale military assistance to Iraq, building up powerful Soviet-style Iraqi armed forces. The Soviet Union and its East European allies also began providing massive

financial and technological support for Iraqi development of a newly discovered and very rich oil field in southern Iraq—the Soviet Union's first major
involvement in an Arab oil project.

Iran was the major target of Iraq's growing military strength. Iran-Iraq
relations began deteriorating with the 1958 Iraqi revolution that overthrew
the monarchy. Iraqi encouragement of antimonarchical, Arab nationalist
movements trying to oust the weak, Western-linked monarchies in the Gulf
ran counter to Iranian efforts to counter those Iraqi subversive efforts and
support the Gulf monarchies. Iran was firmly with the United States, while
Iraq became a close ally of the Soviet Union. Territorial conflicts between Iran
and Iraq over the Shatt al Arab River also intensified, as the Iraqi government
became increasingly nationalist and self-confident, demanding that the entire
width of that lower river belong to Iraq. By the mid-1970s Iraqi-Iranian relations were quite tense.[33] Iraqi relations with India were also quite close.

The Soviet Union also gained a strong position in Ethiopia. A longtime
ally of the West under Emperor Haile Salassie, Ethiopia came under the rule
of a military Marxist group in 1974. Ethiopia's new rulers abolished the monarchy, launched internal class struggle and revolutionary programs, and brought
Ethiopia into alignment with the Soviet Union. Soviet advisors flooded
Ethiopia, followed shortly by a large Cuban military force. The shah was dismayed by the Communist takeover of Ethiopia, demanded that the United
States take firm counteraction, and was troubled when this did not occur.[34]

On the other side of the Red Sea, South Yemen—the People's Democratic
Republic of Yemen (PDRY)—was also a Soviet ally. South Yemen gained independence from Britain in 1967 and its National Liberation Front established
a socialist state aligned with the Soviet Union. The former British naval base
in Aden became a lynchpin for Soviet naval operations in the region, while the
PDRY offered sanctuary and assistance to insurgents in the southern Dhofar
province of Oman in an effort to spread the Arab socialism toward the Strait
of Hormuz.

Moscow gained an anchor on the east flank of the Indian Ocean in 1975
when the U.S. position in Vietnam collapsed. The U.S.-supported Republic
of Vietnam was overthrown by North Vietnamese forces, and Vietnam
united under Hanoi. United Vietnam moved quickly toward alliance with
the Soviet Union, and by 1978, following a Soviet-Vietnamese treaty of
alliance, Soviet military forces had access to U.S.-built air and naval bases in
the former South Vietnam. At the end of 1978 Vietnamese forces occupied
Cambodia (then called Kampuchea), ousting the pro-Chinese Khmer Rouge
regime.

Finally, at the top of the Indian Ocean arch in Afghanistan, Soviet influence also advanced toward the Indian Ocean. In 1973 that country's monarchy was overthrown. The Soviet aid and advisory presence grew. Afghanistan began pressing territorial claims on Pakistan's Northwest Frontier and Baluchistan provinces—claims that the shah felt were Soviet and Indian inspired.[35] Then in April 1978 a Marxist military coup moved Afghanistan fully into the Soviet camp. When popular revolt—assisted by Pakistan, China, and Iran—spread, Soviet forces occupied the country in December 1979. This was the first time Soviet forces had been used to support foreign Communists beyond the frontiers established at the end of World War II. Moscow's aim was to make Afghanistan a permanent part of the Soviet-allied socialist camp. Soviet forces then began concentrating on the borders of both Pakistan and Iran, threatening those countries with dire consequences if they did not suppress activities in support of Afghan resistance to Communist-government and Soviet occupation. India, a Soviet ally, was intensely hostile to Pakistan and might join with the USSR to bring Pakistan into line. Both the shah and Beijing were convinced Moscow's ultimate aim was seaports on Pakistan's Baluchistan coast.

All around the Indian Ocean basin the Soviet Union and its allies were on the advance. There was a meeting of the minds between Tehran and Beijing that this dangerous trend needed to be countered. This was the most important motive for the steadily closer Sino-Iranian relation that evolved during the 1970s, which is reviewed below. Figure 2.1 depicts the adverse regional developments that dismayed Beijing and Tehran in the 1970s and which brought them together in an effort to move events in a more favorable direction.

A final international trend that had a deep impact on Sino-Iranian relations in the early 1970s was rapprochement between the United States and China. For Beijing it was only a small step from the idea of using U.S. power to check Soviet expansionism to similarly using the power of U.S. allies such as Iran for the same purpose. The impact of Sino-U.S. rapprochement on Tehran was even greater and, indeed, may have been decisive. For the shah, U.S.-PRC rapprochement meant that improved Sino-Iranian relations would not be at the expense of Iran–United States ties. United States economic, political, and military support for Iran was vital to the realization of the shah's "great civilization." Had the breakthrough in Beijing-Washington not occurred, in all probability there would have been no comparable breakthrough in Tehran-Beijing relations in the early 1970s. Sino-U.S. rapprochement removed a crucial roadblock for the shah.

There were major differences in Chinese and Iranian attitudes toward both

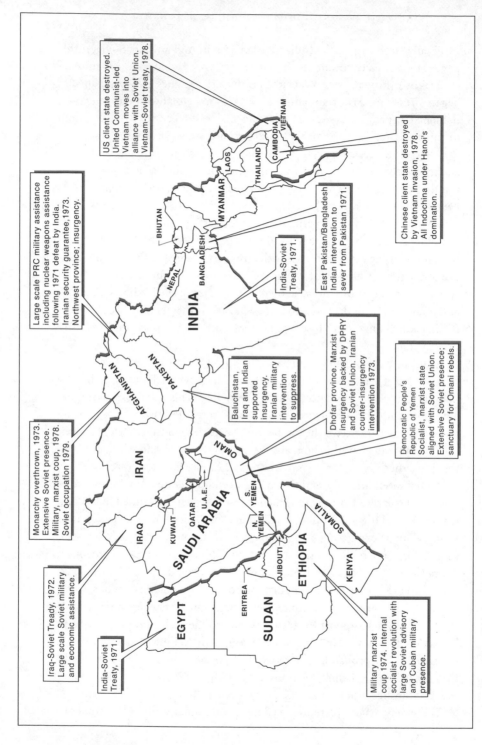

FIGURE 2.1 Geopolitical Underpinnings of Sino-Iranian 1970s Entente

the United States and the Soviet Union in the 1970s. Broadly speaking, Iran was less hostile toward both the United States and the Soviet Union, than was China. Regarding the United States, the shah and his regime were genuinely sympathetic to the West. Many of the leaders of that regime were educated in the West, and, as noted earlier, the Western model of society inspired the shah's modernization drive. China, however, remained profoundly hostile to the West and Western society in the 1970s. From Mao's and the Chinese Communist Party's (CCP) perspective, the United States was a predatory imperialist power, and Western society was exploitative and decadent. Improved relations with the United States made sense to China's Maoists from the standpoint of "using barbarians to control barbarians" or "grasping contradictions" between U.S. imperialism and Soviet social imperialism, but this did not mean acceptance of Western society and values. China's engagement with the United States in the 1970s was basically tactical. Iran's was strategic. The shah's objective was nothing less than to transform Iran into a Western country along the lines of Meiji or Ataturk.

An interesting sub-rosa dispute over U.S. spying on China in Tehran in 1973 symbolized the different approaches of Beijing and Tehran toward the United States. In November of that year China rented several apartments in a newly constructed building to serve as a dormitory for the PRC embassy. When construction was completed but before the Chinese occupants moved in, a Chinese official happened to encounter several intruders in the flats. Chinese embassy personnel forcibly detained the interlopers and turned them over to Iranian authorities. The Chinese soon concluded that the men were Central Intelligence Agency (CIA) agents attempting to bug the yet-to-be-occupied Chinese dormitory, and they believed that Iran's secret police, SAVAK, was of the same opinion. Beijing treated the incident as quite serious and demanded that, at a minimum, the men be punished. Iranian authorities, however, let the men go free—typical imperialist-like behavior of Iran's "western bourgeois politicians," in the view of the Chinese diplomat who apprehended the putative U.S. spies.[36]

Regarding the Soviet Union, the shah's priority was on improving relations with Moscow. Operationally that meant securing greater Soviet economic assistance and political support for Iran's expanded international role in the Gulf and lessening Soviet support for Iraq. Overly close alignment with Beijing's strident anti-Soviet line would not facilitate these ends, but would antagonize Moscow rather than make it more conciliatory. Thus Tehran kept a distance from Beijing's 1970s calls for a Third World united front against the Soviet Union. Nor did Tehran under the shah endorse the Five Principles of Peaceful Coexistence, Beijing's implicitly antihegemonist code of behavior.

THE PROCESS OF SINO-IRANIAN RAPPROCHEMENT

By the late 1960s the shah's thinking about China was changing. He was still intensely anti-Communist and detested China's totalitarian "ant-like society," but he increasingly appreciated China's growing power. In 1967 the shah indicated in a media interview that Iran was prepared to vote for the admission of the PRC to the United Nations if that did not entail the expulsion of Taiwan. Two years later in another media interview, this time with a Pakistani newspaper, the shah said that for any international disarmament agreement to be effective, it would have to include China.[37]

As with U.S.-PRC relations, Pakistan facilitated rapprochement between Beijing and Tehran. In January 1971, Pakistan's Zulfikar Ali Bhutto informed Beijing that Princess Ashraf Pahlavi, a younger sister of the shah, was interested in visiting China as a guest of Premier Zhou Enlai.[38] Mao approved the idea, and Zhou Enlai issued the invitation while the U.S. Ping-Pong team was in Beijing in April. Shortly afterward Princess Ashraf was warmly received in Beijing, as was her sister Princess Fatema, who followed Ashraf to Beijing a mere two weeks later. During both visits Zhou stressed the themes of civilizational commonalties outlined in the previous chapter. Princess Ashraf stressed that while her visit was "personal and non-political," her brother, the shah, "has always maintained that in this world of boundless diversity, coexistence and cooperation based on principles of mutual respect and reciprocal goodwill between countries of differing socio-political systems is perfectly possible."[39] Pakistan provided a convenient venue for talks on the modalities of normalization, and on August 16, 1971, the ambassadors of China and Iran to Pakistan signed in Islamabad an agreement on the establishment of ambassadorial-level relations between the two countries. In that agreement Iran recognized the PRC as "the sole legal government of China," and China supported Iran "in its just struggle to protect its national resources." There was no reference to the Five Principles of Peaceful Coexistence.[40] The *People's Daily* editorial greeting the establishment of diplomatic relations expressed China's "resolute support" for Iran's "effective struggles against the western petroleum monopoly" and to "safeguard national interests and national resources." It also reiterated Beijing's unequivocal claim to Taiwan.[41] Twenty-four hours before the announcement of PRC–Kingdom of Iran normalization, Iran's ambassador in Taipei informed the government there of the forthcoming move—along with the news that Iran would not approve the expulsion of Taiwan from the United Nations. United States and Japanese representatives at the United Nations had earlier indicated support for this position. In an act of monumental diplomatic ineptitude Taipei did not use these indications of support to remain in the General Assembly, thereby saving Tehran from assaying the impact of its support for Taipei on ties with Beijing.

Beijing prepared the way for Sino-Iranian cooperation by cutting off support for the Popular Front for the Liberation of the Occupied Arab Gulf (PFLOAG)—a Marxist-led liberation movement that had been fighting to overthrow the British- and Iran-supported sultan of Oman since the late 1950s. Oman was a monarchy supported by Iran and the West. China began giving *political* support to the Oman insurgency (then known by another name) in 1959 when, under the impetus of domestic and international "antirevisionist" struggles, Chinese foreign policy swung toward endorsement of armed national liberation struggles against Western-aligned Third World governments. In 1967 China began arming the Dhofar Liberation Movement, with Chinese munitions delivered via Tanzania along with Maoist propaganda. Chinese munitions were the first significant foreign assistance secured by the Omani rebels, were offered only after those rebels disavowed support from the Soviet Union, and had a considerable impact on rebel military capabilities.[42] As Oman's China-supported insurgency grew, the shah supported Oman's embattled royal government. In 1973 the shah dispatched troops to Oman to help fight the insurgency. He also deployed aircraft and antiaircraft guns to Dhofar to prevent the PDRY air force from entering Omani airspace to support rebel forces—as had previously occurred.[43] The Omani conflict had regional significance. Soviet-aligned South Yemen, the PDRY, served as sanctuary for the Dhofar rebels. Dismemberment of Oman, or ouster of Oman's pro-Western sultan, would mark a significant gain for the Soviet Union, or for China. China and Iran were involved on different sides of the Oman conflict through 1970.

In 1971 or 1972 Beijing shifted its line regarding the Oman and other insurgencies in the Persian Gulf. Chinese arms aid was cut off, and the Chinese media stopped endorsing the Dhofar rebels and covering their activities. Similar indifference was soon accorded other antigovernment rebel movements in the Persian Gulf. Beijing's dropping of the Dhofar rebels made a deep impression on the shah. In his final testament he recounted that China, "having established diplomatic relations with Iran, withdrew [support for the Omani rebels]. This goes to show that China does not play a double game."[44] The immediate reason for Beijing's dropping the Dhofar rebels was to open the door to Tehran. More broadly, Chinese leaders had concluded that insurgencies created opportunities for Soviet expansionism, and that containing the Soviet Union was better achieved by working with established governments. This shift was a result of Beijing's mounting concern with Soviet expansionism. By late 1976 Oman declared the Dhofar insurgency crushed with Iranian assistance.

A visit to China by Queen Farah in September 1972 provided an opportunity for a fuller exchange of views. Prime Minister Amir Abbas Hoveyda accompanied Farah and engaged Zhou Enlai in extensive talks on Persian Gulf, Indian Ocean, and South Asian issues of mutual concern. Zhou and Hoveyda discovered a near identity of views on a wide range of issues. The two sides also made explicit their support for the other's regime. In his speech welcoming the Pahlavi queen, Zhou extolled the shah not only for his foreign policy line but also for his role in developing Iran. Zhou implicitly equated the shah's role in Iran with Mao Zedong's role in China—a very lofty endorsement in the context of 1972 China. Queen Farah in her speech lauded China's political and social accomplishments under Mao Zedong's rule. As A. H. H. Abidi pointed out, this mutual endorsement of internal regimes represented a significant ideological concession by both sides—the intensely anti-Communist Pahlavi government by endorsing Mao Zedong's totalitarianism, and Cultural Revolutionary China by endorsing the Pahlavi imperial monarchy.[45] Beijing did not comment on but certainly noted that during Queen Farah's visit to Beijing the shah himself was visiting Moscow—testament to the shah's determination not to let improvement of Iran-China relations sour Iran-USSR ties. If Chinese leaders felt slighted by the largely feminine character of Iran's 1971–72 missions to China, Iranian commentators noted that no high-ranking Chinese official reciprocated the visits by the Pahlavi imperial household in those years.[46]

The first high-ranking Chinese official to visit Iran was Foreign Minister Ji Pengfei in June 1973—twenty-six months after Princess Ashraf's initial visit. The key theme of Ji's visit was the need for "the people" of "small and medium sized Third World countries" to "strengthen their unity for their common interests and playing an ever greater role in international affairs" and to oppose "the imperialist and expansionist forces of aggression." "We must not fail to see that certain big powers have not abandoned their hegemonic and expansionist policy of aggression. From the Middle East to South Asia, from the Persian Gulf to the Indian Ocean . . . they are intensifying their expansion and rivalry," Ji warned. In an implicit but unmistakable reference to India, Ji condemned countries that threatened others with "aggression, subversion, and *dismemberment*." As noted earlier, Ji lauded the security agreements reached by Pakistan and Iran the previous month. Regarding the Gulf, "peace and security" was "gravely menaced" by the "intensified expansion, infiltration, and rivalry" of "certain big powers." Iran is an "important country" in the Gulf region, Ji said, and has every reason to "feel uneasy" at the situation there.[47] In private Ji conveyed the message that China no longer supported antigovernment movements in the Gulf. Perhaps the most important element of Ji's visit was China's endorsement of Iran's proposition that Persian Gulf security matters should be handled by the countries of that region, not by extraregional big powers. In this regard Ji said: "We have consistently held that the affairs of a given . . . region must be managed by the countries and people's of that region. . . . Iran and some other Persian Gulf countries hold that the affairs of this region should be jointly managed by the Persian Gulf countries and brook no outside interference. This is a just position and we express our firm support for it."[48]

Although circumstances would later change, this principle would thereafter remain a key element of Chinese policy toward Iran, continuing even into the twenty-first century. In the context of 1973, this principle was directed primarily against the Soviet Union because it was Moscow that was pushing rapidly into the area, while Washington supported Iran as the new policeman of the region. After Iran's Islamic revolution, the same principle would provide the basis for China's opposition to u.s. military intervention in the Gulf and against Iran in the final stages of the Iran-Iraq war. And during the u.s.-iri confrontations over Iran's nuclear programs in the 2000s, the same principle would underpin Beijing's support for Tehran. Most broadly, this principle can be linked to Iran's and China's shared vision of a post-Western-domination era in which the great non-Western nations again play their rightful illustrious roles.

While laying out an ideal end state in which extraregional great powers withdrew from the Gulf and Indian Ocean, both Beijing and Tehran were highly realistic about the role of u.s. power in checking the Soviet Union in the context of the 1970s. Given the vigorous expansion of Soviet activity then under way, and the insufficiency of Iran and other "littoral" powers to counter Moscow's push, Tehran and Beijing both concluded that u.s. withdrawal from the region would dangerously benefit the Soviet Union. Thus when asked during an October 1974 visit to Singapore and Australia whether the growing u.s. presence in the Indian Ocean did not contradict the shah's call for management of Indian Ocean security matters by littoral powers, the shah replied: "I am not opposing the [u.s.] Diego Garcia base as long as there are other powers in the Indian Ocean. That would be silly. . . . some people say that the Russians have a 9,000 ship-day presence in the Indian Ocean. [In that case] how could we tell the Americans to keep away? But we could ask both of them to keep away from the Indian Ocean simultaneously."[49]

A. H. H. Abidi argued that Beijing's endorsement of management of Persian Gulf security by Persian Gulf littoral states *collectively*, implied rejection of Iranian domination over the Persian Gulf region.[50] At the level of principle, Abidi was correct. However, Beijing was certainly aware that because of the reality of Iran's greater national capabilities, the exit of extraregional great powers from the Gulf would leave Iran the dominant country in that region. In fact, Ji Pengfei conveyed in 1973 China's endorsement of Iran's use of its greater power to counter Soviet-backed subversion in the region—in Oman and Baluchistan. Abidi also made the important point that Beijing's emphasis on being a Third World state that would "always stand with the Third World," and "would never be a superpower," placed China in a different moral category from the self-interested "superpowers." Implicitly, China's presence in the Gulf was morally justified, while that of the superpowers was not. In effect, Beijing's call for the exit of extraregional big powers from the Gulf can be seen as an endorsement of Iranian domination of the Gulf in partnership with China. I will return to this proposition in the conclusion.

Returning to Ji Pengfei's 1973 visit, the Chinese envoy endorsed Iran's growing military buildup as "necessary and understandable." He also conveyed Beijing's support for Iran's use of its growing military power to support Pakistan. "We support the stand set forth in the [recent Iran-Pakistan] joint communiqué," Ji said.[51] Immediately prior to Ji's arrival in Tehran, a CENTO conference had met in that city and determined that more vigorous measures were necessary to check subversion in the Gulf region. In effect, Ji's comments conveyed Beijing's endorsement of the regional policeman role assigned by CENTO and the United States to Iran.

Three months after Ji Pengfei's June 1973 visit to Tehran, the Chinese ambassador there conveyed an invitation, signed by Premier Zhou Enlai, for the shah to visit China. The shah very much wanted to accept the visit, but matters of protocol and face intervened. Ji Pengfei's visit might reciprocate the 1971 visits by Princesses Ashraf and Fatema, but certainly could not be seen as reciprocating Queen Farah's September 1972 visit, or so the shah felt. The shah decided to stand on protocol and insist on a visit by Zhou before another imperial Iranian visit to Beijing. Minister of Court Asadollah Alam recounts that, when inviting the shah to visit Tehran, Beijing was "well aware" that the shah expected Zhou himself to visit Iran before the shah could travel to China. "They pretend that [Zhou] is too busy to travel abroad," Alam recorded. By November 1974 the shah faced a dilemma: "I made my acceptance of an invitation to Peking conditional upon their first sending a figure of recognized stature in return for the visit of HMQ [Her Majesty the Queen] to China," the shah told Alam. "I am keen to enforce the rules of protocol," the shah continued, "but they seem to be quite out of fashion. American Presidents . . . travel to China one after another with never a thought for the diplomatic niceties."[52] Eventually Chinese representatives convinced Tehran that Zhou Enlai was actually too ill to travel. (Zhou died of cancer in January 1976.)

Princess Ashraf would pay a brief call on him in May 1975—perhaps to confirm what Tehran had been told about Zhou's illness. In any case, Vice Premier Li Xiannian visited Iran in April 1975 to reciprocate the queen's visit.

Li Xiannian stressed the same themes as Ji Pengfei in 1973, but drew a more dire picture of the threat posed by Soviet expansionism. It followed from this gloomy picture that Third World countries should unite to counter increasingly aggressive Soviet expansionism. Tehran refused to go this far. The shah was not willing to allow Iran-China friendship to sour Iranian-Soviet relations. Iranian representatives carefully abstained from echoing or endorsing Li Xiannian's calls for a Third World united front against superpower hegemony. When Iranian media began speaking of a "Tehran-Peking axis" following Li Xiannian's visit with its stern Chinese anti-Soviet rhetoric, Iranian foreign minister Abbas Khalatbari quickly squelched such talk. Iran-China relations were strictly bilateral and could not be at the expense of a third state, Khalatbari said. More substantially, Tehran improved relations with Moscow throughout the 1970s. The shah's objective was to use Beijing to gain leverage with Moscow and thereby produce more friendly Soviet policies toward Iran, not to make Moscow more hostile to Iran by actually moving into anti-Soviet alignment with Beijing.

The death of Zhou Enlai in January and then of Mao Zedong in September 1976 made Iranian leaders apprehensive about a possible shift in Chinese policy. Might not post-Mao Beijing strive to improve relations with Moscow, thereby allowing Moscow to act more freely in west Asia and making Iran less important to China? CCP chairman and Mao's designated successor Hua Guofeng, Foreign Minister Qiao Guanhua, and Vice Premier Li Xiannian each reassured Princess Ashraf during a July-August 1976 visit to Beijing that there would be no change in China's foreign policy line. Following Mao's death a National People's Congress (NPC) mission led by NPC Standing Committee chairman Ulanfu and Ji Pengfei (by then a member of the NPC) visited Iran. They told the shah that China was increasingly concerned about Soviet advances and supportive of forceful moves to counter those advances. Ulanfu spoke with directness about the Soviet danger:

> The superpowers are frantically contending for world hegemony and *in particular*, the superpower zealously chanting "détente" and "disarmament" *is the more greedy of the two*, extending its tentacles and carrying out expansion everywhere. The Persian Gulf and the Indian Ocean where your country is situated are no exception. *That superpower* has sent numerous warships to these waters, sought to establish military bases wherever possible. . . . And interfered in the internal affairs of other countries, thus seriously endangering the independence

and security of the countries of this area. . . . The cry for a united struggle against hegemony is rising ever higher.[53]

Under these circumstances, Ulanfu continued, "We are happy to note that under the leadership of his imperial majesty the Shahanshah [king of kings, or 'emperor'], the imperial government of Iran has made efforts to strengthen Iran's defense capabilities and build up the country, while at the same time it has actively strengthened Iran's . . . cooperation with other countries in this region . . . thus making a useful contribution to the joint anti-hegemonic cause." To this "we express our support and appreciation," Ulanfu said.[54]

Hua Guofeng's August 1978 visit was the last verse in Kingdom of Iran–PRC relations. It also turned out to be a disaster for PRC diplomacy. The substantive content of the exchanges surrounding Hua's visit was unremarkable, differing little from the line laid out between Ji Pengfei's 1973 and a June 1978 visit by Foreign Minister Huang Hua. It was the symbolic content of Hua's visit, and even more the Iranian domestic background of the visit, that made Hua's visit so momentous and a diplomatic blunder that would weigh heavily on the shah's Islamic revolutionary successors.

After remaining dormant for a number of years, anti-shah activity revived in November 1977 in the form of sabotage, terrorism, and riots. By spring 1978, serious riots began sweeping Iranian cities: Isfahan, Shiraz, Tabriz, Ahyaz, and Tehran. Agitation and confrontation grew in intensity throughout the summer. By August tensions were at fever pitch. One of the worst incidents came on August 19 when arson destroyed a crowded cinema in Abadan, killing 480 people. Movie theaters were being attacked as purveyors of Western decadence. A funeral for the Abadan dead turned into a violent confrontation with police. Similar confrontations spread to other cities. There was considerable bloodshed. On August 27 Prime Minister Jamshid Amuzegar and his cabinet resigned in responsibility for an inability to stem mounting disorder.[55] Two days later Hua Guofeng arrived in Tehran.

Hua's visit would inevitably be high profile. It was the first-ever visit by China's paramount leader and/or CCP head to a non-Communist country.[56] During his visit Hua repeated the endorsements of the shah and his leadership that had become standard for Chinese officials since Ji Pengfei's June 1973 visit. As with earlier visits by Chinese leaders, Hua's visit was carefully choreographed to demonstrate the closeness between the PRC and the Kingdom of Iran—but those demonstrations of closeness now occurred in the context of rising revolutionary upheaval. Hua referred repeatedly and obsequiously to "his imperial majesty" "the Shahanshah" and the accomplishments of his regime. Hua's final words to the shah were emblematic. Bidding farewell at the Tehran airport, Hua told the shah, "We are waiting for the China visits of Your Majesties, the Shahanshah and the Shahbanou [consort of the king]." "So we hope," replied the shah. After takeoff but before leaving Iranian airspace Hua, following diplomatic courtesy, radioed a message of thanks to the shah: "Wishing Your Majesty safety and success."[57] As late as the end of January 1979 Chinese media continued to refer to the "Shahanshah." The shah departed Iran for exile on January 16, 1979. Beijing supported the shah to the very end.

During Hua's visit neither he nor members of his entourage acknowledged, let alone expressed, any sympathy for Iran's anti-shah forces. Nor did PRC media. Chinese media coverage of Iran's anti-shah activity was virtually nonexistent, and what little there was supported the shah's regime. Following indiscriminate police firing on crowds of demonstrators on September 8, 1978, for example, the Chinese press condemned the demonstrators as "financed and organized from abroad."[58] The firm pro-regime loyalty of China's media differed sharply from that of the Soviet Union, which walked a line between showing sympathy for Iran's anti-regime forces and maintaining cordial relations with Tehran. China's leaders were not oblivious to Iran's growing turmoil. It appears, however, that they committed the cardinal sin of believing their own propaganda. When intelligence about spreading disorder in Iran was passed from the embassy in Tehran back to Beijing, people in Beijing tended to see the black hand of the Soviet State Security Committee (KGB) behind that disorder. Given this perception, firmer, not weaker, support for the shah was required.[59] Chinese calculations regarding the U.S. superpower pointed in the same direction. The shah was dismayed by the Carter administration's carping on human rights and its corollary opposition to use of Iranian armed forces to crush the mounting anti-regime movement. Chinese leaders shared the shah's criticism of U.S. policy. One retired Chinese ambassador recounted with incredulity how U.S. ambassador Stansfield Turner made disparaging comments about the shah to the Chinese ambassador seated next to him at a diplomatic banquet as the shah's crisis deepened in 1978.[60] Another authoritative Chinese analyst concluded that the shah's fall was due, in part, to his overdependence on U.S. advice, that is, his failure to use the army to decisively put down the rebellion. In the face of what Beijing took to be the Carter administration's irresolution, firm support for the shah was required. The way to earn a person's friendship was by supporting him when he was in need.

Finally, Chinese analysts and leaders simply miscalculated the durability of the shah's regime. No one in Beijing imagined that the shah's regime, with such powerful and intact armed forces numbering more than four hundred thousand and an impressive record of economic development, would collapse. Beijing would pay heavily for this miscalculation. Beijing succeeded in achieving its objective at the time of Hua's visit—winning the gratitude of the shah. In his final testament the shah declared: "I must also pay homage to the loyalty of the Chinese leaders. When Mr. Hua Kuo-feng visited me, at a time when the Iranian crisis was reaching its peak, I had the impression that the Chinese alone were in favor of a strong Iran."[61] The same Chinese support that won the shah's gratitude produced bitterness among the Islamic insurgent forces soon to take power in Iran.

3 / Revolutionary Iran
and Postrevolutionary China, 1979–88

The Iranian revolution was one of the profound social revolutions of the twentieth century: an uprising of the nonelite masses of ordinary people toppling the institutions that had dominated society for many decades. During the second half of 1978, street demonstrations against the shah and his regime grew in size and militancy. Numerous groups and factions took part in those demonstrations, or supported them from the sidelines, but the most authoritative leader was Ayatollah Ruhollah Khomeini, in exile in Paris after leaving a similar exile in Iraq in October 1978. Secularists and even Marxists increasingly joined the Islamicists in demanding an end to the shah's highly Westernized regime. The shah's police fired on demonstrators, but rather than quell unrest, this application of force further inflamed the demonstrators. On December 11 a demonstration of more than a million people approved a seventeen-point program calling for the establishment of an Islamic government and proclaiming Khomeini as imam (supreme leader). The shah briefly considered ordering the army to repress the demonstrations, but ultimately decided against such a course. Having ruled out repression by brute military force, the shah lifted martial law on January 9, 1979. Demonstrations grew even larger. On January 12 Khomeini, still in Paris, set up the Council of Islamic Revolution and charged it with establishing a transitional government. On January 16 the shah flew into exile under strong pressure from the United States, and on February 1 Khomeini returned to Tehran to the welcome of rapturous throngs. On February 4 Khomeini appointed Medhi Barzargan provisional prime minister of the new government, and on February 11 a revolutionary government was established and proclaimed an Islamic republic. Two days later the Imperial Guards, the elite unit designed by the shah to ensure the survival of his regime, gave up their resistance and surrendered the Niavaran Palace where the crumbling government left behind by the shah had its offices. Revolutionary forces then began the work of repressing enemies and constructing a new order in line with the teaching of Imam Khomeini. In March 1979 a plebiscite led to formal establishment of a new Iranian state: the Islamic Republic of Iran (IRI).[1]

The PRC had also been the product of a profound social upheaval. It too was a state dedicated to destruction of the previous social order. It too was originally a revolutionary state that found its way with violence and turbulence toward construction of a new order. The PRC, like the IRI, was originally a revolutionary state that disdained the dominant international order and sought to replace that order with one fundamentally just—as indicated by the tenets of its ideology. By 1979, however, the passions and utopian visions that had fueled China's revolutionary quest had burned out. China's post-Mao leadership headed by Deng Xiaoping, who consolidated paramount power in August 1978, was dedicated to ending "class struggle" for a Communist society, focusing instead on practical matters of economic development. The institutions and values established by the Chinese revolution were still in place, but the quest now was a pragmatic one for economic improvement, not a visionary quest for a classless and egalitarian society. By 1979 China had entered its postrevolutionary stage. Just as a revolutionary Iranian state was setting out to transform Iranian society, China's state was setting out to derevolutionize Chinese society.

It is ironic that the PRC found itself in 1979 and vis-à-vis the Islamic Republic of Iran in a situation very similar to that of the United States in 1949 vis-à-vis the PRC. The PRC in 1979, like the United States in 1949, bore heavy liabilities because of close association with the ancien régime. In the several years after 1945 the United States gave considerable aid to the government of Chiang Kai-shek, even as that government attempted to suppress the growing forces of revolution. United States support for Chiang Kai-shek created a reservoir of resentment and mistrust among the leaders of the newly founded PRC. As seen in the last chapter, China gave considerable support and comfort to the shah's government during its last years, and this too left a reservoir of resentment and mistrust of China. Beijing was never the main nemesis of Iranian revolutionary fervor. That honor went to the United States, the "great Satan" who had been the shah's major partner since 1953, and to the USSR, the "lesser Satan." But among the leaders of the IRI, and especially with Khomeini, the giant charismatic figure who dominated Iran's revolution, there was considerable mistrust of China. Khomeini vented his distrust of China in late 1978 as the revolutionary movement in Tehran mounted. In a speech in October, shortly after leaving Iraq for exile in Paris, Khomeini warned: "Our youth must know that China and Russia, like the u.s. and Britain, feed on the blood of our people. My request to you is to avoid the slogans that play into the hands of the Shah and try to be independent without any inclination toward East or West. Do not be deceived by international plunders."[2] Two weeks later Khomeini again warned: "Foreign policies of America, England, Russia, and *China* and others support the corrupt regime of the Shah and his crimes. Have destroyed our economy. Have made our army dependent. Have contaminated our culture."[3]

There was also a chasm between the atheistic materialist creed of the ccp and the fervent Islamic faith of the men who founded and led the iri. One of Khomeini's principles guiding foreign policy was "Neither West, nor East." Whether China was included in the "East" was a matter of some debate in revolutionary Iran, but it seems that during the first several years after the iri was established, the ccp's Communist philosophy, combined with ignorance of China by Iran's new leaders, qualified China for inclusion in the "East." In early 1983, for example, when British newspapers reported that China was selling T-69 tanks to Iraq, with which Iran was then at war, with financing from Saudi Arabia, an ally of the United States and Sunni rival of Iran, the *Tehran Times* concluded that this was testament to China's vile nature. "That China like all other superpowers of the East and the West should support Saddam is the proof of the absolute purity of the Islamic Revolution of Iran, as well as the sign of the total bankruptcy of the system of capitalism and socialism and the proof of their shared hostility of Islam."[4] China's diplomats in Tehran during the revolutionary upheaval of 1978–79 noted slogans painted on walls and damning China along with Israel, the United States, and the Soviet Union.[5]

In spite of the profound ideological differences between China's Communist rulers and Iran's new theocratic rulers, interests of state combined with civilizational commonalities to bring the two countries together. On the Iranian side calculations of expediency associated with the war with Iraq that began in September 1980 pushed ideologically reluctant leaders toward renewal of ties with China. Yet once interactions between Iran's new clerical rulers and China's rulers began, at least some of Iran's new leaders recognized in China not only a significant power willing and able to assist revolutionary Iran wage war, but a major non-Western civilization struggling, like Iran, to develop along non-Western lines and resentful of the West's current global domination, interference, and attitude of superiority.

The clerical leaders of the newly established IRI did not know much about China. Many did not know, for example, that China has a Muslim population of twenty or so million, and were delighted to discover this fact once they began visiting China in the early 1980s.[6] As Iran's new rulers learned about China, as they began exchanging views with China's leaders, they discovered a state profoundly resentful of Western global domination, adamant in its rejection of Western notions of cultural superiority, determined to create a new world order in which the non-West would play a far greater role, and with a strong sense of solidarity with other non-Western peoples, especially those with illustrious histories and put upon by Western colonialism and imperialism. Chinese diplomats played on these themes in their efforts to educate Iran's new leaders about China. They also stressed China's post-Mao policy of freedom of religious practice. This was an important and genuine new departure under Deng Xiaoping, and demonstrating to Iranian leaders that China's Muslim's had substantial freedom to practice their religion was a key component of China's diplomacy toward the IRI.

While civilizational factors created the ambience of restored Sino-Iranian relations, the instrumental bonds were based on calculations of power. The leaders of the IRI soon found themselves confronted with a series of monumental problems—war, economic collapse, diplomatic isolation—and learned that China was able and willing to assist the IRI in addressing these problems. Simply stated, the IRI needed assistance and China could provide that help: munitions to conduct the war against Iraq, help in creating jobs and developing the economy, help with Iran's nuclear programs, and a willingness to say a few good words occasionally on Iran's behalf in the U.N. Security Council.

This situation created not only opportunities for Beijing but also distinct dangers. The fact that IRI leaders soon came to see China as a friendly power facilitated Beijing's efforts to restore a cooperative relation with Iran. But PRC alignment with the IRI against the U.S.-led West ran counter to the basic foreign policy line laid out by Deng Xiaoping in 1978. Deng had posited as the overriding goal quadrupling China's 1978 GDP by the end of the century and then lifting China's standard of living to a mid-level (specified to be a per capita GDP of $9,000–$11,000, in 2000 dollars) by the middle of the twenty-first century. Deng understood that achieving this ambitious objective would require access to U.S. markets, technology, and higher education—all predicated on general U.S. goodwill toward China's development effort. The goal was to draw on the assets of the capitalist world to modernize socialist China, and Deng understood that achieving this would require maintaining Sino-U.S. comity.[7] Unless Washington threatened such core Chinese interests as

Beijing's claim to Taiwan or CCP control over Chinese society, China would not confront the United States. China's interests during the present period lay, Deng concluded, in economic modernization, and its foreign policy needed to remain focused on that imperative. China's modernization drive could not afford to confront the United States in the Middle East and the Persian Gulf. The imperative of development imposed constraints on China's cooperation with the IRI.

Association with the IRI also contradicted Deng Xiaoping's efforts to derevolutionize China's diplomacy. Under Mao, China had played the role of patron of the global anti-imperialist revolution. Deng concluded that Mao's approach was contrary to a drive for modernization, and set about systematically derevolutionizing China's international role. Support for foreign revolutionary movements in Southeast Asia, South Asia, and Africa, and for Maoist Communist parties scattered around the world, was dropped. So too was much anticapitalist rhetoric. The philosophy of Khomeini—which became the ideology of the IRI as the Iranian revolution entered its radical phase with the seizure of the U.S. embassy in November 1979 and the war with Iran that started a year later—was as radical as Mao's had been. Khomeini rejected the very notion of sovereignty of states and instead divided humanity into a "camp of oppressors" and the oppressed masses struggling for liberation. The true religion of Islam and the Islamic revolution was the route to liberation, righteousness, and justice, and it was the duty before Allah of Iranians to assist the struggles of the oppressed elsewhere. The governments of virtually all countries, starting with the falsely Islamic governments of Egypt, Saudi Arabia, Iraq, and the Persian Gulf states, had to be overthrown and become part of the true, global Islamic community ruled, like the IRI, by Islamic law and clergy. In line with these precepts, the IRI proclaimed that the "Zionist entity" (i.e., Israel) had to be destroyed by war. Egypt, which had betrayed Islam by making peace in 1978 with the Zionist foe, had to be purified by overthrowing the "pharaoh regime" of President Anwar Sadat. Khomeini in effect excommunicated Egypt from the Islamic world and lauded the assassination of Sadat in March 1981. Iranian pilgrims making the hajj to Mecca undertook revolutionary agitation, even smuggling in weapons. Iran supported Islamic revolutionary movements in several lands. Iraq quickly became the most important target of Khomeini's Islamic revolution; replacing Saddam Hussein's rule with an Islamic revolutionary regime based on Iraq's majority Shiites was the main purpose for which Khomeini sustained war with Iraq for six years.[8]

The IRI's revolutionary approach to world affairs was exactly what China was trying to shed under Deng Xiaoping. China's leaders understood that overly close association with the revolutionary IRI would undercut China's push to normalize its own international role. Yet the IRI was not a tiny Maoist party that could be dropped at little cost. The reality of Iran's very substantial national power remained. This meant that Beijing would strive to befriend the revolutionary IRI, but avoid overly close association with it.

The constraints on China's relations with the IRI had to be conveyed to Iranian representatives with appropriate diplomatic subtlety and indirectness. It would not serve China's interests to anger or alienate Iran's new leaders. One reason for China's stress on civilizational commonalities was probably that this mitigated the rejection of Iranian pleas for stronger, bolder, higher profile Chinese support against U.S. pressure. Beijing's strategic objective was long term: to build a stable, friendly, cooperative relation with a major regional power situated in a very important region of the world. But this could not be achieved at the cost of undermining China's drive for development.

Concerns with Soviet expansionism that inspired China's Iran policy during the shah's era did not dissipate after the establishment of the IRI. If anything those concerns became worse—at least for several years. As discussed in the previous chapter, throughout the second half of the 1970s Moscow's position in the regions south of China expanded dramatically. Moscow's advance was related to a recession of U.S. power. United States military capabilities declined substantially after the Vietnam debacle in 1975, and a major debate unfolded within the United States over whether the country should continue the traditional post–World War II strategy of containing the Soviet Union. President Jimmy Carter's 1978 decisions to veto the shah's use of military force to crush mounting opposition and to pressure the shah to abdicate were important manifestations of the withering of U.S. containment policy. The collapse of the shah's regime—the U.S.-supported bulwark against Soviet expansion for more than a decade—was a devastating blow to the U.S. position in the region.

From Beijing's perspective, the danger loomed that the Soviet Union might achieve preeminence in the vast swath of land and sea between Vietnam and the Persian Gulf, encircling China from the south as well as from the north. If this was to be prevented, Iran had a significant role to play. The same geopolitical interests that had brought China into alignment with the shah's Iran helped bring it into alignment with the IRI. Interestingly, however, as Chinese fears of Soviet expansionism eased in the mid-1980s and then evaporated entirely by the 1990s, Beijing did not lose interest in partnership with Iran. Beijing's new preoccupation became countering U.S. pressure, but in this effort too cooperation with Iran proved attractive to Beijing. The enduring attraction was cooperation with a state with substantial capabilities. The political "weather"—the specific policy objectives sought—changed from period to period, but the utility of an "all-weather" partnership based on national capabilities was constant.

THE DIPLOMACY OF RAPPROCHEMENT

China's diplomacy toward Iran in the several years after 1979 entailed a methodical effort to rebuild the relationship. It began with direct and repeated offers of friendship, including professions of respect for the choice made by the Iranian people in ousting the shah. It apparently included a direct and personal, if private, apology for the perceived transgression of supporting the shah. Mutual friends played a useful role; Pakistan put in a word regarding China's reliable and practical utility as a partner. China's effort to rebuild bridges to Tehran also seem to have included a modification of policy toward the United States in order to assuage Tehran's fears. Beijing's effort included a lot of "face time" with IRI leaders—frequent exchange of delegations provided meetings with IRI's leaders, who were often honored by meetings with China's leaders above the rank of the Iranian visitor. Flattering statements about Iran's importance and greatness also played a role. Demonstrations of respect are important in any culture, but especially so, perhaps, in Chinese and Persian cultures suffering under the psychological burden of "national humiliation" of once-great nations. Stress was on civilizational similarities and common interests as non-Western nations helped create an ambience of cordiality, mitigating the profound cleavage between Tehran's fervent Islam and Beijing's Communism. Perhaps most important of all, Beijing found ways to be useful to the IRI.

On February 14, the day after the Imperial Guards capitulated to revolutionary forces and three days after Iran's revolutionary government was formed, Premier Hua Guofeng sent a cable to Prime Minister Mehdi Barzargan formally recognizing the provisional government of Iran and congratulating Barzargan on becoming prime minister. Hua added this hope: "May the friendly relations between China and Iran continue to grow in strength on the basis of the five principles of . . . non-interference in each other's internal affairs, equality and mutual benefit . . . May the traditional friendship between our two peoples witness a new development."[9] There was no response from Tehran.

PRC ambassador Jiao Ruoyu remained at his post in Tehran throughout the late 1978–early 1979 revolutionary transition of power in Tehran. On April 21 Jiao managed to arrange an interview with Barzargan to convey Beijing's "kind regards and congratulations to the Iranian leaders" and to express the desire to further develop relations between the two countries on the basis of the Five Principles of Peaceful Coexistence. Ebrahim Yazdi, vice premier for revolutionary affairs, and Abbas Amir Entezam, vice prime minister for executive affairs, were present during the interview.[10] After Ambassador Jiao's call on Barzargan in April there were no further public interactions between Beijing and Tehran for nine months. Xinhua and the Chinese media paid very close attention to developments in Iran, however. Xinhua carried extensive coverage of events in Iran during that turbulent year. A key theme of this coverage was the danger that the Soviet Union would take advantage of Iran's instability.

In July Pakistan offered its good offices. In that month Agha Shahi, then an aide to Pakistan's president, reportedly conveyed a personal apology from Hua Guofeng directly to Ayatollah Khomeini. In the message, Hua reportedly said, "I apologize to Imam Khomeini for my visit to Iran during the regime of the deposed Shah and I support the Islamic Republic of Iran." Hua explained that because of his long trip home after visiting Yugoslavia, "I had to stop in Iran." When Iran television announced this news of Hua's reported apology, it added that Ayatollah Khomeini had forgiven Hua because, "Our country likes to have friendly relations with Islamic and non-Islamic countries. Although this trip came at a time when the youth of Iran were being drowned in blood, we and the Iranian nation will forgive him."[11] Other than publicly announcing that the supreme leader Khomeini had forgiven Hua, there was no further initiative toward Beijing from Tehran

Beijing developed an exculpatory explanation for Hua's 1978 visit. The reason for Hua's foreign travel at that time was to give China's paramount leader some international exposure and visit old and new nonaligned friends— Romania and Yugoslavia. Because of the limited range of the Boeing 707 carrying Hua, it was necessary to refuel en route, and since a civil aviation agreement had been concluded with Iran in November 1972, Hua's planners selected Tehran as the refueling stop. The foreign ministry then pointed out that to stop in Tehran without meeting the shah could well have offended him. A brief but "official" visit was thus added, in early 1978, to Hua's return trip. As turmoil mounted in Tehran in mid-1978, the earlier decisions were not revisited. This explanation was conveyed to Iran's new government along with China's wish for friendly, cooperative relation with *any* established government of Iran.[12]

China's close association with the United States circa 1979–80 was a serious problem in PRC-IRI relations. The U.S.-PRC anti-Soviet strategic partnership had deepened rapidly throughout the 1970s, reaching its apogee in 1979 when U.S.-PRC relations were normalized (on January 1, 1979) on the basis of granting China Most Favored Nation (MFN) status—which China actually received when a U.S.-PRC commercial agreement was signed early in 1980. The uncoupling of MFN for China and the USSR was a deliberate U.S. move to form a closer alignment with China against the Soviet Union. (The USSR never received MFN status.) Deng Xiaoping then visited the United States just before China's punitive invasion of Vietnam in February. Chinese polemics against Soviet foreign policy were then very strident. Chinese-American anti-Soviet cooperation even touched directly on Iran when China agreed to provide U.S. intelligence agencies with listening posts in western Xinjiang, replacing posts previously in Iran but closed by the revolution there and used for monitoring Soviet rocket firings in Soviet Central Asia. From the perspective of many of Iran's new leaders, Beijing appeared an ally of the United States. China's cooperation with the United States was a major theme of Soviet propaganda toward revolutionary Iran.

The seizure of the U.S. embassy and sixty-six American personnel by revolutionary Iranian youth on November 4, 1979, forced the issue of China's relation with the United States into the agenda of Iran's new leaders. Respect for the immunity of diplomats is one of the oldest and most basic principles of international law. Beijing tried to walk a middle course between Washington and Tehran, but this failed to assuage Tehran's radicals. A PRC foreign ministry statement issued several weeks after the embassy seizure implicitly affirmed the Iranian radicals' critique of the United States, saying: "We always hold that the internal affairs of each country should be managed by its own people and that there should be no interference in the internal affairs of other countries." It then proceeded to implicitly condemn the Iranian seizure: "But at the same time we hold that the principles guiding international relations and the accepted diplomatic immunities should be universally respected."[13] When the U.N. Security Council voted in July 1980 to condemn the IRI seizure of U.S. diplomats, China abstained.

Beijing understood well the revolutionary origins and political utility of the embassy seizure. There were, in fact, striking similarities between the Iranian seizure of the U.S. embassy and the CCP's own 1948 seizure of the U.S. Consulate in Mukden. Both moves served to radicalize the revolution. But Beijing feared the Soviet Union would take advantage of the Iranian embassy seizure. A long commentary in Renmin ribao two months into the embassy seizure sympathized with the revolutionary origins of the move. The embassy seizure showed "the fierce eruption of the Iranian people's long-suppressed demand for national democratic revolution" and was an "evil consequences of the post-war U.S. Middle East policy." The commentary also explained how the embassy seizure was linked to the internal dynamics of the Iranian revolution: "Stepping up . . . opposition to u.s. imperialism could help iron out domestic differences." Yet the move violated "common international rules of diplomatic practice," and this made it "very difficult" to "win support and sympathy." Most dangerous of all, the commentary emphasized, the embassy seizure created opportunities for the Soviet Union. "Iran's strained relations with the United States and internal unrest have given the Soviet Union a golden opportunity to fish in troubled waters both in this country and in its neighboring areas." With Soviet forces in Afghanistan and concentrating on the Afghanistan-Iran border, it would not be wise to allow the stalemate in Iranian-u.s. relations to drag on, the commentary warned.[14] Reading between the lines, one could see the advice that Iran should negotiate with Washington in an effort to resolve the crisis and improve Iranian-u.s. relations. President Abol Hassan Bani-Sadr resigned in June 1981 in large part over this issue. He had disagreed with the radical's policy of not negotiating with Washington or using u.n. mediation to resolve the embassy seizure issue.[15]

While critical of Iran's seizure of the u.s. embassy, Beijing also condemned the u.s. response of levying economic sanctions against the IRI and the attempted u.s. use of military force in April 1980 to rescue the hostages. A Ministry of Foreign Affairs statement issued following the failed u.s. rescue effort said that "the problem of the American hostages . . . not only causes the anxiety of the American people but also arouses wide international concern." However, "we also consider that the u.s. government's sanctions against Iran and its [military] operation to rescue the hostages in violation of Iran's territorial integrity and sovereignty, are not helpful toward a solution, but would rather worsen the situation."[16] Replying to a briefing by the Italian ambassador to China about the European Economic Community's economic sanctions against Iran, Vice Foreign Minister Song Zhiguang stated that China did not agree that pressure of an economic nature would secure release of the American hostages. On the contrary, Song said, the "hasty American move" endangered sympathy that had emerged for the plight of the American hostages.[17] Beijing's "principled opposition" to u.s.-sponsored economic sanctions would become another consistent element of China's political support for the IRI extending into the twenty-first century.

After keeping a low public profile in Iran throughout 1979, in early 1980 Beijing took the diplomatic initiative. At the end of January 1980 Ye Jianying, chairman of the Standing Committee of the NPC (then the closest equivalent to the office of "president" in the PRC constitutional setup), sent a message extending "warm and sincere congratulations" to Abol Hassan Bani-Sadr on his assumption of the office of the first president of the IRI. "We wish Your Excellency and the fraternal Iranian people many new successes in the noble cause of safeguarding state sovereignty and independence and turning Iran into a prosperous country." "May the friendship and relations of amicable cooperation between China and Iran and between our two peoples continue to grow in strength and develop," Ye wrote.[18] When the IRI embassy in Beijing held a reception in February commemorating the first anniversary of the establishment of Iran's revolutionary government, Chinese foreign minister Huang Hua, vice minister of foreign trade Cui Qun, and vice chairman of the China Islamic Association Haji Iliyas Shen Xiaxi attended. When a second reception was held two weeks later commemorating essentially the same event, Vice Premier Ji Pengfei and Vice Foreign Minister He Ying attended along with leading members of the Islamic Association of China and various departments under the State Council. In February 1980 the Chinese Red Cross Society donated two thousand blankets and two hundred tents for flood victims in southern Iran. Periodic relief contributions in the aftermath of natural disasters also became a consistent element of China's courting of the IRI over coming years.

The first Chinese delegation to the IRI was a group of Chinese Muslims in February 1980 led by the vice president of the China Islamic Association, Al-hajji Mohammad Ali Zhang Jie—a longtime core cadre in CCP united front work. The delegation traveled to Iran at the invitation of the IRI foreign ministry to celebrate the beginning of the fifteenth century of the Islamic era and the first anniversary of Iran's Islamic revolution. The delegation stayed two weeks, was received by Ayatollah Khomeini and President Bani-Sadr, visited holy sites at Qom and Mashhad, and participated in several seminars on Islamic matters.[19] Zhang Jie's mission seems to have been an important step in educating Iran's new clerical leaders about China's partially Muslim character. Zhang was a member of China's Hui (Han but Muslim) minority from Hebei province in north China. After finishing Islamic studies in the late 1930s, Zhang became involved in anti-Japanese nationalities propaganda work in cooperation with the CCP. In 1941 he became vice director of the Yan'an mosque—Yan'an being the capital of the CCP's base area on the Shaanxi-Gansu-Ningxia border region in north China—and acting director of the Hui Association of that base area. After 1949 Zhang held a number of important positions in the China Islamic Association and the China Islamic Studies Association. He also participated in Chinese delegations to more than ten Islamic countries, thereby "making contributions to friendly relations" between those countries and China, according to an online biography.[20] Zhang was well versed in CCP policy and explained to Iran's new leaders that China's Muslims enjoyed freedom of religion while participating in the building of new China under the leadership of the CCP.

Shortly after the return of Zhang Jie's Chinese Islamic Association delegation from Iran, a new ambassador, Zhuang Yan, took up his post in Tehran. Zhuang was able to arrange the first high-level meeting between IRI and PRC officials in Belgrade during the funeral for Yugoslav leader Josip Broz Tito. On May 6 Hua Guofeng, en route by air to Yugoslavia to attend Tito's funeral, radioed a message of greetings to President Bani-Sadr while passing through Iran's air space. "I would like to express sincere wishes for the safety and good health to [sic] Your Excellency, security for your country, and continued cooperation between the PRC and Iran," Hua's message said.[21] On May 9 IRI foreign minister Sadeq Qotbzadeh, also attending Tito's funeral, met with Hua for a half hour at the Intercontinental Hotel in Belgrade. Hua and Qotbzadeh discussed and agreed on the expansion of Sino-Iranian relations on the basis of mutual respect and noninterference in each other's internal affairs. They also agreed that Soviet forces should withdraw immediately from Afghanistan, leaving the destiny of Afghanistan to be decided by its people. At the end of the meeting, Hua invited Qotbzadeh to visit China.[22] Before that could happen, Qotbzadeh was purged and executed in September 1982 as part of the rupture between moderate and radical camps in the Iranian revolution. An IRI foreign minister would not visit China until September 1983—thirty-six months into the Iran-Iraq war. Barzargan, Bani-Sadr, and Qotbzadeh, Iranian leaders more responsive to China's initiatives in the months immediately after the revolution, were leaders of a "realist" faction advocating diplomatic openings toward major countries in pursuit of Iran's national interests. They were opposed, and ultimately defeated, by an "idealist" faction that placed Islamic values above national purposes and favored export of the revolution and disassociation with any country linked to the superpowers—such as China was to the United States.[23] Iran's response to Beijing's overtures was held hostage to this elite factional struggle.

CHINA AND THE IRAQ-IRAN WAR

Iran's eight-year-long war with Iraq created powerful exigencies for Iran and thereby opportunities for Beijing's diplomacy. The war was a searing experience for Iran. In all of its wars from the 1920s through the 1970s (mostly domestic insurgencies), Iran had suffered some 3,000 soldiers killed. In the first two weeks of the war with Iraq, its losses were more than ten times that.[24] By the end of the war, Iran's total war dead would number 262,000, with another 600,000 wounded, or combined, 2.2 percent of the 1980 population of 39 million.[25] In 2004 the main roads of many Iranian villages were lined with photographs of the soldiers from that village who died in the war.

Full-scale war began on September 22, 1980, when Iraqi forces attacked into Iranian territory along a seven-hundred-kilometer front. Saddam Hussein saw an opportunity to displace Egypt (discredited by its "traitorous" peace with Israel) as leader of the Arab camp. He also calculated that disorganiza-tion within Iran would render it a soft target, permitting him to seize Iran's oil-rich and Arab-populated southwestern province of Khuzistan. But things did not go as Saddam Hussein planned. Iranian forces put up stiff resistance. By late 1981 Iraqi forces had run out of steam. Iran then took the offensive and in a series of attacks between March and May 1982 virtually eliminated Iraqi forces from Khuzistan. Faced with mounting battlefield setbacks and growing financial difficulties, Hussein decided to withdraw his forces to the international border and adopt static defense along that line, using the June 1982 Israeli invasion of Lebanon as a pretext. Thus, by mid-1982 Iranian ter-ritory had been cleared of Iraqi forces.

Iran could have declared victory and made peace at that point, but its lead-ers decided to continue the offensive into Iraq in expectation that the Iraqi military would collapse in the face of determined attack, triggering an upris-ing of Iraq's long-oppressed Shiites. An Islamic revolutionary regime in Iraq would then extend the realm of the true faith. Iran's leaders also believed that Iraq's attack had been instigated by the United States as a way of weakening Islamic revolutionary Iran. The appropriate counter to this, they concluded, was a revolutionary jihad to sweep across Iraq, the Persian Gulf, and Arabia, finally destroying the "Zionist entity that western imperialism had implanted in the heart of the Islamic world" (i.e., Israel). In July 1982 a major Iranian offensive opened in the direction of Basra in southern Iraq with the Iranian high command announcing that Iran was "going to liberate Jerusalem, pass-ing through Karbala."[26] Revolutionary zeal sustained Iran's offensive efforts for several years, although those offensives gained little territory at the cost of very high Iranian casualties.

Beijing's formal position on the Iran-Iraq war was neutrality combined with professions of friendship and continued commerce with both belliger-ents. The day after the war erupted Premier Zhao Ziyang outlined China's stance, laying out three principles that would guide Chinese policy through-out the war: (1) the conflict was not in the interests of either Iran or Iraq, and disputes between the two should be settled peacefully via negotiations; (2) the superpowers should not intervene in the conflict; and (3) the fighting should not expand, lest it threaten peace and stability in the Gulf area.[27] A

Renmin ribao commentary elaborated on China's position. Iran and Iraq were both Muslim countries belonging to the Third World. "Hence, there is no conflict of fundamental interests between them." Conflict between these two Third World countries would be of no help in finding a solution to complicated problems, "but will only sadden their own people and gladden their enemy." War, the commentary warned, would "provide excuses for outside interference and consequently involve this region in the contention between big powers."[28] Beijing feared that the United States would use the pretext of protecting Gulf shipping to use force against Iran, further expanding its military position in the Gulf. Peace would deny the United States this opportunity and hinder the development of u.s. military hegemony in the Gulf. Peace was thus in accord with Iran's own interests, with the Third World's interest, and with China's interest. In line with this, throughout the Gulf war Beijing urged Tehran to conclude a swift, compromise peace with Iraq.

On September 28, 1980, the Security Council unanimously adopted a resolution calling on Iraq and Iran "to refrain immediately from any further use of force and to settle their disputes by peaceful means." China voted for the resolution. This stance of the Security Council outraged Khomeini and his brethren in Tehran. By placing Iran and Iraq on the same moral level, the Security Council failed to differentiate between the aggressor and the victim of aggression, between an aggressive and a self-defensive resort to military force. The Security Council and its resolutions were devoid of justice and reflected the greedy self-interest of the great powers. The ringleader of those "arrogant powers," the United States, had itself instigated Saddam Hussein's attack against Iran, or so IRI leaders believed. Now the United States and the other "arrogant powers" were using the United Nations to mask Saddam Hussein's aggression, and using that aggression to pressure the IRI. By following the lead of the other permanent members of the Security Council on the issue of the Iran-Iraq war, by refusing to distinguish between the aggressor and the victim of aggression, Beijing confirmed many of Khomeini's negative stereotypes of China. Beijing talked about Third World solidarity but was in fact a junior partner of the Great Satan. It was such sentiments that led to the issue in 1983 of the IRI postage stamp depicted on the cover of this book. Overcoming these deep suspicions required a significant adjustment of China's relations with the United Sates circa 1982—a matter discussed below.

Beijing's policy of neutrality was partially intended to avoid spoiling China's relations with the Arab countries—most of which supported Arab, Sunni Iraq against Persian, Shiite, and revolutionary Iran. China's calculations in this regard were expressed very well by Vice Premier Ji Pengfei during a visit to the Yemen Arab Republic days after the onset of the Iran-Iraq war: "With a population of 150 million and rich oil resources, the Arab countries are of strategic importance. They are playing an increasingly important role in international affairs. We sincerely hope that the Arab countries will become even more prosperous and stronger. . . . China maintains friendly relations with both Iraq and Iran. . . . Superpower attempts to meddle and interfere should be guarded against."[29]

Framed in terms of Beijing's Three Worlds theory, Ji Pengfei's words meant that the true interests of both Iran and Iraq, and indeed of the entire Middle East, lay in countering u.s. and Soviet hegemony. Any contradiction between Iran and Iraq should be settled in a fashion that did not undermine the Third World's antihegemony struggle by giving the superpowers a chance to expand their domination by "meddling and interfering." From Khomeini's perspective, however, Beijing's refusal to draw a clear distinction between aggressive and defensive resort to force merely because to do so might alienate "a population of 150 million and rich oil resources," manifested the same sort of self-interested, amoral mentality that afflicted all "arrogant powers" such as the United States. Khomeini's philosophical starting point was not calculation of national self-interest, but divinely revealed moral principles. It would take considerable diplomatic effort by Beijing to explain to the leaders of the Islamic revolution that China too, and unlike the base superpowers, acted on the basis of high moral principle, in this case the principle of opposing superpower interference to emancipate the Third World from superpower hegemony. At a more practical level, the combination of heavy logistic requirements associated with a large, high-intensity war, plus the alienation of Iran's traditional Western military suppliers, created severe problems for Iran. Tehran had to find new sources of military supply quickly. Into this vacuum stepped China.

The first high-level iri delegation to visit China was in February 1981 and led by Majlis member (and future president and successor to Khomeini as supreme leader) Seyed Mohammad Ali Hoseyn Khamenei. When the delegation arrived in Beijing, the Iraq-Iran war had been raging for five months and the magnitude of the logistic problems faced by Iranian forces was apparent. According to official announcements, the purpose of Khamenei's visit was to brief Chinese leaders on Iran's position on the war. The fact that China had declared neutrality in the conflict, Khamenei told the press shortly after arriving in Beijing, did not mean that the Chinese government was not sympathetic to Iran. In fact, Khamenei said, China sympathized with Iran.[30] Iran cherished China as a close friend, Khamenei told vice chairman of the Standing Committee of the npc Ulanfu. The two countries shared common ground in international affairs and had many common interests. Ulanfu replied that China and Iran enjoyed a traditional friendship and should expand their relation. Third World countries should unite to oppose imperialism, colonialism, and hegemonism and to safeguard world peace, Ulanfu said.[31] An array of Chinese officials graced a "tea party" given for Khamenei by the Iranian embassy in Beijing.

By 1982 U.S. officials were charging that China and North Korea together accounted for 40 percent of Iran's arms supplies.[32] By 1987 that number had risen to 70 percent.[33] Sino-Iranian economic cooperation also began to expand in 1982. In July of that year an Iranian economic delegation led by acting agriculture minister Abbasali Zali visited Beijing to discuss "economic, commercial, and technical relations" and "investigate Chinese economic facilities." While economics was the main thrust of Zali's visit, he also explained Iran's stance on the war with Iraq, the "general position of the Islamic revolution," and "the interference of foreign powers in the region."[34] In December that same year, a Chinese economic delegation visited Iran. An agreement was signed providing for an increase of total bilateral trade from $200 million in 1982 to $500 million for 1983.[35] With war, sanctions, and Iran's revolutionary activism isolating it from traditional trading partners, Tehran needed new partners. Again China seized the opportunity.

CHINA'S 1982 FOREIGN POLICY
ADJUSTMENT AND SINO-IRANIAN RELATIONS

In 1982 China adjusted its global alignment, away from close alignment with the United States against "Soviet expansionism" and toward a more independent stance. No longer did Beijing identify the Soviet Union as the most dangerous source of war or call for a global united front of all antiexpansionist forces to check Soviet advances. Rhetorically, Washington and Moscow were now placed on a nearly equal plane as superpowers seeking hegemony and as equivalent sources of hegemonic superpower misdeeds. Chinese media became more critical of U.S. policies and started laying greater stress on the Third World. Beijing also began to respond positively to gestures from Moscow, beginning a process that would lead ultimately to Sino-Soviet rapprochement and Mikhail Gorbachev's May 1989 visit to Beijing.

The standard explanation of this 1982 adjustment is in terms of Chinese anger over the Reagan administration's arms sales to Taiwan, combined with a Chinese assessment that the revitalization of U.S. anti-Soviet containment policy under Ronald Reagan had halted the previous dangerous drift toward Soviet global primacy. With Moscow on the defensive, it was unlikely to launch new aggressive ventures. There is no reason to discard these standard explanations. But an additional "Iran factor" (actually an Iran *and Indian* factor) seems to have part of the mix of Chinese considerations underlying the 1982 shift.[36]

There are several bodies of evidence suggesting an Iran factor in the 1982 shift. First of all, China's relations with Iran circa 1979–81 suffered because of Beijing's close association with the United States. China's more "independent" line responded to Soviet propaganda attacks on China's "alliance" with the United States—attacks that apparently had some resonance in Iran. The 1982 shift in Chinese policy, however, ameliorated Iranian concerns about China, thereby expediting Sino-Iranian rapprochement. Nearly as soon as Beijing's "independent foreign policy line" had been enunciated, Chinese leaders began using that line, along with marginally more assertive Chinese opposition to u.s. policy, to strengthen Sino-Iranian relations. Iran noted and was happy about China's increasing alignment with the Third World circa 1982.[37] Finally, and most important, the 1982 adjustment in China's line extricated Beijing from close alignment with the United States just as Iranian-u.s. ties were spiraling downward. Given the reality of mounting u.s.-Iranian tension in the 1980s, Beijing had little realistic hope of a close relation with Tehran as long as China remained in close strategic alignment with Washington.

The iri faced rapidly mounting u.s. military pressure primarily because of the u.s. response to the collapse of its key regional ally, Iran under the shah, combined with increasing Soviet aggressiveness. As noted earlier, traditional u.s. policy toward the Gulf was to rely on a proxy power, first Britain and then Iran, to police that region. That policy collapsed with the shah's regime. President Carter's response was a decision to deploy u.s. military forces to the region and to build up an infrastructure that could sustain operations to deter or, if necessary, defeat a move to seize Persian Gulf petroleum or close the Strait of Hormuz. Henceforth the United States itself would serve as guardian of the Gulf. Originally the "Carter Doctrine," as this radical departure in u.s. policy was dubbed, was directed against possible Soviet expansionism. But as the radical, expansionist nature of the Iranian revolution became apparent, and once Iraq and Iran were embroiled in war with pressures toward escalation in the form of attacks on oil commerce in the Gulf, the doctrine was extended to apply to potentially aggressive regional powers. This meant that Iranian moves against the flow of oil through the Persian Gulf brought it into direct military conflict with the United States.[38]

From the iri's perspective, the purpose of the u.s. buildup in the Gulf was to pressure and ultimately destroy Iran's Islamic revolutionary regime. As noted earlier, Iran's Islamic leaders believed that the United States had instigated Saddam Hussein's attack on Iran in September 1980, while the hostage crisis was in its tenth month, as a way of punishing and weakening Iran. Eliminating or at least limiting the rapidly expanding post-1979 u.s. military presence in the Persian Gulf thus quickly became a major Iranian objective. In this situation, continued Chinese alignment with the United States in the Persian Gulf constituted a major obstacle to Sino-Iranian rapprochement.

Chinese propaganda toward Iran during 1979–80 had had the effect of stressing China's alignment with the United States in the global struggle against the Soviet Union. A *Renmin ribao* article in early January 1979, for example, while the shah was still in power, warned that Moscow was deploying a division of Persian-speaking troops to Iran's northern border. Soviet MiG-25 aircraft were increasingly intruding into Iran's airspace, while seventeen Soviet cruisers and a flotilla of submarines stood off the Strait of Hormuz. Landing craft were on "standby" at a nearby Soviet base. Soviet leader Nikita Khrushchev had once described Iran as "a ripe apple." Leonid Brezhnev "now seems rather impatient in his eagerness to pick the 'ripe apple,'" the article said.[39] A Beijing radio broadcast in April 1979 explained that Moscow was "bent on placing Iran under its control so as to lay hold of the Persian Gulf outlet and cut off the West's petroleum supply line." Achieving an unstable condition in Iran was part of Moscow's strategy: "Particularly worth noting is the fact that Soviet social imperialism does not want a stabilized Iran."[40] Still another commentary in *Renmin ribao* in June 1979 explained,

> The Soviet Union is always glaring like a tiger, ready to pounce on Iran. This is because Iran not only has abundant petroleum and natural gas but also occupies the most important strategic position. If the Soviet Union can dominate Iran, it will be able to go southward through the Persian Gulf and Indian Ocean and extend its aggressive forces right into the Middle East oil-producing region. It will then achieve a great superiority over the United States in their contention for world hegemony.[41]

To foster instability in Iran, the Soviet union was infiltrating "its agents into Iran in an attempt to usurp the leadership of the people's struggle," conducting a "massive propaganda offensive" via radio and television broadcasts, and secretly shipping weapons into Iran.

Within a couple of years, as part of Beijing's shift in global alignment, this sort of gloomy and implicitly antirevolutionary rhetoric would disappear from the Chinese media, probably because it roused rather than eased Iranian suspicions of Beijing. This commentary illustrated, of course, the geopolitical outcome that Beijing sought to avoid as it engaged the IRI. But it also implicitly underlined the fact that China stood with Washington in the global struggle against Moscow.

It may be that the conjunction between Beijing's adoption of an "independent foreign policy" and Sino-Iranian rapprochement was pure serendipity and that the improvement of Sino-Iranian relations that flowed from Beijing's distancing itself from the United States was an unintended consequence of that policy. Scholarly prudence requires that one defer final judgment until Beijing declassifies primary documents regarding the proposed inspiring 1982 shift. However this may ultimately prove to be, it is clear that China's 1982 shift in policy substantially enlarged the areas of commonality between Beijing and Tehran.

THE "NEW START" IN SINO-IRANIAN RELATIONS

In May 1982 the IRI's first ambassador in Beijing took up his post. Dr. Ali Khorram had been a doctoral student in physics at the University of Chicago as Iran's revolutionary movement burgeoned in 1978. He became part of a small group of Iranian students in the United States who reported to and advised Khomeini's Paris headquarters on the American and international situation. As the Islamic revolution moved toward victory in February 1979, the Paris headquarters directed Khorram's group to contact and secure the allegiance of Iran's several diplomatic missions in the United States. This Khorram's group did with some success. Establishment of an Islamic regime necessitated a major change in diplomatic personnel, and Khorram was drawn into the diplomatic corps as part of this reshuffling. He was first posted to the United Nations, then to Libya. Beijing was his third posting. Khorram was still in his twenties when he assumed his post in Beijing.[42]

Before taking up his new post, Khorram spent several weeks in Tehran studying foreign ministry documents on Sino-Iranian relations. A hostile view of China prevailed in Iran at the time, largely because of Hua's August 1978 visit. Khorram's study of the record convinced him that Hua's visit had not marked a special Chinese endorsement of the shah's regime, but that the exculpatory explanation of that visit being advanced by China's representatives was essentially accurate. Once in Beijing Khorram concluded that China was not like the United States, Britain, or the Soviet Union, but that it identified and sympathized with the Third World. He began reporting this conclusion to Tehran. Khorram also discovered in Beijing mistakes in Chinese thinking about developments in Iran: many people greatly exaggerated the danger of Soviet influence in Iran. Khorram attributed this to U.S. influences. United

States agents had passed this misinformation to China, presumably in an effort to spoil IRI-PRC relations.

In January 1983 Chinese foreign ministry advisor He Ying called on Khorram and stated he wanted to confess a mistake in previous Chinese thinking about Iran. Previously China had viewed Iranian developments through the prism of the global anti-Soviet struggle and, consequently, overestimated the role of Soviet instigation and subversion in Iranian affairs. China had undertaken a reappraisal of events and now recognized that the earlier view was mistaken. Beijing now had a very different analysis of the Iranian situation. He Ying asked Khorram to convey to Tehran this Chinese acknowledgment of its previous "mistaken views." Khorram suggested that He Ying himself convey this important message to Tehran.

He Ying was the first high-level PRC envoy to visit the IRI. He traveled to Tehran in late January 1983 to "exchange views" and discuss the "common struggle against imperialism and colonialism." In talks with He Ying, Khamenei (then Majlis speaker) stressed the "crimes all over the world" being committed by the United States. By attacking Iran, Saddam Hussein was fulfilling U.S. objectives of destroying Muslim nations, stabilizing the Zionist regime, and establishing U.S. military bases in the region. The two sides concluded He Ying's visit with a pledge of a "common stand in the struggle against imperialism and colonialism."[43] He Ying's visit prepared the way for a set of reciprocal foreign minister visits, the first since the establishment of the IRI: Ali Akbar Velayati to China in September 1983, and Wu Xueqian to Iran in October 1984. According to one highly authoritative Chinese source, these visits marked a "new beginning" in Sino-Iranian relations.[44]

In Beijing, Velayati met with President Li Xiannian and told him that Iran deemed China "a country of strategic importance" that held "an important place" in Iran's foreign policy.[45] Li Xiannian replied that China and the IRI had two principles in common. Both were "neither West, nor East," and both followed a policy of independence. China appreciated Iran's independent foreign policy, Li said. Velayati met also with premier Zhao Ziyang, who said possibilities for further cooperation existed because there was no conflict of interest between the two countries, while both faced the common tasks of economic development and fighting hegemonism.[46] Iran's policy of safeguarding its independence could check the rivalry of the superpowers in the Persian Gulf (and thereby implicitly serve China's own interests), Zhao noted. Velayati replied that the IRI had "suffered at the hands of one superpower without allowing the hands of another superpower to take their place."[47] In talks with Wu Xueqian, Velayati said that Iran did not seek or submit to hegemony, supported the nonaligned movement, and advocated stronger relations with Third World countries. Wu said that China did not depend on or submit to pressure from foreign powers. China's foreign policy was founded on the principles of antihegemonism, maintaining world peace, and strengthening relations with Third World countries. Both sides expressed support for the Palestinian people.[48] Velayati and Wu signed a five-year agreement on cultural, scientific, and technological cooperation.

Wu Xueqian's return visit in October 1984 evoked a similar tone. China attached "great importance" to cooperation with Iran, Wu told Khamenei (by then president), who replied that the Iranian people respected the Chinese people and cast an eye of hope toward China as they struggled in the revolution. Majlis speaker Ali Akbar Hashemi Rafsanjani was also enthusiastic about the possibility of expanded political cooperation with China. Iran appreciated China's policy of independence from the superpowers and seeking close ties with other Third World countries, Rafsanjani told Wu. Many similarities existed between Iran and China, Rafsanjani said, notably their independent foreign policies, and they should be friends.[49] At the end of Wu's visit the two sides issued a joint communiqué for the first time.[50] It called for expanding and strengthening "bilateral relations and international cooperation." Wu Xueqian told reporters that Iran and China "share common views on many major international issues *although they pursue independent foreign policies.*"[51] This last phrase was an early statement of a consistent theme of China's policy: hesitation to align too closely with revolutionary Iran.

China did not accept several of Tehran's proposals for cooperation. Foreign Minister Velayati had developed a plan to expel Israel from the United Nations as a step toward destruction of that "Zionist entity" and "liberation of Palestine." Velayati requested that China, with its Security Council veto, support the plan.[52] China declined. Velayati also felt that the 1978 Camp David peace treaty between Egypt and Israel "only served to trample on the rights of the Palestinian people" and protect the "Zionist regime."[53] China should use its U.N. veto to support more actively the Palestinian cause, Velayati urged. Chinese representatives again demurred. Beijing was in fact moving in the other direction—toward expanded ties and ultimately (in 1992) ambassadorial relations with Israel. Velayati also called on China to "cut . . . unjust ties with the superpowers" and increase its support for Third World countries.[54] Needless to say, Beijing was not interested in the Sino-Iranian cooperation that entailed cutting PRC-U.S. ties.

One aspect of China's independent foreign policy explained by Wu was U.S. president Ronald Reagan's high-profile visit to China in April–May 1984. Iranian media had been very critical of that visit, and China was upset with Iran's criticism of China's policy toward the United States. Such criticism could endanger execution of a recently concluded PRC-IRI billion-dollar arms sale, the Chinese side suggested.[55] Beijing felt that just as Washington should not attempt to dictate PRC-IRI relations, Tehran should not attempt to define PRC-U.S. ties.

China was more interested in low-profile, economic cooperation with Iran. In February 1985 a large and high-power PRC economic delegation led by state councilor Zhang Jingfu made an eight-day visit to Tehran to find ways of expanding cooperation in agriculture, fisheries, animal husbandry, irrigation, rural industries, and dam building. The result was the establishment of a vice ministerial–level joint committee on cooperation in economics, trade, science, and technology to "explore in detail possibilities for cooperation."[56] Zhang also signed a hefty arms sales agreement.

An Iranian view of the political context of expanding economic cooperation at this juncture was conveyed to Zhang Jingfu by President Khamenei. The Iranian people had learned to differentiate between friends and potential foes and realized that China had no "domination seeking tendencies." Regarding the United States, Iran would employ every opportunity to criticize its "support for the Zionist regime and its interference in the affairs of other countries. We deem it our right to defend the oppressed countries and in this respect there is a common view between the Islamic Republic of Iran and the People's Republic of China," Khamenei said.[57] There were "broad prospects" for cooperation between China and Iran even though they have different social systems. Third World countries could not expect help from the superpowers, but could only "rely on unity and cooperation among themselves."[58] In his reply to these fulsome words by Khamenei, Zhang Jingfu hinted at some of the limits to China's alignment with Iran. Zhang would go only as far as to say that expanded Sino-Iranian cooperation was in the interest of the Third World.[59] Privately Chinese officials informed *Far Eastern Economic Review* reporter James Clad at the time of Zhang Jingfu's visit that they hoped for the same degree of cordiality in Sino-Iranian relations as existed in Sino-Pakistani relations.[60]

In June 1985 Majlis speaker Rafsanjani visited China. As will be discussed in a subsequent chapter, an agreement on nuclear cooperation was concluded during Rafsanjani's five-day visit. China's commitment of support for Iran's nuclear energy programs signified a very significant deepening of the Sino-Iranian relationship. In talks with Rafsanjani, Deng Xiaoping started with the theme of ancient civilizational contacts and moved to the "major common point" between China and Iran—both sought development.[61] Premier Zhao Ziyang was Rafsanjani's primary host. In his banquet speech welcoming Rafsanjani, Zhao lauded the overthrow of the Pahlavi dynasty as a "new leaf" in Iran's history, and paid tribute to Iran for its opposition to hegemonism and contributions to safeguarding the interests of the Third World.[62] Rafsanjani pressed for closer Sino-Iranian cooperation, telling Zhao: "We view relations and economic cooperation between Iran and China from a high strategic perspective. We believe that China is the best country for Iran to cooperate with. Politically we are without apprehensions in cooperating with China. China does not have a colonialist mentality. In the process of cooperating with Iran, China absolutely will not aggress against or injure Iran's interests."[63]

Rafsanjani apparently sought more than loose alignment based on common interests. He sought, rather, a united front against both superpowers, but especially against that superpower most threatening to the IRI, the United States. Speaking to state counselor Zhang Jingfu, Rafsanjani said that the emergence of independent countries such as China and Iran opposing both superpowers was a "very important phenomenon" new to world history. These countries should "create further solidarity among the Third World and oppressed nations" to oppose the superpowers. While the United States was "tempted to use the one billion strong market of China for the sake of its trashy stuff," Rafsanjani told Zhang, Washington did not want a strong China. China and Iran should establish friendly relations with "the big powers" only on the condition that they "not keep their presence" in "our regions . . . in the Indian Ocean and around China." Iran and China together should "remove the cancerous tumors of imperialism in their regions."[64] Rafsanjani made a similar pitch to India in August 1982.[65] This was the sort of anti-U.S. ideology that China had just abandoned in the post-Mao era and had no intention of returning to.

Chinese leaders gently indicated to Rafsanjani that, while they sympathized with many of Iran's perspectives and ardently desired expanded cooperation, there were limits to how far China could go in aligning with Iran against the United States. Zhao Ziyang told Rafsanjani that while the two countries enjoyed many similarities and both fought against superpower dominance, they pursued *independent* policies in that fight.[66] Thus, by 1985 a fundamental dilemma had been posed for Beijing: how far should China go in aligning with Iran against the United States? The desire of many Iranian leaders for strategic partnership with China was very useful to Beijing. It offered Beijing the opportunity of rebuilding a multidimensional, cooperative relation with a major power in the Middle East. Yet going too far in aligning with Iran against the United States could put China in a position in which it would have either to default on its professed support for Iran or confront the United States over Middle Eastern issues peripheral to China's own vital interests. China's leaders concluded that China could not allow cooperation with Iran to undermine its broadly cooperative and nonconfrontational relation with the United States. While sharing many interests and perspectives with Iran, China would pursue an independent foreign policy eschewing membership in any bloc, including, especially, anti-u.s. blocs.

CHINA'S ARMS SUPPLY RELATION
WITH IRAN DURING THE IRAN-IRAQ WAR

During the 1980s, arms sales constituted the most important element of the Sino-Iranian relation. China's arms supply relation with Iran will be discussed in detail in a subsequent chapter, but a general consideration of those sales during the Iran-Iraq war is essential here because they played such an important role in normalization of PRC-IRI relations. Beijing's willingness to meet Iran's needs for munitions during its desperate struggle against Iraq, and its resistance to u.s. demands to end those sales, earned considerable goodwill in Tehran. It demonstrated in a very practical way that China was independent of the United States and could and would resist u.s. pressure. The approach of China's arms sales representatives was also "businesslike." Chinese representatives were not concerned with human rights issues or proliferation. They were willing to accept and work with Iranian demands for indigenization of production and find ways of surmounting constraints on Iran's ability to pay cash. Interactions between Chinese and Iranian representatives negotiating arms deals were larded with rhetoric about Third World, anti-Western solidarity and revival of cooperation between two ancient civilizations. There was much promotion of "friendship" via red-carpet treatment, banquets, and organized touring. While it is easy to be cynical about such Chinese "barbarian handling" techniques, evenhanded analysis requires recognition that, in this case at least, these techniques seem to have served Chinese interests quite will. Iran's newly empowered Islamic officials, treated as pariahs by much of the world and deeply concerned with regime and national survival, apparently came away from arms-driven interactions with Chinese representatives during the early 1980s convinced that China was different from the other major powers.

China's wartime arms sales demonstrated to Tehran that Beijing was an able and reliable partner. These demonstrations provided leverage for expansion of postwar Sino-Iranian cooperation. For example, in August 1988 as Tehran was finally moving to end the war and beginning to draw in China as its preferred partner in postwar economic reconstruction, deputy prime minister for executive affairs Hamid Mirzadeh told Deputy Foreign Minister Qi Huaiyuan that, while Iran had received many proposals for postwar reconstruction, these proposals would be studied in the light of past relations. Those countries that had cooperated with Iran during the war, such as China, would enjoy priority.[67] China was one of the countries that "maintained its position when our country was facing [difficult] conditions," Mirzadeh said.[68] China's military assistance to Iran during its war with Iraq was an important step in building a broader Sino-Iranian partnership—comparable, perhaps, in Sino-Pakistani relations to China's support for Pakistan during the 1965 Indo-Pakistani war.

According to one authoritative Iranian source, China took the initiative in opening the arms supply relation. Several years into the Iran-Iraq war a Chinese representative indicated to Ambassador Khorram that China had become aware that Chinese arms were making their way to Iran by various countries. Given its policy of neutrality, China found this situation "unbalanced" and wanted to rectify it. If Iran wished to purchase Chinese military equipment, a proposal would be welcomed.[69] In April 1983 a high-level Iranian military delegation reportedly made a secret visit to Beijing to negotiate arms purchases. A $1.3 billion deal resulted, with North Korea serving as the intermediary.[70] A second agreement worth $1 billion was signed in March 1985 in Tehran by Zhang Jingfu and Iranian chief of staff Colonel Ismail Suhrabi. This contract provided for Chinese delivery over a period of two years of a complete arsenal of Chinese copies of Soviet-designed equipment, including fighter aircraft, tanks, artillery, multiple rocket launchers, and surface to-air missiles. Two-thirds of the value of the deal was to be paid for by Iranian oil shipments over a period of two years. The remaining one-third was to be paid in hard currency.[71] Still another agreement was negotiated by the head of the procurements office of Iran's Supreme Defense Council, Shokrollah Reyzai, and signed by Majlis speaker Rafsanjani during the latter's June 1985 visit to Beijing. It was reportedly worth $1.16 billion. A reporter for the *Middle East Defense News* obtained access to the two volumes constituting that contract and found that it specified a Hong Kong firm headed by a British national to serve as intermediary for the sale, thus allowing Beijing to claim with narrow accuracy that *China* had not sold weapons to Iran. (I will return in a later chapter to the problem of indirect sales.) The June 1985 contract also illustrated the marketing strategy of selling the initial hardware at very low prices, while the follow-on package of spare parts, maintenance, and training ran three times the purchase price of the hardware.[72] China also reportedly agreed to receive and train annually two hundred Iranian pilots and aviation technicians. Still another arms sales contract was reportedly concluded in early

1986 worth $3.1 billion and including HY-2 Silkworm antiship cruise missiles.[73] The supply of Silkworm antiship cruise missiles was especially significant, giving Iran the ability to strike effectively at oil tankers plying Gulf sea-lanes. Yet another agreement was concluded in mid-1987 and reportedly concluded Chinese construction of several factories to produce bombardment rockets, artillery, helicopters, ammunition, and spare parts for tanks.[74]

Parallel with arms sales to Iran, China sold substantial amounts of munitions to Iraq—although the USSR, France, and other Western countries, including the United States, were Iraq's major arms suppliers. It is testament to Chinese diplomatic skill that, in spite of the fact that China also served as a major arms supplier for Iraq, Beijing was able to parley its arms sales to Iran into the beginnings of renewed partnership. Iranian intermediaries apparently did not come away from their arms dealings with China with a bad taste of trucking with cynical "merchants of death." One factor mitigating Iranian ire at Beijing's truck with Iraq during the war was Chinese willingness to help Iran solve its problems as defined by the Iranian government. Whatever Beijing might be doing or allowing to happen in terms of Baghdad, toward Tehran it proved very useful in helping Iran solve pressing military problems. Chinese punctiliousness in execution of its contracts with Iran may also have helped form an impression that the Chinese were reliable partners with whom one could do business. It is also likely that China's assistance to Iran's nuclear programs helped mitigate Iranian displeasure at Chinese arms sales to Iraq. The primary objective behind Iran's nuclear program (at least at that point) was fear of Iraqi possession of nuclear weapons, and in this crucial area Beijing was willing to assist Tehran.

CHINA'S U.N. DIPLOMACY DURING THE IRAN-IRAQ WAR

At the U.N., China balanced between staying in step with the other permanent members of the Security Council (the "Perm Five") and demonstrating solidarity with Iran. On the one hand, Beijing sought to demonstrate that China was now a responsible great power willing to work with its peers in dealing with problems of international peace and security. On the other hand, Beijing found ways to differentiate itself from the other Perm Five by supporting an angry and isolated Tehran.

Security Council intervention in the Gulf war was driven by escalating Iraqi and Iranian attacks on oil facilities and commerce in the Gulf. This fact itself rankled Tehran. First the Security Council shirked its responsibility under the U.N. Charter to punish an aggressor. Then it intervened only for the sake of its own, selfish, material interests (to protect "its" oil supply). Moreover, although Iraq took the initiative in expanding "the tanker war," Security Council resolutions targeted Iran.[75]

To understand the politics of the tanker war, it is necessary to begin with the geography of that conflict. Both Iran and Iraq declared war zones in the Persian Gulf adjacent to their own and the other's coast, but left corridors in the central Gulf for commerce of neutral countries such as Saudi Arabia and Kuwait. Since Iran had large oil production facilities in the Gulf, and since most of its oil exports were via the Gulf, Iraqi warplanes found abundant Iranian targets and were able to prey on tankers carrying Iranian oil within the war zone declared by Iraq. Iraq, however, exported its oil via pipeline through Turkey once the war began, or piped it to Kuwait or Saudi Arabia, and then via the Gulf on neutral, third-country ships. This meant that Iranian warplanes and warships found no Iraqi oil production facilities or tankers in the Gulf, or even third-country vessels carrying Iraqi oil, in the Gulf war zone around Iraqi territory. Thus, if Iran was to reciprocate Iraqi attacks on Iran's Gulf oil production and commerce, it would have to strike not at Iraq-bound ships inside the war zone declared by Iran, but at third-country traffic traveling along international sea-lanes outside declared war zones and visiting neutral ports in the Gulf.

Under principles of international law, belligerent countries at war are required to respect the freedom of commerce and navigation of neutral countries. From Tehran's perspective this was a distorted interpretation of international law that blatantly favored Iraq. Submission to it would leave unavenged Iraqi attacks against Iranian commerce. Thus Tehran decided to strike at neutral commerce in the international sea-lanes of the Persian Gulf. In September 1981, in response to Iraqi attacks on Iranian oil facilities in the Gulf, Iranian aircraft attacked a Kuwaiti oil-loading facility. Washington responded by declaring that it expected both Iran and Iraq to respect the unrestricted flow of oil from the Persian Gulf even while they continued to war with one another.

As attacks on neutral oil traffic in the Gulf mounted, and as Iran shifted from defensive to offensive in the war, Washington began pushing for an arms embargo against Iran. By 1983 Washington had concluded that Iran rather than Iraq was the party least willing to end and most responsible for continuation of the war. Washington also concluded that Iran was largely responsible for attacks on neutral commerce in the Gulf. Part of Washington's strategy for pressuring Tehran to end the war was an international embargo on arms sales to Iran—a policy formalized as Operation Staunch on December 15, 1983. Its purpose was to persuade all countries to cease sales of arms to Iran in order to force Tehran to the negotiating table. Iraq, which Washington did not deem responsible for continuation of the war, was not the target of u.s. arms embargo pressure. As State Department testimony to Congress said: "Because Iraq for several years has sought the earliest possible end of the war, in contrast to Iran's intransigence, we do not urge third countries to withhold arms from Iraq."[76]

Beijing and Tehran would have noted that as soon as China began supplying arms to Iran, Washington began trying to end those sales. From Beijing's and Tehran's perspective, this was a clear example of u.s. hegemonism. Washington was ignoring Iran's sovereign right to defend itself and to procure such arms as it felt necessary for that purpose—and to dictate the terms of relations between China and Iran, two sovereign states. Moreover, Washington had appointed itself guardian of Gulf sea-lanes. All of this was arrogant hegemonism. Of course, China could not say this openly or too directly lest it spoil relations with the United States. But there was certainly a meeting of minds when Chinese and Iranian leaders "exchanged views" in private.

Balancing carefully between Washington and Tehran, Beijing condemned attacks on neutral shipping in the Gulf and supported u.s.-sponsored Security Council resolutions to this effect. But it married this cooperation with the other Perm Five with calls for u.s. military withdrawal from the Persian Gulf, leaving management of that region's security affairs to the countries of the region. This Chinese statement of principle did not have any practical effect other than to flatter Iranian pride. The one element of China's position that *did* matter substantively was its refusal to go along with Washington's Operation Staunch.

In June 1984 the United States secured unanimous passage by the u.n. Security Council of Resolution 552 calling on Iran and Iraq to cease attacks on neutral commerce in the Persian Gulf. China voted for the resolution, but after the vote its representative, Mi Guojun, added this implied caveat: "Any action the Security Council takes must be conducive to bringing about the participation of the two sides in a process of peaceful negotiations."[77] Added to China's long-standing view that sanctions only intensified conflicts, Mi's statement was a subtle warning that China would not be willing to move from Resolution 552 to sanctions.

In late 1984 Washington tilted further toward Iraq as Iran gained the upper hand on the battlefield and u.s. leaders increasingly feared Iranian victory resulting in Iranian domination of the Gulf. Tehran, of course, saw Washington's tilt toward Baghdad as further manifestation of u.s. conspiracy against it. Prospects for u.s.-Iranian military conflict mounted as Washington increasingly aligned with Iraq, and Iran remained determined to reciprocate Iraqi attacks in the Gulf. By 1986 growing Iraqi desperation prompted increased attacks on tankers visiting Iranian—that is, belligerent—ports. Iran responded in kind by targeting neutral vessels (primarily Kuwaiti). From ten Iranian attacks on Kuwaiti vessels in 1986, the number jumped to forty in 1987. China's supply of Silkworm antiship missiles threatened to involve Beijing in the escalating conflict in alignment with Iran and against the United States and the broader international community. Early in 1987 u.s. satellite reconnaissance indicated that Iran was installing Chinese Silkworm antiship missiles along the Strait of Hormuz, raising the prospect that those weapons might attack tankers transiting that strait.[78]

In February 1987 Mohammad Javid Larijani, vice foreign minister and special envoy of the prime minister, visited Beijing to discuss developments in the Gulf. Briefing Vice Premier Wan Li, Larijani said that a situation at the front had been reached in which "even countries backing Iraq are now questioning their assistance to that regime."[79] As for peace terms, Larijani said Iran hoped to end the war as soon as possible but in a way "ensuring the punishment of the aggressor." Iran's foreign policy was based on resisting aggression, and it would never give up this legitimate right. The region was on the threshold of a great development, Larijani said, with "observers" convinced that Saddam Hussein "will indeed go."[80] In other words, defeat of Iraq and peace via defeat of the aggressor was in the offing. Tehran still sought regime change in Baghdad. Wan Li expressed the hope that Iran and Iraq would quickly end their conflict on conditions acceptable to both sides. This was an implicit rejection of Larijani's argument of peace through victory. Foreign Minister Wu Xueqian told Larijani that China supported the efforts of the u.n. secretary-general to establish peace and security in the region.[81] Here too China's indirect message was that Tehran should end the war on compromise terms acceptable to Baghdad. Beijing was nudging Tehran toward ending the war.

To deter Iranian attacks on neutral shipping in the Persian Gulf, in March 1987 Washington authorized the Kuwaiti-proposed "reflagging" of eleven Kuwaiti tankers. Flying the u.s. flag and under u.s. registration, these vessels would be protected by u.s. armed forces. Parallel to reflagging was an effort to secure a u.n. push for a negotiated end to the Iran-Iraq war, an effort that would eventually culminate in Security Council Resolution 598 of July 1987.

In May 1987, just after an Iraqi attack on the u.s. destroyer *Stark* off Bahrain and while the Security Council was beginning to move toward forcing an end to the war via what became Resolution 598, Iranian deputy foreign minister for political affairs Hussein Sheikholeslam traveled to Beijing to exchange views on the "latest developments" in the war. Sheikholeslam said Iran planned to continue the war until victory, while Wan Li called for an early end to the war under conditions that both sides could accept.[82] The extent of divergence between Tehran's and Beijing's views was indicated by Sheikholeslam's comments to the media during his Beijing visit that Iran was prepared for confrontation with the United States. Whenever the United States had intervened, it had been badly defeated, the Iranian envoy said.

The next month Foreign Minister Velayati stopped in Beijing on his way home from a nonaligned conference in North Korea. This visit coincided with Chinese consideration of a Kuwaiti request that Beijing cooperate with Washington in the reflagging effort.[83] Security Council deliberations over Resolution 598 were also under way. Velayati conveyed to President Li Xiannian an "oral letter" from President Khamenei saying that the aggression of the superpowers was causing instability and tension in the Persian Gulf. Iran felt that the security of the Gulf region should be upheld by the countries of that region. This was probably a bid for China to bloc the movement toward UN-endorsed u.s. intervention against Iran in the Gulf. Li Xiannian responded by turning in a different direction Iran's stress on danger posed by the superpowers in the Gulf. There indeed existed the danger of "internationalization" of the Iran-Iraq war, Li Xiannian told Velayati. To avoid a situation in which the "clam and the gull fight to the fisherman's advantage" (i.e., creating a situation of which the superpowers could take advantage), the first thing was for Third World countries not to fight among themselves, thereby giving the superpowers an opportunity. China's greatest wish was that all its friends in the Persian Gulf (i.e., Iran and Iraq) live together in peace.[84] Beijing feared that escalation of the war would lead to military conflict between Iran and the United States, which the United States was certain to win, leaving Iran in a weaker situation and the United States in a more hegemonic position over that vital region.

Foreign Minister Wu Xueqian and Iranian ambassador Alaeddin Broujerdi discussed the reflagging project in June. The United States and the Soviet Union were seeking to secure their own interests in the region, Wu warned, and the situation would become even more dangerous if the current tension was not defused. The superpowers never think of the interests of the Third World countries, Wu opined. Broujerdi declined Wu's advice to avoid confrontation with the United States. Iran was daily strengthening its military strength to face any challenge. "We are getting prepared to confront the u.s.," Broujerdi told Wu.[85]

RESOLUTION 598, MANDATORY SANCTIONS, AND SILKWORMS

During Security Council debate in July 1987 over Resolution 598 demanding an immediate cease-fire, China gave Iran a degree of support, once again balancing between staying in step with the other Perm Five and befriending Tehran. China was "seriously concerned" about possible "internationalization" (i.e., u.s. intervention) of the Iran-Iraq war, Chinese representative Huang Jiahua told the Security Council. "The five permanent members bear a special responsibility for maintaining international peace and security," Huang said, and "their endeavors must be consistent with the important principle that the [Security] Council is an organic whole." In plain speech, the United States should not resort to military moves without approval of all permanent members of the Security Council. Huang went on to say that China "also expects that other countries concerned, the major powers in particular, will exercise restraint and refrain from doing anything to exacerbate the situation."[86] This too should be read as criticism of u.s. preparations to confront Iran militarily.

IRI representatives at the United Nations found China most responsive of the Perm Five. When the draft of Resolution 598 was published, China's representatives worked with those of Iran to make it more "balanced and fair" in terms of recognition of responsibility for initiation of the war and punishment of those responsible. Item six of the eventual resolution provided for the secretary-general to appoint an impartial commission to investigate the matter of war guilt, while article seven provided for a mechanism to ascertain and compensate for war damages. IRI representatives had sought Soviet assistance in modifying the 598 draft, but were told that such assistance would require a lessening of Iranian criticism of Soviet policy in Afghanistan.[87] China demanded no such quid pro quo.

On July 20, 1987, the Security Council unanimously passed Resolution 598 calling for an immediate cease-fire, withdrawal of military forces without delay to internationally recognized boundaries, and UN-sponsored peace talks. This was the first time in the history of the United Nations that the five permanent members of the Security Council acted in concert to end an ongoing war. Several weeks before the vote, u.s. ambassador to the United Nations Vernon Walters had visited Beijing to solicit Chinese support.[88] While staying in step with the other Perm Five, China again found ways to support the IRI in the Security Council. During the debate over Resolution 598, Washington, London, and Paris pushed hard for mandatory arms embargo against any country unwilling to accept a cease-fire, that is, against Iran. China and the Soviet Union refused such a proposal. All those two powers would agree to was future *consideration* of *possible* sanctions.[89] Moscow's refusal gave

Beijing considerable political cover, but since China was Iran's major munitions supplier, it was Beijing's refusal that was more important to Tehran.

For nearly a year Iran rejected Resolution 598. Not until July 18, 1988, did
Tehran accept it. During the intervening year, China and Iran "exchanged
views" many times on the Gulf situation.[90] In the words of an official Chinese
diplomatic history, when it became apparent that Iran would not embrace
Resolution 598, China "stepped up its urging of Iran to accept peace."[91] China's
nudging, in fact, seems to have played a significant role in prompting Tehran
to agree to bring the war to an end.

Contrary to China's advice to avoid a military clash with the United States,
Tehran refused to back down before U.S. pressure and continued to strike
at neutral oil traffic in the Gulf. On July 24, 1987, the first Kuwaiti ship escorted
by U.S. naval forces hit an Iranian mine while well inside neutral waters in
the main commercial channel of the Gulf. Iranian forces also began conducting
"martyrdom maneuvers"—small ship and commando attacks on U.S. ships.
"The Persian Gulf will be the graveyard of the United States," declared Iran's
Revolutionary Guard headquarters.

As Iran and the United States moved toward military confrontation,
Deputy Foreign Minister Qi Huaiyuan traveled to Tehran in August. China
desired expanded relations with Iran, Qi told his Iranian hosts, and was concerned over the security and stability of the region. In other words, continued or expanded war would make difficult expanded Chinese cooperation with
Iran. Qi also spoke out against "big power interference" in the Persian Gulf.
The security of that region should be maintained by the countries of the region,
Qi said.[92] What China declined to do at this juncture was as significant as what
it did. Beijing declined to participate in the Kuwait-inspired, U.S.-led reflagging
effort. Kuwait had invited Chinese participation, even giving Beijing the
options of allowing Kuwait to hire Chinese ships or having Kuwaiti tankers
registered with Chinese authorities. Beijing declined all options. "The size of
the Chinese fleet of cargo ships is small and we have no more ships to lease,"
Qi Huaiyuan explained. "On the other hand, the service of registration of foreign ships is not yet available in China."[93] Qi's responses were diplomatic foils.
The bottom line was that participating in the reflagging effort would have put
China into de facto alignment with the United States and Kuwait against Iran.
Beijing was not interested in such an option.

By mid-1987 China alone among the Permanent Five did not have warships in the Persian Gulf region as part of the collective effort to ensure safe
passage of oil traffic through the Gulf. Several of the European states (Holland,
Italy, France, Belgium, and Britain) sent warships to the Indian Ocean / Persian
Gulf region as the threat to commercial traffic grew in 1987. Germany dis-

patched warships to the eastern Mediterranean, replacing u.s. ships shifted farther east. The Soviet Union too dispatched warships to the Persian Gulf area. China did not follow suit. Had Chinese leaders desired, dispatch of a symbolic naval force to the Arabian Sea would have been well within the capabilities of the People's Liberation Army (PLA) Navy. PLA-Navy ships had made their first visits to foreign ports in 1985 by calling at Karachi, Colombo, and Chittagong. China alone among the Perm Five had no interest in military involvement in the Persian Gulf in de facto alignment against Iran.

In October Beijing's Silkworm sales to Iran threatened to drag China into the mounting confrontation between Iran and the United States. In the middle of that month after u.s. forces captured and publicized an Iranian mine-laying vessel operating in commercial sea-lanes, Iran retaliated by firing its Silkworms missiles at u.s. ships. One u.s.-escorted tanker was hit. United States forces retaliated by striking and destroying an Iranian oil production platform in the Gulf. Interestingly, the October 1987 attack was Iran's last use of Silkworms. Henceforth it would rely on mines.[94] Almost certainly Beijing insisted that Iran not use its Silkworms to strike at u.s.-escorted Gulf commerce. Rhetorically Beijing stood with Tehran. A Xinhua "news analysis" shortly after the October Gulf clashes said, "The military involvement of big powers has aggravated tension" in the Gulf, creating a more "explosive situation" by adding fuel to the flames. "In particular, the u.s. attack against Iranian oil platforms [came] at a time when the Secretary General . . . was about to start a new round of mediation for peace. This worries international society."[95] Beijing was in a delicate situation. The costs of China's pro-Iranian neutrality were mounting. If, on the one hand, China supported Iran, it could turn American, Arab, and European opinion against it by convincing people that China was perpetuating the Iran-Iraq war, or even conclude that China was helping Tehran militarily challenge the United States. On the other hand, if Beijing supported Washington's efforts, it could estrange Tehran, perhaps derailing its increasingly successful efforts to reconstruct a partnership with that country.

Beijing was convinced that Washington's reflagging of Kuwaiti tankers was "not a real step to protect international shipping in the [Persian Gulf] for the Gulf nations' interests," as a Xinhua commentary of September 1987 explained. Rather, "The Reagan administration believed that it was a good time to increase its military presence in the Gulf" since the Arab nations there "were eager to get u.s. help." The continuation and escalation of the Iran-Iraq war was leading to a "military push into the Gulf region by outside powers."[96] Another article in *Jiefangjun bao* (Liberation Army Daily—the newspaper of the PLA) quoted a putative 1984 comment by Henry Kissinger to the effect that "if both sides (Iran and Iraq) lose in the war, this will be advantageous to the West."

The United States "showed a lot of concern about safety in oil transportation," but was really concerned about control of the Persian Gulf. Both superpowers should withdraw their military forces from the Gulf, the article concluded.[97]

In early 1988 Washington, London, and Paris renewed their push for an arms embargo to press acceptance of Resolution 598. During talks on this subject with President Ronald Reagan and Secretary of State George Schultz in Washington in March, Foreign Minister Wu Xueqian avoided commitment. China would support an arms embargo against Iran only if "the overwhelming majority" of the Security Council supported it, Wu told Schultz. Efforts by Schultz the next month in Moscow to secure Soviet endorsement failed. Thus Moscow and Beijing jointly declined the u.s. move to cut off Iran's arms supplies. The Soviet Union was Iraq's major arms supplier, while China was Iran's. In effect, Beijing and Moscow joined to protect each of their special relations with Gulf clients against what both perceived as u.s.-led Western efforts to bring those clients under greater Western control. However, if Moscow shifted position and accepted an embargo, China would be compelled to do likewise. Beijing did not want to put itself in opposition to the other Perm Five and appear to desire to keep the war going. Beijing certainly informed Tehran it could well be compelled to go along with an arms embargo if Tehran continued to reject Resolution 598 and Moscow shifted position.

As Washington was pressing for an arms embargo of Iran, the United States–Iran military confrontation reached its climax. On April 14 a u.s. frigate hit a mine and very nearly sank. Several days later u.s. and allied warships discovered Iranian-laid mines in the central Gulf sea-lanes. Washington authorized retaliation, and Iranian forces prepared to confront the u.s. Navy. The largest naval battle undertaken by the u.s. Navy since the end of World War II was the result. Two Iranian oil production platforms were destroyed and several Iranian fast attack small craft, a fast attack missile boat, and a frigate were sunk by u.s. forces. Following this battle, Washington declared that it would no longer tolerate hostile attacks on commercial traffic outside declared war zones. One important factor pushing Iran to end the war was the perception that it was drifting toward war with the United States. Chinese warnings to this effect over the previous months may have reinforced this Iranian conclusion.

Again China stood rhetorically beside Tehran following the April United States–Iran clash. The day after the clash, China's foreign ministry expressed "grave concern over the renewed u.s.-Iranian military conflict . . . and the resultant heightened tension there." "China is always opposed to big powers' military involvement and intervention in the Gulf and stands for maintaining Gulf security and freedom of navigation," the statement said.[98]

From April 1988 onward Iran's military position vis-à-vis Iraq deteriorated.

Iraqi forces recaptured several areas along the border, while Iraqi chemical attacks caused demoralization among Iranian forces. Internal dissent and opposition began to mount and the economy declined. Iran was virtually isolated. European allies of the United States had joined the u.s.-led effort to clear mines and maintain maritime commerce in the Persian Gulf. The Arab League unanimously condemned Iran's refusal to accept Resolution 598.[99] China was Iran's only significant friend (although Germany was beginning to reach out to Tehran), and Beijing had indicated that there were major limits on China's ability to assist Iran under wartime circumstances.

In July—while China was serving as chair of the Security Council—Tehran finally accepted Resolution 598. China's foreign ministry quickly issued a statement "welcoming" this move.[100] After Secretary-General Javier Perez de Cuellar announced on August 8 that the two sides had agreed to a cease-fire, Beijing quickly issued a statement "welcoming" this "significant progress."[101] Active hostilities between Iran and Iraq finally ceased on August 20, 1988. Five days later u.n.-sponsored talks between Iran and Iraq began in Geneva.

China continued to nudge Tehran toward peace with Iraq. Shortly after Tehran accepted Resolution 598 but before the UN-sponsored peace talks began in Geneva, Qi Huaiyuan arrived in Tehran for discussions. Qi expressed appreciation of Iran's acceptance of Resolution 598, spoke highly of Iran's decision to hold peace negotiations with Iraq, and hoped the Geneva talks would achieve positive results. Prime Minister Musavi replied that China should "play its active and just role in fully implementing the u.n. resolution." This was a call for China to move the United Nations toward identification of Saddam Hussein as aggressor, his punishment as a war criminal, and awarding reparations. "Iran gives a priority to China-Iran relations," Musavi said.[102] Qi urged Velayati and Rafsanjani to make peace with Baghdad. The Iranians refused to budge. Qi concluded that Velayati and Rafsanjani simply did not have the authority to moderate Iran's position and that only Khomeini had this power.[103]

In October Vice Foreign Minister Mohammad Hoseyn Lavasani arrived in Beijing for further discussions. To Premier Li Peng, Lavasani explained the Iran-Iraq situation since the Geneva talks began and the view of the Iranian government about settling the Iran-Iraq conflict and restoring peace. In Tokyo, prior to arriving in China, Lavasani had informed his hosts about the "obstacles created by Iraq" in implementing Resolution 598, and he probably conveyed the same message in Beijing.[104] Again a plea was issued for Chinese pressure on Iraq at the United Nations. Li Peng replied that China's "clear and consistent" position on the Iran-Iraq war was "strict neutrality and enthusiastic persuasion for peace." China hoped, Li Peng said, that Iran and Iraq would be able to "talk matters through" in a spirit of mutual understanding. Regarding China's role in the Security Council, China would "exercise its appropriate role," Li Peng promised vaguely. Li offered a carrot in the form of a promise of postwar development assistance. China hoped, Li told Lavasani, that after the war was ended, Sino-Iranian economic, trade, and other relations would "continue to grow."[105]

In December Velayati again went to Beijing to discuss the Iran-Iraq peace talks. Li Peng told Velayati that China hoped Iran and Iraq would continue the momentum of the peace talks, utilize the mediation of the U.N. secretary-general, and implement Resolution 598 at an early date. Regarding China's U.N. role, Foreign Minister Qian Qichen told Velayati that China would "make due contributions" to the realization of an early peace between Iran and Iraq.[106] Velayati conveyed to Zhao Ziyang a letter from Majlis speaker Rafsanjani calling for expanded Sino-Iranian cooperation. "Bilateral cooperation between Iran and China is incontestably advantageous to the maintenance of regional and Asian peace, stability, and security, and is even helpful to world peace," Rafsanjani's letter said. "We hope that cooperation between Iran and China will become the model for cooperation between non-aligned developing countries of the Third World."[107] Velayati and Qian Qichen also discussed prospects for China's participation in Iran's postwar economic reconstruction. Following the Iran-Iraq cease-fire and beginning of peace talks, a series of high-ranking Chinese economic officials began visiting Iran to discuss China's role in postwar reconstruction.

Tehran reported again to Beijing in April 1989 on "Iraqi impediments in the way of the peace negotiations." No progress had been achieved in the implementation of Resolution 598 because of these impediments, explained Deputy Foreign Minister Javad Mansuri. The Iranian envoy hoped that China and Iran could reach common stands on key issues, that is, that China would agree to use its Security Council seat to press Iraq to make concessions. Qian Qichen replied blandly that the cease-fire provided the ground for peace.[108] In October 1989 Qian Qichen made the first visit by China's foreign minister to Iran in five years. Qian again urged a compromise settlement at Geneva. Iran should realize "protracted peace" in the Persian Gulf. A continuation of war was "unimaginable" and the present situation of no war, no peace was not advantageous to the reconstruction of either Iran or Iraq, Qian said.[109]

In spite of Beijing's efforts, the Iran-Iraq talks at Geneva yielded little progress. Only as international pressure mounted on Iraq in the aftermath of its August 1990 seizure of Kuwait would Iraq's attitude become more conciliatory and Iranian-Iraqi relations begin to improve. What is most important for our purposes, however, is that by 1987–89 Tehran turned frequently to China for advice and support on such critical issues as war and peace. A relationship that had begun as cold estrangement in 1979 had within a decade become one of valued consultation and support.

SKILLFULLY SEIZING AN OPPORTUNITY
TO RECONSTRUCT A PARTNERSHIP

Comparing the state of Sino-Iranian relations in 1979 and in 1988 is instructive. Beijing's relations with early, revolutionary Iran were extremely poor, soured by Beijing's close embrace of the shah, by ignorance compounding a religious-ideological chasm, and by Beijing's quasi-alliance with Washington. As indicated by the chronology appended to this study, there were no high- or mid-level interactions at all during the first two years of the revolutionary Iranian state, and only one per year for the next four years. By 1985 interactions were beginning to become frequent, with three exchanges in that year, followed by six exchanges in 1986, ten in 1987, and ten again in 1988. In 1979 and 1980 Iran's leaders deeply distrusted China. By 1987–89, Beijing was one of Tehran's most valued interlocutors. By the last two years of the Iran-Iraq war, Tehran devoted considerable energy to securing China's support. Such support was not as unequivocal as Tehran desired, but it was adequate to keep Tehran happy and coming back for further consultation.

Beijing gave Tehran important substantive support. It stepped in to become Iran's major arms supplier and refused to bow to Washington's demands to suspend such sales. Beijing occasionally spoke out in the Security Council on Iran's behalf—the only Permanent Five member to do so. Beijing criticized Washington's military moves against Iran. Beijing seconded Tehran's call for the withdrawal of all "big power" military forces from the Gulf and for management of the security affairs of the Gulf by regional states. Beijing also initiated cooperation with Iran's nuclear research programs in 1985, a program predicated on a desire to acquire a nuclear deterrent against Saddam Hussein and his ambitious nuclear weapons program.

The crux of Beijing's advice to Tehran was a message of realistic prudence in dealing with the United States. Tehran should end the war with Iraq and avoid military confrontation with the United States, because to do otherwise would only strengthen u.s. domination of the Persian Gulf. United States hegemony over the Gulf was not in the interests of Iran, China, or the Third World, and peace between the Gulf states and avoidance of military confrontation with the United States was the most effective way of thwarting u.s. hegemonist designs. Tehran did not accept Beijing's advice at the time. In retrospect, China's advice may have seemed like the wise words of a sincere friend.

There was a strong emotive component to the reconstructed Sino-Iranian relationship. Chinese and Iranian representatives shared similar views of the world. Both resented and feared the great power of the United States, the West, and the USSR. China's leaders understood the logic and dynamics of social revolution; China's veteran leaders had themselves made such a revolution. While separated by the chasm between atheism and religious faith, the leaders of both states shared resentment of Western dominance over world affairs. Effusive, even flattering, Chinese rhetoric about the greatness of Iran and Iranian civilization decorated these interactions, indicating that China viewed Iran as an important country. One can only speculate about the manner used by Chinese representatives to express views divergent from those of Iran, but probably it was one of frank but friendly disagreement couched as divergent perspectives among Third World brothers. Revolutionary Tehran had other friends: Syria, Libya, North Korea, and Pakistan. But none of those countries had the substance of power and influence that China possessed. In short, China established itself over the course of a decade as the IRI's most influential and trusted friend.

This in itself was a considerable diplomatic achievement. But on top of this is the fact that Beijing repaired its ties with Tehran without creating major problems in its relations with either the United States or the Arab countries. Tensions emerged in U.S.-PRC relations because of Iran—and these will be discussed in a later chapter. But those conflicts were contained and did not undermine Sino-U.S. cooperation. Objectively speaking, one must conclude that Beijing got just about right the balance between conciliating Washington and supporting Tehran. The mix of Chinese policies served Chinese interests quite well.

Beijing was in the advantageous position of being courted by both Tehran and Washington. Moreover, Beijing seems to have kept both suitors reasonably happy. Beijing protected its investment in Iran without alienating Washington or the Arab countries. It is interesting that the discrepancy between Washington's pro-Iraqi neutrality and Beijing's pro-Iranian neutrality caused relatively little tension in the U.S.-PRC relation during the 1980s. This was probably due to Beijing's willingness to subordinate its ties with Tehran to its ties with Washington when expediency required it. It was also due to the priority both Beijing and Washington placed on developing a cooperative relation between them.

4 / Sino-Iranian Partnership and Post–

Cold War u.s. Unipolar Preeminence, 1989–2004

Several factors came together circa 1989 to produce closer Sino-Iranian relations. The end of the Iran-Iraq war in August 1988 allowed Iran to turn to the task of economic construction, thereby opening new vistas for Sino-Iranian cooperation. The death of Ayatollah Khomeini on June 3, 1989, strengthened demands within Iran for improved living conditions after long war years of scarcity, while ushering in a period of increased pragmatism among Iran's clerical rulers. In all, Khomeini's passing precipitated changes so sweeping that specialists refer to post-Khomeini Iran as "the second republic."[1] In his final testament—a document he specifically endorsed three times before his death—Khomeini had called on his followers to reject "the atheist East" as well as the "oppressor West" and rely only on other Islamic countries.[2] Khomeini's wishes notwithstanding, his death eliminated an authoritative veto against closer cooperation with the "atheist East," while unleashing a popular longing for better living conditions that compelled Iran's leaders to seek quick and effective ways of achieving economic improvements. Beijing offered help in this regard.

On the Chinese side, the deterioration of relations with the United States and the West in the aftermath of military suppression of popular demonstrations, also on the night of June 3–4, had a deep impact on Sino-Iranian relations. The mammoth demonstrations in Beijing in April–June 1989 were the strongest challenge to rule by the Chinese Communist Party (ccp) since 1949. Those demonstrations roused great attention and sympathy in the United States, and when they were crushed by military force, u.s. public opinion, previously broadly positive toward China's government, shifted dramatically in a negative direction. As Western criticism mounted and as sanctions followed criticism, China's leaders sought support from Third World friends. In mid-1989 the CCP Politburo met to decide on countermeasures. The first two of these would soon be superseded by events—exploiting the United States–China–Soviet Union triangle to China's advantage and developing relations with the USSR and the socialist countries of Eastern Europe. The third policy would prove more durable and more relevant to relations with Iran: China would henceforth put more effort into developing relations with Third World countries.[3] Iran, of course, was one of the more powerful Third World countries.

Tehran was more than willing to join Beijing in rebutting Western "interference in the internal affairs" of non-Western countries. Then as anti-Communist revolutions in Eastern Europe and in Russia gathered strength during the second half of 1989, fears of geostrategic encirclement were added to Chinese apprehensions. Then the USSR itself succumbed to peaceful, anti-Communist revolution. Henceforth the geopolitical imperative of checking Soviet power—an imperative that had previously limited U.S. proclivities to criticize the harsh aspects of China's internal regime—no longer operated. In early 1991—the same year that the USSR disappeared—a U.S.-led war against Iraq expanded still further U.S. influence in the Persian Gulf. Chinese leaders saw in these events the specter of a world dominated by the United States. In such a world, Communist-ruled China could easily become a pariah and target of U.S. containment. Iran too was dismayed by the strengthened position of the United States. Opposition to U.S. unipolar domination created considerable common interests between China and Iran.

Expanded partnership with Iran was useful to Beijing in two main ways. First, Iranian support could be used internally and internationally to substantiate Beijing's argument that Western criticism of the repression of June 1989 was a form of interference and cultural arrogance. More important, Chinese support for Iran penalized Washington for its "anti-China policies" and demonstrated to Washington the U.S. need for China's cooperation in the Middle East. Through its assistance to Iran, China demonstrated its ability to confound or to facilitate U.S. objectives in the Middle East. China could facilitate Iran's nuclear programs, missile programs, and military modernization efforts, for example, or it could abstain from such cooperation with Iran. It was Washington's choice, China's leaders would tell their American interlocutors. And should Washington choose confrontation with China, a strong link with a strong Iran would be a useful hedge against a hostile United States.

By the early 1990s China and Iran shared an interest in moving the world in the direction of multipolarity. The disappearance of the Soviet Union had created, from Beijing's perspective, a seriously "unbalanced" international system. Without the USSR to check the United States, U.S. hegemonism was increasingly aggressive. This was an unhealthy situation that endangered regional and international peace, including the peace of both Iran and China. Some within the CCP leadership believed that the United States was following a secret, long-term strategy that sought destruction of all socialist states as a means to global hegemony. Since Communist-led states were resistant to U.S. domination, they had to be eliminated, these Chinese leaders believed. Other Chinese leaders tended to believe that once the USSR was eliminated, U.S. leaders saw China as the major obstacle to U.S. global domination. Washington therefore sought to weaken China by overthrowing the CCP, instigating internal chaos via liberalization, and fragmenting China by supporting various independence movements in Taiwan, Tibet, and Xinjiang. With a strong China out of the way, the United States would dominate the world. In this context, American subordination of other centers of world power would further embolden U.S. hegemony and allow it to focus on China. But if U.S. hegemony met resistance and/or got bogged down in other regions of the world, say in the Middle East, it would be more reluctant to confront China directly. There were also important commercial motives behind Beijing's push for expanded cooperation with Tehran. The opening and marketization of China's economy was gaining steam, and Chinese enterprises were increasingly going abroad, including to Iran, in search of profit.

But there were still dangers associated with a close Chinese alignment with Iran. Such an alignment could easily earn for China the onus of being the friend of pariah regimes. China might gain a reputation as an irresponsible, possibly even a rogue, state. Following the events of June 1989, a high ranking Chinese objective was to rehabilitate China's name, to reestablish China's reputation as a sober, responsible power that could be trusted and that would not use its increasingly great power for aggressive purposes or in a reckless manner. Too close association with revolutionary Iran could work against this objective.

Iran's radical Islamic nature, and for that matter its Shiite character, increased the potential costs of close Chinese association with it. In an influential 1993 essay, "Clash of Civilizations," Harvard professor Samuel Huntington argued that there was a natural anti-Western alignment between Chinese Communist-Confucian civilization and Islamic civilizations. The article attracted great attention (and uniform criticism) in China, as well as considerable praise in the United States. In the context of the 1990s, aside from aligning with radical Islamic Iran, there would have been few things that China could have done that would have more confirmed to Americans that China was indeed their new main enemy. The u.s. advocates of abandonment of traditional (since Richard Nixon) engagement policies toward China and adoption, instead, of containment policies pointed to links between China and Iran as a key dimension of China's threatening behavior toward the United States.[4] One of the most cogently argued of these pro-containment positions (that by Edward Timperlake and William Triplett) maintained that China's persistent support for the missile and nuclear programs of Iran and other anti-u.s. nations of the Middle East constituted a sort of strategic diversion of u.s. strength away from the Far East centers of China's own concern.[5] With such arguments percolating through the u.s. national security apparatus, close alignment with Iran could be potentially very dangerous to China's ties with the United States.

China's anti-u.s. hegemonist solidarity with Iran carried the danger of provoking a backlash from the United States. Iran was a card that had to be played very carefully against Washington. If used carefully, China's support of Iran could push Washington toward greater cooperation with China. But if overplayed, it could convince Washington that Beijing was seeking to support and arm the world's anti-u.s. forces, acting as a "peer competitor," if only a covert one. Once Washington reached this conclusion, there could be a strong reaction and potentially the adoption of a genuine containment policy that would undermine China's post-1978 development drive.

The principle of keeping a low profile and avoiding international blocs was reiterated by Deng Xiaoping in April 1990 when he issued a twenty-four-character guideline on foreign affairs. While directed primarily at those within the ccp who were then arguing that China should criticize the "revisionist errors" of Gorbachev in "betraying the proletariat" by abandoning the East European Communist regimes, Deng's guideline applied equally well to close solidarity with countries like Iran. This was Deng's guideline: "Observe the situation calmly. Stand firm in our positions. Respond cautiously. Conceal our capabilities and await an opportune moment to make a comeback. Be good at guarding our weaknesses. Never claim leadership."

Foreign analysts know little about China's foreign policy decision-making process at this juncture. Informed conjecture suggests that China's leaders were not of one mind about playing the Iranian card in the 1990s. The crisis of 1989 brought to the fore in China the ccp's most hard-line leaders. These included Premier Li Peng and a cortege of elderly ccp "veterans" returned to the political arena by Deng's effort to overcome resistance within the Politburo to use the PLA to crush popular opposition to martial law. The PLA also played an unusually prominent role in setting policy toward the United States in the years after the Beijing massacre. The hard-liner and PLA mentality partook of the paranoid worldview outlined earlier that saw the United States pursuing a long-term strategy of overthrowing the CCP. From this perspective, China was in a state of undeclared and "smokeless war" with the United States. In such a situation, China had to be tough, wage a "tit-for-tat struggle" against Washington. Weakness would invite only stepped-up U.S. aggression.

But if hard-line leaders helped forge the close Sino-Iranian relation of the 1990s, it is also the case that Qian Qichen, client of hard-liner Li Peng, played a key role in distancing Beijing from Tehran circa 1997–98.[6] This may be a "Nixon goes to China" phenomenon. Just as Nixon, an arch–anti-Communist, was relatively immune to domestic criticism for opening relations with "Red China," hard-liner Li Peng's support may have helped protect Qian from criticism for moving Beijing away from Tehran in 1997. My *guess* is that Qian Qichen played a key role in persuading his patron to distance China from Iran circa 1997 and that Li Peng's hard-line credentials gave Qian protection against internal criticism. This jumps considerably ahead of the narrative here, however. A final point to be made about China's "Iran card," is that use of Iran as leverage against the United States implies preparedness to strike a deal with Washington if and when the price is right. Concluding such a deal implies some modification of China's relations with the "card" country, Iran.

Tehran also made a strategic decision for expanded partnership with China. The Iranian leadership had made a strategic choice to develop relations with China and was now satisfied with that decision, President Rafsanjani told Chinese ambassador Hua Liming in October 1995.[7] An analyst at Shanghai's Academy of Social Sciences offered an astute analysis of the reasons for Tehran's decision to seek partnership with China.[8] Khomeini's death had opened the door to expanded relations with China. As long as the supreme leader lived, his principle of "Neither West, nor East" had been translated into policies of isolationism. Iran's post-Khomeini leaders had reinterpreted that doctrine to mean mere rejection of dominance or control by other countries. As Rafsanjani told visiting Wan Li in May 1990, "China is one of the few countries in the world that can be a good friend to those Third World countries who are keen on independence. . . . Our choice of establishing relations with your country was a correct choice."[9] Tehran was also impressed by China's successful development record during the 1980s and hoped, as Mahdi Karubi told Wan Li in May 1990, that "in the process of implementing post-war reconstruction, Iran hopes to borrow China's experience."[10]

Finally, Tehran appreciated China's strength and hoped to borrow that strength to constrain American threats against Iran, according to the Shanghai analyst.

China was not Iran's only hope for support against the West circa 1989–90. Tehran apparently hoped that the USSR too would be a strategic partner in countering the United States. Iran's post-Khomeini supreme leader, Ayatollah Seyed Mohammad Ali Hoseyn Khamenei, had studied as a youth at Moscow's Patrice Lumumba University. The way to Soviet-Iranian rapprochement was opened by Soviet agreement to withdraw its forces from Afghanistan—a move formalized in agreements signed in Geneva in April 1988 and completed by the following May. Peace between Iran and Iraq also reduced Soviet-Iranian tension, since Moscow had been Iran's major arms supplier during the war. In February 1989 Imam Khomeini had sent a letter to Soviet president Mikhail Gorbachev lauding his courage in reforming the USSR and encouraging him to study Islam as a solution to his country's mounting problems. Under the new circumstances, Khomeini believed that strong relations between Iran and Moscow would "help [both] confront the West."[11] Soviet leaders saw the opportunity and dispatched Foreign Minister Eduard Shevardnadze to Tehran. This was the first visit by a high-ranking Soviet official to Iran since the 1979 revolution. In Tehran Shevardnadze stressed Moscow's desire for expanded cooperation in all areas.[12] Several agreements were signed, and Iranian observers expressed great hopes for a new era of Iranian-Soviet cooperation. Unfortunately for Iranian strategy, the USSR soon slid into its terminal decline. Once Russia emerged as successor to the Soviet state in January 1992, it was far weaker and less concerned with foreign affairs than the Soviet Union had been. It was also far less interested in confronting the West. The demise of the Soviet alternative further encouraged Iran to turn to Beijing.

FORGING A BROADER PARTNERSHIP

The end of the Iran-Iraq war and the resulting Iranian push for economic development provided impetus for a visit by Deputy Premier Tian Jiyun in early March 1989. Tian was the highest-ranking Chinese official to visit Iran since Hua Guofeng's 1978 visit. The purposes of Tian's visit were to discuss China's role in Iran's postwar reconstruction and prepare the way for a visit to China by the president and soon-to-be successor to Khomeini as supreme leader, Khamenei. Tian delivered an invitation to Khamenei from President Yang Shangkun indicating China's willingness to contribute to Iran's postwar reconstruction. Expressing "deep sympathy" toward Iran's financial and manpower losses during the war, Tian told Khamenei that China was keen on contributing to Iran's reconstruction. "Although China's financial strength is limited, the desire for cooperation with Iran is sincere," Tian said.[13] Khamenei told Tian, "We prefer to cooperate with those countries of which Iranian people have no unpleasant memories." Prime Minister Hoseyn Musavi, who accompanied Khamenei, told Tian: "In the light of China's friendly attitude toward the Islamic Republic of Iran during the war, Tehran and Beijing can draw a solid and constant plan for expansion of mutual cooperation." These statements were testament to the political capital accrued by Beijing as a result of its support for Iran during the 1980–88 war. Cooperation in a range of industrial sectors was discussed during Tian's visit.[14]

While Tian Jiyun was in Beijing, the IRI broke diplomatic relations with the United Kingdom because of conflict arising out of Ayatollah Khomeini's fatwa calling for the assassination of British writer Salman Rushdie, the author of the book *The Satanic Verses*, which Khomeini deemed blasphemous. The fatwa against Rushdie threw Iranian-European ties into a deep chill for several years, further isolating Tehran and making ties with Beijing attractive. Majlis speaker Rafsanjani commented to Tian on the rupture with Britain, indicating that Iran hoped to expand ties with China as a consequence. "One does not have the concerns it has in ties with big powers when it comes to expanding relations with you," Rafsanjani told Tian.[15] "Our people and officials know that China has had effective cooperation with us in special circumstances." "Special circumstances" apparently referred to China's arms sales to Iran during the war with Iraq.

In May 1989 President Khamenei finally reciprocated Hua Guofeng's 1978 visit. Khamenei's visit (his second, following his first in February 1981) was the first ever by an Iranian head of state to China and came just before the visit by Gorbachev to Beijing. Khamenei's entourage included officials from IRI ministries of commerce, mines and metals, roads and transport, industry, housing and urban development, oil, energy, culture and Islamic guidance, the Islamic Revolutionary Guards Corps, and defense.[16] Khamenei's visit represented the beginning of overt Sino-Iranian military cooperation. It was apparently China that took the initiative here. The day Khamenei left for Beijing, China's ambassador in Tehran, Wang Benzuo, told the Iranian news agency that China was ready to hold talks on military cooperation with Iran: "If our Iranian friends are interested in this area we are ready to hold talks in this regard."[17] Regarding Iran's concern about China's recent sale of medium-range missiles to Iran's Arab rival Saudi Arabia—an issue Wang said he recently discussed with Deputy Foreign Minister Javad Mansuri—those missiles were sold to Saudi Arabia only "after the needed guarantees were given by Riyadh," Wang said. The military relation that began in May 1989 with Khamenei's visit would grow in importance over the decade and will be discussed in a subsequent chapter.

A set of agreements had previously been worked out for signature during Khamenei's visit. These agreements ranged from banking arrangements, to visa-less travel for holders of government service passports, to exchange of university students and teachers with provisions for scholarships, to creation of a "joint research center." China agreed to double its purchase of Iranian oil, thereby "paving the way for a substantial increase in bilateral trade."[18] Iran was "interested in joining hands with China in research and scientific fields," Khamenei told the press, and there was plenty of room for expanded cooperation in the fields of mines and energy. Premier Zhao Ziyang told Khamenei that China was willing to participate in Iran's reconstruction efforts on a wide scale.[19]

Khamenei's visit was not without friction. When he arrived in China his schedule did not include a meeting with Deng Xiaoping, a fact that apparently miffed Khamenei and caused him to fail to meet as scheduled with Li Peng for an initial round of talks. A meeting with Deng was quickly arranged.[20] Deng, thirty-five years older than Khamenei, underlined China's determination to pursue friendly relations with Arab countries as well as with Iran and the importance of Third World countries not wasting their strength on disputes between themselves. We hope to see a stable Middle East that facilitates development, Deng told Khamenei.[21] Khamenei told Deng that Iran had with great interest watched China for some time as a country where "great changes have taken place in the past four decades." Khamenei was allowed to "perform religious services" in Beijing's Ox-street Mosque. He also met with the prayer leader of that mosque, leaders of the Islamic Association of China, and a group from the Beijing Muslim community. These Chinese Muslims assured Khamenei that the new policies of the Chinese government allowed Muslims freedom to practice their religion.[22]

Following the Beijing massacre, Beijing and Tehran found common ground in opposing Western efforts to impose Western values and institutions on non-Western peoples. On June 18 the head of the East Asian section of Iran's foreign ministry told a *Tehran Times* reporter that outsiders had no right to interfere in China's internal affairs. The recent "anti-China declaration" by the Group of Seven Western countries was "naked interference in China's domestic politics," the Iranian official said.[23] Even stronger Iranian support was forthcoming during Foreign Minister Qian Qichen's October 1989 visit to Tehran. Had China not been firm in responding to Western pressure, Foreign

Minister Ali Akbar Velayati told Qian, the Western powers would have been even bolder. The attitude of the West toward China was regrettable, Velayati said, and based on the West's own selfish interest. President Rafsanjani told Qian that, if Western pressure toward China was this intense, one could imagine what the Western attitude would be toward a small country. Beijing and Tehran also supported one another in the effort to exclude Westernizing influences. In an interview with Iran's IRNA news agency during PRC president Yang Shangkun's visit to the IRI in October 1991, for example, PRC ambassador Hua Liming urged "Third World countries" to "discriminate and resist things that are the cause of corruption in Western societies."[24]

Sino-Iranian rejection of Western attempts to impose "Western" values went beyond support on specific events and included common rejection of the "new world order," proposed by President George H. W. Bush in September 1990. In July 1991, when Premier Li Peng visited Tehran, he and President Rafsanjani had "broad and deep" discussions on the new world order. After those discussions, Li declared that the new world order that needed to be built was one in which "the selection of whatever social system by a country is the affair of the people of that country."[25]

THE 1991 IRAQ WAR

The 1991 Gulf War deepened the Sino-Iranian partnership. The confrontation between Iraq and the international community that began with Saddam Hussein's seizure of Kuwait on August 2, 1990, strengthened the parallelism between Chinese and Iranian interests and thereby the partnership between the two countries. Beijing and Tehran quickly reached the same conclusions: Iraq's invasion and occupation of Kuwait was unacceptable and should be undone by withdrawal, but the United States should not intervene militarily. The United States should not marshal military forces in the region or resort to military force. Both Tehran and Beijing saw the U.S. military campaign against Iraq as part of a broader hegemonist drive to bring the Middle East under U.S. domination.

Iran's minister of posts and telecommunications, Mohammad Gharazi, arrived in Beijing two weeks after Iraq's seizure of Kuwait. Gharazi discussed the Iraq-Kuwait issue with Li Peng. Iran opposed the Iraqi aggression *and* favored the pullout of foreign forces from the region, Gharazi said. Li Peng said that China's policy was "identical" to Iran's.[26] China opposed the Iraqi invasion of Kuwait and opposed "military involvement by big powers because such involvement will do nothing but complicate and intensify the situation."[27] The situation should be resolved by peaceful means, Li Peng told Gharazi.

The two sides discussed the issue further and again reached agreement during a visit to Beijing in October by former prime minister and political advisor to President Rafsanjani, Hoseyn Musavi. Li Peng again emphasized that the seizure of Kuwait by Iraq *and* the presence of alien forces in the Persian Gulf were major threats to the region. China favored a political solution to the crisis. Musavi agreed: "We insist on the withdrawal of Iraqi forces from Kuwait *as well as* U.S.-led troops from the region."[28] The same month President Yang Shangkun told visiting defense minister Ali Akbar Torkan that while China and Iran both opposed the Iraqi invasion of Kuwait, they believed that the problem should be resolved *by regional countries* through peaceful means. China, Yang said, was against a military solution to the crisis. Yang also stressed Iran's "important role" in the Gulf and the Middle East.[29] At the end of the year China's foreign policy veteran Wu Xueqian told a visiting Majlis delegation that the only rational way to solve the crisis was for Iraq to withdraw *and* for the presence of U.S. and other "alien" forces to be eliminated from the region. In effect, and from Beijing's and Tehran's perspective, while Washington was pushing to bring the Gulf under fuller U.S. control, Beijing stood with Tehran in opposing that effort.

While forming an anti-U.S. partnership with Iran, Beijing also seized the opportunity presented by the Gulf crisis to leverage an end to U.S. sanctions imposed after the Beijing massacre. The Bush administration was moving toward war to liberate Kuwait from Iraqi occupation, and greatly desired U.N. Security Council authorization for such an effort. As a veto-holding permanent member of the Security Council, China could block such an authorization. Washington therefore needed China's support.

Foreign Minister Qian Qichen noted Washington's strong desire for China's support. Qian believed that after a spate of U.S. diplomatic efforts to maintain amicable Sino-American relations immediately after the Beijing massacre, the Bush administration lost interest in that effort later in 1989 as the Communist regimes in Eastern Europe crumbled. Iraq's invasion of Kuwait had revived Washington's interest in cooperative ties with China, Qian believed. This created, in Qian's words, an "advantageous opportunity to promote the normalization of Sino-American relations."[30] Stated simply, U.S. needs in the Middle East gave China leverage. China's top leaders decided to send Qian on a mission to Egypt, Saudi Arabia, Jordan, and Iraq (and not Iran!) in November 1990 in order to "seek a peaceful solution" to the Gulf crisis and "increase China's international stature and regional influence."[31] As Beijing perhaps anticipated, Qian's mission further roused Washington's interest in securing China's cooperation. With China paying active attention to the Middle East, it was important to secure its support for U.S. policy. Thus, while Qian was in Cairo on November 6 as the first stop on his Middle East tour, Secretary of State James Baker, also in Cairo at the time, sought and secured a meeting with him at the Cairo airport. Baker pleaded for Chinese support for Security Council authorization to use force. Qian argued in favor of giving sanctions a longer time to work, although he declined to estimate how long it might take sanctions to secure Iraqi withdrawal from Kuwait. Qian was struck by what he took as American impatience and desire for quick results. Eventually a deal was struck. Beijing would support, or at least not veto, a Security Council resolution, in exchange for a u.s. promise to "find an opportunity to cancel sanctions against China."[32] Premier Li Peng met with IRI ambassador Mohammad Tarumi Rad in late November to explain China's abstention on the crucial Security Council vote.[33] As with Beijing's suspension of Silkworm missile sales in 1987, Tehran was being educated in the pragmatic limits of China's support for Iran in the face of u.s. pressure.

Beijing saw the u.s. war against Saddam Hussein's Iraq as a "struggle between global and regional hegemonisms." The PRC State Council and representatives from the General Office of the Central Committee reportedly held a secret meeting in mid-January 1991 to evaluate the Gulf situation. The document produced at that meeting and distributed to high-level party, government, and military leaders reached this conclusion and determined that the United States had two objectives: first, to teach Saddam Hussein a lesson, and, second, to dominate the world. Washington's war against Iraq was a move to bring the oil resources of the Middle East under u.s. control. In terms of response, China would refrain from openly criticizing the United States and maintain a neutral position in its propaganda.[34] China's "principled stance" was to oppose that war, in cooperation with its friends in the region such as Iran. But China's ability to influence events was limited, and it would use the opportunity to restore relations with the United States and build influence in the Middle East region.

The swift victory of u.s.-led forces over Iraq in February 1991 surprised and dismayed Beijing. Chinese military analysts had expected Iraq's large, well-armed, and battle-hardened army to tie down and inflict heavy casualties on u.s. forces, thereby protracting the war. In the event, u.s. superiority over Iraqi forces was so overwhelming that the superior numbers of Iraqi troops and tanks were essentially irrelevant, and u.s. forces won swift, decisive, and low-cost victory. From Beijing's and Tehran's perspective, the outcome of the 1991 Gulf War was a major advance for u.s. hegemonism in its efforts to dominate the Middle East and the world.

On February 21, after three weeks of intense u.s. air war against Iraq and less than a week before u.s.-led forces launched their four-day ground offensive, Chinese deputy foreign minister and "special presidential envoy" Yang Fuchang arrived in Tehran to convey China's support in this precarious situation. Iran and China have very friendly relations and take common stands regarding the Persian Gulf crisis, Yang told the Iranian media. China deeply admired Iran's efforts to solve the Gulf crisis via diplomatic means and would support all efforts to prevent the war from spreading, Yang said.[35] In the midst of the 1991 Kuwait crisis, Tehran was virtually isolated, but Beijing offered understanding and support. As the Chinese saying "to deliver coal when it is snowing" (*xue zhong song tan*) indicates, a true friend is one who gives help when it is needed.

Strengthened partnership with Iran was a major gain for Beijing from the 1991 Gulf War. All the Arab countries in the region had climbed on the u.s. bandwagon to force Iraq out of Kuwait. Other than Iraq, Iran was the sole pariah, and it turned to Beijing for solace. China lost considerable credibility with the Arab countries by arguing to Saudi Arabia, Jordan, and Egypt that the Iraqi seizure of Kuwait could be undone by peaceful means. This simply was not credible. Ellis Joffe has pointed out that the fact that making such an incredible argument did not seriously undermine China's position was testament to its near irrelevance. Arab leaders could and did ignore China's incredible argument, because what China said simply did not matter very much.[36] In the isolated Iranian market, however, China's "principled position" had somewhat higher value.

THE APOGEE OF THE ANTIHEGEMONY PARTNERSHIP, 1991–96

In the several years after the 1991 Gulf War the Sino-Iranian antihegemony partnership reached its apogee. In July 1991 Premier Li Peng made a three-day official goodwill visit to Iran as part of a six-country Middle East tour. Li was the first Chinese premier to visit Iran since Hua Guofeng's August 1978 visit. Li Peng explained the purpose of his visit in these terms: "I have come to visit your country with the purpose of deepening understanding, enhancing friendship, promoting cooperation, and maintaining peace. . . . As a big country in Asia, Iran plays an important role in both regional and international affairs. China is ready to join Iran in the common efforts for maintaining peace and stability in the region and establishing a just and rational new international order."[37]

Li Peng elaborated in his banquet speech:

> In the current ever-changing international situation, the further strengthening of friendly and cooperative relations between the two countries in all fields

not only accords with the fundamental interests of the peoples of our two countries, but also is conducive to peace and development in the region and the world. . . . The current world situation is undergoing a deep change, and the situation is still turbulent and keeps changing. Hegemonism and power politics are the cause of world tension and turbulence, as well as the major threat to world peace and security.[38]

Comments by Li to the Iranian media were more pointed: "We are against the domination of the U.S. or of a minority over the world, and against the creation of the new order by the U.S. in international relations, and we are in complete agreement with the Islamic Republic of Iran on this point."[39] Iranian leaders asked Li to give substance to his anti-U.S. rhetoric by playing a more forceful role in the global anti-U.S. struggle. China should act as a counterweight to the United States in the Middle East and play a more active role in "resolving the Palestinian problem," in the Iranian view.[40] Together "freedom fighters and justice-seeking people" should prevent the efforts of "some" to "stabilize their unrivaled domination in the world," Supreme Leader Khamenei told Li. Third World countries, "especially those which are in sensitive areas of the globe should have closer cooperation with each other to resist the U.S. drive for 'absolute domination,'" Khamenei urged the visiting Chinese premier.[41] In effect, Tehran was inviting Beijing to join Iran in militant struggle against the United States in East and West Asia. The "freedom fighters" and "justice-seeking people" closest to the hearts of Tehran's leaders were, of course, the Hezbollah in Lebanon seeking destruction of "the Zionist entity" Israel. It is unclear how much indication Li Peng gave that China was willing to go down such a path. However this may be, Beijing declined Tehran's advice regarding Palestine. The next year China normalized relations with Israel. Simultaneously Beijing offered substantive benefits to Tehran in other areas.

During Li Peng's visit, Iran and China signed an agreement on a two-year plan for cultural, scientific, and educational exchanges. China also agreed to launch a satellite for Iran for radio and television transmission. As will be discussed in later chapters, China was supplying huge amounts of munitions to Iran. According to estimates of the Stockholm International Peace Research Institute (SIPRI), deliveries in 1993 and 1994 topped $200 million each year, the highest level since the end of the Iran-Iraq war. Nuclear cooperation also expanded rapidly.

Strategic discussions continued in September 1991 when an NPC friendship delegation, led by NPC Standing Committee member and China's longtime Iran-hand He Ying, visited Iran in the immediate aftermath of the failed hard-liner coup in the USSR and as that state was sliding rapidly toward its demise. Again Tehran proposed a firm anti-U.S. partnership to China. Drastic changes were currently under way in the international situation, Foreign Minister Velayati told He Ying. Some countries were trying to impose their own "patterns" on other countries. Both China and Iran were independent countries taking their own road and hoped to strengthen their nations in this effort. A unified, powerful, and independent China could make greater contributions to the world than other countries, Velayati said.[42] The furthest He Ying would go was to pledge that China would not form an alliance or establish strategic relations with the superpowers.[43]

The dialogue continued when president Yang Shangkun visited Iran in October 1991. In a written interview with IRNA shortly before his departure for Tehran, Yang broached a key theme of his upcoming visit: "Being an important country in West Asia and the Persian Gulf region, Iran plays a significant role in maintaining regional peace and security."[44] When meeting Khamenei, Yang returned to the theme: "China attaches importance to Iran's position in the Middle East and the Persian Gulf region, and hopes Iran would play a greater role in preserving peace and stability."[45] In talks with president Rafsanjani, Yang declared: "The Chinese government prizes its friendship and cooperation with Iran and genuinely hopes to develop . . . cooperative relations further in all areas . . . while making contributions to safeguarding regional stability and world peace." Yang and Rafsanjani agreed that the current international situation was "unbalanced" with "intensified contradictions." The task was to establish a new just and rational international political and economic order, and the two sides should cooperate in this process.[46] Rafsanjani was very positive about the result of Yang's visit: "After the victory of the Islamic revolution, we chose China as our partner. . . . On the whole it seemed that we could regard China as one of our good partners. But with this trip we have come close to our goals of expanding scientific, economic, cultural, and international (cooperation) especially regarding Asian issues. . . . We believe that our talks could be effective and affect the situation."[47]

China and Iran began cooperating in third countries. In late 1991 Iran agreed to underwrite Chinese arms sales to Sudan, where an Islamic government had taken power in Khartoum in June 1989. China's arms sales contract with Sudan predated that coup d'état, but Tehran stepped in to provide financial support to Sudan's cash-strapped Islamic government, permitting the Sino-Sudanese arms deal to move forward. Tehran reportedly underwrote the sale of $300 million in Chinese arms to Sudan.[48] Further Iranian-financed Chinese arms sales to Sudan occurred in the mid-1990s—as Sudan confronted possible U.N. sanctions because of its involvement in a 1995 attempted assassi-

nation of Egyptian president Hosni Mubarak.[49] The parties to these trian-
gular arms deals tried to keep them secret, but they inevitably came to the
surface. They posed a fundamental question for China and the international
community. Was China a responsible member of the international community fit to sit at the high table of nations? Or was it still a rebel that chose to
associate with pariah states conniving at violating basic norms of the international community like nonassassination of leaders of states? Similar questions about China's relations to the nuclear nonproliferation regime were
equally troubling. Debate over these questions intensified among China's foreign policy elite in the mid-1990s.

High-level Sino-Iranian discussions continued in April and September 1992
when Foreign Minister Ali Akbar Velayati and President Rafsanjani respectively visited Beijing. During Velayati's visit the two countries "harmonized"
their positions "on major world issues." The "polarization" of power during the post–Cold War era provided favorable grounds for promotion of
cooperation between Iran and China, according to an Iranian radio broadcast. Regarding the "new world order" recently proposed by U.S. president
George H. W. Bush, China and Iran had a "relatively similar" approach. Both
believed, unlike the United States, that all countries should enjoy an equal
right in international decision making. The U.S.-proposed "new order" was
not in accord with the national interests and independence of Third World
states.[50] "Regional cooperation" between China and Iran in Afghanistan and
Central Asia in light of "changes in the former Soviet Union and independence of Central Asia" was also discussed during Velayati's visit. China and
Iran shared concerns about the spread of U.S.-supported Turkish influence
into post-Soviet Central Asia, and Beijing was prepared to accept Iran as a
counter to more pernicious Turkish influence.[51] In Afghanistan, where civil
war had erupted following the withdrawal of Soviet forces, China and Iran
both supported a political settlement and an end to the fighting.

Rafsanjani's visit in September took place, according to Voice of the Islamic
Republic of Iran radio, "at a time when hegemonistic powers, notably America,
have recently started extensive propaganda attacks against Iran and China in
various forums, [taking] maximum advantage of the consequences of the dis-
integration of the former Soviet Union." China and Iran were "new powers
capable of affecting world events, and it was precisely for this reason that
America was trying to weaken the pivotal Tehran-Beijing and Tehran-
Islamabad role" in order to strengthen its "self-professed unchallenged domination." America's very opposition to Sino-Iranian cooperation demonstrated
the "importance and constructive role" of that cooperation in "world equations."[52] In line with these sentiments, Rafsanjani pressed during his visit for

closer antihegemony cooperation. Iranian leaders apparently envisioned a bloc including Iran, China, Russia, India, and Pakistan challenging the United States, thus rectifying the "unbalanced" international situation. Beijing was not prepared for such a course and proposed measures that deflected Iranian enthusiasm into bureaucratic deserts. Three months after Rafsanjani's visit Beijing and Tehran announced an agreement to survey ways and means of establishing an organization of Asian countries, including Russia, Pakistan, and India and eventually the Central Asian republics. The two sides were to undertake research and then inform the other of the results of their investigations.[53]

While not prepared to align closely with Tehran, Beijing was prepared during Rafsanjani's visit to strengthen Iran's nuclear and military development efforts—in exchange for Iranian oil. Nuclear cooperation was especially significant. During Rafsanjani's visit, Defense Minister Ali Akbar Torkan and China's science and technology minister, Song Jian, signed an agreement providing for extensive nuclear cooperation, including construction of several large nuclear power plants. By late 1991 Washington had concluded that Iran was seeking nuclear weapons, and thwarting that effort became a major objective of u.s. policy. China's expanding nuclear cooperation with Iran constituted a major and direct challenge to this u.s. policy. A large munitions sales agreement was also signed during Rafsanjani's visit. A major part of payment was to be in crude oil, an arrangement favorable to Iran, which was suffering liquidity problems because of a decline in oil prices.[54] Queried by the media about his talks in China, Rafsanjani reported they "were clear-cut and free of trouble, and therefore went ahead very fast."[55]

Beijing was clearly using links with Tehran as a way of hitting back at Washington for what Beijing deemed u.s. policies hostile to China—criticism, sanctions, and such. A subsequent chapter on linkages between Sino-u.s. and Sino-Iranian relations will explore the ways in which Beijing used u.s. displeasure with Sino-Iranian cooperation to move u.s. policy in directions favorable to Beijing. One result of Beijing's constant balancing between building a long-term, all-weather relation with Iran and using China's ties with Iran to pressure Washington was than neither Tehran nor Washington was fully satisfied with China's Iran policies.

THE INTENSIFICATION OF IRANIAN-U.S.
CONFLICT AND CHINA'S RESPONSE

The Clinton administration (inaugurated in January 1993) announced a new policy of "dual containment" of Iran and Iraq in May 1993 premised on objection to both countries' foreign and domestic policies. Internationally both countries opposed the Arab-Israeli peace process, sponsored terrorism and assassination of foreign leaders, and were pursuing weapons of mass destruction—at least so the Clinton administration concluded. Internally, the two states ruled by coercion, repressed human rights, opposed popular political participation, and fostered a siege mentality and radical political ideologies—all of which made them unable to engage constructively with other countries, again according to the new U.S. policy. In response to these defects, the United States would now seek to isolate both Iran and Iraq via international economic boycotts and restriction of technological and military capabilities.[56] This new, tough policy reflected, in part, a hardening of congressional views. In October 1992 Congress had passed the Iran-Iraq Arms Non-Proliferation Act, which provided that the United States would "oppose, and urgently . . . seek the agreement of other nations also to oppose, any transfer to Iran or Iraq of any goods or technology, including dual-use goods or technology," that could "materially contribute to either country's acquiring chemical, biological, nuclear [weapons] or destabilizing numbers and types of advanced conventional weapons." "Nations and persons" who transferred such "goods or technology" were to be subject to sanctions.[57]

From Beijing's perspective, dual containment and the Iran-Iraq Non-Proliferation Act were brazen U.S. hegemonism. The United States had no grounds to concern itself with Iran's internal governance. Regarding nuclear issues, Iran was a signatory of the Non-Proliferation Treaty (NPT) and as such had the right to the peaceful use of nuclear energy. Iran had cooperated with the International Atomic Energy Agency (IAEA—the NPT's watchdog body), and the IAEA had never found Iran in violation of its NPT obligations. Yet the United States, acting on the unilateral basis of its own domestic law and unilateral policy decisions, was presuming to regulate relations between Iran and other countries, which were in full accord with international law.

As U.S. policy toward Iran hardened, Deputy Foreign Minister Mohammad Javad Zarif visited Beijing in July 1993 for consultations with Qian Qichen over U.S. moves. Iran attached great importance to cooperation and exchange of views with China, Zarif told Qian. "Certain countries" were unhappy with the existing friendly relations between Iran and China, Qian replied, but despite that vicious propaganda, the two countries would continue their cooperation to the benefit of both countries and to consolidate world peace and security. The two leaders dismissed as "unjustifiable" the idea of using human rights for political gains and imposing views held by one group on others.[58] Consultations continued in March 1994 when Qian visited Tehran. The U.S.-PRC confrontation over China's Most Favored Nation (MFN) status and its human rights deficiencies was then reaching a climax, with the United States threatening to revoke MFN status unless China improved its human rights record, and China adamantly rejecting U.S. demands. Different countries should respect each other and refrain from imposing their social systems and ideology on others, Qian told Velayati. The world was not homogeneous but made up of countries having different political and social systems, pursuing different ways of achieving economic progress, and having different religious and cultural traditions. Velayati agreed, telling Qian that the states of the Persian Gulf region should manage the affairs of the region by themselves and oppose hegemonist intervention and policies of coercion.[59] Both sides agreed that the present era was not one in which a superpower or a few big countries could give orders to others, and that the developing countries needed to strengthen their unity and cooperation to maintain peace and uphold their own interests. Qian emphasized that countries with different social systems, paths of economic development, religions, and cultural traditions should respect each other and not seek to impose their systems and values on other countries. In the future, if China "became powerful" (*qiang-dale*), it would never become hegemonist, Qian pledged.[60] The same themes characterized discussions between first vice president Hasan Habibi and Jiang Zemin and Li Peng in Beijing in August.

Early in 1995 U.S. pressure on Iran intensified further. In March Clinton barred U.S. companies from producing oil in Iran, blocking an effort by Conoco to invest $1 billion in oil and gas projects in Iran—a move that would have been the first U.S. oil company project in Iran since the revolution.[61] Two months later Clinton cut off all U.S. trade and investment with Iran, including U.S. company purchase of Iranian oil for resale overseas.[62] Explaining the new trade embargo, U.S. Secretary of State Warren Christopher called Iran an "outlaw state" that had been trying for a decade to develop nuclear weapons.[63]

As U.S. pressure on Iran intensified, Foreign Minister Velayati visited Beijing in March 1995 for talks with Qian Qichen on the first stop of a four-nation East Asia tour. (Vietnam, Thailand, and Malaysia were Velayati's other stops.) Velayati's most important goal in undertaking the tour, according to the Voice of the Islamic Republic of Iran radio, was to counter the U.S. policy of isolating Tehran in political and economic spheres. Since China pursued a firm policy in the face of America's hegemonistic strategy, Beijing was giving greater attention to Iran in recent years, the radio said. In order to counter America's expansionist policy, Iran had close cooperation with China in its capacity as a permanent member of the U.N. Security Council.[64]

During their talks, Qian and Velayati agreed that certain Western countries should not misuse human rights to pressure other countries whose views were different from those of the West. Regarding the situation in the Persian Gulf, Qian said that the presence of alien forces there would be of no help in improving relations among regional countries, and that regional security could be maintained only through cooperation among those regional states.[65] During a meeting with Li Peng, Velayati underlined the need for expanded Sino-Iranian cooperation, noting that certain countries were using human rights and disarmament to pursue political objectives. Li Peng noted that no country is allowed to interfere in the internal affairs of another country.[66]

Tehran appreciated Beijing's support in the face of mounting U.S. pressure. "China has proven that it is a reliable friend and partner . . . that won't surrender to the U.S.—which considers itself the only power in the emerging world order," stated a *Tehran Times* article in May. The article went on to explain that "Iran–China cooperation can play a very crucial role in paving the way for a comprehensive cooperation among Asian countries to emerge as a monolithic bloc. . . . The Tehran-Islamabad-New Delhi-Beijing axis can constitute the backbone of this cooperation."[67] A partnership among key Asian countries and Russia was needed to counter U.S. domination in the current state of global geopolitical imbalance, according to Iranian deputy foreign minister Alaeddin Broujerdi in June 1996. Many powerful countries—China, Russia, India, and Iran—were dissatisfied with U.S. foreign policy, Broujerdi said. Relations between those aggrieved countries were growing closer, and they should now work together to play a major global role.[68] Six months earlier, Iran's ambassador to India had called on India, China, and Iran to unite to counter the U.S. threat. "[The] U.S. is posing a threat not only in the [Persian Gulf] region but all over the world. It wants to play the role of policemen and a judge at the same time," the Iranian representative said. The United States dreamed of becoming the ruler of the world, but that dream would never be fulfilled. The countries of Asia—China, India, and Iran—with their "rich cultural and historical background had contributed immensely to the growth of human civilization" and should now work together for the good of humanity.[69] Tehran still wanted Beijing to work toward a grand Eurasian coalition to balance the United States.

Again Beijing was not willing to join an overt anti-U.S. coalition. From the perspective of China's mainstream leadership, doing so was too risky. It might prompt a strong and vigorous U.S. reaction, perhaps directed primarily against China, which most Chinese leaders suspected the United States saw as the greatest, long-term challenge to American global dominance. Such a strong u.s. reaction could have severe adverse consequences for China's ongoing development and modernization drive. The Iran card was useful for pressuring Washington. But it should not be overplayed.

Beijing was willing to support Iran with declarations by Chinese officials and media commentary. When Washington decided on tougher economic sanctions against Iran in April 1995, a Ministry of Foreign Affairs (mfa) spokesman called the move futile and not conducive to settlement of existing issues between the United States and Iran. Such moves would only worsen tension, according to the spokesman. Differences between countries could be resolved only through negotiation and mutual respect, not through pressure and threat.[70] When the Iranian vice foreign minister visited Beijing in May, Chinese vice foreign minister Tian Zengpei reiterated the same points.[71] Further u.s. moves the same month brought another denunciation along the same lines by an mfa spokesman.[72] Articles in *Renmin ribao* argued at length that the new u.s. economic sanctions against Iran would fail.[73] An article in July 1995, for example, maintained that u.s. sanctions against Iran would have a "pathetic outcome" since they would have the support of neither u.s. European allies nor u.s. corporations:

> The world is moving toward multi-polarity, so it is becoming increasingly unworkable to be posturing as the "only superpower" giving orders to everybody whenever it pleases. . . . One country will not be willing to be subject to another country's political will and sacrifice its own major economic interests for it. One wonders if certain people in power in the United States will be able to learn something from the failure of its act of imposing sanctions on Iran.[74]

Another article in January 1996 condemned a u.s. appropriation of $20 million for "subverting the Iranian government," arguing that "the United States wants to unsettle the Gulf states in order to reap unfair gains." The real u.s. goal was "controlling the world's most important energy resources, expanding arms exports, and safe-guarding its strategic political, military, and economic interests." The most recent u.s. move was "brazen interference in Iran's internal affairs" that "once again demonstrated" that

> the world is not very peaceful, primarily because hegemonism and power politics refuse to leave the international arena. Some major powers . . . always resort to such old weapons as interference, containment, encirclement and checking, and threaten others with isolation, sanctions, or even subversion. However,

such hegemonist moves . . . run counter to the world trend since the end of the Cold War and become increasingly incompatible with the times.[75]

Such statements were useful to Tehran in legitimizing its policies to Iranian opinion. They may also have influenced world opinion to some degree. Most important, they indicated to IRI's leaders that they did not stand alone, but had a powerful friend. There was also China's U.N. Security Council veto and the implicit promise to wield it, if necessary, on Tehran's behalf. China's most substantial support came in the areas of nuclear assistance and modernization of Iran's military.

BEIJING'S 1997 PARTIAL DISENGAGEMENT

Just as Sino-Iranian antihegemony cooperation was most intense, Chinese policy underwent an abrupt shift as a result, apparently, not of anything that transpired in Tehran-Beijing relations, but of deteriorating U.S.-PRC ties. Successive and increasingly severe crises rocked Sino-American ties in the 1990s: over the Beijing massacre of 1989, the 1993–94 confrontation over linkage of Most Favored Nation and human rights, and the 1995–96 face-off over Taiwan. These intense confrontations apparently precipitated debate within the CCP over management of Sino-U.S. relations and a derivative decision to partially disengage from Iran. Avery Goldstein identified a major shift in China's diplomatic orientation circa 1996. Increasingly concerned that China's own policies might push other countries into alignment with U.S.-inspired China-containment schemes, spoil Sino-U.S. ties, and perhaps even push Washington into a preemptive military strike against China, Beijing adopted a more conciliatory approach after intense debate.[76] Beijing's partial disengagement from Iran in 1997 seems to have been part of this package of more conciliatory, less confrontational policies.

In fall 1997 Beijing struck a deal with the United States terminating Chinese nuclear cooperation with Iran, and ending Chinese sales to Iran of advanced antiship cruise missiles, the weapons most threatening to oil tankers and U.S. warships. Since this adjustment of Chinese policy was closely tied to Sino-U.S. ties, it is discussed in a later chapter on Sino-U.S. bargaining over Iran.

As Beijing moved toward accommodation with Washington, it gave warning to Tehran. In April 1997 negotiations between Qian Qichen and U.S. deputy assistant secretary of state Robert Einhorn led to China's agreement to suspend cooperation with nuclear facilities not safeguarded by the IAEA. While this referred primarily to China's nuclear cooperation with Pakistan, not Iran, it was the first step in intensified negotiations leading to the deal revealed during Jiang Zemin's October visit to the United States. While Sino-U.S. talks were under way Vice Foreign Minister Ji Fengding visited Iran in June for an exchange of views on international and regional issues.

Needless to say, Iranian leaders were disappointed by Beijing's capitulation to U.S. pressure. Iranian anger was, however, directed primarily against Washington. The United States' pressure on China was yet another manifestation of the Great Satan's hostility toward Iran and hegemony over world affairs. Nothing was to be gained by pique toward Beijing. That would only further isolate Iran, thereby serving U.S. imperial objectives. China was still willing to cooperate with Iran in important areas, especially economic development and military modernization. China could still offer support in the Security Council. Nothing would be gained and much potentially lost by directing Iranian anger against Beijing. Yet, following Beijing's 1997 partial disengagement there was far greater realism in Iranian appraisal of China and its role. Gone were earlier extravagant, romantic visions of China joining a Eurasian bloc against the United States. Henceforth, Tehran would manifest a much more sober assessment of the limits of China's willingness to align with Iran against the United States. One Tehran commentator noted during Jiang Zemin's 2002 visit, for example:

> Ever since the Islamic revolution, the Islamic Republic has tried to obtain most of its technological requirements from countries such as China and Russia . . . Of course, China has not always provided a green-light for these demands, because China has been under American pressure in this connection. . . . Iran has always been hoping that China's desire to have relations with Iran would not be overshadowed by the pressures and interference of a third party, namely America. Of course, this desire has not always produced positive results.[77]

Other Iranian commentators noted during Jiang's 2002 visit that one motive behind China's renewed courtship of Iran at that point was a desire to gain increased leverage with the United States: "Of course, it must be emphasized . . . that China is also trying to use its expanding relations with Tehran as a winning card and a potential winner of concessions from America."[78] Other Iranian commentators noted that China's relations with the United States trumped its ties with Iran. One Tehran newspaper explained, for example, during Jiang's visit: "The Chinese have certain strategic priorities, such as the return of Taiwan to the mainland and preserving Tibet as part of the . . . PRC. For the attainment of these objectives, they need the support of the United States. They also need advanced technology from the United States. . . .

Therefore the PRC will never sacrifice its relations with the United States for Iran."[79] Still another Tehran paper said that Iran could hope China would use its Security Council veto on behalf of Iran, should that become necessary. "At the same time, it must be borne in mind," the paper explained, that China never gets involved in military or political blocs for or against the interests of another country."[80] Beijing's 1997 policy adjustment had a sobering effect on the Tehran-Beijing partnership. It also cost Beijing in terms of status and influence in Tehran.

As indicated by the chronology of Sino-Iranian interactions in the appendix of this study, high-level Sino-Iranian interactions fell in 1998 to the lowest level since the "new start" in relations that began with Wu Xueqian's 1984 visit. There were only two vice ministerial–level exchanges in 1998, compared to ten high-level visits in 1997 and eleven in 1996. A six-year hiatus in military exchanges also began in 1998. After Defense Minister Mohammad Firouzandeh's visit in September 1997, there was not another public military exchange until the visit by Revolutionary Guards commander Mohammad Hejazi in October 2003. The suspension of military exchanges and sharp scaling back of visits by high-level leaders were indications of the estrangement of Sino-Iranian relations following Beijing's accession to U.S. pressure over Iran.

RENEWED SINO-PERSIAN PARTNERSHIP AND U.S. HEGEMONY

In 1999 Beijing began repairing ties with Tehran. A sharp deterioration of Sino-U.S. relations in that year was one factor in the initiation of this effort. In May U.S. warplanes had bombed China's embassy in Belgrade, Yugoslavia, during the brief war to stop Serbian ethnic cleansing in Kosovo. Angry mobs besieged the U.S. embassy in Beijing and burned U.S. diplomatic properties in Chengdu, Sichuan province. Beijing declared and professed to believe that the U.S. attack had been deliberate. While that attribution of malevolent intent to the United States was probably more an effort to placate nationalist anger within China, U.S. intentions seemed genuinely sinister to Beijing. The Kosovo intervention was conducted by NATO and without authorization by the U.N. Security Council (because of Russia's veto), thus setting a precedent for military intervention without U.N. authorization into what Beijing deemed the internal affairs of a sovereign state.

Vice Foreign Minister Ji Fengding got the ball rolling in August 1999 during a three-day visit to Tehran. Ji called for both countries to "climb higher and look further" (*deng gao wang yuan*) and work jointly to expand cooperation. There was not, Ji said, merely one form of cooperation between the two countries—implicitly referring to the now-suspended nuclear cooperation—but many forms. There was great potential for expanded cooperation, Ji said, putting great stress on both being ancient civilizations, Asian, and developing countries. Both sides should realistically appraise their interests, identify areas of possible cooperation, explain doubts, and strive to increase mutual confidence. Ji sweetened his pitch by indicating Chinese willingness to support construction of several power stations, copper mines, and a second phase of the Tehran metro project. Ji's group left Tehran feeling they had secured Iranian understanding and reached a mutual desire for expanded cooperation on the basis of common interests.[81]

Establishment of a "political consultation mechanism" in the form of regular vice foreign ministerial visits was another element of the restored Sino-Iranian partnership. Foreign ministers Tang Jiaxuan and Velayati discussed such an arrangement during their meeting at u.n. headquarters in New York City in September 1999, and the "consultation mechanism" was formally agreed to during Tang's visit to Tehran the next February. The first regular "consultation" took place in May–June 2001 in Beijing. The second came three months later—two days before the September 11 attacks on the United States. Tang's February 2000 visit was the first visit by a Chinese foreign minister to Iran since 1994. Its key purpose was to open the completed first phase of the Tehran subway project, thereby highlighting Chinese support for Iran, and smoothing the way for a visit by President Khatami to China several months later. A second round of high-level visits—President Khatami to China in June 2000, Vice President Hu Jintao to Iran in January 2001, and President Jiang Zemin to Iran in April 2002—followed as part of the effort to resuscitate the partnership.

Khatami's June 2000 visit was the first visit by an Iranian president since May 1989. His 170-person entourage included Foreign Minister Kamal Kharazi and Defense Minister Ali Shamkhani. Chinese defense minister Chi Haotian met with Shamkhani, even though that meeting was not publicly announced.[82] Open military exchanges resumed seven months after the Shamkhani-Chi talks. The joint communiqué issued at the end of Khatami's visit attested to the broad convergence of Chinese and Iranian views. The communiqué stipulated that Beijing and Tehran agreed to establish "a twenty-first-century-oriented, long-term and wide-ranging relationship of friendship and cooperation in the strategic interests of the two countries on the basis of mutual respect for sovereignty and territorial integrity, equality and mutual benefit, and peaceful co-existence."[83] Significantly, the words *partnership* or *strategic partnership* were not used. Those words would have signified a closer relationship than Beijing was prepared to commit to. Yet the communiqué alluded to the anti-u.s. aspect of the renewed relationship when it stipulated that "both sides stand for world multipolarization" and "stressed the need to establish an equitable, just, fair and reasonable new international political economic order that is free of hegemonism and power politics and based on equality," free from "the use or threat of force and imposition of economic sanctions to settle disputes between countries," and in which human rights should not be used as a pretext for interfering in the internal affairs of other countries. All these phrases were oblique references to u.s. policies. The communiqué also "emphasized that the security and stability of the Persian Gulf should be safeguarded by the countries in the region free from outside interference." This too carried an implicit message: the u.s. military role in the Persian Gulf should end and the Iranian role increase. This reiterated China's traditional position tracing back to Ji Pengfei's 1973 visit.

In January 2001 high-level and public military exchanges resumed after a hiatus of six years when China's minister of the State Commission for Science, Technology, and Industry for National Defense, Liu Jibin, visited Iran for talks with Shamkhani. Stronger ties were in the interest of both countries, Liu told Shamkhani, and the leaders of the two countries had "the political will" to expand cooperation further. The stand of the two countries as described in the joint communiqué issued during President Khatami's visit provided "the main bases" for China-Iran cooperation in all fields, Liu Jibin told Shamkhani.[84] When Liu met with the commander of Iran's army, Major General Mohammad Salim, the two sides "called for the expansion of bilateral relations in the area of science and technology."[85] In meeting with oil minister Bijan Namdar Zangaheh, Liu called for increased Iranian oil exports to China, terming Iran a "reliable and stable power in the region."[86] In 2000 China's oil imports from Iran increased by 84 percent over the previous year. In 2001 they increased another 55 percent. Overall two-way trade increased by 73 percent in 2000. China's increased oil purchases transformed a previous chronic Chinese surplus in bilateral trade into a steady Iranian surplus. Chinese arms for Iranian oil was a major component of the renewed Sino-Iranian relationship.

China also supported Iran's effort to launch a "dialogue among civilizations" during 2000 and 2001. That campaign was then a major thrust of Iranian diplomacy, aimed against the philosophy of "clash of civilizations" that was putatively popular in the United States. Significantly, the dialogue among civilizations was part of reformist president Khatami's effort to dethaw Iran's relations with the United States. Beijing endorsed Iran's effort in the General Assembly to declare 2001 a year of dialogue among civilizations and later organized or participated in several academic and cultural events in association with the United Nation's Year of Dialogue among Civilizations. China also supported Iran's efforts to join the World Trade Organization (WTO), though not being a member itself, China did not have very much clout on this question. Iran first applied to begin membership talks with the WTO in 1996, but the United States vetoed discussion of that application and the issue was never put to a vote. Iran's application was first discussed by the WTO in May 2001 after "several emerging economies" spoke out in favor of Iran's application.[87] The United States vetoed several subsequent efforts to begin membership talks with Iran—in October 2001 and again in February 2002. But in May 2004 China's ambassador Lio G. Tan told Expediency Council chairman Rafsanjani that China still backed Iran's accession to the WTO.[88] China officially became a WTO member in December 2001.

The media of both Iran and China indicated considerable enthusiasm for renewed antihegemony partnership. An Iranian analysis of President Khatami's 2000 visit to China found the following:

> The resistance that emerged [among] the Chinese leadership level in the face of America's incursions, and the endeavors by Washington to transform international relations and world politics into a unipolar world, brought about the hope among many of the world's independent countries that by strengthening their cooperation . . . the aim of confronting the unipolar world being considered by America, will be consolidated. Therefore, at present, the strengthening of the Tehran-Beijing axis is of great importance. We must not lose sight of the fact that China is a country that emerged as an absolute power in Asia . . . [and its] ideologically consolidated leadership have caused it to emerge as a party that many countries in the world can consult and depend on.[89]

On the Chinese side, Iran's role in the antihegemonist strategy of at least some Chinese analysts was reflected in a 2000 article in the influential journal *Strategy and Management*.[90] According to this article, the United States already controlled the entire west bank of the oil-rich Persian Gulf through its relations with the pro-American states on that bank (i.e., Saudi Arabia and the small Gulf states). So powerful was U.S. control that the Gulf had become, in effect, an "internal sea" of the United States. Challenges to that position were likely to fail. But if China and Russia together expanded relations with Iran, they could together maintain "a minimum balance" that could thwart evil U.S. moves. Since secure export of oil from the Gulf required nonbelligerence by both banks (i.e., the U.S.-controlled west bank and the China-Russia–supported Iranian east bank), the fact that China, Russia, and Iran were strongly positioned on the east bank would "prevent the U.S. from implementing oil embargoes against other countries in special times." In plain speech, in the event of a u.s.-prc clash over Taiwan, the United States would not dare to shut off China's Gulf oil supplies, because if it did so, China, Russia, and Iran on the Gulf's "east bank" would retaliate by closing down the flow of Gulf oil to Western states. Thus, the *Strategy and Management* article continued, close links with Iran would provide "insurance against a remote contingency" (*fang wanyi de baoxian*). The purpose of such an arrangement was not to challenge the United States, but to maintain a minimum balance. This final caveat was probably directed against opponents within China's foreign policy elite who argued that alignment with Iran against the United States was too risky.

The common opposition to u.s. hegemonism that provided inspiration for renewed Sino-Iranian partnership in 1999–2000 became stronger still as the administration of George W. Bush took over in Washington in January 2001. In its first months in office, the Bush administration charted a foreign policy course more assertive and less deferential to objections of other countries than the policies implemented under Clinton over the previous eight years. Toward Taiwan, the Bush administration modified the long-standing policy of "strategic ambiguity" about u.s. preparedness to defend Taiwan against mainland attack and offered to sell increased amounts of sophisticated arms to Taiwan while initiating unprecedented military-to-military links between the United States and that island state. In South Asia, Bush continued the new partnership with India initiated by Clinton, but scrapped the taboo against military cooperation with India maintained by the Clinton administration. India–United States military ties expanded rapidly, much to Beijing's dismay. The new administration also scrapped the 1972 antiballistic missile treaty with Russia and pushed ahead with the development of missile defense. (Announcement of intention to terminate the treaty came on December 13, 2001, with actual termination taking place six months later as provided by the terms of the treaty.) Chinese analysts were convinced that u.s. missile defense programs were intended to nullify China's nuclear retaliatory capability vis-à-vis the United States. Then came September 11 and the subsequent u.s. intervention in Afghanistan to remove the Taliban government. United States military ties with the Central Asian states expanded rapidly, much to Beijing's dismay.

The more assertive foreign policies of the Bush administration did not cause renewed Sino-Iranian partnership. As demonstrated above, the renewal of that partnership traces to the last years of the Clinton administration. Yet, Washington's more assertive course under Bush certainly did validate for both Beijing and Tehran the wisdom of rejuvenated antihegemony partnership.

China supported Iran in January 2002 when President Bush included Iran, North Korea, and Iraq in an "axis of evil." China "disapproves of the use of such words in international relations," said an MFA spokesman. There were bound to be "serious consequences if the logic of the wording" "axis of evil" was followed. Use of such terminology was contrary to "the principle that all countries should be treated on an equal footing" and to the "long term peace and stability of the world and various regions."[91] Bush's characterization of Iran as part of an axis of evil was a form of impermissible bullying. Nor was the war on terrorism to be expanded unilaterally and arbitrarily by any country; U.S. charges of "terrorism" could be based only on "irrefutable evidence." Regarding U.S. efforts to "cloud" China's relations with Iran, China and Iran were "independent states and follow their own measures," the MFA spokesman said.[92]

President Jiang Zemin's high-profile visit to Iran in April 2002—three months after Bush's inclusion of Iran in an axis of evil—was a clear rejection of Bush's inclusion of Iran in that "axis." The visit was the first by China's paramount leader to Iran since Hua Guofeng's ill-fated 1978 visit. As noted earlier, Jiang's visit had been in planning since 1999, but Bush's "axis of evil" speech elevated the visit's political significance. A PRC foreign ministry spokesman explained the rationale of Jiang's five-nation tour in this way:

> Under the pretext of counter-terrorism, the U.S. has stepped up the unilateralist global strategic layout . . . It has expanded targets of attack by categorizing the so-called "dissenting forces" as "axis of evil countries" . . . and is determined to eradicate them by force. [In the name of counterterrorism, the United States was establishing] "military security platforms" in Central, South, and Southeast Asia, and attempting to monopolize oil, natural gas, and mineral resources abundant in those regions. The U.S. pursuit of imperial hegemonics under the pretext of counter-terrorism has seriously upset the global strategic balance. . . . Therefore, the international community has to oppose unilateralism, in addition to terrorism. . . . President Jiang's five-nation tour will be conducive to a better common understanding of the international community on condemning terrorism and maintaining the global strategic balance.[93]

During a meeting with Supreme Leader Khamenei and President Khatami, Jiang said that U.S. policy was based on bullying and a quest for global hegemony. Washington had, however, encountered widespread resistance throughout the world.[94] Commenting on Jiang's visit, a spokesman of Iran's foreign ministry stressed the common opposition of China and Iran to a "unipolar world," and their common belief that "participation by all members of the international community" is necessary to establishing peace and security.[95] An Iranian newspaper explained the situation this way: "Tehran and Beijing share identical political views. . . . Both take pride in the fact that they are in no way subservient to Washington. . . . Although Beijing supports America's war against terrorism, it has made no secret of its disgust over America's attempts to assert global supremacy, a fact that Iran has repeatedly denounced over the past two decades."[96]

As the United States moved toward another war with Iraq in 2003, China and Iran both opposed that war. China endorsed an effort in January by Turkey, Iran, Egypt, Jordan, Saudi Arabia, and Syria to convene a meeting in Istanbul to avert a new Gulf war. (The u.s.-led invasion of Iraq began on March 20.) Regarding the common position adopted by the foreign ministers of those six nations to avert a u.s. attack by pressuring Hussein to "intensify cooperation with United Nations arms inspectors," an MFA spokeswoman said: "We hope the . . . meeting can achieve progress. Our consistent position is to solve the Iraq issue through diplomatic and political means."[97] In early March, China indicated its willingness to participate in a "Three plus Five" conference intended to abort the impending war. The "three" were Security Council permanent members France, Russia, and China—all opposed to the impending u.s. war. The "five" were Iraq's neighbors, Turkey, Iran, Saudi Arabia, Syria, and Kuwait. Speaking on March 9, China's ambassador to Iran, Liu Zhentang, commented: "Our viewpoint vis-a-vis the Iraq crisis is exactly like Iran's. We believe the American unilateral policies have met with global opposition. Iran and China wish to navigate the world toward peace. We shall, therefore, try to form a coalition with all advocates of peace worldwide."[98]

On the heels of the u.s. ouster of Saddam Hussein's regime in early 2003, and as information about previously undisclosed Iranian uranium enrichment activities came to the surface, the United States began pushing to bring the issue of Iran's nuclear programs before the u.n. Security Council for consideration of sanctions. Many Chinese analysts saw this as the next step in the American drive to dominate the Middle East: the IRI was the next u.s. target.[99] Shortly after Baghdad fell to u.s. forces, for example, the director of the South Asian and Middle East Research Center of the MFA-affiliated China Institute of International Studies, Li Guofu, wrote that after the u.s. defeat of Iraq, Iran would be the next target the United States would seek to force into submission.[100] Another article in the Chinese Academy of Social Sciences journal *American Studies* maintained that the u.s. defeat of Iraq would lead to increased u.s. pressure on Iran.[101] The conflict over Iran's nuclear activities was "basically a test of strength between the United States and Iran." "The development of Iranian military strength, especially the nuclear question, causes great uneasiness in the United States." Washington hoped to use the nuclear issue to "suppress" (*da zhen*) the Iranian regime, thereby encouraging Iranians to overthrow the current regime and drawing Iran into the "system of u.s. values." This was the next step in u.s. strategy after the destruction of Saddam Hussein's regime and was part of the u.s. effort to draw the Middle East into a "new world order" under u.s. domination. The elimination of Hussein's regime had removed one major "threat" to u.s. hegemony in the Middle East. Now, "the United States definitely does not want Iran to become hegemonic and challenge its position in the region." Washington's strategy toward Iran was to "demonize" the Tehran regime, while using internal contradictions between conservatives and reformers to strengthen "peaceful evolution." Simultaneously, Washington would "manipulate international society," tighten embargoes and sanctions against Iran, and "thus gradually disintegrate Iran's current regime." The final u.s. objective was for Iran to abandon "nuclear energy," install a democratic regime, and abandon confrontation with the United States. The United States' strategy sought to "cause the Middle East countries to abandon their own historical cultural tradition and pursue u.s.-style democracy." The authors were confident that u.s. efforts would fail. The people of the Middle East countries would not accept "u.s.-style democracy." Russia opposed Washington's approach, and the European countries saw Iran as an opportunity to assert their independence of Washington. Iran could use the European Union and Russia as a "bargaining chip" with Washington. There was no reference to China's role in the article, but by implication China would support Iran's resistance to u.s. hegemony.

THE LIMITS OF THE SINO-IRANIAN ENTENTE

Beijing's support for Iran has been carefully circumscribed. Beijing eschewed explicit formation of a "partnership" with Iran. Beginning with Russia in 1996, China formed partnerships (*huoban guanxi*) with a number of countries and regional organizations: Russia, the United States, Canada, Mexico, the Association of Southeast Asian Nations (ASEAN), India, Pakistan, the European Union, the United Kingdom, Japan, and South Africa.[102] The partnerships with Russia and the United States were dubbed "strategic," while those with Egypt and Saudi Arabia were called "strategic relationships." The others were merely "cooperative partnerships." Iran was absent from this retinue of China's international "partnerships." The joint communiqué issued at the end of Khatami's 2000 visit to China was larded with rhetoric about the closeness of Sino-Iranian relations, but carefully avoided the word *partnership* and avoided calling the relationship "strategic," although it found a way to use that word in a more qualified fashion. The operative clause of the 2000 joint communiqué read: the just-concluded meeting of the two presidents opened up "new prospects" for "establishing a twenty-first-century-oriented long-term and wide-ranging relationship of friendship and cooperation in the *strategic* interests of the two countries."[103] No joint communiqué was issued at all in association with Jiang Zemin's April 2002 visit to Iran.

China also evaded Tehran's repeated entreaties to join an anti-u.s.-Eurasian bloc. Beijing also avoided the sort of direct, joint policy declarations that it had issued jointly with Russia explicitly condemning various u.s. moves.[104] Nor has Beijing concluded a "friendship treaty" with Iran such as it did with Russia in July 2001. Moreover, much of Beijing's most substantial assistance to Tehran—help with military modernization efforts and transfer of dual-use technology—has been conducted covertly or semicovertly. In other words, while rendering Tehran a degree of support, Beijing has kept considerable distance between itself and Tehran. Beijing provided a degree of support for Iran against u.s. pressure, but has also limited its commitment to Iran to minimize the adverse impact of ties with Iran on China's links with the United States and the Arab and European states, and on China's international reputation generally. Beijing has carefully avoided putting itself in a position in which it would be obligated to assist Tehran against u.s. pressure.

Beijing has been very cautious about open military cooperation with Iran. It avoided open cooperation entirely during the Iran-Iraq war. It suspended military cooperation for several years as part of the 1997 disengagement. When reviving military exchanges with the Shamkhani-Chi Haotian talks in June 2000, Beijing kept the matter secret and did not initiate open military exchanges for another nine months. A contrast between China's dense military relation with Pakistan and China's far thinner relation with Iran is also instructive. Table 4.1 provides such a comparison and makes clear that Sino-Pakistani military relations are far thicker than Sino-Iranian military ties.

Nor were Iranian ports visited by PLA-Navy squadrons, as were ports of many other countries in the Indian Ocean region. Between 1985 when PLA-Navy warships began calling at Indian Ocean ports and 2004, Chinese warships reportedly called at these ports: Karachi in Pakistan (1985, 2001), Bombay (2001), Colombo in Sri Lanka (1985), Chittagong in Bangladesh (1986), Sittwe in Myanmar (2001), Lumut and Kelang in Malaysia (1997, 2000), Dar Es Salaam in Tanzania (2000), and Simonstown in South Africa (2000). The absence of visits to Iranian ports came in spite of the explicit antihegemony cooperation between China and Iran. Almost certainly Iranian leaders would have welcomed PLA-Navy visits to Chabahar or Bandar Abbas, but

TABLE 4.1

Comparison of China's Military Relations
with Iran and Pakistan

(Number of Military Exchanges)		
	Iran	*Pakistan*
1990	2	4
1991	2	3
1992	3	6
1993	3	5
1994	0	9
1995	0	10
1996	1	5
1997	0	11
1998	1	5
1999	0	6
2000	0	7
2001	0	4

SOURCE: *Zhongguo waijiao gaijian* [Overview of China's Diplomacy],
1991–95; *Zhongguo waijiao*, 1996–2001. The title changed in 1996.

Chinese leaders concluded the costs of higher-profile military cooperation
with Iran would be too great.

China's caution in conducting open military relations with Iran is probably a function of several factors. The first is that China faces far heavier risks
and penalties from military ties with Iran than from military ties with
Pakistan. Over Iran, Beijing confronts the United States. Over Pakistan, Beijing
antagonizes primarily India. The U.S. ability to penalize China is infinitely
greater than India's ability. Moreover, Washington typically has a tough mind-
set in which it uses whatever means best make sense to pursue its interests.
New Delhi, for reasons that cannot be explored here, has traditionally been
loath to pressure China. Consequently, the costs of open military links with
Iran are greater than for military links with Pakistan. It should be noted, however, that this applies to open military exchanges; nonpublic military
exchanges and sales could be a different matter.

The reaction of India's neighbors to a Chinese military presence is also
somewhat different from the reaction of Iran's neighbors. India's smaller
neighbors, viewing themselves as suffering from various forms of Indian domination, often welcome a Chinese presence as a way of demonstrating inde-

pendence from the local behemoth, India. Iran's Arab's neighbors, however, are fearful of the IRI and might take a more negative view of Chinese military links with Iran.

It is also likely that China has a far weaker commitment to Iran's security than to Pakistan's. Beijing judges sustaining a strong Pakistan vital to constraining India, a potentially dangerous regional rival with whom China shares a long border and who may harbor revanchist dreams about Tibet. China's interest in a militarily strong Iran is more remote. China's interest in a strong Iran is in creating a favorable regional balance in an area fairly distant and not bordering on China, as a way of moving the world in a multipolar direction. Stated simply: China might go to war to uphold Pakistan, but not for Iran. This difference in gravity of interest is reflected in different bilateral military relations.

Tehran apparently understands the limits of China's support. One Iranian report on discussions between Jiang and Khatami in April 2002 concluded that while China and Iran shared common views of the world order, "no one expects the Chinese to become united with Tehran in international equations." However, the report continued, Tehran "expects that the relationship between Iran and China will be safe from the intrusion of any third parties."[105] Another commentary noted that while Iran might benefit in certain situations by involving China in Iranian-U.S. tensions, such a tactic could easily backfire. "It would be more to Iran's national interests to keep Tehran-Beijing relations free of third party considerations," the paper concluded.[106] In other words, since Tehran understands that China's interests with the United States trump China's interests with Iran, securing Beijing's necessarily limited support against the United States will not be served by conspicuous efforts to draw China into alignment against Washington. Iran's interests would be better served by attempting to insulate Sino-Iranian relations from Iranian-U.S. tensions. The principles of mutual benefit and equality require that the reverse also hold: Sino-Persian cooperation will continue regardless of U.S.-PRC conflicts.

The gist of the anti-U.S. entente of Iran and China seems to be twofold. First, there is a convergence of views that the United States is a hegemonist bully bent on dominating the Middle East and that the world would be better off if the U.S. effort fails. In fact, things would be better if the United States withdrew from the Gulf region. Second, Tehran counts on its importance to China to secure a degree of Chinese support and to insulate Sino-Iranian cooperation, to some degree, from U.S. pressure. Tehran can expect Beijing not to go along with sanctions against Iran. Sino-Iranian cooperation will continue in spite of U.S. pressure. This depends, of course, on the intensity of U.S.

pressure and how much it threatens the broader u.s.-prc relation. It also depends on how clear the evidence is of Iranian nuclear weapons programs and on the alignments of the European powers, Russia, and India and, by extension, how grave the dangers are to China's reputation as a responsible power of going against the consensus of the international community. China, for its part, knows that because Tehran values its relation with China, Iran will resist u.s. efforts to cut China's oil flow in the event of a "special situation" between China and the United States. China's ability to secure the oil it needed in such an eventuality would be highly problematic, but cooperation with a large, powerful, and friendly Iran would be a major Chinese asset in that effort.

5 / The Xinjiang Factor in PRC-IRI Relations

THE ISLAMIC REVOLUTION AND CHINA'S MUSLIMS

A significant variable influencing IRI-PRC relations has been Iranian involvement with China's Muslim communities. The impulse of Islamic revolutionaries in Iran to support the struggles of their putatively oppressed Muslim brethren in foreign lands, including China, has occasionally come into conflict with Chinese Communist Party (CCP) internal security concerns especially in China's sprawling western province of Xinjiang. This Iranian propensity to dabble in the affairs of China's Islamic community seems to have been most pronounced in the early 1990s—precisely as China's post-USSR—era internal security concerns in Xinjiang intensified. Chinese apprehension over existing or possible Iranian involvement with Islamicist elements in Xinjiang was probably one factor persuading Beijing to avoid too close an association with the IRI.

China's Muslim population of more than 20 million includes two main groups: the Hui who are Chinese-speaking, practice many Chinese customs, and belong to the Mongoloid racial group—and the Uighurs—who speak a Turkish-derived language, practice a culture broadly derived from Islamic Central Asia and the Middle East, and belong to the Caucasian racial group. In 2000, 45 percent of Xinjiang's population of 18.5 million (or 8.4 million) were Uighurs, while 0.8 percent of China's entire population of 1.3 billion (or 9.8 million) were Hui.[1] Both groups have a sharp sense of their separateness from the dominant Han culture of China. As Muslims they tend to reject the common Han assumption of Han cultural superiority, and indeed themselves claim their own Islamic superiority over the "heathen" or atheist Han. China's

Muslims have long resisted state efforts at Sinicization.[2] Both groups also have long histories of rebellion. Rebellions by Hui Muslims in China's northwest and southwest in the nineteenth century played a role in undermining the Qing dynasty, while perennial revolts by Xinjiang's Turkic Muslims created opportunities for Soviet advances. By 1940 Xinjiang was a de facto Soviet protectorate, based in part on support for Uighur anti-Han sentiment.

Beijing's apprehensions concerning anti-regime activities among China's Muslims intensified following the events of 1989–91. The powerful challenge to the CCP in spring 1989 put a sharper point on questions of loyalty of all groups, but especially groups with strong identities, traditions of independence from the CCP regime, and histories of rebellion. Moreover, the collapse of the USSR in 1991 carried ominous implications for Xinjiang's internal security. While ethnic nationalism among the peoples of Central Asia did not play a major role in achieving independence of that region from Soviet rule, the example of that independence could, and in fact did, inspire some of Xinjiang's Muslims to strive for a similar achievement in Xinjiang. The withdrawal of Soviet forces from Afghanistan in early 1989, after a decade of pounding by Islamic mujahideen, similarly inspired dreams of independence among Xinjiang's Uighurs. If even the seemingly mighty USSR could be defeated, could not PRC rule of Xinjiang be overthrown? Some Muslims in Xinjiang and elsewhere began to ask that question.

The newly independent, post-Soviet governments of Central Asia were also fragile. Myriad monumental problems confronted these post-Soviet Central Asia states, and failure in dealing with those problems could well result in economic collapse, ethnic conflict, civil war, or even interstate war. The Soviet withdrawal from Afghanistan was followed by a civil war, with militant Islamicist groups supported by Pakistan increasingly gaining the upper hand. Tajikistan too slid in 1992 into a full-scale civil war between hard-line Communists and Islamicists. Such economic and political instability could spread across the region, giving the ideology of Islamic revolution an opportunity to spread. Post-Soviet Central Asia witnessed a swift revival of Islam. The collapse of Soviet power lifted a seventy-year-long reign of militant atheism and opened the way to a reemergence of the long-suppressed Islamic faith of the Central Asian peoples. Islam had survived underground during the decades of Soviet rule and reappeared powerfully with the end of the Soviet era. The historic links between Central Asia and the Muslim Middle East—severed by Russian conquests in the nineteenth century but dominating Central Asia's relations with the world for a millennium before that—began to revive. The "Islamic renaissance" of Central Asia was heterodox and influenced by diverse strains of Islam. Radical Islamicist ideology, the ideology of

Islamic revolution as expounded by Ayatollah Ruhollah Khomeini, was one influential strain.[3]

During the 1990s Islamicist separatist activity in Xinjiang increased substantially. Xinjiang Uighur militants sought aid from groups like Osama Bin Laden in Afghanistan, the Islamic Movement of Uzbekistan, the Islamic Renaissance Party of Tajikistan, and the Chechnya rebels. According to one detailed PRC account, during the early 1990s Xinjiang's Islamicists concentrated on recruitment, organization, indoctrination, and training. By 1996 operations shifted to military actions. Religious leaders who cooperated with the CCP, grassroots government cadre, and Han people generally became targets of assassination. Buses were bombed, buildings set afire, and major economic development projects attacked. Bridges were favorite targets. Riots were instigated and often turned into armed clashes with the police. In one incident at Yining in February 1997, eighty people died in several days of fighting. During 1996 PRC police engaged in intense gunfights with Uighur separatists ten times.[4]

Iran, or more properly speaking the Islamic foundations and political organizations of Iran, was not Beijing's only or most serious concern in this regard. Wahhabi groups from Afghanistan, Saudi Arabia, and Pakistan and terrorist groups like Bin Laden's and the Chechnyan rebels, as well as moderate secularist proponents of Islam as propounded by Kemalist Turkey, were all attempting to influence the evolution of post-Soviet Central Asia. Nor did Beijing's foreign policy response to China's Islamic internal security problem focus on Iran. Cooperation with the Russian Federation (the recognized successor state to the Soviet Union) to support the Communist Party–derived and secular governments of post-Soviet Central Asia was the major element of Beijing's response. Our concern here, however, is with Iran.

THE IRI AND THE EXPORT OF THE ISLAMIC REVOLUTION

Export of the revolution was an explicit and important tenant of Khomeini's Islamic Revolution (in IRI publications the words are always capitalized) that founded the IRI in 1979. Khomeini was a genuine Islamic internationalist, believing that Islamic belief transcended any lesser national or ethnic loyalty. For a true Muslim, loyalty to Islam and Allah took precedence over loyalty to one's nation. Indeed, the very division of the Islamic community into nation-states was heretical, according to Khomeini. Allah had arranged events so that the Islamic revolution and Islamic government triumphed first in Iran; but Iran's duty, before Allah, was to spread that revolution to other lands.[5]

In only two cases—Lebanon and Bahrain—was IRI intervention "blunt, concrete, and important," in the words of Sohail Mahmood.[6] In Lebanon the IRI sent a contingent of a thousand elite Islamic Revolution Guards in June 1982, just after the Israeli invasion of Lebanon, to support the Islamic cause. (Planning for that move had preceded the Israeli invasion.) This cadre became the nucleus around which Hezbollah—an organization of Lebanese Shiites that embraced Khomeini's ideology—formed. Hezbollah expanded its influence in Lebanon with substantial Iranian support. The Iranian embassy in Damascus, Syria, was the center for dispensing money, training, and weapons to Hezbollah. By 1987 Tehran was providing Hezbollah with assistance worth $100 million a year. In Bahrain, with a majority Shiite population, Tehran supported the Islamic Front for the Liberation of Bahrain. Demonstrations organized by that group and calling for Islamic government after the Iranian model began in Bahrain in 1979 and led to several coup attempts in the following years. Kuwait and the other small Gulf States and Saudi Arabia were also targets for Iranian-backed Islamic revolutionary activity in the 1980s. As noted earlier, bringing to power a revolutionary Islamic regime in Iraq was a major reason for Tehran's continuation of the war with Iraq.

In East Asia the Moro National Liberation Front (MNLF) based on the southern Philippine island of Mindanao was supported by Tehran. In October 1979 the Islamic Revolutionary Guards Corps (IRGC) announced the goal of liberating Muslim lands in the Philippines. About the same time the IRI announced an embargo on sales of Iranian oil to the Philippines. The MNLF opened an office in Tehran to coordinate Iranian support, while the IRGC trained some MNLF soldiers and even sent some military instructors to the southern Philippines for that purpose. Iranian support for the MNLF continued until 1989.[7] The IRGC also supported the Islamic Renaissance Party of Tajikistan as that country slid into civil war.[8] The Tajiks spoke a Persian-derived language (the only major group in Central Asia to do so) and shared many cultural affinities with Persia.

Xinjiang too was a target of Iranian revolutionary activism.[9] During the early period of the IRI, Iranian Islamic organizations had sometimes funded the construction of mosques or madrasses (religious schools) in Xinjiang in a clandestine manner and without official Chinese permission. Such unauthorized mosque construction was a major source of conflict between Uighur Muslims and Xinjiang authorities. Madrasses in Iran had also sometimes set aside quotas for students from Xinjiang and recruited students for those seats by clandestine methods and without official Chinese permission. Some Xinjiang students were sent to Iran, where they were instructed in the tenets of extremist Islam. Such Iranian involvement in Xinjiang was quite limited. The Sunni faith and Turkish-derived culture of most of Xinjiang's Muslims limited the appeal of Persian speakers and Shiites. Moreover, other Islamic countries—Saudi Arabia, Libya—engaged in similar and more widespread subversive activities in Xinjiang. Be that as it may, Chinese representatives made clear to Iranian representatives the unacceptable nature of such illegal activities; they stressed that Sino-Iranian cooperation in other areas would be impossible if "interference" in the internal affairs of China continued. Iranian representatives got the message, and the government took measures to stop such activities. Some objectionable activities continued to occur, but Chinese officials concluded that these transpired without the knowledge of Iran's government. When brought to the attention of Iran's government, corrective measures were usually taken.

During the exchange of foreign minister visits in 1983 and 1984, Beijing sought and secured assurances regarding "noninterference" in Xinjiang province. In 1989, as the two sides moved to establish an expanded postwar relationship, Chinese officials drove home the point that Iranian interference in the affairs of China's Muslim community was unacceptable. In September the first-ever officially invited Iranian religious delegation—a delegation from the Islamic Propagation Organization led by that body's president, Ayatollah Ahmad Jannati—visited China. Jannati, a theologian with the conservative watch-guard body the Council of Guardians, stressed that the IRI "is desirous of cementing ties with the Muslim world, especially the Muslim community of China."[10] CCP elder Li Xiannian made clear to Jannati that China, although it was willing to develop relations with all nations on the basis of the Five Principles of Peaceful Coexistence, would never allow any foreign interference in its internal affairs. China was determined to battle any attempt at subversion, even though it recognized that it would be a long fight.[11] Li cast his comments in terms of an attack on Western interference, but Jannati would have gotten the point. Another CCP elder, PRC president Wang Zhen, drove home the same message. Wang Zhen explained to Jannati that freedom of religion and insistence on noninterference in China's internal affairs were longstanding Chinese policies. China did not interfere in the religious affairs of other countries and did not permit other countries to interfere in China's religious affairs. On this basis of mutual respect China was prepared to actively expand friendly interactions with religious circles of all countries, Wang explained to Jannati.[12]

Pakistan probably helped educate Iran's new leaders about China's political facts of life. Pakistan was a country founded on Islam in 1947 and that adopted an increasingly Islamicist orientation in the 1970s under Mohammad Zia ul-Haq. Yet Pakistan had also forged a long-lasting and close strategic and military partnership with China. One of the ways in which Pakistan safeguarded its strategic partnership with China was by carefully eschewing

Islamicist activity in China. During the 1980s and 1990s, when problems of Islamicist subversion in Xinjiang periodically arose, Beijing would sometimes turn to Islamabad for help. Pakistan's good offices probably made clear to Iranian officials that "noninterference" in Xinjiang's Islamic community was a precondition for the expanded Sino-Iranian relationship that developed in the second half of the 1980s.

In spite of Chinese warnings, during the early 1990s the IRI mission in the PRC recruited several dozen Chinese Muslims from various regions of China (not only in Xinjiang) for study in Qom—Iran's great religious center 125 kilometers south of Tehran. Offered full scholarships to cover expenses of study in Iran, the Chinese students were interviewed at an IRI mission in China, were granted an innocuous-seeming tourist visa to Iran, and left for Iran without attracting official Chinese attention. At Qom, the students spent the first year learning Farsi before concentrating on Islamic studies. Most of the Chinese students, being Muslims required to read the Koran Arabic script, could at least read Arabic, and this facilitated their study of Farsi and Islamic philosophy.[13] The arrangements came to the attention of the Chinese government when one of the students, overwhelmed by the isolation and boredom of Qom, telephoned the PRC embassy in Tehran. A representative of that embassy then met with the student, and the entire matter came to light. Such activity ceased in the mid-1990s. Iranian Islamic foundations—many of which were immensely wealthy from property seized at the time of the 1979 revolution and operation of vast swaths of Iran's economy under state protection—were also involved in China. These foundations, and especially the Poverty Foundation, were enthusiastic about contributing money to local governments in Muslim areas of China to build schools or start Islamic businesses. These contributions were in accord with central government policy and were welcomed by local governments, but bore close supervision by state security agencies.[14]

Ali Akbar Omid Mehr, an IRI diplomat who eventually broke with the regime and found political asylum in Europe, offers a fascinating account of IRI revolutionary activism.[15] According to Omid Mehr's account, following the "success" of the Islamic revolution in Lebanon, IRI leaders decided that the next target would be Afghanistan. That country, however, was to be merely a springboard for Islamic revolutionary operations in Central Asia and Xinjiang, the latter being "the only mostly Muslim-population district of China." Further guidance was given by Iran's ambassador to Pakistan during a "seminar" in September 1993 for heads and political analysts of IRI missions in Pakistan. Omid Mehr was a political analyst in the IRI consulate in Peshawar at the time and says he personally participated in the seminar. Prospects for the Islamic revolution were good, according to the ambassador. "Ten years from now China will disintegrate or at least the Muslim populated district will separate itself," he told seminar participants. "The Muslims will not under any circumstances accept the Chinese regime because they are virgin Sunnis," he continued. "Virgin Sunnis" refers to a historically early form of Sunnism, which Shiites believe is purer and thus closer to Shiism.

Omid Mehr's account also alludes to some of the trade-offs faced by Iran between promoting Islamic revolution in Xinjiang and fostering cooperative relations with Beijing. At one seminar organized by the IRI embassy in Islamabad, attendees watched videotapes of President Rafsanjani. In one speech Rafsanjani stated, "In relations with China and North Korea we have been fortunate in being able to deepen our relations and strategic coopera-tion, and these are now at a very satisfactory level." Omid Mehr explained that "the left wing of the IRI regime" was enamored by the prospect of eco-nomic and military unity with China. "For this aim, they tried to navigate each event of the region, especially in Afghanistan and Tajikistan, in a way permitting the establishment of [nonmilitant?] regimes in that region, so as to create a powerful bloc with China." In Tajikistan, Iran joined with Russia to mediate and end the civil war in 1997. Iranian efforts to build influence among the Islamic Renaissance Party in Tajikistan had come to naught, and Tehran, along with Moscow and Beijing, increasingly feared the spread of Sunni–Taliban–Osama Bin Laden radicalism.

Omid Mehr does not say how IRI leaders attempted to balance efforts to export Islamic revolution to Xinjiang and the formation of a "powerful bloc" with China. Presumably, Tehran scrapped export of the revolution to China for the sake of cooperation with China's government, especially when Chinese leaders told them this was the choice they faced, and especially since Iranian leaders valued China's military, political, and economic support. There was by 1997 increasing convergence between Chinese and Iranian interests in coun-tering Sunni fundamentalism in Central Asia. As the Taliban gained control over most of Afghanistan in 1996 and formed alliances with Osama Bin Laden's group and with the equally extreme Islamic Movement of Uzbekistan, Iran, in tandem with Russia, began supporting the anti-Taliban forces led by Ahmad Shah Masood and his Northern Alliance. China too maintained links to that group and also began providing military assistance to Kyrgyzstan and Uzbekistan to help them gain control over their borders so as to counter militant traffic across them.[16] Tehran's interests in Islamic revolution in Afghanistan faded as the Sunni Taliban directed their fury at Afghan Shiites and at Iranian influence in Afghanistan.

Events in the Balkans during 1992–95 revealed further divergences in Chinese and Iranian perspectives, plus some of the dangers for China from too close an association with Tehran. Both Tehran and Beijing opposed Western-led u.n. intervention in disintegrating Yugoslavia, but from very different perspectives. Communist-led, socialist Yugoslavia was an old friend of China—estranged during the Mao era, but warmly embraced by Deng Xiaoping's China after 1978. During the 1980s Sino-Yugoslavian relations were quite close. The breakup of Yugoslavia began with Croatian and Slovenian declarations of independence in June 1991. The following February referenda in Bosnia-Herzegovina also voted for independence. Forty-three percent of Bosnia-Herzegovina's population was Muslim, about 1.9 million people. Serbia began arming ethnic Serbs in Bosnia-Herzegovina to resist independence, and ethnic cleansing of Muslims by Serb militias quickly followed. In May 1992 the u.n. Security Council levied sweeping economic sanctions against Serbia, and in August authorized use of military force to protect delivery of relief supplies to enclaves in Bosnia besieged by Serb forces. China abstained on both Security Council votes—the only Perm Five member to do so.[17]

Yugoslavia was still China's good friend. When a reconstituted Yugoslav Republic (including Serbia and Montenegro) was proclaimed in Belgrade in February 1992, China was the only major country to swiftly recognize it. Indeed, Chinese representatives participated in the founding ceremonies. Even more dangerous for the prc than the demise of yet another socialist state—and one that had not been a Soviet satellite—was the precedent of u.n.-sponsored Western intervention in an ex-socialist state faced by deep ethnic cleavages. Such a precedent might someday be applied against China in Tibet or Xinjiang. Yet Beijing's concern for its reputation—its desire not to be seen as an outcast, obstructionist power—led it merely to abstain rather than veto Western-sponsored Security Council intervention in former Yugoslavia.

Tehran was opposed to Western military intervention, but even more to the persecution of Bosnian Muslims. Tehran wanted Beijing to play a forceful role, including use of its Security Council veto power, to assist the persecuted Bosnian Muslims. When Iranian deputy foreign minister Alaeddin Broujerdi met in Tehran with his visiting prc counterpart Yang Fuchang in February 1993, he called on China to take necessary steps to stop Serbian atrocities. At a minimum the u.n. embargo on arms imports by Bosnian Muslims should be lifted, Broujerdi said, so they could defend themselves. Yang replied to Broujerdi by turning the discussion toward bilateral economic cooperation.[18]

Iranian Islamicists groups adopted more direct means of assisting Bosnian Muslims. In September 1992 an Iranian plane ostensibly carrying relief supplies for Bosnia via Zagreb was discovered to be carrying four thousand guns and one million rounds of ammunition disguised as relief supplies. Again in 1994 Iran was found to have supplied military goods to Bosnia in violation of U.N. sanctions.[19] From Beijing's perspective, Iranian covert arming of Muslims within another country was as dangerous as overt Western military intervention. Nor would China's effort to restore its good name after the blemish of June 1989 be served by association with Tehran on Balkan issues. China's leaders concluded that China had nothing to gain and potentially much to lose by complying with Tehran's request for China's exercise of its Security Council veto on behalf of Bosnian Muslims.

Returning to Xinjiang, in spite of concern about Iranian meddling in China's Islamic affairs, Beijing arranged visits to Xinjiang for high-ranking IRI visitors. These visits were valued by Iranian leaders, and by granting them Beijing bestowed a favor that fostered feelings of friendship. Thus, when President Khamenei visited China in May 1989, he was permitted a two-day visit to Xinjiang, though apparently not to Xinjiang's famous Islamic center of Kashgar (Kashi in Chinese). (It is possible that a visit to Kashgar transpired but was not publicly announced.) In Urumqi, Khamenei "performed religious services with the teachers and students" of the Institute of Islamic Theology and "met noted religious figures of various nationalities." He was happy to see that the Chinese people enjoyed freedom in religious activities, Khamenei said.[20] When Rafsanjani visited China in 1992, he was permitted a visit to Urumqi and Kashgar, although his visit to Kashgar was not announced by China's media. Visiting Kashgar's main mosque for afternoon prayers, Rafsanjani received tremendous applause from a large crowd there.[21] During his June 2000 visit to China, President Khatami was also allowed to visit Urumqi and Kashgar. In Urumqi, Khatami held talks with the chair of Xinjiang's regional government, Abulat Abdurixit, and met with members of the Xinjiang Islamic Association. Abdurixit accompanied Khatami on a visit to the tomb of Xiangfei, an imperial concubine of the Qing dynasty.[22] In Kashgar, Khatami was allowed a visit to the Grand Mosque. Controls were tight during Khatami's visit. The week before Khatami arrived, five Muslims were executed in Urumqi for separatist crimes. An earlier imam of the Kashgar Grand Mosque had been shot and wounded in 1996, and two other imams killed the same year for perceived collaboration with Chinese authorities.[23] All of these Xinjiang visits by Iranian leaders were certainly arranged by China's waishi ("foreign affairs") system to put China's foreign guests in contact only with pro-CCP Muslims who testified to the genuine nature of CCP policy of religious freedom for Muslims.[24]

Allowing high-ranking IRI officials to visit Xinjiang had both positive and negative implications for China's internal security. On the one hand, such visits might inspire Xinjiang's Islamic secessionists. On the other hand, they demonstrated Beijing's confidence in its control over that region. Perhaps most important and in line with the typical modus operandi of China's foreign affairs system, allowing Iranian leaders to visit Xinjiang granted those leaders a favor they ardently desired, thereby fostering "friendship" and creating a sentimental obligation that would make them more willing to comply with Chinese policy requests. Beijing's objective in this case was noninterference in the affairs of China's Muslim communities. The implicit point of these visits was that Beijing was willing to allow contact between Iranian Islamic leaders and China's Muslim communities as long as such contact was supervised by Chinese authorities, and as long as Iran abstained from interference in China's internal affairs. Visits by ranking Iranian officials allowed them to confirm the freedom of Xinjiang's Muslims to practice their religion and provided opportunities for Islamic leaders loyal to the CCP to drive home this point. Visits to Xinjiang also provided opportunities for "friendly and frank" discussions about the impermissibility of foreign interference in China's religious affairs. It is also possible, as Michael Dillon suggests, that Beijing's desire to win Iranian goodwill (as well as that of other Muslim countries) may impose limits on Chinese repression in Xinjiang.

Iran's Islamic revolutionary activism had broader implications for China's relations with the IRI. That activism alienated a large number of countries— the Sunni, secular, or nationalist governments of the Arab, post-Soviet, and Southeast Asian regions targeted by Iranian militants, and also the Western powers that supported those targeted states. Indeed, Tehran's friends included only a few states: Libya, Syria, North Korea, and, by the mid-1990s, Russia. The first three of these states did not enjoy a good reputation or exercise much influence in the international community. China, however, was in a very different class. It was respected and recognized as a great power. To protect that reputation, Beijing had to watch the company it kept. Iran's pariah status cut both ways in Sino-Iranian relations. On the one hand, it made Chinese support more valuable to Tehran and thereby created opportunities for Beijing. On the other hand, too close association with the IRI could tarnish China's own international image and hinder its quest for international respectability. Tarnishing by association with Iran could also endanger Chinese achievement of other goals, ranging from securing "permanent normal trade relations" with the United States, to keeping investment pouring into China, to securing Beijing's hosting of the 2008 Olympics Games.

6 / China's Assistance to Iran's Nuclear Programs

Support for Iranian nuclear programs was a key element of Beijing's effort to forge a partnership with Iran in the 1980s and 1990s. From 1985 to 1997 China was Iran's major nuclear partner. While China was *not* Iran's only foreign nuclear partner during that period, it was by far the most important. During that period, China in effect assisted Iran in circumventing u.s.-led international opposition to Iran's nuclear efforts. Iranian leaders viewed their nuclear programs as extremely important, and China's support in this area made Beijing valuable to Tehran. Eventually, in 1997, China abandoned its nuclear cooperation with Iran under intense u.s. pressure and in order to safeguard China's vital relation with the United States, a disengagement that tells much about the role of Iran in China's overall diplomacy and which will be examined in a later chapter.

The nuclear relation between China and Iran was denied by both parties for six years and was publicly acknowledged beginning only in 1991. Even then many aspects of the relationship remained secret and were revealed only more than a decade later. Important documentation on the relationship was provided by Iran and China to the International Atomic Energy Agency in 2003.[1] While IAEA reports of 2003–4 refer only to unnamed "foreign suppliers" and "foreign states," these references can often be triangulated with other information to ascertain with fair certainty which of those foreign states was China.

China's early experience with nuclear nonproliferation was not positive. As the Soviet Union and the United States began to recognize common interests in restricting the proliferation of nuclear weapons during the late 1950s,

China's nuclear effort was a major target of the incipient nonproliferation regime. Soviet assistance to China's nuclear efforts began in 1955, and in 1957 it was embodied in a comprehensive nuclear cooperation agreement that included Soviet assistance in Chinese manufacture of atomic weapons. By mid-1959, however, Soviet leader Nikita Khrushchev had concluded that Soviet interests were best served by keeping nuclear weapons out of Mao Zedong's hands, and Moscow abrogated the 1957 nuclear agreement. Shortly afterward, in August 1959, Khrushchev made the first-ever visit to the United States by a top Soviet leader, thereby opening the period of Soviet-U.S. "peaceful coexistence" that lead to the first element of the global nonproliferation regime, the Nuclear Test Ban Treaty of 1963. Beijing saw, with considerable justice, Soviet-American antinuclear proliferation efforts as directed against China.

As the United States and the Soviet Union began mobilizing international support for a Non-Proliferation Treaty (NPT, signed in 1968 and brought into effect in 1970), Beijing saw that treaty as a joint "superpower" (U.S. and USSR) effort to maintain global military dominance. The five "nuclear weapons states" recognized by the NPT were free to possess and develop nuclear weapons as they saw fit, while other countries were prohibited from acquiring such weapons. Significantly China was one of the five nuclear weapons states legitimized by the NPT—testament to recognition by Washington, Moscow, and London when the NPT was being drafted that China would someday need to be incorporated into that regime. (China tested an atomic bomb in 1964 and a hydrogen bomb in 1967.) The standing invitation to China to become a legitimate nuclear weapons state under the NPT meant that Beijing had the option of acting on the same realist logic (i.e., maintaining military superiority) that inspired Moscow and Washington, at least in Beijing's view, to establish the NPT. China would move decisively along these lines in 1997 when it finally disengaged from Iran's nuclear effort. China under Mao, however, wanted nothing to do with such an arrangement. The purpose of the NPT regime, Mao concluded, was to uphold the ability of the two superpowers to threaten or even use nuclear weapons against other states without fear of retaliation. The NPT was an attempt by the U.S. "imperialists" and the Soviet "social imperialists" to uphold their ability to exercise "nuclear blackmail" against Third World countries, which were the major victims of superpower aggression. From this standpoint the more Third World countries that acquired nuclear weapons, the better.

China's large investments in nuclear weapons production starting in 1955 meant that when the "opening to the outside world" began under Deng Xiaoping in 1978, China had a very large nuclear industry, entirely military but underpinned by an array of basic know-how and technologies regarding the production, conversion, and handling of fissile materials. Moreover, the individuals running China's nuclear industry were politically very influential, typically linked to the People's Liberation Army. With the marketization and opening of China's economy after 1978, the enterprises constituting China's nuclear industry were under great pressure—both political and economic—to earn foreign currency via exports. They soon found that China's nuclear goods and services had a significant market in such countries as Pakistan, Iraq, Algeria, Bangladesh, Syria, Egypt, India, Ghana, Argentina—and Iran. The contracts for these transactions were usually negotiated on a purely commercial basis by representatives of the Chinese supplier and the foreign purchaser, with little or no supervision by China's central government.[2] China's swift transition from a centrally planned to a market economy meant that China lacked government institutions for supervision and regulation that existed in more mature market economies. There was also little knowledge and even less acceptance in China in the late 1970s or early 1980s of international nonproliferation norms rooted in the NPT. Still more, China's nuclear industry viewed international sales as a mechanism for advancing its own technological level. Sale of Chinese nuclear goods and services would generate foreign currency, which could be used to upgrade the technological level of China's nuclear industry. While very large and competent in military applications, China's nuclear industry was backward in comparison to many other countries in the areas of civilian utilization of nuclear energy, that is, using the intense heat produced by concentrated uranium to make steam to turn generators to produce electricity. Cooperation with foreign nuclear research centers would allow China to raise its own level, while fostering sentiments of "friendship" for China among Third World countries. The outcome of these forces was China's emergence as a major nuclear supplier to developing country markets during the 1980s and 1990s. As this process unfolded, the United States focused increasing attention on bringing China within the global nonproliferation regime.

Several factors played a primary role in accomplishing China's gradual socialization to the nonproliferation regime: (1) China's desire for u.s. civilian nuclear technology; (2) development of a cohort of Chinese specialists on nonproliferation affairs; (3) sustained u.s. pressure combined with a desire to stabilize relations with Washington; (4) a desire to be recognized as a sober, responsible leading nation of the world; and (5) recognition that as an NPT nuclear weapons state, China's interests were served by limiting the number of states that possessed nuclear weapons.

The possibility of acquiring u.s. nuclear electrical power generation technology was the major lever used by the United States to nudge China away from nuclear cooperation with Iran. Energy had long been a developmental bottleneck in China. Preferences for investment in heavy industry during the Maoist years had left energy (along with all other infrastructure) grossly under-invested. Power outages were a way of life and a major cause of lost production in Maoist China. Then as marketization deepened after 1978, government revenues (and thus the ability to build new power facilities) fell, while demand for energy skyrocketed. Moreover, China's domestic oil reserves first stagnated and then by the 1990s went into decline. Imported oil was available on global markets, of course, but was expensive, drained currency that might otherwise go to import equipment and technology, and put China in a position of increased vulnerability vis-à-vis the U.S. Navy in the event of a conflict over Taiwan. Nuclear generation of electricity offered a solution to these manifold problems. If China's large but military-oriented nuclear industry could be used to produce electricity, a critical bottleneck on China's development might be eased. To achieve this, China needed to import foreign civilian nuclear technologies. The United States' technology in that area was among the most advanced and safest in the world. Consequently, China's nuclear industry ardently desired access to that technology. The terms the United States set for access to that technology were Chinese compliance with global nonproliferation norms—and in the case of Iran, cooperation with the United States *beyond* those global norms.

Development of a cohort of Chinese nonproliferation specialists during the 1980s spread within China's elite a better understanding of the NPT regime. This process unfolded as Chinese scholars and students began going abroad for study and returned to China with new perspectives. Officials from the United States and Japan also consistently engaged their Chinese counterparts on nonproliferation, thereby putting these issues onto the agenda of China's leaders. Foundations and universities in the United States sponsored seminars and workshops on nonproliferation issues. By the end of the decade proliferation issues were increasingly debated and understood in Beijing. China's new nonproliferation specialists began to argue that China's interests would be best served by restricting the number of nuclear weapons states in the world, especially around China's own periphery. If China continued to dispense nuclear technologies freely around the Third World, it would become known as an irresponsible proliferator, perhaps even as a rogue state. This would place China in opposition to widely accepted international norms, tarnish its reputation, and cause it to lose status. However, if China brought itself into conformity with global nonproliferation norms, it would prove itself a responsible country, a proper partner for the United States and other leading powers. It would also permit cooperation on an issue much stressed by Washington.

Gradually these forces brought China into the global nonproliferation regime. In 1984, just prior to beginning nuclear cooperation with Iran, China joined the IAEA. As discussed below, most, though not all, of China's nuclear cooperation activities with Iran were declared to the IAEA and periodically inspected by the IAEA, and thus technically in line with NPT and IAEA requirements. In August 1991 China indicated its willingness to accede to the NPT, which it did in 1992. Step-by-step, China drew back from its early role of nuclear supplier to Third World states suspected of harboring covert nuclear weapons programs. Regarding Iran, this process of withdrawal took twelve years.

CHINA'S ASSISTANCE TO IRAN'S NUCLEAR PROGRAMS

Iran under the shah had extremely ambitious nuclear programs in cooperation with the United States, France, and Germany. Khomeini suspended those programs in 1979, but ordered them revived as the war with Iraq raised the specter that Iraq might use nuclear weapons against Iran.

In 1984 Iran opened at Esfahan the Nuclear Research Center (ENRC) to research reactor technology, the nuclear fuel cycle including uranium enrichment, and the chemical reprocessing of depleted uranium to extract plutonium. (Plutonium is a fissile material used, like uranium, in atomic bombs.) Prior to 1979 France was under contract to construct a research reactor for the Esfahan center, but Paris abandoned that contract after the revolution.[3] In 1985 Iran decided to launch a covert uranium enrichment program, revealed to the IAEA only in 2003.[4] In June 1985, during Rafsanjani's visit to Beijing, China and Iran secretly concluded a protocol for cooperation with Iran on the peaceful uses of nuclear energy.[5] The 1985 agreement was not announced or officially acknowledged at the time, but under the agreement China helped Iran develop the ENRC. Most of Iran's China-assisted nuclear activities under the 1985 agreement were based at ENRC. The ENRC was not declared to the IAEA as a nuclear facility until 1992. Once declared to the IAEA, it was inspected and deemed innocuous, but a more thorough inspection in 2003 found it included a number of massively built secret rooms used for covert nuclear activities not previously declared to the IAEA. Would Chinese specialists working at ENRC have known of these secret facilities and programs?

Under the 1985 agreement, China supplied Iran with four small teaching and research reactors for ENRC: a subcritical assembly using natural uranium fuel, moderated by light water; a subcritical assembly using natural uranium fuel, moderated by graphite; a zero-power reactor using natural uranium fuel and moderated by heavy water (i.e., a zero-power heavy-water reactor); and a 27-kilowatt, miniature neutron source reactor using less than one kilogram of highly enriched uranium.[6] Construction of the first reactor began in January 1988, and the reactor went critical in January 1992. Construction of the other three all began in January 1990, and those reactors went critical in January 1992, March 1994, and June 1995, respectively. China supplied the fissile material for all four reactor cores.[7] These four research reactors and their related nuclear fuel were later declared and made subject to IAEA safeguards and regularly inspected by the IAEA. In the view of the U.S. government, none of the four reactors supplied to Iran by China posed a "direct proliferation risk" since they did not produce significant quantities of plutonium. They did, however, enable Iranian personnel to learn design principles that could be used to construct indigenously larger reactors for plutonium production. Under the June 1985 agreement, engineers from the Atomic Energy Organization of Iran (AEOI) and mostly from ENRC went to China for training in nuclear reactor design.[8] By 1987 fifteen AEOI engineers were reportedly training in China.[9] As reports of nuclear cooperation between China and Iran began to emerge, China's Ministry of Foreign Affairs denied, in February 1986, the existence of any nuclear cooperation between China and Iran.

In 1987 Iran received from Abdul Qadir Khan of Pakistan drawings of centrifuges for uranium enrichment, that is, the separation of fission-capable $U235$ isotopes from nonfission-capable $U238$ isotopes. Such enrichment can yield either low-enriched uranium (LEU) suitable for use in electricity-generating nuclear power plants, or highly enriched uranium (HEU) that can be used to make fission bombs. The centrifuge design supplied in 1987 was based on West European, not Chinese, sources. It is germane to note, however, that in 1987 China had yet to sign the NPT and Sino-Iranian nuclear cooperation was expanding rapidly. Sino-Pakistani relations were also extremely close, and a large part of both Pakistan's and Iran's nuclear technology had come from China. About that time reports appeared in Western media that China and Pakistan were assisting Iran in setting up a centrifuge-based uranium enrichment facility at Moallem Kalayeh near Qazvin, a hundred kilometers west of Tehran.[10] In 1991 Chinese engineers were reported working at Darkhovin, near Ahvaz, and at Moallem Kalayeh near Qazvim, installing uranium enrichment equipment.[11] It thus may have been that Chinese engineers assisted Iran with development of the Qadir Khan–supplied centrifuge designs. Whatever China's involvement in Iran's covert centrifuge enrichment program, production of the components for those centrifuges and mechanical testing of the assembled devices began a decade later in 1997 and continued until 2002, according to Iran's subsequent report to the IAEA.[12]

In 1987 China agreed to supply to the ENRC a machine known as a calutron (for California University electron, after the University of California, which invented the device in the early 1940s). The device was delivered two years later. A calutron uses magnetism to separate ion beams of uranium isotopes with slightly varying atomic nuclei and thus masses, hence its proper name electromagnetic isotope separation, or EMIS. The U.S. World War II atomic bomb project had used calutrons to produce fissile bomb material.[13] Iraq's covert nuclear program, revealed after Iraq's defeat in the 1991 war, had also included EMIS. Iranian personnel had difficulty making the Chinese calutron function according to design, and Chinese personnel assisted in resolving those difficulties. Iran's China-supplied calutron was inspected by IAEA in February 1992 and found to be different from the EMIS used by Iraq in attempted weapons production. Iraq's EMIS had been modified with a far higher electrical current to provide a high enrichment capability. Iran's had not. Iran's China-supplied EMIS was of "desktop" size and of the standard configuration using natural zinc to produce stable isotopes for medical purposes. As a Chinese spokesman said, Iran's China-supplied calutron was suitable for "nuclear medical diagnoses and nuclear physics research, isotope production education, and personnel training."[14] Skeptics pointed out, however, that Iraq too had started with small calutrons and then indigenously developed larger ones for enrichment purposes. Iran could have hidden facilities where enrichment-capable EMIS machines could be located, these skeptics noted.[15] The small China-supplied calutron could be used as a model for reverse engineering of larger machines that could separate amounts of fissile material adequate for bombs. Moreover, the partially enriched uranium produced by calutrons could be fed into centrifuges, substantially reducing the number of centrifuge cycles necessary to achieve high levels of enrichment. Iran's China-supplied calutron could enrich uranium to 36.5 percent U235.[16] In 2003 IAEA inspectors found Pakistan-supplied centrifuges, and not EMIS reverse engineered from the China-supplied calutron, in the secret rooms at ENRC.

In 1989 Chinese geologists began assisting AEOI explore for uranium. Joint Chinese-Iranian teams were formed to prospect for uranium in eastern Iran. In September AEOI head Reza Amrollahi announced that prospecting had been successful and that uranium mining operations would begin at eleven sites. One deposit in Yazd province held an estimated thirty-five hundred tons of uranium.[17] Amrollahi also said that Iran planned to build a mill to convert uranium ore into yellowcake.[18] The ore from the Yazd Saghand uranium mine was transformed into yellowcake and later became the feedstock for a uranium conversion facility built at Natanz in 2001.[19] Chinese experts also assisted opening a number of uranium mines. Uranium mining is not reportable to the IAEA nor subject to IAEA safeguards.[20] As shown in a later chapter on economic relations, China assisted Iranian mining of a number of minerals during the postwar period. Iran's mining sector generally was targeted for development after the Iran-Iraq war, because it was seen as capable of producing foreign-currency-generating exports.

In January 1990 the deputy director of China's Commission for Science, Technology, and Industry for National Defense, General Jiang Hua, and Iran's minister of defense Ali Akbar Torkan concluded a ten-year agreement including provisions for further nuclear cooperation.[21] In a departure from earlier efforts to keep Sino-Iranian nuclear cooperation secret, the January 1990 agreement was announced by Xinhua news agency shortly after it was signed. The announcement also explained the logic of the deal: China was rich in uranium, and the export of nuclear fuel and nuclear fuel technology "earned foreign exchange for the country" and had "great attraction to the developing countries." Pakistan, Syria, and Ghana were mentioned along with Iran as potential customers.[22] This was an important departure: China was starting to defend rather than conceal and deny its international nuclear cooperation.

The China National Nuclear Company (CNNC) was the Chinese principal for implementing the January 1990 agreement, and in June 1990 it signed a contract with AEOI for delivery of the 27-kilowatt, subcritical, neutron source reactor for ENRC mentioned earlier. CNNC also agreed in 1990 to supply a much larger, 27-megawatt reactor for installation in ENRC. This reactor was called a "plutonium production reactor" in the West since it could produce an estimated six kilograms of plutonium per year.[23] That plutonium could be extracted via chemical processes to obtain bomb-capable fissile material, a route to bomb making that eliminated the technically difficult requirement of enriching uranium, but required large quantities of burnt uranium reactor fuel for reprocessing.

During 1991 China secretly sent to Iran 1,600 kilograms (1.6 metric, or 1.8 English, tons) of uranium products. This transaction was not reported to the IAEA until 2003, when it was reported by China itself once the transfer was discovered by IAEA investigators.[24] This Chinese uranium provided the input for a large number of Iranian "benchmark" reprocessing and enrichment experiments, mostly at the ENRC, over the next decade. The shipment included 1,005 kilograms of uranium hexafluoride, 402 kilograms of uranium tetrafluoride, and 401.5 kilograms of uranium dioxide. Uranium hexafluoride (UF6, or "hex") is a gaseous form of uranium used as the feedstuff for enrichment processes. Uranium tetrafluoride ("green salt") is the feedstuff for production of either metallic uranium or uranium hexafluoride, which is then enriched via centrifuges. The large amount of uranium materials supplied by China in 1991 enabled Iranian scientists to become familiar with a number of steps integral to the nuclear fuel cycle. Most of the uranium tetrafluoride supplied by China in 1991 was converted into uranium metal via 113 experiments carried out in the early 1990s. These experiments were covert and not declared to the IAEA until 2003. A small portion of the uranium tetrafluoride was converted into uranium hexafluoride in benchmark experiments. The uranium dioxide was used to test "pulse column process" and production of uranium fuel pellets. Some of the uranium dioxide was irradiated and used for isotope production experiments. The facility at ENRC in which these various conversion experiments were performed was declared to the IAEA only in 2003.[25] China's supply of the raw material for these covert experiments, plus its extensive nuclear cooperation with Iran at this juncture, strongly suggests that China knew of Iran's covert nuclear experiments.

A major step forward in Sino-Iranian nuclear cooperation came in July 1991 when Premier Li Peng visited Iran. Li discussed nuclear cooperation between the two countries with President Rafsanjani. They agreed in principle that China would complete a large nuclear power plant at Bushehr, on Iran's Persian Gulf coast, begun by France and Germany in the mid-1970s but abandoned after the 1979 revolution. Li and Rafsanjani also agreed that technical committees in trade, technology, military, and scientific cooperation would draft specific agreements.[26] In October PRC president Yang Shangkun visited several of Iran's China assisted nuclear facilities during his visit to that country. Yang also reiterated China's pledge to assist the completion of the Bushehr reactor.[27]

Following Li Peng's and Yang Shangkun's visits, Western media began reporting on China's willingness to substitute for Germany and France to build large reactors for Iran. Some of these media reports charged China with knowingly assisting an Iranian covert nuclear weapons program.[28] Confronted by mounting Western suspicion, Beijing publicly defended its nuclear cooperation with Iran. Early in November an MFA spokesman replied to a question about reports of nuclear cooperation between China and Iran by saying that such cooperation was entirely for nonmilitary purposes and that reports of cooperation in the area of nuclear weapons development were "utterly groundless." Chinese nuclear cooperation with Iran, and with all other countries, was conducted in accordance with three principles, the spokesman said. First, it was solely for peaceful purposes; second, it was open to international inspection; and third, the recipient country pledged not to transfer China-supplied materials or technologies to a third country without China's permission.[29] A few days later the MFA issued a statement outlining, and officially admitting for the first time, China's 1989 supply of a calutron and 1991 supply of a 27-kilowatt reactor to Iran. Both transfers had been "guided by internationally observed regulations, and China had requested the International Atomic Energy Agency to enforce safeguards before these facilities were shipped," according to the MFA.[30] China's decision to admit nuclear cooperation with Iran came just prior to a visit by U.S. secretary of state James Baker to Beijing to discuss this and other issues—a visit that was the first to China by a top-level U.S. official since June 4, 1989.

In September 1992 President Rafsanjani made a four-day visit to China accompanied by Defense Minister Ali Akbar Torkan and other top military officials. During the visit Rafsanjani and Yang Shangkun presided over the signing of a twelve-point agreement by science and technology minister Song Jian and AEOI head Reza Amrollahi. The agreement provided for cooperation in designing, building, and operating nuclear power plants; research on reactors; exploration for and mining of uranium ore; radiation safeguards; and ecological protection.[31] Under the agreement China was to assist in construction of at least four 300-megawatt nuclear power stations modeled after a recently constructed nuclear plant at Qinshan, Zhejiang province. These reactors would have produced large quantities of plutonium-rich depleted uranium fuel. Dates for delivery of the Qinshan-model power plants to Iran were not specified in the agreement. Both Chinese and Iranian officials stated that all reactors transferred under the agreement would be fully covered by IAEA safeguards.[32]

U.S. intelligence sources believed Rafsanjani had chosen China as Iran's principle nuclear partner.[33] At a news conference following the signing of the September 1992 agreement, Rafsanjani noted, "Our cooperation with China has constantly been increasing" and the fruits of the current visit "will help to enhance our cooperation and make it more comprehensive in many new areas." The Iranian ambassador to China stressed the political, as opposed to merely the commercial, significance of the agreement. Cooperation between China and Iran in the nuclear field was "one of the good types of cooperation between the two countries [and] emphasizes the sincere and profound trust that exists between the nations," the ambassador said. Nuclear cooperation was "long term in nature and not short term such as cooperation in the import and export areas." This "calls for each of the two sides to be well acquainted with each other and to trust each other to a great extent," the ambassador continued.[34]

About two weeks after the Song-Amrollahi agreement, the deputy director of the Bureau of International Cooperation of China's Ministry of Energy, Liu Xuehong, announced that "for technical reasons" China "could not supply" Iran with the 20-megawatt "plutonium production" reactor agreed to in 1990.[35] The temporal relation between China's agreeing to supply four 300-megawatt power plants and cancellation of delivery of a single 27-megawatt reactor raises several questions, which will be discussed in the next chapter on Sino-u.s. negotiations over the nuclear issue.

Twice in the six months after the Song-Amrollahi agreement (in November 1992 and again in February 1993) cnnc president Jiang Xinxiong visited Iran to work out details for supply of the 300-megawatt power plants. At the end of Jiang's second visit he signed an agreement with Amrollahi stipulating that cnnc would build two 300-megawatt nuclear power plants. Spokesmen for both China and Iran stressed that the plants would operate under iaea safeguards and be used entirely for peaceful production of electricity.[36] President Rafsanjani declared, "All the world should believe that Iran and China cooperate in the field of nuclear technology for the purpose of peaceful utilization of nuclear energy—not for military purposes."[37] During negotiations over the 300-megawatt power plants, China indicated it had no interest in recovering spent fuel from the reactors. Planning about waste disposal would be left to Iran, according to Chinese nuclear industry officials familiar with the negotiations.[38] That would leave the burnt uranium fuel available for reprocessing to extract plutonium.

In February 1993, the same month the Jiang-Amrollahi agreement was signed, the Chinese Academy of Science (cas) agreed to provide Iran with an HT-6B Tokamak laser nuclear research apparatus. The Tokamak is an electromagnetic containment machine used to generate, heat, and concentrate plasmas of hydrogen isotopes deuterium and tritium in an attempt to achieve controlled nuclear fusion. It was developed by Soviet scientists circa 1960. It is similar in operation to the familiar fluorescent light, with an electrical current passed through a gas-filled tube to ionize the gas causing it to discharge energy. In the case of the Tokamak, however, the tube is circular and surrounded by an electromagnetic coil whose magnetic field confines the gas molecules to the center of the tube, thereby intensifying the impact of the electrical current, which is also considerably more powerful than in a familiar fluorescent bulb.[39] The Tokamak is not related to weapons design or production. It is, however, a very sophisticated device near the frontier of nuclear science and testament to the ambitious nature of both China's and Iran's nuclear programs.

The Tokamak supplied to Iran in 1994 was China's first-ever international transfer of nuclear fusion research technology and, as such, a testament to China's steady advance in the nuclear area.[40] It had been designed and built in the mid-1980s by the Institute of Plasma Physics of cas, and operated by that institute for ten years before transfer to Iran. The laser device was installed in Iran at the Plasma Physics Research Center of Azad University in Tehran.

Teams of Chinese scientists went to Iran on two occasions to help with the installation and fine-tuning of the device. In February 1995 the device was successfully tested. CAS's Institute of Plasma Physics prided itself as the "Third World Research Center for Nuclear Fusion" because of its role in assisting Third World countries developing nuclear fusion research.[41] In March 1996 China, Iran, India, and Russia signed a protocol in Moscow establishing an Asian Fusion Research Foundation to cooperate in the study of fusion.[42] Many scientists believe that controlled nuclear fusion offers the best hope for supply of humanities' post–fossil-fuel-era energy needs.

China also helped Iran with atomic laser technology—another cutting-edge nuclear technology and one that promises an extremely efficient and easily concealable means of uranium enrichment. Atomic vapor laser isotope separation (AVLIS) was pioneered in the United States and the Soviet Union in the 1970s. It involves the vaporization of uranium metal and bombardment of that vapor by intense laser light of a precise frequency to separate U235 and U238 atoms. It is an extremely efficient form of isotope separation/enrichment with only one per one hundred thousand atoms collected being other than the desired fissile U235. Different types of lasers have been used, but copper vapor lasers provide the most appropriate wavelength. The United States' research in AVLIS was abandoned in 1994 because large existing stockpiles of U235 made it unnecessary.[43]

Iran had begun working on laser isotope separation under the shah. An American scientist had then persuaded scientists in the shah's nuclear program of the great potential of laser isotope separation, and Tehran contracted to purchase four infrared lasers for uranium enrichment on a large scale. The lasers arrived in Tehran in October 1978, just before the revolution.[44] In the late 1980s China provided Iran with laser systems suitable for laser isotope separation.[45] In 1992 a "foreign supplier" provided Iran with a laser separation lab.[46] This supplier was apparently Russia.[47] The Russian-supplied lasers were poor quality, with beams too scattered to separate uranium isotopes effectively. Iran then turned to China. In the 1980s China had obtained from Israel a copper vapor laser gun sight for use on the Russian-model T-54 tank. China transferred this technology to a laser research institute in Hefei, which was able to adapt the Israeli-supplied technology to AVLIS use. In 1994 China transferred its now-indigenized copper vapor laser to Iran, where it was installed at the Tehran Nuclear Research Center.[48] With Chinese and Russian assistance Iran was able to establish a pilot plant for laser isotope separation using copper vapor lasers in 2002.[49] When IAEA inspectors visited that facility in 2003, they found Iranian specialists working with copper laser devices. Those activities did not involve enrichment, but U.S. and foreign intelligence suspected that Iran was using this method elsewhere in covert enrichment programs.[50] Iranian scientists later admitted to IAEA that they had enriched small amounts of uranium via copper vapor laser processes. South African and Russian, not Chinese, scientific personnel were reported to have assisted Iran with those copper vapor laser projects.[51] AVLIS enrichment facilities would be relatively easy to conceal both because of their small size and because relatively low electricity consumption means there is not an unusual number of electrical lines leading into the facility for spy satellites to observe.

China also undertook to assist Iran with zirconium tube production during the mid-1990s. Zirconium is a corrosion resistant metal used to make tubes that hold the uranium fuel pellets in the extremely hot and corrosive core of a nuclear reactor. Production of zirconium or zirconium tubes is not controlled by or reportable to the IAEA. Mastery of zirconium metallurgy is, however, another step in development of a self-reliant nuclear capability. China also cooperated with Iran in the area of heavy water. Heavy water is rich in the hydrogen isotope deuterium and when bombarded by radiation from a reactor produces plutonium. United States officials considered a heavy-water reactor to be a plutonium production plant and as further evidence of Iran's intention of acquiring nuclear weapons. In 1992 CNNC began negotiations with Iran for construction of a 25–30-megawatt heavy-water reactor. According to CNNC Bureau of International Cooperation director Liu Xuehong, the reactor under consideration for sale to Iran in 1992 was of the same sort sold by China to Algeria several years earlier.[52] U.S. intelligence agencies intercepted telephone calls between Tehran and Beijing discussing possible Chinese sale of a heavy-water reactor. After the United States confronted Beijing with the matter, China's government investigated and squelched the proposed deal.[53] This sale was never consummated. Specific agreement not to sell a heavy-water reactor was one element of the 1997 Sino-U.S. agreement regarding Sino-Iranian cooperation.

After the collapse of China's offer of a heavy-water reactor, Iran proceeded on its own with the design, construction, and operation of such a plant. Construction began in 1996 at Arak, 250 kilometers southwest of Tehran. Initially there was speculation that China's offered design may have provided the basis for Iran's subsequent independent effort, but later U.S. and non-U.S. intelligence reports concluded that Russian entities, not Chinese, were the crucial foreign partners in Iran's Arak heavy-water plant. After China withdrew from the project, Iran turned to Russian specialists.[54] Still, it is likely that Iran gained much technical knowledge of the reactor through its negotiations with CNNC over the previous several years.

While declining to supply Iran with a heavy-water reactor, China reportedly supplied it with substantial amounts of heavy water in the early 1990s. China reportedly shipped to Iran, by cargo planes operating from restricted air bases, "militarily significant quantities" of heavy water in batches of less than twenty tons. Twenty tons was the threshold requiring report of such transactions to the IAEA.[55] In addition to allowing Iranian personnel to conduct benchmark experiments with heavy-water processes, this China-supplied heavy water could have been paired with Iran's reactors to produce plutonium. In 1994 China also supplied Iran with an unknown quantity of tributylphosphate, a chemical used for extracting plutonium from depleted uranium. At the same time, China may have supplied to Iran technical data on plutonium separation.[56] Later China reportedly sold Iran anhydrous hydrogen fluoride that can be used in production of uranium hexafluoride.[57]

According to information supplied to the IAEA in October 2003, between 1981 and 1993 Iran produced in laboratories "bench scale" (kilogram) quantities of nearly all the materials important to the production of enriched uranium: ammonium uranyl carbonate, uranium trioxide, uranium tetrafluoride (UF4), and uranium hexafluoride (UF6). All of these activities were covert and unreported to the IAEA. In 1993 Iran decided to terminate domestic research and development efforts on UF4 and UF6, because a "foreign supplier" indicated willingness to design and construct a uranium conversion facility (UCF).[58] That foreign supplier was China. In 1994 China agreed to provide Iran with large facilities for the production of uranium hexafluoride— a UCF, or "hex plant." As noted earlier, UF6 is a gaseous form of uranium containing both U238 and U235 isotopes and constituting the input for centrifuge enrichment. In June 1994 there were reports that Chinese nuclear engineers who were assisting AEOI construct a small-scale, pilot uranium conversion plant at Rudan, Shiraz, had been kidnapped. These reports were at least partially confirmed by Iranian authorities. As part of negotiations over the sale of a UCF, China supplied Iran with blueprints, test reports, and design information on equipment for two facilities. The first facility was designed to convert uranium ore concentrate into natural uranium dioxide and then into uranium hexafluoride, UF6. The designed capacity of this hex plant was two hundred tons of UF6 per year. The second facility was designed to produce uranium metal.[59] The explosive cores of atomic bombs are uranium metal. In March 1996 a team of Iranian nuclear specialists went to China to study technical documents. The next month a Chinese team went to Tehran to begin detailed design work.[60] In 1996 Iran formally notified the IAEA Safeguards Department that it planned to purchase a uranium hexafluoride conversion plant from China.[61] By mid-1997 a large number of Chinese nuclear technicians were engaged in preliminary work in Iran on construction of the two facilities.[62]

The United States protested "at the highest levels" China's sale of a hex plant to Iran. After several years of bargaining with Washington, Beijing finally agreed to suspend the hex plant deals, and this undertaking was embodied in the October 1997 Sino-U.S. agreement.

According to Iran's 2003 report to the IAEA, before the equipment for the UCF was delivered by the "foreign supplier," that supplier cancelled the contract in 1997. After China backed out, Iran then proceeded to use the foreign supplier's design data to produce all necessary equipment domestically. Construction of the plant began in 1999, and the first production line was expected to begin operation in November 2003.[63] Some "well placed sources" said that China "sold" the blueprints for the UF6 plant to Iran when it withdrew from the project.[64] Even if such a sale did not take place, the technical information and understanding acquired by Iranian personnel over the previous two years of negotiations provided a solid basis for independent Iranian construction of the UF6 plant. Iran's China-designed hex plant would provide the feedstock for the Natanz centrifuge enrichment facility.[65] In 1983 the United States had prevented the IAEA from assisting Iran in the production of UF6. A decade later China helped Iran acquire that capability.

CHINA'S DISENGAGEMENT FROM IRAN'S NUCLEAR EFFORTS

Even as China-Iran nuclear cooperation was reaching its high point in the mid-1990s, China was beginning to back away from that cooperation. Talks regarding the implementation of the February 1993 agreement signed by Jiang Xinxiong and Amrollahi regarding the two 300-megawatt power plants continued throughout 1993 and 1994. Several problems emerged. Key components of the Qinshan-model reactor offered to Iran were originally supplied by Western third parties—Germany, Japan, and the Netherlands. Those original third-party suppliers would not sell components for transfer to proliferation suspects such as Pakistan and Iran, so it was necessary for China to reverse engineer and produce these components itself. CNNC was confident this could be done, but indicated to Iran that it would take several years and considerable money. Iran, for its part, failed to provide China with detailed information on how it expected to pay China the initial installment of £1.2 billion for initial work on the first plant. In other words, China demanded money up front as a guarantee. Tehran probably wanted China to carry this cost out of antihegemonist solidarity. There was also disagreement over the siting of the first plant. China preferred the original site selected in the 1970s, at Darkhovin, near the Iranian-Iraqi border and the head of the Persian Gulf. Iran rejected this site because of proximity to Iran's nemesis, Iraq, and insisted on building the plant at Bushehr, partially completed by Germany prior to 1979. China, however, felt the Bushehr site was seismologically unsound, prone to earthquakes, and thus not a good place to build a nuclear reactor. Iranian representatives suspected that Chinese equivocation was due, at least in part, to U.S. pressure on Beijing to suspend the project.[66] As U.S. pressure on China mounted, Beijing at first dug in its heels. In September 1995 PRC ambassador to Tehran Hua Liming responded in this way to an Iranian reporter's query about U.S. pressure on Sino-Iranian nuclear cooperation: "Yes. It is true that they exert pressure on our government with regard to our relations with Iran. However, we believe that the PRC is an independent country with an independent foreign policy. The PRC is free to choose its own friends and it will not allow its actions to be supervised by other countries. We have always considered the Islamic Republic of Iran our friend."[67] In January 1996 First Deputy Premier Tian Zengpei announced that "China will continue its cooperation with Iran on the peaceful use of nuclear energy within the framework of regulations set by the International Atomic Energy Agency and considers this a principled and correct policy."[68] Shortly afterward, and in the midst of intense U.S.-PRC negotiations, China announced the "suspension" of China's agreement to build the 300-megawatt reactor.

In the fall of 1996 Iranian military sources disclosed that Iran had requested the dispatch of an observation team to watch China's next scheduled nuclear weapons test, and also Chinese training of ten or more Iranian personnel in the conduct of nuclear explosion tests.[69] It may well have been that evidence of the ultimate weapons orientation of Iran's nuclear program was accumulating and becoming increasingly apparent. China's leaders must have asked themselves the political costs of being associated with Iran's nuclear program as its large and covert and military dimensions came into public view. In any case, in October 1997 during President Jiang Zemin's state visit to the United States and summit meeting with President Clinton, China delivered a pledge not to sell nuclear power plants, a uranium hexafluoride plant, heavy-water reactors, or a heavy-water production plant to Iran. China also agreed not to undertake new nuclear cooperation with Iran. China was allowed to minimize its loss of political capital in Tehran by completing two low-proliferation-risk projects already under way: (1) the zirconium tube factory, and (2) the zero-power research reactor using heavy water and natural uranium and scheduled for completion by the end of 1997.[70] These moves were outcomes of intense U.S.-PRC negotiations, which will be considered in a later chapter. It is important to note that while capitulating to u.s. demands regarding Iran, Beijing rejected similar demands regarding Pakistan. This difference tells much about the limits of China's support for Iran and, therefore, about the role of Iran in Chinese calculations. It also suggests a stronger Chinese commitment to Pakistan's security than to Iran's.

Iran was bitter about its abandonment by Beijing. China lost considerable credibility in Tehran. It would take Beijing several years to rebuild its ties to Tehran, and then with a far greater element of strategic realism in Tehran. But there was not much that Iran could do. Railing against Beijing would only further isolate Iran before u.s. pressure. Moreover, Beijing still indicated a willingness to support Iran in other areas, and Chinese support in the Security Council or the IAEA might be useful in checking u.s. moves.

Iranian denunciation of the October 1997 PRC-U.S. agreement thus focused on the United States. "America's effort to pressure China into stopping peaceful nuclear cooperation with Iran is interference in other countries' internal affairs," Iranian media said. The United States, motivated by "political intentions and self-interest," had embarked on a campaign of "false propaganda" against Sino-Iranian nuclear cooperation.[71] Sino-Iranian nuclear cooperation was purely of a peaceful nature and closely scrutinized by the IAEA. China had never transferred nuclear weapons or nuclear weapons technology to Iran. The u.s. campaign against Iran's nuclear programs was an effort to divert attention from Israel's growing nuclear stockpile and an attempt to damage Iranian-Russian nuclear cooperation. Chinese capitulation to u.s. pressure was unfortunate and would only increase u.s. pressure in this area. AEOI deputy head Asadollah Saburi later commented on China's 1997 capitulation to u.s. pressure. Iran had severed ties with China on nuclear projects, Saburi stated, because "the Chinese reached a conclusion to work on nuclear matters with other countries, not Iran. Our contract was cancelled partly for political reasons."[72]

THE ORIGINS AND TERMINATION
OF CHINA'S NUCLEAR COOPERATION WITH IRAN

Table 6.1 lists various components of Chinese-Iranian nuclear cooperation discussed earlier. Clearly this cooperation was extensive, sustained over a fairly long period, and of crucial importance to Iran's nuclear effort.

What motivated China's support for Iran's nuclear programs? Desire to earn profits and foreign currency clearly inspired both China's politically influential nuclear industry and the central state organs issuing directives to that industry. Evidence cited earlier indicates that China's nuclear industry

TABLE 6.1

Sino-Iranian Nuclear Cooperation

Activity	Date	Location	Nature of activity	Result
Secret agreement re cooperation re peaceful uses of nuclear energy	June 1985	signed in Beijing	assist establishment ENRC	systematized and expanded nuclear cooperation; declared to IAEA only in 1992
Supply of subcritical light-water moderated reactor	1986?	ENRC	natural uranium fuel; open tank; vertical assembly	familiarization with reactor operation and design principles completed
Training 15 AEOI nuclear engineers	late 1980s	in China	training in reactor design and nuclear research	
Supply of electromagnetic isotope separation machine	agreement 1987, delivery 1989	Karaj	Calutron enrichment to 36.5%	experimental separation of uranium isotopes enrichment experimentation
Uranium exploration and mining	agreed to 1989, continued for decade	Yazd, Khurasan, Kerman provinces	prospecting and opening of mines joint teams formed circa April 1996	very successful; major deposits opened
Secret ten-year agreement re nuclear cooperation	January 20, 1990	signed in Beijing	extensive cooperation	provided for major expansion of nuclear cooperation
27 Kw miniature neutron source reactor	agreement re June 1990; went critical March 1994	ENRC	isotope production under IAEA safeguards	familiarization with reactor operation and design principles

Activity	Date	Location	Nature of activity	Result
Secret sale of 1.8 tons of uranium products	1991	used mostly at ENRC	provided raw material for wide array of uranium conversion experiments over decade	allowed Iranian engineers to conduct benchmark experiments on virtually all stages of uranium fuel cycle conversion processes
Supply of subcritical, graphite-moderated reactor	early 1990s	ENRC	natural uranium fuel; horizontal configuration	familiarization with reactor operation and design principles
Supply of zero-power reactor	1991	ENRC	natural uranium fuel; heavy water moderated under IAEA safeguards	familiarization with reactor operation and design principles grandfathered under October 1997 U.S.-PRC deal
Cyclotron operations	circa 1991	Karaj	Chinese engineers assist with operation of Belgium-supplied machine	
Nuclear medicine research center	May 1991	Karaj	Chinese technicians observed working at site	research in nuclear medicine and agriculture
Atomic laser assistance	July 1991	Qazvin	assistance with laser equipment	reported site of nuclear weapons research center
Supply of copper vapor laser	circa 1994	?	?	adapted to AVLIS use
Agreement to supply four 300 MW pressurized water reactors and nuclear center	initial agreement July 1991; Sale agreement September 1992	Beijing and Tehran	modeled after Qinshan reactor	Met intense U.S. pressure because of potential for plutonium production. "Suspended" September 1995, cancelled January 1996

TABLE 6.1 (*continued*)

Activity	Date	Location	Nature of activity	Result
27 MW reactor	1992	ENRC	capable of producing 6 kg plutonium per year	cancelled September 1992 under U.S. pressure
Supply HT-6B Tokamak laser	February 1993	Az'ad University, Tehran	obstensibly for laser fusion research experiments	diverted and used covertly for uranium enrichment
Heavy water production plant	1992	Arak	plutonumium production	suspended under U.S. pressure October 1997
Heavy water supply	mid-1990s		shipments in "militarily significant" quantities	shipments reportedly completed (evidence weak)?
Supply of uranium conversion facility	1994	Rudan?	UF6 "hex" plant and uranium metal plant; both large-scale	cancelled under U.S. pressure October 1997 PRC designs and technical data allow Iran construction
Supply of zirconium tube facility	mid-1990s?	Esfahan	corrosion-resistant tubes containing nuclear fuel pellets	grandfathered under October 1997 U.S.-PRC deal
Anhydrous hydrogenfluoride sale	1996	ENRC	"100s of tons" possible use in UF6 production	sale "suspended" February 1998, cancellation "reaffirmed" March 1998

SOURCES: Nuclear Threat Initiative and Center for Nonproliferation Studies, Monterey Institute of International Studies, "Iran Nuclear Chronology," http://www .nti.org/e_research/e1_iran-nch.html.

"An Iranian Nuclear Chronology, 1987–1992" and "Nuclear Facilities" in *Middle East Defense News* 5, nos. 17–18 (June 8, 1992), via LexisNexis.

Agreement for Nuclear Cooperation between the United States and China, report to the U.S. Congress, February 3, 1998. 105th Cong., 2nd sess., H. Doc. 105–197.

"China's Nuclear Exports and Assistance to Iran," Nuclear Threat Initiative, http://www.nti.org/db/china/niranpos.htm.

saw nuclear exports as an excellent profit-earning opportunity. China's top leaders and central planning agencies probably gave little scrutiny to the profitable deals arranged by China's nuclear enterprises, at least as long as they were not directly military. When China's top leaders thought about China's nuclear exports during the nineteen years after 1978, they saw those exports as among China's few high-technology, high-value-added exports, generating hefty revenues that went to modernize China's large but archaic nuclear energy industry so that it could contribute to easing a crucial developmental bottleneck.

Developing with Iran a relationship of influence and trust was also served by nuclear cooperation. Following the 1979 revolution, France, Germany, and the United States all withdrew from nuclear cooperation with Iran. Under the shah those Western countries had been quite happy to cooperate with Iran's extremely ambitious nuclear programs. After the overthrow of the shah, the Western countries abandoned nuclear cooperation with Iran and began trying, instead, to thwart Iran's nuclear cooperation with other willing partners such as China, Russia, or India. From Beijing's and Tehran's perspective, the Western powers apparently felt that only pro-Western countries were qualified to possess nuclear capabilities. Countries and states that chose to follow a non-Western course of development or that were opposed to Western policies were apparently not to be trusted with nuclear capabilities—to exercise their rights under the NPT to peaceful research and use of nuclear energy. China refused to go along with this hegemonic Western arrogation of authority to determine which states were and were not to be trusted with nuclear capabilities. Tehran clearly valued greatly China's willingness to undertake nuclear cooperation with Iran in spite of strong U.S. pressure. Iran's leaders, having made a series of decisions to forge ahead with nuclear programs, found many avenues of international cooperation closed, but found China willing to extend a hand of friendship and cooperation. This undoubtedly gained significant influence for Beijing in Tehran. Cultivating "friendship" with Iran was an important Chinese motive.

It is also significant that Beijing saw U.S. hegemonism on the offensive in the Gulf, striving to bring that region under U.S. domination. From Beijing's perspective, the United States had seized the opportunity of the Iran-Iraq war to expand its position in the Gulf and corral the Arab Gulf states into the U.S. camp. Then in the "unbalanced" post–Cold War period, it struck at Iraq in 1991 to teach it a lesson, thereby further strengthening the U.S. position. Iran as well as Iraq was a target of U.S. hegemony à la dual containment. Under such circumstances, should the government of Iran decide that nuclear weapons were necessary to check U.S. aggression, would China not be sympathetic? Would China's interests in foiling u.s. ambition to dominate the Persian Gulf not be served by Iranian acquisition of nuclear weapons? This is a surmise, but it seems more plausible to me than the alternate notion that China's leaders *would not have* examined the implications of nuclear assistance to Iran and the linkage between that assistance and what they perceived as u.s. hegemonist policies in the Gulf.

China's nuclear technology sales took place within a Chinese political culture that viewed the global nonproliferation regime as a product of "superpower collusion." The idea that the "first world" superpowers "colluded" in using the nonproliferation regime to uphold their nuclear supremacy was instilled in China from 1963 to at least 1978. This idea was no longer explicitly enunciated after Deng took over, but neither was it explicitly renounced. Beliefs accruing from years of indoctrination do not evaporate overnight.

It is also significant that most of China's nuclear cooperation with Iran, at least in the 1990s, was in compliance with the then-existing norms of the international nonproliferation regime. China's assistance in setting up the ENRC that began in 1985 was not reported to the IAEA until 1992, and China's 1991 sale of 1.8 metric tons of uranium materials was not reported to the IAEA until 2003. These would seem to be clear violations of IAEA rules. Aside from these actions, China's other nuclear cooperation with Iran fell within the then-existing IAEA regime. That regime prohibited work only on directly weapons-related activity and production of highly enriched fissile material. All other activities were permitted—or at least were not prohibited—as long as they were reported to and supervised by the IAEA. IAEA inspectors investigated Iranian nuclear facilities in February 1992, November 1993, April 1994, October 1995, and July 1997 and found no evidence of violations of the NPT or efforts to produce nuclear weapons.[73] As shown here, there is no evidence China was involved in nuclear weapons activities. Indeed, there is no absolute evidence that Iran itself was. Regarding the reporting requirement, China was clearly lax in this regard. From the standpoint of 2004 it is apparent that the old NPT regime was deeply inadequate. Yet those were the rules of the game at the time, and the IAEA never objected to Sino-Iranian nuclear cooperation. Most, though not all, of that cooperation was within the letter of the NPT regime.

Some analysts have argued that China's assistance to the nuclear programs of Iran and other Islamic countries has been used by Beijing to divert u.s. and Western attention away from East Asia, thereby increasing China's relative position in East Asia. China's liberal distribution of nuclear technology to countries that in all probability have aspirations of acquiring nuclear weapons has not been based on naïveté or mere profit motive, according to this point of view, but premised on awareness that Islamic nuclear powers in North Africa or the Middle East would tie down greater Western military strength in that region, weakening Western ability to concentrate on East Asia.[74]

It seems likely that *some people* within China's leadership did harbor such ideas of strategic diversion of the United States away from East Asia via support for Iran's nuclear programs. The militant antihegemony statements made by Li Peng during his 1991 visit to Tehran, for example, suggest such a conclusion. This assumption is several steps away from saying that the Chinese government had and pursued a policy of strategic diversion. Within any organization's decision-making process, different people agree on a particular decision for different reasons. It may not be necessary and would be divisive to attempt to sort out the various reasons for approving or disapproving of a particular action. As shown here, there is abundant evidence that powerful Chinese interests had economic reasons for exporting nuclear materials and technologies. People acting on the basis of those motives may well have joined with others moved more by geopolitical strategizing. However, China's 1997 disengagement from nuclear cooperation with Iran suggests a break with this sort of geopolitical diversionary strategy.

How much did China's intelligence services know about Iran's covert nuclear activities? The secret sale of 1.8 metric tons of uranium products in 1991—a transfer that made possible an array of clandestine reprocessing and enrichment experiments—strongly suggests that China's leaders knew of Iran's extensive covert programs. The sale of the copper vapor laser for AVLIS use points to similar conclusions. Large numbers of Chinese nuclear specialists traveled to Iran to participate in a wide array of nuclear activities. Iranian nuclear specialists traveled to China, some for long periods, and some probably shared with Chinese analysts their knowledge of Iran's nuclear programs. China's intelligence services certainly had many opportunities to learn about Iran's covert activities. Moreover, Pakistan, Iran's other major nuclear partner, was supplying crucial centrifuge technology for uranium enrichment and perhaps even a bomb design (as Qadir Khan supplied to Libya). China presumably had good intelligence in Pakistan as well. My informed guess is that China's leaders knew at least the broad contours of Iran's covert nuclear programs. For a number of years China's leaders turned a blind eye to those activities because to do so served China's interests of forging a multidimensional partnership with Iran while earning foreign currency.

China's decision to disengage was probably made, in part, on the basis of injury to China's reputation anticipated upon discovery of Iran's covert nuclear programs. If Iran went nuclear and China was deemed the key foreign power making that possible, the losses for China's reputation could have been very heavy. China's decision to disengage from nuclear cooperation with Iran also protected China's relations with the United States.

China's disengagement decision was also a function of a shift in Chinese thinking about the global nonproliferation regime. Over the course of twenty years China had shifted from being a rebel trying to subvert the NPT regime, to an established power working to uphold it. By 1996–97 there was mounting evidence of Iran's covert and possibly weapons-oriented programs. The United States undoubtedly put this information on the table before PRC representatives. It may be that China's leaders concluded that Iran was in fact pursuing nuclear weapons and did not want to be associated with that effort once it exploded into public view. The basic question was, where does the PRC stand? Was China a rogue state attempting to subvert the global nonproliferation regime? Or was it a leading, established state, willing to work with the United States and other respectable powers to uphold that regime? China's exclusive status as a nuclear weapons state under the NPT suggested that fewer rather than more states with nuclear weapons was in China's interest. Cooperation with the United States to uphold the global nonproliferation regime would help protect China's vital economic cooperation with the United States, and possibly help build a strategic partnership with Washington. Perhaps most fundamental, China's craving for international respect was better satisfied by recognition as a leading, established power, cooperating as an equal with the United States, rather than by playing the role of anti-Western rebel.

CHINA'S SUPPORT FOR IRAN DURING THE 2004 IAEA DEBATES

Even after its 1997 nuclear disengagement from Iran, Beijing found ways of demonstrating China's friendship for Iran and support for its nuclear efforts. A clear example of this came during the IAEA debates over Iran's nuclear programs in 2004. Iran's nuclear activities came under increased international pressure in 2003. In August 2002 an Iranian opposition group announced that Iran was constructing two undeclared nuclear facilities—a uranium enrichment plant at Natanz and a heavy-water plutonium production reactor at Arak. IAEA inspection verified those claims. Then in May 2003, the same group announced still another undisclosed uranium enrichment facility under construction west of Tehran. This was followed in June by the European Union calling on Iran to allow IAEA inspectors access to any facility, not merely to facilities previously declared by Iran to be part of its nuclear program—the latter being the normal arrangement under IAEA protocol. Also in June, an IAEA report documented various undeclared nuclear activities by Iran.[75] Washington seized on revelations of Iranian covert nuclear programs to push for strong IAEA condemnation of Iran followed by referral of the Iranian nuclear issue to the U.N. Security Council for possible sanctions. In this situation, Beijing gave Tehran a degree of support, while calling on Iran to convince the international community of the veracity of its repeated professions of nonproliferation of nuclear weapons.

Beijing's starting point was Tehran's profession that it did not intend to produce nuclear weapons. Ambassador Hua Liming exemplified this in his September 1995 interview. Asked by an Iranian reporter whether, in light of recent nuclear weapons tests by France and China, the ambassador would "give Iran the right to have nuclear capacity," Hua replied:

> Your country's officials have repeatedly announced that the Islamic Republic of Iran is not seeking nuclear weapons but the peaceful utilization of nuclear energy. Thus, I believe that all the countries of the world have the right to pursue peaceful objectives with regard to their nuclear energy programs. . . . the United States has hundreds of nuclear power plants and so does France. . . . Thus it would be illogical to deprive a developing country like Iran of a nuclear power plant.[76]

Similarly, when asked about China's stance on the Iranian nuclear issue before the IAEA during the 2004 debates, Foreign Minister Li Zhaoxing replied that China was confident that Iran was pursuing a peaceful nuclear program.[77] Beijing took Tehran's words at face value—in itself a dramatic demonstration of Chinese goodwill toward the IRI. Tehran said its nuclear programs were not aimed at nuclear weapons, and that was enough for Beijing. Accepting Tehran's word was a manifestation of mutual trust in the Sino-Iranian relationship.

From this initial assumption, it followed for Beijing that Iran was essentially meeting its obligations under the NPT and was entitled to the peaceful use of nuclear energy. Iran had an "absolute right" to the peaceful use of nuclear energy, PRC ambassador Lio G. Tan declared in mid-2004.[78] To the IAEA Board of Governors in September, PRC representative Zhang Yan called on the international community to respect Iran's reasonable concern and legitimate right with regard to peaceful use of nuclear energy. A uranium enrichment program was not in itself evidence of nuclear weapons intent. Enriched uranium could be used either to generate electricity or to make bombs, Zhang said. Enrichment per se was not banned by the NPT.[79] Zhang also urged Tehran to cooperate with the IAEA. China hoped, Zhang said, that Iran would continue to cooperate fully with the IAEA, fulfill its obligations, clear up unresolved issues, and ratify the NPT supplemental protocol at an early date. Iran should take new measures to build confidence and increase transparency, said China's ambassador for disarmament to the United Nations, Hu Xiaodi, in November 2004.[80] Beijing "welcomed" Iran's signature of an additional protocol with the IAEA in December 2003 that provided for enhanced inspections of Iranian nuclear facilities.

Beijing also opposed Washington's effort to have the Iran nuclear issue passed by the IAEA to the Security Council. "The IAEA Board of Governors is the proper venue and place to settle the [Iran nuclear] issue," said PRC IAEA board member Zhang Huazhu in September. There was "no necessity for the issue to go anywhere else," Zhang said.[81] Shortly before visiting Tehran in November Li Zhaoxing telephoned U.S. secretary of state Colin Powell and British foreign secretary Jack Straw to say that the Iranian nuclear issue would "become more complicated" if referred to the Security Council. The IRI has good, constructive, and positive cooperation with the IAEA, Li told Powell and Straw.[82] Beijing also opposed the U.S. push for sanctions, insisting that the issue be solved through peaceful negotiations. "The Chinese government is against any threat and hegemony on the international scene," Li Zhaoxing said during his November 2004 visit to Tehran. An article in *Renmin ribao* was more blunt. The international community "opposes the handling of international disputes often and always with sanctions and armed threats by dent of its [the U.S.] superpower status."[83]

Tehran apparently pushed for assurance that Beijing would exercise its veto on behalf of Tehran should U.S. pressure to take the matter to the Security Council succeed. Li Zhaoxing flew to Tehran in November 2004 to convey Beijing's somewhat equivocal answer. When asked at a joint press conference with Foreign Minister Kharrazi whether China would use its veto if Tehran was hauled before the Security Council, Li replied: "Veto cannot be used extensively since there are special limits to that. We must see if there is any ground for such a referral or who has the prerogative to do this."[84] Li's words led one Iranian paper to conclude, "We should not set any hopes [on] China in the Security Council."[85] Between the lines of Li's words was this message: China's stance in a Security Council debate would depend on the strength of the evidence of Iranian nuclear weapons programs and the attitudes of the other Perm Five. Early in 2005 reliable reports said Iran's IAEA representative visited Beijing to urge that China use its influence with Pakistan to prevent Pakistan from cooperating with the IAEA on the Iranian nuclear issue. There was strong international pressure on Pakistan to have Abdul Qadir Khan reveal the full scope of his secret activities with Iran, and Tehran wanted Beijing to counter that pressure. Tehran reportedly linked Chinese support on the nuclear issue to more than one hundred proposed joint economic projects.[86]

China's diplomacy during the 2004 Iran-IAEA debate balanced between supporting Iran and upholding the NPT regime in tandem with the other Perm Five. Tehran indicated to Beijing that support on the nuclear issue was the quid pro quo for cooperation in other areas. After conferring with Li Zhaoxing during his November 2004 visit to Tehran, Rafsanjani, chairman of the IRI Expediency Council, lauded China's support on the nuclear issue. Given the global responsibility of China, it was expected that Beijing would back Iran's legitimate rights in international forums, Rafsanjani said. He also called for implementation of agreements signed earlier between the two countries.[87] Shortly before Li Zhaoxing's visit the Chinese oil firm Sinopec had been awarded rights to develop the Yadavaran oil field, China's first major involvement in the development of Iranian oil resources. China's need for imported energy was huge and growing rapidly. Iran offered large quantities of energy under conditions that promised maximum insulation of China's international energy supply from U.S. pressure. There may not have been an explicit quid pro quo between oil and nuclear issues. But implicitly, at least, solidarity in one area facilitated cooperation in other areas.

7 / China and Iran's Military Development Efforts

PARAMETERS OF IRAN-CHINA MILITARY COOPERATION

China has consistently assisted the military development of the Islamic Republic of Iran. During the 1980–88 war, China became Iran's most important foreign supplier of munitions and munitions-producing capital goods. During the postwar period, first the Soviet Union and then Russia superseded China as Iran's major military supplier, but Beijing continued to be important. Throughout, Beijing refused to go along with u.s. efforts to cut off Iran's munitions imports or—with several important exceptions—to hobble Tehran's access to what Washington termed "advanced conventional weapons." Chinese assistance in the military arena has been highly valued by IRI leaders. Military cooperation has been an important area of the PRC-IRI partnership, and Beijing's determination in persisting with this cooperation in spite of u.s. pressure has enhanced Beijing's stature in Tehran. China's consistent support in this area offset the loss of political capital Beijing suffered by its termination of nuclear cooperation in 1997.

When the war with Iraq began in September 1980, Iran found itself in the position of fighting that war with military forces largely equipped with u.s.-made weapons, but with resupply and replacement of those weapons unavailable from the United States. Vietnam, with huge stockpiles of u.s. arms inherited from recently defeated South Vietnamese forces, was able to meet some of Tehran's needs. But Tehran also began urgently to equip its forces with non-u.s. weapons.[1] Access to West European arms was restricted by European fears of Tehran's revolutionary objectives, by u.s. pressure, and by a conclusion after 1982 that Tehran was largely responsible for the continuation (if not the outbreak) of the war. Access to Soviet munitions was limited by Moscow's alliance with Iraq—which Moscow activated as Iran assumed the offensive circa 1982—by Soviet actions in Afghanistan, and by Khomeini's view of the sinister nature of the Soviet system. That left China among major arms producers. Beijing did not fail to grasp the opportunity.

There was a serendipitous meshing of Iranian demand and Chinese supply. The post-1978 marketization reforms introduced by Deng Xiaoping created powerful incentives for Chinese industrial enterprises to export. Chinese defense industrial firms were large, politically influential, and among the most technologically advanced in China's industrial sector. Deng's reforms allowed those enterprises to seek out foreign customers independently and retain a large portion of the profits from foreign sales. Expanded arms exports also helped Beijing meet an urgent need for *Chinese* military modernization. China's war against Vietnam in February 1979 had exposed serious inadequacies in the People's Liberation Army (PLA). Fighting only against Vietnam's regional forces (and not against Hanoi's much tougher main forces), the PLA had prevailed only by brute manpower and at extremely heavy cost. This experience highlighted for China's leaders the urgent need for defense modernization. But at the same time, Deng wanted to cut China's defense budgets, reversing the Mao-era militarization of the economy and freeing funds for investment in long-neglected civilian sectors of the economy. Where would funds for military modernization come from? Revenues from exports of arms and defense capital goods offered one important source. Iran, with its large wartime demand for military goods and with rich petroleum resources to pay for imports, offered an important customer.

In 1980 China's defense industry was granted permission to sell surplus arms and military equipment on international markets. As noted in an earlier chapter, when the Iran-Iraq war began Beijing quickly called for an end to fighting, restraint by both sides, noninvolvement by outside powers, and settlement of the conflict by peaceful negotiations. In line with this moral high ground, and probably in an effort to minimize the impact of arms sales to Iran on China's ties with Arab countries, China's leaders decided that Chinese entities should not sell munitions *directly* to either Iran or Iraq. Indirect sales—sales to third parties who might then resell goods to Iran or Iraq—were, however, permissible. As it turned out, Jordan became the major transshipment point for Chinese munitions to Iraq, a development manifest in an explosive growth in China's exports to Jordan during the war. Syria and North Korea became the major intermediaries for the sale of Chinese munitions to Iran. China's Ministry of Foreign Affairs (MFA) was empowered by China's central leaders to clear all "sensitive" exports to either belligerent, even indirect sales. Direct sales of munitions (usually involving missiles) to either Iran or Iraq were permitted only in special cases, which had to be cleared by the MFA and approved by Deng Xiaoping.[2]

There was also a fit between the requirements of Iran's wartime strategy and the sort of arms that China could supply. IRI leaders decided early in the war to conduct it without large foreign borrowing. Iran would not, unlike Iraq, attempt to import large quantities of expensive, high-technology weapons. It would rely, instead, on Iran's numerically superior manpower and revolutionary-religious ardor. Iran would also, its leaders decided, attempt to indigenize defense production to the greatest extent possible. Both requirements pointed toward somewhat lower-tech weapons.[3] Chinese munitions met these requirements. Chinese weapons were relatively simple, low-tech, but rugged, and appropriate for the large numbers of men being mobilized and quickly trained by Iran. Chinese weapons were cheap and yet effective on the battlefield against Iraq's largely Soviet-equipped forces. Chinese firms were also willing to transfer technology and manufacturing equipment to Iran. Nor did Chinese firms attach political conditions.[4] Beijing, unlike potential Western suppliers, was not concerned by the harsh, revolutionary aspects of the IRI's internal regime—or even by Iran's revolutionary aspirations for the Persian Gulf and the Middle East.

BEIJING'S POLICY OF PLAUSIBLE DENIAL

China in the early 1980s was still far away from becoming either a major petroleum importer or a major participant in the global market economy. This meant that China's material stakes in the stability of the Persian Gulf were still small. Beijing was concerned, however, that too close and too public Chinese military support for Iran would damage Beijing's image among Arab public opinion. The war between Shiite Persian Iran and Sunni Arab Iraq broadly rallied Arab opinion to Iraq's side—a trend assiduously encouraged by Iraqi propaganda. With the exception of Libya and Syria, Arab governments and public opinion supported Iraq. Egypt and Saudi Arabia, two major Arab powers, were especially important supporters of Iraq. China had courted Egypt since the mid-1950s out of recognition of Egypt's leading role in the Arab world. As far as Saudi Arabia was concerned, that state then remained one of only three major states recognizing the Republic of China on Taiwan. (The two other states were South Africa and South Korea.) Given Saudi support for Iraq, drawing Saudi Arabia away from Taipei would not be facilitated by large-scale Chinese arming of Iran. Chinese arms sales to Iran might anger Riyadh, inclining it to remain in Taipei's embrace. This concern did not preclude highly lucrative arms sales to Iran, but it did mean that those sales should be kept as low profile as possible. Arab governments such as those in Cairo and Riyadh understood the reality behind China's diplomatic cant denying sales to Iran (and Iraq), but those denials perhaps had some effect on public opinion in the Arab countries.

Official denials of arms sales to either Iran or Iraq offered Chinese representatives convenient refuge when pressed on those arms sales. Rather than having to justify those sales or explain how they fit with China's call for restraint or noninvolvement of external powers, Chinese representatives could simply deny such sales existed. China also sold large amounts of arms to Iraq during the war, although China's role in this regard was well behind the Soviet Union and France. Denial of sales to either belligerent protected China's claim to high moral status that otherwise might be impugned by charges of being an amoral "merchant of death" selling arms to both sides of a conflict. Thus foreign ministry information director Qi Huaiyuan told the press in April 1983, just as China was signing its first major arms supply agreement with Iran, that China had not supplied any weapons to either party during the Iran-Iraq war.[5] Following further press reports of weapons sales in 1985, the foreign ministry again issued a denial: "We have stated many times that we are not engaged in any arms transactions with Iran. China's position on the issue of the Iran-Iraq war is neutral, and we strictly adhere to this neutral position."[6] In November 1985 Vice Premier Yao Yilin said that China had not supplied arms or missiles to Iran. In line with the strict neutral stance in the Iran-Iraq war, Yao told reporters from an Arab newspaper, China had not sold arms to either side.[7] Further reports in 1987 prompted another foreign ministry statement: "China's position of selling no weapons to Iran in the war between Iran and Iraq is consistent." Reports in Arab papers that China had become Iran's biggest source of weapons were "groundless."[8] In fact, those reports were quite accurate, as figures presented below will attest. Two years later President Li Xiannian told Egypt's minister of state for foreign affairs, Butrus Ghali, that China had not sold arms or missiles to Iran. Rumors to the contrary were attempts by the United States to divert world and Arab public opinion from the scandal the United States suffered as a result of its own recent secret arms sales to Iran.[9] In a March 1988 speech to the National Press Club in Washington, and after agreeing with the Reagan administration to end Silkworm missile sales to Iran, Wu Xueqian again denied "direct arms sales" to Iran.[10] In 2004 Chinese foreign affairs specialists continued to deny China had sold arms to Iran during the 1980–88 war.

Reliance on third-country intermediaries may have rendered China's denials accurate in a narrow sense. Chinese firms sold arms to North Korean, Hong Kong, Pakistan, British, or Turkish entities. Those entities in turn sold the items to Iranian agencies.[11] As evidence of Chinese sales to Iran mounted, Chinese foreign ministry spokesmen began referring to the "complicated" nature of the international arms market in relation to the matter of "through what channel Iran has obtained what kind of weapons."[12] Interestingly, Beijing's refuge in fine legal distinctions was in line with u.s. policy at that time. Secretary of State George Schultz stated in June 1983 that while u.s. policy was not to sell weapons to either belligerent, some items may have gotten through via indirect channels.[13] As critics, including Iranian critics, of u.s. policy pointed out, considerable war-relevant u.s. materials reached Iraq during the conflict.[14] After Iraq withdrew to the international boundary and abandoned offensive operations in 1982, Washington concluded that Iran, rather than Iraq, was mainly responsible for continuation of the war. Washington also feared that an Iranian victory over Iraq would lead to an unfavorable balance of power in the Gulf. Thus Washington *may* have deliberately turned a blind eye to transfers of u.s. munitions to Iraq. China's policy of plausible denial was then in line with the u.s. approach, although most Chinese weapons went to Iran, while most u.s. weapons went to Iraq.

THE POSTWAR ARMS RELATIONSHIP

With the end of the Iran-Iraq war, and again following Iraq's 1991 defeat, Iran's defense requirements, and consequently Sino-Iranian military cooperation, changed. With Iraq partially disarmed under u.n. supervision, Iran's defense budgets fell sharply. Iran's leaders also opted after the war with Iraq to forgo major increases in conventional arms, concentrating instead on the development of key advanced, sophisticated technologies, especially missile, chemical, and nuclear capabilities. Tehran now sought to develop a self-sufficient indigenous production capacity for these key technologies.[15] China again helped Iran achieve its objectives.

China's role in Iran's post-1988 military development effort was secondary but still significant. During the 1990s Russia, and perhaps even North Korea, surpassed China in importance as Iran's preferred military development partner. This was due to Moscow's new willingness to sell very advanced military technologies to Iran at bargain-basement prices. Regarding North Korea, that country was most willing to ignore u.s. and international restrictions on transfer of missile technology. Yet China ranked third as Iran's military supplier during the post-1988 period.

Following preliminary discussions during Khamenei's 1989 visit, China's deputy director of the State Commission for Science, Technology, and Industry for National Defense (COSTIND), General Jiang Hua, traveled to Tehran in January 1990 to sign, with Iranian defense minister Lieutenant General Ali Akbar Torkan, a ten-year agreement on military technology exchange.[16] Missile cooperation was a key focus of the agreement. Torkan then led a "senior military delegation" to China in October. This was the first visit by a defense minister on either side since the Sino-Iranian relationship was established in 1971. In Beijing Torkan met separately with PRC defense minister Qin Jiwei, chief of staff (and future defense minister) Chi Haotian, deputy chief of general staff He Qizhong, and minister in charge of COSTIND Ding Henggao. During a forty-minute meeting, president Yang Shangkun told Torkan, "Our two sides should work for a closer relationship in various fields." Torkan conveyed to Yang a letter from President Rafsanjani and told Yang that Iran's leaders attached importance to Sino-Iranian ties.[17] In March of the next year Ding Henggao reciprocated Torkan's visit.[18] Reports in Arab media at the time of Torkan's visit to Beijing asserted that Iran and China were discussing joint production of M-11 and M-9 ballistic missiles.[19] As shown below, cooperation in the missile area did intensify following Torkan's visit. As shown in an earlier chapter, so too did Sino-Iranian nuclear cooperation.

Table 7.1 illustrates publicly announced, high-level PRC-IRI military interactions between 1989 and 2003. Those exchanges were densest in the early 1990s, when Sino-Iranian antihegemony cooperation was also most intense, and then fell off in the second half of the 1990s. There were probably extensive military exchanges before 1989 that remained nonpublic. Given the extensive arms transfers and missile and nuclear cooperation that existed during the pre-1989 period, it is almost certain that talks between responsible PRC and IRI military officials were necessary. Until the end of the Iran-Iraq war, however, military exchanges were kept secret, probably because they contradicted China's policy of neutrality.

Between 1982 and 2004 China supplied Iran with $3.8 billion in conventional weaponry, a yearly average of $171 million, according to the Stockholm International Peace Research Institute (SIPRI) data presented in table 7.2. Beginning in 1982, the second year of the Iran-Iraq war, as Iran shifted to the offensive and Iran's Western arms suppliers (Italy, Britain, France, and the Netherlands) fell away, China became Iran's major supplier—a position it held until 1990 when Soviet sales surpassed those of China. During the wartime period, North Korea was Iran's second-largest supplier—again as indicated by table 7.2—selling Iran nearly $1 billion in arms. Some unknown portion of those ostensibly North Korean sales were in fact made in China. Even after

TABLE 7.1

Publicly Acknowledged High-Level

PRC-IRI Military Exchanges, 1989–2003

May 1989	Military officials talk during President Khamenei's visit to PRC
Jan. 1990	Deputy director of Science and Technology Commission, Gen. Jiang Hua, to IRI
Oct. 1990	Defense Minister Ali Torkan with "senior military delegation" to PRC
Mar. 1991	COSTIND head Ding Henggao to IRI
Oct. 1991	PLA General Logistics Department delegation to IRI
Sept. 1992	IRI Army logistics chief, Gen. Alastu Tuhidi, to PRC
Sept. 1992	Chief of Iran's Joint Chief of Staff, Maj. Gen. Ali Shahbazi, to PRC
Oct. 1992	PRC defense minister Qin Jiwei to IRI
Jan. 1993	IRI Revolutionary Guards commander Mohsen Rezai to PRC
July 1993	IRI vice defense minister to PRC
Aug. 1993	IRI "strategic representatives" group to PRC
Aug. 1993	IRI naval staff command college group to PRC
Sept. 1993	PLA meteorological group to IRI
Aug. 1996	IRI defense minister Mohammad Forouzandeh to PRC
June 2000	IRI defense minister accompanies President Khatami to PRC
Dec. 2000	Minister for Science, Technology, and Industry for National Defense Liu Jibin to IRI
Oct. 2003	IRI Revolutionary Guards Corps commander Mohammed Hejazi to PRC

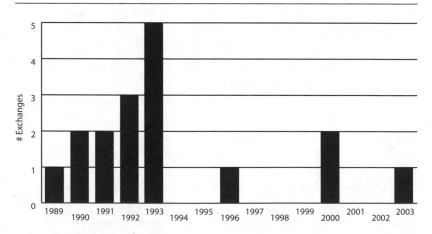

Moscow's emergence as Tehran's top supplier in 1990, China remained important, ranking number two in seven of the fifteen years after 1988, and number one in 1994 and 1996.

A large portion of China's military assistance to Iran during the war consisted of small arms and ammunition, befitting the IRI's "labor-intensive" style of warfare. Yet China also supplied a substantial quantity of heavy weapons. As indicated by table 7.3, heavy artillery and tanks were among the most important items.

Beijing also cooperated with Tehran's effort to develop an indigenous defense industrial capacity. In this regard, the IRI had a good basis to build on. Since the 1920s the Pahlavi governments (first of Reza and then of Mohammad Pahlavi) strove for indigenous defense industrial capacity, seeing that as one way of increasing Iran's regional status. Creation of a self-reliant defense industrial base in all areas but airplanes and warships was one dimension of the shah's ambitious post-1968 military modernization drive. Substantial progress was made in that direction before the Islamic revolution brought things to a complete halt. After the outbreak of the Iran-Iraq war, Iran's new regime sought to revive the shah-era defense industrial base, but did so under conditions of international isolation. Iran's need for foreign assistance can be estimated from the fact that sixty-five thousand foreign advisors and their dependents were in Iran to support the shah's military and industrial programs shortly before the revolution.[20] With Iran's Western advisors gone, Tehran urgently needed to find replacements to gin up production for the war against Iraq.

Iran's initial emphasis on reviving the prerevolutionary defense industrial base was on ammunition production. Then came production of infantry weapons. By 1987 Iran had achieved 75 percent indigenous production of infantry arms and ammunition. Iran also indigenized production of artillery and rockets. One hundred and twenty new defense industrial projects were launched in the years after 1979. Although figures are unavailable, it is clear that Chinese specialists were involved in many of these defense industrial projects.

The Sino-Iranian military technology exchange relation was not entirely one-way. China received some advanced military technology via cooperation with Iran. It is important to remember that in the early 1980s the PLA was far from the technologically sophisticated force it would become twenty years later. The PLA then desperately needed technological upgrading. Early during the Iran-Iraq war, Iran promised to give China access to late-model Soviet weapons captured from Iraq.[21] Iran also captured French-made missiles from Iraqi forces and may well have shared that technology with Chinese engineers. Iran reportedly let Chinese engineers study the F-4 Phantom, a sturdy and

TABLE 7.2

Iran's International Arms Suppliers, 1975–2003

(us$ millions in 1990 constant price)

	1975	1976	1977	1978	1979	1980	1981	1982	1983	1984	1985	1986	1987	19
Argentina										8	6			
Austria											285			
Belarus														
Brazil														
China							2	229	260	216	156	546	625	32
Czech.												90	90	9
Ethiopia											27			
France	8		105	367			157							
GDR														
Israel											22	22		
Italy	97	113	87	192	105	38	97	42						
Japan					146									
N. Korea								141	241	65	39	47	188	19
S. Korea											45			
Libya						26	104			1	36		20	
Holland	23	30	38	28			27			11	22			2
Pakistan						15	30	30						
Poland														
Romania														
ussr			740	740								22	6	
Russia														
Sweden											22			
Switzerland							25	75	77	143				
Syria								177	46					
uk	587		52	229	175					119	52			
Ukraine														
usa	4,401	3,125	4,703	1,568	41					9	97			
Total	**5,116**	**3,268**	**5,725**	**3,124**	321	225	442	694	624	563	676	869	929	63

SOURCE: Stockholm International Peace Research Institute arms transfer project, Stockholm, Sweden. Courtesy of Dr. Siemon Wezeman. Updated November 18, 2004, via sipri arms transfer database, http://www.sipri.org/contents/armstrad/atira_data_html.

1989	1990	1991	1992	1993	1994	1995	1996	1997	1998	1999	2000	2001	2002	2003
											8	15	16	
4	6	40												
74	138	113	81	287	204	42	323	36	51	36		8	12	12
155	21													
							2							
8														
11		107	129	144	9	9	4	4	2					
22	22	22		10	10	20								
0	1	2												
					88	182								
97	97													
	397	1001												
			176	516	76	53	234	235	252	244	323	352	319	423
				23					30			75	75	
371	682	1285	386	980	375	290	547	241	296	242	294	410	371	324

TABLE 7.3
China's Conventional Arms Sales to Iran, 1982–2004

Item	Description	Year ordered	Number ordered	Year delivered or licensed	Number delivered
F-6	fighter aircraft	1982	100	1982–83	100
F-6	fighter aircraft	1985	12	1985–86	12
T-59	main battle tank	1985	200	1985–86	200
Type 59/1	130 mm towed gun	1985	100	1985–86	100
Type 60	122 mm towed gun	1985	100	1985–86	100
CSA-1	surface-to-air missile	1985	100	1985–86	100
Hong-ying 5	portable SAM	1985	300	1985–86	300
F-7	fighter	1985	60	1986	20
CSA-1 SAMs	mobile SAM	1985	6	1985–86	6
Hong Ying-5	portable SAM	1985	300	1985–88	600
F-6	fighter	1985	24	1986–87	24
F-7	fighter	?	?	1985	24
T-59	main battle tank	1986	?	1987	120
Type 59/1	130 mm towed gun	1986	120	1987	120
Type 63	107 mm multiple rocket	1982	?	1982–87	900
C-801	antiship cruise missile	1986	8	1987	8
Hai Ying-2 L	antiship cruise missile	1986	?	1987–88	96
Hong Jian-73	antitank missile	1982	?	1982–87	6,500
Hong Ying-5	portable SAM	1986	?	1987	300
T-59	main battle tank	1986	?	1987–88	240
Type 501	armored personnel carrier	1986	?	1986–88	300
Hai Ying 2	antiship cruise missile	1986	?	1987–88	124
PL-2A	air-to-air missiles	1986	?	1986–88	540
PL-7	air-to-air missiles	1986	?	1986–88	360
HQ-2B	SAM system	1989	48	?	?

Item	Description	Year ordered	Number ordered	Year delivered or licensed	Number delivered
Hai Ying 2	antiship cruise missile	1989	?	?	?
Hong Ying-5	portable SAM	1985	?	1985–88	600
HQ-2B	coastal defense SAM system	1989	8	1990–93	8
"	"	1989	96	1990–93	72
CSS-8 TEL	SSM launcher	1989	25	1990–96	25
CSS-8	SSM	1989	200	1990–96	200
Hugu missile boats	fast-attack craft	1991	10	1994	5
F-7m Airguard	fighter	1991	75	1992–94	68
ESR-1	surveillance radar	1992	10	1994–96	10
Rice Lamp	fire-control radar	1992	10	1994–96	10
C-802	antiship cruise missile	1992	80	1994–96	80
C-801	antiship cruise missile	1992	64	1996	64
Y-12	transport aircraft	1993	9	1994–95	9
Y-7	transport aircraft	1994	2	1998	2
Hudong	fast-attack craft, missile	1995	10	1994–96	10
C-801	antiship cruise missile	1995	24	1997–98	24
F-7M Airguard	fighter aircraft	1995	5	1996	5
C-802	antiship cruise missile	1995	80	1996–99	80
Y 7	transport aircraft	1996	14	1998	2
China Cat	fast-attack craft, missile	2000		2001–04	
TL-10/FL-8	antiship missile	2002	?	?	10
TL-6/FL-9	antiship missile	2003	?	?	

SOURCE: SIPRI Yearbook, 1981–2002 (New York and Oxford: Oxford University Press, 1981–2002). Also, SIPRI Web database, http://www.sipri.org/contents/arstrad/atira_data_html (accessed November 15, 2005).

capable fighter-bomber supplied by the United States to Iran in the 1970s. China also acquired air-refueling technology from Iran. For many years the PLA had sought this technology to extend the operational time of PLA aircraft over the Spratly Islands. After years of failure in this effort, in 1991 China obtained this technology from Iran. It had been provided to Iran under the shah by the United States, reverse engineered by Iranian personnel, and manufactured in Iran.[22] Iran also sold China a batch of 115 MiG-29s flown by Iraq to Iran during the 1991 Gulf War to avoid their destruction by U.S. forces and later claimed by Iran as compensation for damages suffered in the 1980–88 war. China reportedly planned to use the MiG-29 engines, along with new engines purchased from Russia, to produce a modernized fighter, the Jian-7, Chinese efforts to indigenously develop an adequate engine having hit snags.[23] Iranian engineering capabilities are quite advanced in certain discrete areas, for example, in robotics, a field crucial to development of unmanned combat systems. Russia was also generous in certain areas of missile technology transfer to Iran. This meant that joint development with Iran might allow China to acquire an additional increment of advanced Russian or Iranian weapons technology.

Arms apparently constituted China's major export to Iran until the late 1990s. This conclusion is suggested by comparing the estimates of Chinese arms sales to Iran calculated by SIPRI with data on bilateral trade published by the United Nations' *Directions of Trade Statistics*. This is done in table 7.4. The methodologies used by SIPRI and the United Nations to reach their respective annual figures are different, but comparison produces a rough estimate. From a very modest 1 percent in 1981, arms skyrocketed to more than five times the value of regular Chinese merchandise sales the next year, and then to twenty-one times, twelve times, and nine times that value respectively during the last three years of the Iran-Iraq war. Thereafter arms sales declined, but still stood at an average of 50 percent of total Iranian civilian imports during the ten years after the war. As shown below, the largest component of China's imports from Iran was oil. In effect, China was exchanging arms for oil. This helps explain why arms sales to Iran were so important, and why China resisted so tenaciously U.S. efforts to restrict that trade.

MISSILES AND AMERICAN HEGEMONY: THE CHINESE VIEW

Before looking at Chinese assistance to Iran's missile programs, it is useful to look briefly at China's view of U.S. efforts to restrict the international dissemination of such technology. Chinese analysts tend to see arms-control agreements as instruments through which powers attempt to achieve mili-

TABLE 7.4

China's Arms Sales to Iran as Percentage of Regular Chinese Exports to Iran

Year	Arms sales PRC to Iran*	Iran imports from PRC*	Arms as percentage of PRC exports to Iran
1981	2	179	1
1982	229	45	509
1983	260	294	88
1984	216	170	127
1985	156	48	325
1986	546	26	2,100
1987	625	53	1,179
1988	325	36	903
1989	74	48	154
1990	138	321	43
1991	113	322	35
1992	81	335	24
1993	287	326	88
1994	204	147	139
1995	42	232	18
1996	323	242	133
1997	36	395	9
1998	51	655	8
1999	36	613	6

* (Millions U.S. $)

SOURCES: Stockholm International Peace Research Institute Database; Arms Transfer Database; data provided by Dr. Siemon Wezeman; and *Direction of Trade Statistics,* (Washington, DC: International Monetary Fund, 1982–2000).

tary advantages over rivals. During the Cold War, for example, Washington emphasized in its arms-control talks with Moscow reduction of land-based intercontinental ballistic missiles (ICBM's) in which the Soviet Union had a lead, while attempting to exclude from limitation submarine-launched mis siles in which the United States had a lead. With the end of the Cold War, the United States focused increasingly on "regional conflicts," but the essential principle of gaining military advantage remained. Preventing the "proliferation" of weapons of mass destruction and missiles that could deliver such weapons was now a key U.S. objective—and also a key means of maintaining U.S. military superiority. The Missile Technology Control Regime (MTCR) setup by the United States and six other Western nations in 1987 was, in China's view, a mechanism of this u.s. effort at continued military domination.[24] The MTCR was, in the words of another Chinese analyst, "formulated to protect the unilateral interests of the Western countries."[25] The MTCR sought "to limit the transfer of missiles but not to limit the transfer of other offensive weapons such as fighter bombers." For Third World countries without advanced air forces or adequate air defenses, advanced fighter-bombers were a greater threat than missiles. By trying to impose the MTCR on the world, the United States and its Western allies were, in effect, trying to maintain the ability to attack from the air potential enemies in the Third World, while limiting the ability of those adversaries to retaliate from the air with missiles.[26]

Chinese analysts felt that advanced bomber aircraft were, in fact, more lethal than missiles. A u.s. F-15E fighter-bomber, for instance, could deliver 11,000 kilograms of explosives, while a Chinese M-9 carried a mere 500-kilogram warhead. Yet, proliferation of aircraft was not restricted, only missiles. Advanced performance aircraft were, of course, produced by the United States and its Western allies, and since Western sale of such aircraft was unrestricted, the West was free to sell them to whomever they liked. This meant that countries friendly to the United States received such aircraft, while countries deemed unfriendly did not. If the United States could deny missile capabilities to disobedient developing countries, while supplying its friends with advanced aircraft, the United States would maintain a favorable balance of power.[27]

From Beijing's perspective, missiles are the equalizer of developing countries. In the era of modern warfare, air power predominates. The power that controls the air has a great advantage over its opponents and is able to strike with suddenness, great destructive force, and from a great distance. United States military forces, with large and extremely advanced aerospace forces, would enjoy such a decisive advantage in a contest with any developing country. The vast fiscal resources of the United States, its huge spending for defense research and development, and the advanced levels of u.s. technology mean that no developing country could hope to field air forces capable of challenging those of the United States or its Western allies. Were u.s. military forces then to be left invulnerable to swift, devastating counterattack from the sky? Not if a developing country adversary was armed with missiles. Ballistic and cruise missiles offered Third World forces a means of punishing u.s. forces from the air. Unlike advanced fighter aircraft, the technology of combat-effective missiles is within reach of many developing countries. Missiles offered developing countries a way of striking effectively at enemy troop concentrations, logistic nodes, transport lines, bases, and ships or at enemy population centers.

The u.s. propensity to use force against developing countries further encourages developing countries to acquire missiles, in the Chinese view of things. The u.s. resort to air bombardment against developing countries clearly demonstrates the danger: Yugoslavia in 1999, Iran in 1987, Afghanistan in 1998 and again in 2001, Iraq in 1991 and again from 1997 to 2003, and threats of aerial attack against China itself in 1996 when Washington ordered two aircraft carriers to the vicinity of Taiwan. It was u.s. "gunboat diplomacy" that stimulated demand for missiles among developing countries, in China's view. In the words of one Chinese participant in a Track Two Sino-American conference on proliferation, developing countries hope through acquisition of missiles to acquire the capability "to retaliate against their adversaries with their distant strike means with the intention of getting control of the initiative of war."²⁸ A better way for the United States to deal with international problems, in the view of another Chinese analyst, would be to "abandon power politics and settle regional conflicts according to the principles of the u.n. Charter."²⁹ That, of course, would require the United States to abandon hegemony and treat other countries, even weak Third World countries, as equals to be dealt with without use or threatened use of force. The United States also acted as the self-appointed judge and enforcer of the mtcr. The United States claimed the power to determine what was and was not "destabilizing." Chinese missile technology sales to Iran were "destabilizing," while u.s. sale of missile technology to Japan, Singapore, or Taiwan was not.

Beijing saw an even more fundamental flaw in u.s. efforts to restrict proliferation of missile technology: it was a violation of the sovereign right of Third World states to self-defense. A core element of sovereignty is, in Beijing's view, the ability of a state to defend itself and to acquire such means as it deems necessary for that defense. Sovereign states have the right to arm themselves for self-defense as they deem necessary, except insofar as they themselves limit those rights by signing various sorts of treaties. Such determinations regarding a state's self-defense requirements are a core part of the sovereign power of a state. "Interference" in this area by the United States and its Western allies is a manifestation of hegemony. Of course it is in the interest of the United States and its allies to limit the military capabilities of Third World states, especially ones unwilling to accept Western dictates. But this was hegemonist logic, contrary to China's respect for the sovereign power of states to decide what is necessary for national self-defense. In effect, Washington was saying that Tehran did not have the right to do what its government determined was necessary to defend itself. Again the question was, did the United States run the world?

CHINA'S ASSISTANCE TO IRAN'S
POST–IRAQ WAR NAVAL WARFARE CAPABILITIES

Iran's post-1988 military modernization focused on countering the United States. Throughout that period Tehran was deeply apprehensive of possible u.s. military moves against the IRI. Tehran's fear was *not* of a large-scale u.s. invasion and occupation intended to overthrow the IRI, but of possible u.s. disruption of Iran's oil production and shipments in the Persian Gulf. Iranian analysts noted that the u.s. Navy's post–Cold War doctrine emphasized "littoral warfare" in which u.s. forces would confront enemy forces in confined coastal waters, with the anti-u.s. forces expected to use mines, diesel submarines, cruise missiles, and light fast-attack boats.[30] Much of Iran's postwar military modernization was designed to counter u.s. littoral war against Iran.

Beijing assisted Tehran's effort to strengthen its antilittoral warfare capability. While each element of China's assistance to the development of that capability was modest, taken in aggregate they represented a very substantial enhancement of Iranian antilittoral warfare capability. Moreover, while Russia and North Korea were Iran's major partners in the area of ballistic missile development, China played the key role in the naval area.[31]

China's first contribution to Iran's naval warfare capabilities was two hundred HY-2 antiship cruise missiles—known as "Silkworms" in the West—delivered to Iran in 1986. Modeled after a Soviet antiship missile (the Styx) of the 1960s, the Silkworm had a range of 100 kilometers at a speed of 0.9 mach and carried a 450-kilogram warhead. It did not constitute a serious threat to u.s. warships, but it did pose such to the large, slow-moving oil tankers plying the Gulf. China supplied Silkworms to Iran while the "tanker war" between Iran and Iraq was escalating. The range of the Silkworm easily covered the 30-kilometer-wide Strait of Hormuz. Soon after China's initial 1987 sales, Beijing apparently provided Iran with machinery and technology to manufacture Silkworms indigenously.[32]

In the mid-1990s China provided Iran with a new generation of substantially more capable antiship missiles, the C-801 and the C-802, modeled after the French Exocet. The C-801 is powered by a solid-fuel rocket, has a range of 40 kilometers at a speed of 0.9 mach, and can be fired from submarines via torpedo tubes and from airplanes. The C-802 is powered by a more fuel-efficient turbojet and has a range of 120 kilometers. The C-802, first unveiled by the PLA in 1989, weighed less than a quarter and had a diameter of less than half the Silkworm, cruised at a lower altitude than the Silkworm (20–30 meters compared to 30–50 meters), and had a somewhat shorter minimum range than the Silkworm. These characteristics made the C-801 and C-802 considerably more capable and more difficult to defend against than the Silkworm.[33] China agreed to sell 150 C-802s to Tehran, but only 75 were delivered before the deal was frozen under intense u.s. pressure.[34] Iran first tested its C-801s in June 1997, when three were fired from an Iranian F-4 Phantom. Two of the C-801s reportedly hit their targets at a range of 40 kilometers (25 miles).[35] Chinese specifications accorded the C-801 and C-802 85 percent accuracy.[36] In 2002 the China Aerospace Science and Technology Corporation (CASTC) reportedly collaborated with an Iranian firm to produce indigenously the C-801.[37] The C-802 was also soon indigenously produced by Iran and known as the Karus.[38]

China also supplied Iran with launch platforms for the C-802s. In 1995 and 1996 China sold Iran ten Hudong missile-armed fast-attack craft. These 171-ton, steel-hulled, 110-meter-long craft were based on a Soviet missile boat design and were capable of a speed of 35 knots. In themselves they were not particularly potent. Armed as they were with four C-802s, they were considerably more lethal. Acquisition of C-802-armed Hudongs made Iranian forces capable of launching antiship cruise missiles from ships, as well as from shore batteries and from airplanes. During 1996–98 Iran modified its fleet of ten 1970s French-built Kaman class fast-attack boats to carry C-802s, giving Iran a fleet of twenty such missile boats. The upgrading of the Kaman class boats also included installation of China-supplied fire control and air-sea search radars.[39] Iran also continued to expand throughout the early 1990s the number of shore-based launch sites for its Silkworm, C-801, and C-802 antiship cruise missiles. China also supplied Iran, and helped Iran indigenously produce, a variant of the turbojet-powered C-802 configured for delivery by aircraft, surface ships, or submarines. Named the YJ-2, the Iranian version of this missile extended the range to 120 kilometers. Like the C-802 it traveled at 0.9 mach and skimmed the sea at only 5–7 meters during its terminal approach phase.[40] With Chinese help, Iran could attack u.s. ships from multiple vectors, greatly complicating defense.

In the late 1990s CASTC undertook joint development with Iran of a new generation of antiship missiles. In 1998 China unveiled a short-range (15-kilometer) antiship missile, the C-701. Shortly afterward Iran deployed a similar missile named the Noor, apparently a result of joint development efforts with CASTC.[41] In the mid-1990s China reportedly sold a batch of modern torpedoes to Iran. These were used for the first time by the Iranian navy during exercises in the Gulf in April 1996.[42] In 1999 China agreed to help Iran modify a Chinese FL-7 antiship missile, extending its range from 30 to 50 kilometers and rendering it fireable from either helicopters of fast-attack craft.[43]

In 2000 China provided Iran with yet another class of missile-armed fast-attack craft, the China Cat, a small (19 tons displacement) and fast (50 knots compared to the Hudong's 35 knots) vessel with a catamaran hull and four Chinese FL-10 antiship missiles.[44] Iran was expected to acquire ten China Cats.

China may have supplied Iran with two variants of rocket-propelled rising mines: the EM-52 and the EM-55. These are highly sophisticated weapons derived from Soviet-designed naval mines and developed by China circa 1987. Deposited on the seafloor at depths of up to 200 meters, the mines contain a computer that processes acoustic, magnetic, and pressure data under different environmental and operational states specified to the computer before laying the mine. Once triggered, a rocket propels the explosive charge to the target in one of several modes specified by the central processing unit.[45]

China also helped Iran modernize its air defense system. In 1985 China began supplying Iran with HQ-2B surface-to-air missiles (SAM) for air defense. According to SIPRI, 150 of these missiles were delivered during the Iran-Iraq war, and another 200 after. The HQ-2B had been derived from Soviet SA-2 SAM delivered by Moscow to China in the 1950s. They were designed to hit bombers flying at high altitudes and were virtually obsolete by the 1980s, when most air forces favored low-altitude bombing.[46] During the 1990s, however, Iran was able to use the HQ-2B as a base, incorporate modern Russian technology, and produce a more advanced SAM, the Sayed-1(A), which could be used against either low- or high-altitude targets. China also provided Iran with assistance in developing a man-portable, shoulder-fired low-altitude SAM, the Misagh-1—a sophisticated second-generation missile for low-altitude defense.[47] Circa 1996, the China National Electronics Import Export Company began shipping to Iran components for JY-14 radar systems, according to a CIA report. The JY-14 is a sophisticated system that can track up to 100 aircraft and missiles simultaneously and feeds data to computer systems, which sort and pass it on to batteries of interceptor missiles. The JY-14 has the ability to track targets at altitudes of 75,000 feet and at a range of up to 186 miles even when subjected to high electronic clutter or jamming. Construction of several JY-14 radars in Iran began about 1998.[48]

While this list of Chinese assistance to Iran is impressive, it should be kept in mind that Russia with its advanced electronics and missile capabilities, and not China, was Iran's preferred military partner during the post-1988 period. Nonetheless, taken together Beijing's contributions helped Iran accomplish a very considerable enhancement of antinaval capabilities. This military modernization improved Iran's defenses against regional rivals Iraq and Saudi Arabia and against the United Arab Emirates (UAE), with whom Iran was locked in chronic disagreement over ownership of three small islands in the Strait of Hormuz. Iraq, however, was progressively weakened starting with its 1991 defeat followed by u.n. sanctions, and by 1997 Iraq was stumbling toward another confrontation with the United States. Saudi Arabian–Iranian relations were improving. It was also extremely unlikely that Riyadh or the u a e would challenge Iran militarily. As noted earlier, the United States constituted Iran's major security concern and the primary hypothetical opponent targeted by Iran's China-assisted military modernization efforts.

CHINESE ASSISTANCE TO IRAN'S BALLISTIC MISSILE PROGRAMS

When the Iraq-Iran war began in 1980, Iran had no surface-to-surface missiles (s s m). As that war reached a stalemate by 1983 and evolved into a war of attrition with both sides trying to wear down the other, missiles became increasingly important. Unfortunately for Iran, Iraq had a substantial lead in this area. Iran adopted a two-track solution to its missile deficiency. First, it purchased s s m from Libya, Syria, North Korea, and probably the Soviet Union. Second, it began developing an indigenous production capacity for various sorts of missiles. In this latter area, China and North Korea became Iran's key partners.[49] Tehran established a division of labor in its missile cooperation with North Korea and China. In its quest for all-round missile capability, Tehran wanted to master both liquid-fuel and solid-fuel technologies. North Korea met Iran's needs in the liquid-fuel area, while China supplied Iran's needs regarding solid fuel rockets — a technology that tended to be more accurate, fast firing, reliable, and safer for the launch crew. China's assistance with missile development and manufacture was apparently agreed to during Rafsanjani's June 1985 visit to Beijing.[50]

Regarding the relation between Beijing and Pyongyang in their common support for Iranian missile development efforts, exceedingly little is known. Presumably it was Tehran that worked out the division of labor between those two countries and that brought in one or the other, or some third country, as Iranian needs dictated. Yet Beijing facilitated North Korea's missile cooperation with Iran. According to u.s. intelligence reports, China repeatedly allowed Iranian cargo planes bound for North Korea to transit Chinese airspace to travel to North Korea to pick up missiles and/or missile components.[51] In 1983 Iran reportedly agreed to contribute funding to North Korea's Scud-B reverse-engineering effort.[52] The Scud-B that had become operational with Soviet forces in 1967 was a single-stage, liquid-fuel rocket with a 300-kilometer range. In late October 1983 i r i prime minister Ruhollah Musavi and defense minister Mohammad Salim held talks in Pyongyang about long-term

Iranian financial support for the North Korean Scud-B program. Agreement was reached with Iranian financing securing Tehran an option of purchasing production models when available.[53] During the course of the war with Iraq, Iran purchased two to three hundred North Korean Scud-B. By the late 1990s Iran would domestically produce, with North Korean and Chinese assistance, an advanced version of the Scud-B with a range of 500 kilometers.[54] China provided engineering support for North Korea's Iran-supported Scud-B development effort—supplying technical training for North Korean personnel in engine design and production, air frame design, and metallurgy, as well as supplying high-quality machine tools for precision manufacture of components.[55]

China's direct ballistic missile assistance to Iran during the 1980s war focused initially on unguided, mid- and short-range, heavy artillery rockets needed for immediate use against Iraqi forces. China helped Iran copy and indigenously produce the Chinese Type-83 artillery rocket. That Chinese-assisted reverse-engineering effort apparently began in 1985 as part of the agreements reached during Rafsanjani's visit.[56] By 1987 that effort provided Iran with a 320-millimeter rocket with a range of 45 kilometers and a warhead of 70 kilograms and named the *Oghab* ("eagle" in Farsi).[57] China also provided Iran with machinery, technology, and technical expertise to manufacture the Oghab indigenously. An Iranian Oghab factory went into operation at Seman, 175 kilometers east of Tehran, in 1987 with an output of up to one thousand of the rockets per year. By December 1986 Iranian forces began using the Oghab on the battlefield against Iraqi forces. A more accurate version of the Oghab named the Fajr 3 went into production in Iran in late 1989.[58]

China also assisted Iran in developing and manufacturing another class of solid-fuel, unguided, heavy artillery rockets—the Nazeat. These rockets were of 356–450 millimeters, with ranges from 80 to 120 kilometers. They went into production in early 1988 at a factory established by North Korea at Esfahan. In March of the same year Nazeat missiles were first fired at Iraqi cities. China also constructed for Iran facilities to manufacture solid propellants, including the key ingredient ammonium perchlorate. Ability to produce indigenously this critical ingredient greatly reduced Iran's vulnerability to sanctions.[59] In 1989 Iran purchased two hundred HQ-2J (CSS-8) missiles from China. These were originally antiaircraft missiles, but had been modified for ground attack. The range was limited to 150 kilometers and the warhead was relatively small; however, the missile was cheap and this purchase allowed Iran to replenish its SSM inventory after depletion during the "war of the cities" that characterized the final stage of the Iran-Iraq war. The missile could also serve as a terror weapon against cities in Iraq or the Gulf states. HQ-2J were assembled in Iran, with China providing components plus production equipment and machinery.[60]

With the end of the war, Sino-Iranian missile cooperation entered a new stage. During 1988 China reportedly agreed to provide Iran with technology required to produce SSM comparable to Iraq's Al Hussein (with a 600-kilometer range) and Al Abbas (with a 900-kilometer range) missiles. (China's M-9 has a range of 600 kilometers with a 500-kilogram warhead—a Category I missile under the MTCR.) The 1988 agreement reportedly included Chinese training of Iranian engineers and technicians and provision of PRC technical advisors. China also agreed to provide equipment and technical assistance in developing the infrastructure to design, test, and manufacture such missiles. By 1989 China was reportedly assisting Iran in establishing a missile factory at Shahroud, in northeastern Iran, to produce an 800-kilometer SSM. China also reportedly assisted in the construction of a missile test facility and launch range near Seman.[61]

During the 1990 talks between COSTIND deputy director Jiang Hua and Defense Minister Ali Akbar Torkan, China apparently agreed to help Iran set up production lines for M-11s and M-9s at the Esfahan missile factory.[62] The M-11 has a range of 280 kilometers, thereby falling just short of the 300-kilometer Category I threshold. Both missiles were solid-fuel and had been explicitly designed by the PLA for export. The M-11 was designed as a solid-fuel replacement for the Scud-B and could be fired from standard Scud-B launch vehicles, but was superior to the liquid-fuel Scud in that it was quicker, easier, and safer to fire. Iran and Syria had reportedly contributed financially to China's development of the M-9 and had even made a deposit on purchase of M-9s when they became available.[63] China apparently reneged on any commitment to sell whole M-9s to Middle Eastern countries, but moved ahead with assisting Iran (but apparently not Syria) with indigenous development and production capability for missiles closely comparable to the M-9. China apparently did not transfer whole M-11 missiles to Iran as it did to Pakistan in 1992. A spokesman for the Iranian embassy in Beijing stated in September 1992 that China was "ready to dispatch" five hundred M-11s to Iran.[64] Such a transfer apparently did not occur because of U.S. pressure.[65] Israeli intelligence reported Iranian agreement with China to fund development of a new missile based on the M-9, but with more advanced guidance systems. Iran was to assemble the missile indigenously.[66]

During his July 1991 visit to Iran, Premier Li Peng traveled to Esfahan and reportedly visited several complexes where Chinese experts were working, along with Iranians and North Koreans, to produce various sorts of missiles.[67] In 1994–95 the CIA determined that China had delivered to Iran dozens, perhaps hundreds, of missile guidance systems and computerized tools for missile production. This equipment and technology reportedly allowed Iran to increase the accuracy of its North Korean Scud missiles and facilitated development of an indigenous missile production capacity.[68]

In the early 1990s Iran initiated development of a new series of ballistic missiles, the Zelzal ("earthquake"). Solid-fuel and resembling Chinese missiles, the Zelzal-1 had a range of 100–150 kilometers and the Zelzal-2 a range of 350–400 kilometers. Technology for the new missile came from Russia, China, North Korea, and Germany, with Chinese experts providing assistance with solid-fuel technology and guidance.[69] China also secretly delivered to Iran in the early 1990s between twenty and ninety M-7 missiles, a 160-kilometer range, combined liquid-fuel and solid-fuel ssm with antiship capability.[70]

A new round of missile cooperation began in August 1996 when Iran's defense minister Mohammad Firouzandeh, along with a number of other high-ranking officers of the Revolutionary Guards ground forces, visited Beijing for discussions with Defense Minister Chi Haotian. According to press reports in Tehran, the two sides concluded a protocol for the purchase of $4.5 billion worth of weapons and military technology over three years. Of that package, $1.5 billion was for ballistic missiles, missile production technology, electronics production equipment, and military training. C-802 antiship cruise missiles, HQ-2 SA missiles, and multiple rocket launchers, gyroscopes, accelerometers, and equipment to build and test missile guidance systems were part of the package.[71] China reportedly agreed under the protocol signed by Firouzandeh and Chi to assist Iran in establishing factories to produce missiles, helicopters, and artillery, as well as to provide Iran with aircraft, missiles and missile launchers, armored vehicles, and trucks.[72] The cia reported that during the second half of 1996 China was providing a "tremendous variety of assistance to Iran and Pakistan's ballistic missile programs."[73]

In May 1997 Iranian missile technicians traveled to China to observe a ground test of a 450-millimeter-diameter rocket motor to be used in yet another new short-range solid-fuel rocket, the NP-110, being developed jointly by Iran and China, according to u.s. intelligence reports. The joint development effort also reportedly involved Chinese supply of X-ray equipment for examining missile castings and solid-fuel propellants. Acquisition of this X-ray technology marked a significant advance in Iran's ability to produce and use solid-fuel rockets.[74] A few years later China reportedly set up a factory in Iran to manufacture the NP-110 engine.[75] By the end of the 1990s China was training ten Iranian scientists in inertial guidance techniques and providing Iran with specialty steel for missile fabrication.[76]

China also supported Iran's effort to produce indigenously a new single-stage missile with an 800–1,240-kilometer range, the Shahab-3. (*Shahab* is Farsi for "meteor.") While the Shahab was based on North Korean liquid-fuel technology and incorporated mainly Russian and North Korean technology, China apparently provided guidance and control technology, plus specialty steel for the missile.[77] In 1997 China's Great Wall Industrial Corporation—a firm specializing in satellite launches—provided the entire telemetry and missile flight-testing infrastructure to support the Shahab program.[78] More than one hundred Chinese and North Korean rocket specialists were reportedly working in Iran on development of the Shahab rockets in the late 1990s.[79] In July 1998 Iran conducted an initial test of the Shahab-3. Final tests of the Shahab-3 were conducted in July 2003, and the weapon was formally turned over to Iranian armed forces. In May 2002 five Chinese companies were sanctioned by the United States for supplying technology for the Shahab-3. The 930-kilometer range of the Shahab-3 brought Israel and u.s. bases in Turkey within range of Iranian missiles

A cia report reviewing the second half of 2003 stated that Chinese entities continued to help Iran "move toward its goal of becoming self-sufficient in the production of ballistic missiles" as well as providing Iran with dual-use missile-related items, raw materials, and assistance.[80] In November 2003 Tehran announced that it was developing booster rockets for use with the Shahab-3 that would enable Iran to launch an earth satellite. In January 2004 Iran's defense minister Ali Shamkhani announced Iran would become the first Islamic country to launch a satellite into space by mid-2005 using "its own indigenous launch system."[81] More than a decade before, in December 1988, China had agreed to sell Iran satellite and communications technology, and an agreement to that effect was finalized during Li Peng's July 1991 visit.[82] In 1998 Iran had joined a China-led consortium including Mongolia, Pakistan, South Korea, and Pakistan to undertake joint manufacture of multipurpose satellites.[83]

CHINA AND IRAN'S CHEMICAL WARFARE CAPABILITIES

During the mid-1990s China began assisting Iran develop dual-use chemical facilities. China has long experience with chemical warfare (cw—an abbreviation standing for both "chemical weapons" and "chemical warfare"). In spite of denials, it is virtually certain that China developed in the 1950s and maintains today strong chemical warfare capabilities for self-defense.[84]

The Geneva Protocol of 1929 banned the use of chemical weapons in war, but not their production and stockpiling. China signed the Geneva Protocol on chemical weapons in 1929, and the prc reaffirmed China's commitment in 1952. After joining the U.N. Committee on Disarmament in 1980, China began participating in negotiations of the Chemical Weapons Convention (CWC) intended to ban production and stockpiling of chemical weapons. During CWC negotiations, and inspired by its skeptical view toward disarmament generally, China was concerned that the existing great powers would use the CWC to consolidate military advantages over Third World countries. China deemed especially pernicious Western countries' demand for challenge inspections. Such inspections would allow states to demand inspection of facilities suspected of producing or stockpiling chemical warfare agents—whether or not those facilities had been declared to the CWC monitoring authority. China viewed such an inspection regime as overly intrusive and constituting a violation of the sovereignty of suspect (and probably Third World) countries. China felt that control over information was especially important for weak countries and that Western powers could use these intrusive inspections to gain access to military or commercial secrets. In the words of one authoritative Chinese analyst:

> During the [CWC] negotiations, the Western developed countries, viewing challenge inspections as a means to better enable them to be the world's policeman, actively strengthened the power of the challenge inspections and limited the rights of the inspected state. They tried to establish a challenge inspection mechanism, taking liberties with the rights of the Convention, and used it to do as they pleased in terms of initiating challenge inspections. China conducted a resolute boycott against this. We considered that making appropriate and effective challenge inspections was necessary for the Convention to have teeth, but they ought not to harm the national security interest of the state parties by turning them into a means by which the great powers could wantonly infringe on the sovereignty of other nations.[85]

To ameliorate what it deemed the unfair aspect of challenge inspections, Beijing introduced and secured incorporation into the CWC of a "balance mechanism," whereby a challenge inspection could be denied, while allowing sanctions to be employed against countries that abused this right of denial. When the completed CWC was opened for signature in January 1993, China quickly signed it and ratified it in December 1996. Yet in China's view the CWC was deeply flawed. While it reflected a developing trend toward peace, it was also a product of U.S. efforts to uphold the U.S. lead in the area of chemical warfare. The CWC was "imbalanced," having a miniscule controlling effect on the United States, while giving the Western countries a legal mechanism for intervening in the internal affairs of Third World countries.

Iran, for its part, signed the CWC in January 1993, the same month as China. Several years later Iran admitted that during the later stages of the war with Iraq and in response to Iraq's widespread use of chemical weapons against Iranian forces, Iran had developed chemical warfare agents. According to Anthony Cordesman, by the end of the Iran-Iraq war, Iran was producing mustard and nerve gas and loading those agents into special artillery shells.[86] With the end of the Iraq war, Tehran unilaterally terminated its CW programs—according to Tehran. United States intelligence believed, however, that Iran had stockpiled large quantities of CW agents and was seeking to acquire a self-sufficient indigenous capability to produce CW materials.[87] China was Iran's major partner in this CW effort, or so Western intelligence agencies believed.

The unbalanced and discriminatory nature of the Western-run CWC inspection regime was exemplified in the Yinhe ("Galaxy") incident that occurred in July 1993, only several months after China signed—but also several months before it ratified—the CWC. The Yinhe incident had a deep impact on Chinese views of U.S. policies toward China. It is also an incident that underlined for Beijing what China deemed the unreasonable, arrogant, and hegemonistic way in which Washington tried to regulate Sino-Iranian ties. The Yinhe incident became enshrined in the Chinese nationalist narrative of U.S. containment, bullying, and efforts to dominate China. It remains a very emotional issue in China, and it could well continue to influence China's determination to continue chemical cooperation with Iran even in the face of great U.S. displeasure.[88]

The Yinhe was a Chinese owned ship that in July 1993 took on cargo in Dalian. It left that port headed for Bandar Abbas. United States intelligence received highly detailed information indicating that the loading registries for the Yinhe contained thiodiglycol and thionyl chloride, chemicals that can be used to make mustard and nerve gas.[89] Assuming the loading manifests signified the cargo was actually loaded—an assumption that in retrospect proved mistaken—U.S. officials determined that the Yinhe was carrying forbidden chemical warfare agents to Iran. On July 23 the U.S. embassy in Beijing told the MFA that the Yinhe was carrying the two chemicals for Iran and asked the Chinese government to halt the delivery. Otherwise, China would face sanctions under U.S. law. After several further representations to the MFA, the United States demanded that China either order the Yinhe to return to Dalian or allow Americans to board and inspect the ship. Meanwhile U.S. military aircraft and ships had begun trailing and photographing the Yinhe.[90]

An MFA statement on the episode pointed out that the Convention on Chemical Weapons had not yet taken effect and would not take effect until at least 1995. Nor had the United States or China yet ratified the CWC. Moreover, "No international organization has ever empowered the u.s. to conduct unilateral inspection of other countries," the MFA statement said. "People cannot help wondering what legal basis the u.s. has got to justify its actions," it continued. "If such behavior of a self-styled 'world cop' is to be condoned, can there still be justice, sovereign equality and normal state-to-state relations in the world?" u.s. actions "have seriously infringed upon China's sovereignty and its right to freedom of navigation in international waters," acts constituting "blatant contempt of the norms governing international relations."[91]

In spite of the fact that China was under no valid legal obligation not to export the two chemicals, the MFA statement said, China's government had issued as early as 1990 "clear-cut orders against their export" to relevant regions.[92] Chinese authorities had carried out an investigation of the matter, MFA officials said, and found that the two chemicals were not, in fact, aboard the Yinhe. President Jiang Zemin gave a face-to-face assurance to this effect to u.s. ambassador Stapleton Roy. For Roy that was good enough. He felt it unlikely the Chinese president would put his credibility on the line in this fashion if he were not confident he would not be embarrassed. Washington did not accept Roy's analysis, but warned the Yinhe against entering an Iranian port, and continued to demand that the vessel submit to inspection. For some twenty days the Yinhe rode at anchor outside the Strait of Hormuz, running low of drinking water and food. Eventually China agreed to inspection by Saudi Arabian inspectors. The Yinhe docked at the Saudi port of Ad Dammam, where Saudi inspectors, watched closely by American and Chinese representatives, went through its entire cargo. The suspect chemicals were not found. United States inspectors had to sign, together with Chinese and Saudi inspectors, a statement declaring the vessel void of banned chemicals. Throughout the incident u.s. media had asserted that China was involved in proliferation.

Chinese officials and public opinion were outraged by the Yinhe episode. "This is a show of hegemonism and power politics pure and simple," said the MFA statement. Beijing demanded a public apology from the United States, compensation for financial losses, and a commitment from the United States "to strict compliance with international laws and norms governing international relations in future handling of its relations with other states."[93] None of these was forthcoming.

As noted earlier, the Yinhe incident entered the anti-American nationalist narrative of China. From the Chinese perspective, it was as though the Americans believed they could do whatever they felt best and order other nations to comply—or face American punishment. International law did not matter to the Americans, or at least that law was easily overridden by U.S. policy and domestic legislation. This was the sort of arrogance at the core of hegemonism, most Chinese, guided by China's media, concluded. There is no direct evidence linking the Yinhe episode to subsequent Chinese support for Iran's chemical capabilities. But at least at a purely emotional level, such a connection is virtually certain. Chinese cooperation with Iran was payback for the Yinhe incident and a practical demonstration to the Americans that they did not rule the world.

By the second half of the 1990s, U.S. and other Western intelligence agencies began to detect fairly frequent episodes of Chinese support for Iranian dual-use chemical capabilities. In February 1995, after a nearly two-year probe by Hong Kong authorities and the United States, the Hong Kong government dissolved three companies involved in shipment from China to Iran of precursor chemicals for mustard gas and sarin. All three companies had been set up by an Australian man, apparently as cover for such transactions. The day after Hong Kong's move, the U.S. State Department banned the three Hong Kong firms from doing business in the United States and put them on a watch list for proliferation of chemical weapons. The United States did not make a determination that China's government or Chinese enterprises had committed a sanctionable offense in connection with these incidents. An MFA spokesman rejected as "utterly irresponsible" U.S. charges that China had exported chemical weapons to Iran. "China has never exported any missile components or chemical weapons to Iran," the spokesman stressed. He added that instead of making "unwarranted accusations against China" regarding proliferation, the United States should take "concrete and effective measures to remove the grave aftermath and consequences" caused by Taiwan's seated president Lee Teng-hui's recent visit to the United States.[94] The link between U.S. relations with Taiwan and China's relations with Iran is important and will be discussed in the next chapter.

Throughout 1995 U.S. intelligence monitored a "steady flow" of Chinese chemical-related equipment to Iran where it was installed in factories ostensibly to produce chemicals for industrial or commercial use. Washington believed that these factories had at least a latent military purpose. Tehran's objective, Washington suspected, was to develop the capability to produce all components necessary for chemical warfare, as well as the indigenous capability to manufacture the equipment necessary to turn those ingredients into finished chemical weapons. Early in 1996 U.S. intelligence determined that China was providing Iran with several virtually complete factories that could be used to produce CW agents. The factories were ostensibly meant to produce industrial chemicals, but again U.S. officials believed the factories had a covert CW use. The transfer of Chinese technology to Iran was helping what one U.S. official described as "the most active chemical weapons program" in the Third World.[95] In testimony to Congress in November 1995, deputy assistant secretary of defense Bruce Reidel said that Chinese companies were helping Iran develop chemical weapons. Iran promptly denied the charges. Under no circumstances would it "go after chemical weapons," an Iranian foreign ministry official said.[96]

In late 1996 Chinese entities were believed to have supplied Iran with up to four hundred tons of nerve, riot-control, and tear gas precursor chemicals. Early the next year a shipment of forty thousand barrels of chemicals used for CW decontamination was disclosed by U.S. intelligence. Chinese firms also sold glass-lined vessels for use in production of CW agents. In June 1997, U.S. agencies announced that Iran had completed the construction, with Chinese assistance, of a factory to manufacture indigenously these glass-lined vessels. In May 1997 Washington for the first time invoked sanctions against PRC firms for assistance to Iran's CW efforts. Seven PRC and one Hong Kong firms were sanctioned for "knowingly and materially" contributing to Iran's CW programs. Many of the transfers of China-made CW-related items were conducted by front companies set up in Hong Kong.[97] Early in 1998 it was reported that a Chinese chemical company had completed construction of a new large production facility at Qazvin, on the outskirts of Tehran, and which was capable of producing nerve gas. In April Iran's Defense Industry Organization reportedly took delivery of five hundred tons of materials to be used as input for the plant—and banned under the CWC. China's SinoChem was the supplier of the feedstock. To express Iran's thanks for Chinese assistance, a high-level Chinese military delegation was invited to tour a number of Iran's top-secret military installations.[98] Assistance continued into the 2000s. The CIA report to Congress for the second half of 2003 stated that "evidence" indicated Chinese firms continued to supply to Iran dual-use "CW related production equipment and technology."[99]

CHINA'S CONTINUING POLICY OF PLAUSIBLE DENIAL

China continued into the postwar period the policy of denial it developed early in the Iran-Iraq war. In 1992, shortly after the January 1990 talks between Jiang Hua and Ali Akbar Torkan providing for cooperation in setting up missile production lines in Esfahan, a foreign ministry spokesman denied as "a totally groundless and fabricated allegation" press reports that China was selling intermediate-range ballistic missile production technology to Iran.[100] In July 1995 while Chinese engineers were assisting Iran develop its Zelzal class of missiles and providing solid-fuel and guidance technology for that effort, and while China was providing C-801 and C-802 cruise missiles plus production facilities to Iran, a foreign ministry denounced as "utterly irresponsible" u.s. government charges that China had exported missile technology to Iran.[101] Yet again in 2000, while Chinese companies were supplying technology for Iran's Shahab-3 missile, a foreign ministry spokesman denounced as "totally unfounded" u.s. imposition of sanctions for the "sale of missiles" to Iran.[102] As u.s. sanctions over China's chemical assistance to Iran became more frequent during the George W. Bush administration, a foreign ministry statement condemned those sanctions as "unreasonable." "China does not export chemicals, technology, or equipment used to make chemical weapons," the statement said.[103]

Here the scholar striving for objectivity faces a dilemma. Should he credit Beijing's denials or the contrary assertions of u.s. government agencies? In the case of missiles, there seem to be three reasons for crediting u.s. government assertions over prc denials. First, u.s. official assertions are substantiated by reports from a very wide range of independent journalists working for British, Arab, and Hong Kong publications—the publications cited in the endnotes attached to the paragraphs above. Second, multiple, independent expert analysts (Swedish, British, and Israeli) of weapons systems have compared the characteristics of Iran's new missiles to those of China's and found Chinese parentage probable. Third, assumption of Chinese transfers makes intelligible subsequent years of hard bargaining between Washington and Beijing over this issue (a matter examined in the next chapter). Would China have resisted tenaciously u.s. demands and then, after years of u.s. pressure, taken moves addressing u.s. concerns if there had been no basis for those concerns? Evidence regarding the commercial modalities of Chinese assistance to Iran's missile programs is currently unavailable, and it is possible that reliance on third parties could render China's denials technically correct—as during the Iran-Iraq war. Be that as it may, it seems likely that in the missile area, Beijing has followed a policy of plausible denial similar to that used during the Iran-Iraq war.

It is also is important to note that China apparently did not transfer whole missiles to Iran after the secret M-7 transfers in the early 1990s. Chinese assistance was rather in the form of scientific and engineering know-how, industrial technology, and capital goods. As shown in the next chapter, China did not recognize the mtcr annex listing sensitive dual-use technology. In other words, China felt it was under no obligation not to export general industrial capital goods and technology to Iran merely because Washington felt it might be used to produce missiles. In the area of chemical warfare, the situation seems similar. Here much (and perhaps all) of what China has transferred seems to have been dual-use industrial facilities—facilities that could be used to produce pesticides, herbicides, industrial chemicals, or chemical weapons agents. Tehran has probably given assurances that these facilities are for purely civilian, nonmilitary use, and Beijing has probably accepted those assurances at face value.

Again one can only infer the rationale for China's policies of plausible denial. My sense is that the main reason has to do with Beijing's effort to manage the contradiction between fostering a meaningful relation with Iran on the one hand, and minimizing friction in Beijing's relation with Washington, the Arab countries, and Israel on the other. Beijing was able to assist Tehran in an area Tehran deemed important and thus garner influence, while doing this in a fashion that confused and divided the United States and thus mitigated U.S. pressure. Strengthening Iran's military also moved the world in a multipolar direction, while denying this assistance obfuscated that fact and diminished adverse U.S. reaction.

FRICTIONS IN THE SINO-IRANIAN ARMS SUPPLY RELATION

As might be expected in any robust relationship, there were frictions in the Sino-Iranian arms supply relation. The relatively low technological level of Chinese weapons was acceptable to Tehran during the war with Iraq when neither Western nor Soviet suppliers were willing to sell to Iran. After the end of the war, however, the Soviet Union, and after 1991 Russia, entered the picture and was quite willing to supply Iranian needs. As Iranian military leaders began comparing Chinese and Russian equipment, they recognized the inferiority of Chinese items. "We just don't like Chinese armaments anymore," a senior Iranian official told one source, who followed the observation with a suggestion that Russia would be a better supplier for Iran.[104]

China had the advantage of being willing to take Iranian oil in exchange for its weapons and defense industrial capital goods. This was difficult for Russia, which had itself become a major oil exporter and had to find customers for its own oil. China, however, was increasingly confronting the need to import ever-larger quantities of petroleum and was more than happy to swap Iranian oil for whatever Chinese goods Iran was willing to take. Bargaining must have been hard in the various Sino-Iranian deals, with each side seeking to maximize its own advantage. The Iranian side sought to push as low as possible prices on goods it imported, while Chinese suppliers resisted unprofitable prices.[105] Iranian representatives probably pleaded for lower Chinese prices and more generous financial underwriting by the Chinese government on grounds of antihegemonist solidarity. This must have met with the reply that Chinese firms now operated on the basis of profit-making and markets, that cooperation needed to be mutually beneficial, and that only limited financial support was available from China's government agencies. One suspects that below the rhetoric of Third World solidarity there lay difficult and tough bargaining. The shift from sale of end-use weapons to sale of munitions-related capital goods may have been an outcome, at least partially, of these factors. Creation of an indigenous Iranian defense industry moved Iranian calculations of interests from the narrower sphere of quality of weapons to a broader sphere of industrialization and job creation. Joint weapons development efforts were probably a response to Iranian dissatisfaction with the quality of Chinese weapons. Transfer of engineering and manufacturing capabilities created the basis for *future*, indigenous Iranian effort.

OBJECTIVES OF CHINA'S ASSISTANCE
TO IRANIAN MILITARY DEVELOPMENT

There is abundant evidence substantiating a commercial explanation of China's arms sales to various countries, including Iran. China's politically well-connected military industrial firms profited handsomely from such sales, and this profit served various individual, institutional, and national interests. Earning money is certainly part of the explanation of China's long and robust support for Iran's military development efforts. But it is not the entire explanation. Given nearly constant u.s. (and Israeli) pressure on China over its arms cooperation with Iran (yet again, a topic discussed in the next chapter), periodic top-level decisions to continue arms sales are certain. Noncommercial considerations must have figured prominently in these deliberations about whether purely commercial gains should be set aside for the sake of smoothing u.s.-prc relations.

Support for Iran's military development effort was advantageous to China's own military modernization drive. The role of arms exports in financing China's military research and development efforts was mentioned earlier. Direct financial contributions to certain of those efforts by countries such as Iran and Syria were probably minor, but still count as inputs to China's military modernization effort. So too did the occasional transfer of military technology from Iran to China.

Building with Iran a multidimensional, cooperative partnership tested by adversity and founded on mutual understanding, trust, and common interests was another high-ranking Chinese objective underlying its military cooperation with Iran. Iran was a major regional power and it was in China's interests to gain influence with the power. Tehran placed great emphasis on military development, and helping Tehran realize its goals in that area, in spite of u.s. pressure and threats, earned Beijing considerable political capital in Tehran. United States pressure was not without some influence on China's military relation with Iran. But in spite of American pressure, Beijing persisted at least long enough to give Iran self-reliant indigenous nuclear, missile, and cw capabilities. With several significant exceptions, Beijing did not capitulate to u.s. objections regarding China's transfer of "advanced conventional weapons" to Iran. And even when China capitulated to u.s. pressure, as in the nuclear, cruise missile, and Category I ballistic missile areas, it did so only after protracted resistance, and then found other areas in which to be helpful to Tehran. Repeated Chinese pledges to Washington regarding nonassistance to Iran in the missile area did not, in fact, mean the end of such assistance. By circumventing in various ways u.s. pressure, Beijing demonstrated to Tehran its reliability as a military partner; it demonstrated that China was willing and able to help Iran meet major objectives even when those objectives made unhappy the arrogant u.s. superpower. The Sino-Iranian military relation was thus tested by adversity and emerged stronger from the forge.

China's assistance to IRI military modernization also rested on the belief that a militarily strong Iran served China's interests by constraining the United States. Following the revolution in the international system in 1989–91, China's leaders concluded that u.s. hegemony—no longer deadlocked with the Soviet Union—was now on a rampant offensive and constituted the most serious threat to China's security. Chinese analysts developed a long litany of u.s. moves in a purported drive for global domination: attempts to subvert CCP rule of China via "human rights," thereby replicating in the PRC the u.s. success in disintegrating the USSR; maintaining NATO when it was no longer necessary and admitting the new ex-socialist states of Eastern Europe into the Western military bloc (a development Chinese analysts styled "the Eastern expansion of NATO"); encouragement of Japan to play a larger role in Asia and the world; encouragement of Taiwanese "independence" and separation from China; development of antimissile defenses designed to nullify China's nuclear retaliatory capability; forging a strategic and military partnership with India; and drawing Central Asia into the u.s. military system. In the Chinese view of things, the Middle East constituted a crucial arena of the post–Cold War u.s. hegemonist offensive. The aim of u.s. policy in that region was to bring its rich energy resources under u.s. control as a stepping-stone to global domination. This, Beijing believed, was the true rationale behind the 1991 war against Iraq and the "dual containment" of Iraq and Iran. Washington was determined either to compel those regimes to bend to u.s. will or to replace them with more pliant regimes. Were this achieved and the energy resources of the entire Persian Gulf brought under secure u.s. control, the u.s. dream of global domination would come closer to realization. United States global domination was antithetical to China's interests since the closer the United States moved toward that goal, the greater would be u.s. pressure on the PRC.

Beijing also believed that Washington would fail to achieve its dream of global hegemony. The prime cause of this failure would be, according to Beijing's analysis, the desires of the world's people for freedom from foreign, American domination. In the Middle East, for example, Iran's government and people were determined to resist u.s. demands, threats, and bullying. It was in China's interests that this resistance succeed.

China's support for Iran's antihegemony struggle had to be conducted in such a way as not to undermine China's relation with the United States. China's overriding foreign policy interest was in ensuring that the United States continued benevolent, friendly policies toward China's post-1978 economic development drive. There was a contradiction between this objective and China's support for Iran's antihegemony struggle, and this contradiction had to be handled correctly. When absolutely necessary, the secondary goal of moving the world toward multipolarity by supporting Iran's antihegemony resistance would be subordinated to the primary goal of protecting the Sino-u.s. relationship. Within that framework, China would do what it could to support Iran. In fact, this policy seems to have been fairly successful. As demonstrated earlier, China's support for Iran's nuclear and military modernization programs was thick, significant, and long lasting. While that support generated chronic friction in China's relations with the United States, it did not lead to collapse of that vital relationship. Washington, whatever its displeasure toward Beijing's cooperation with Iran, continued its policy of support for China's modernization drive.

Chinese policy toward Iran is predicated on strengthening the military capabilities of the IRI. Washington does not like that policy or its result, but American desires do not govern Chinese policy. China will cooperate with Iran, even if Washington does not like it. If mid-range power Third World countries such as Iran cannot defend themselves against u.s. bullying, intervention, and pressure, then Washington will come much closer to global domination. In such a situation China would be much more isolated in its resistance to American pressure and hostility. Nor will Beijing bow to American use of nonproliferation regimes to emasculate states like Iran. While Beijing will obey the letter of its obligations under these regimes, it will not accept arbitrary, unilateral u.s. interpretations of those obligations.

Another significant if still potential advantage to China of arming Iran to confront the United States is that the PLA may have the opportunity to test its weapons on the battlefield against u.s. military forces. Intuition suggests that this is a high-order goal in the case of assistance to Iran's anti-naval warfare capabilities. By providing Iran with China's most advanced anti-ship systems, and working out with Iranian military people how best to employ those systems, and by watching closely and probably with Iranian assistance in the event of a u.s.-Iranian clash, the PLA will be in a position to learn a good deal about how to prosecute a war against u.s. naval and air forces. Preparing for a war with the United States over Taiwan has been a key objective of China's military modernization since the early 1990s. In such an eventuality China's situation will in key aspects resemble Iran's; both will need to strike effectively at u.s. warships conducting littoral operations from some distance offshore. By observing the performance of China's weapons in Iranian hands, and by noting what does and does not work, the PLA will become significantly more effective should it someday be ordered by China's leaders to bring Taiwan under Beijing's control.

There is another implicit link between Taiwan and China's military relation with Iran. That relationship gives Beijing leverage with Washington over Taiwan. If the United States does not like China's relations with Iran, Washington will have to pay heftily to end that cooperation. Satisfaction of Chinese demands regarding Taiwan would probably be the coin of the realm.

8 / China-Iran Cooperation and the United States

D uring the 1970s Chinese and u.s. interests toward Iran converged. Both countries looked on Iran as a friendly power and sought to bolster it as a bulwark against Soviet influence. The Iranian revolution of 1979 ended that felicitous congruence of Chinese and u.s. interests. Henceforth, Chinese efforts to strengthen Iran clashed frequently with u.s. policy. This conflict was most acute in areas where Sino-Iranian cooperation threatened to diminish the military advantages the United States enjoyed vis-à-vis Iran and/or increase Iran's ability to threaten the sea-lanes and/or oil-supplying states of the Persian Gulf. This conflict between Beijing and Washington was manifest in the areas of nuclear energy, guided and ballistic missiles, and dual-use goods relevant to production of chemical or advanced conventional weapons. The conflict between Beijing and Washington in this area would intensify for a decade, becoming quite acute by the mid-1990s. Eventually China would subordinate its cooperation with Iran to its overriding interest in comity with the United States. Beijing refused, however, to abandon its quest for influence with Tehran and resisted u.s. efforts to push China in that direction. Beijing managed its 1997 partial disengagement from Iran adroitly, minimizing the damage to Sino-Iranian relations. Nonetheless, Beijing paid a price in terms of its reputation and influence in Tehran.

The new leadership that took control of China in 1978 was dedicated to a sustained drive for economic development to raise the Chinese people out of poverty and make China strong by drawing on the resources of the world economy. Deng Xiaoping recognized that success in this drive would depend on the goodwill of the United States, the power that for better or worse dominated that global economy. This dependence posed the danger, however, that Washington would use it to compel China to acquiesce to u.s. policies injurious to China's interests. The most egregious u.s. challenges in this regard involved u.s. human rights demands, which China's rulers perceived as undermining the ccp's control over Chinese society, and u.s. relations with Taiwan. It was these two areas that u.s. moves produced the deepest Sino-u.s. conflicts. The issue relevant to this study, however, is China's ties with Iran. United States pressure on China to draw back from cooperation with Iran in various areas was a secondary but significant source of conflict in the Sino-American relationship after 1979. Washington attempted to use China's dependence on u.s. support for China's modernization drive to compel Beijing to abandon elements of Chinese-Iranian cooperation that Washington deemed especially objectionable. Senator Alphonse D'Amato, one of the strongest congressional advocates of sanctions against Iran during the 1990s, explained China's situation in regard to Iran in this way: "China cannot have cooperation with the United States while it sells materials used for making chemical weapons to Iran, and China could lose its trade surpluses with the United States that way. You cannot trade with u.s. and . . . build a relationship of mutual respect, and then because [you're] going to receive a half a billion dollars in hard currency sell weapon's technology to Iran."[1]

Beijing resisted and evaded u.s. pressure over Iran while attempting to use China's ties with Iran as leverage on Washington's Taiwan policy. Beijing viewed u.s. efforts to restrict China's cooperation with Iran as American hegemony. Washington's efforts to restrict the military capabilities of Iran were nothing less than part of Washington's effort to achieve world domination. It might be in the interests of u.s. hegemony to keep Iran militarily weak, but that was not China's interest. China's interests required that developing countries of the Third World have strong self-defense capabilities better able to resist Western and u.s. power politics, bullying, and hegemony. China would determine for itself what its interests were and would not accept dictation of those interests by the United States. As China's 1995 white paper on arms control put it, "All nations have the right to maintaining an appropriate national defense capability . . . international arms control must not impair the independence and sovereignty of any nation."[2]

In the nuclear area, Beijing believed that Iran, as a signatory of the npt, had a right to the peaceful use of nuclear energy. Again citing the 1995 white paper: "Preventing the proliferation of nuclear weapons should not proceed without due regard for the just rights and interests of all countries in the peace-

ful use of nuclear energy, particularly in the case of developing countries."
There could not be a "double standard" whereby "anti-proliferation is used
as a pretext to limit or retard the peaceful use of nuclear energy by developing nations."[3] The International Atomic Energy Agency had not found Iran
to be involved in nuclear weapons development activities in violation of its
NPT obligations, and the United States could not simply substitute its own
judgments for that of the IAEA and expect other sovereign states to comply
with such unilateral determinations. Nor could a state via its own legislation
or executive declarations determine what sort of defense preparations or international arms transfers were permissible. These things could be determined
only by agreement among sovereign states. No state could unilaterally legis-
late or declare restrictions for other states. Sovereign states might agree to
restrict transfer to other countries of certain technologies. China, for example, had done this with its accession to the Non-Proliferation Treaty in 1992
and via agreements with the United States in 1987, 1994, and 1997 regarding
transfer of missiles and nuclear materials. But in the absence of such agreements, no legal restriction existed. Nor could one state determine unilaterally the meaning of the provisions of agreements and treaties. When there
was disagreement about the meaning of international agreements, authoritative determinations regarding meaning could be arrived at only multilat-
erally, via negotiation between relevant parties. For one party simply to declare
the meaning of ambiguous clauses and proceed to attempt to force other states
to submit to those interpretations was, again, hegemonism and power politics. Again the 1995 white paper: "All nations should endorse . . . and support
the arms control . . . measures adopted after voluntary consultation and
agreement between nations."[4]

From Beijing's perspective, U.S. objections to China's nuclear and missile
cooperation with Iran were, at bottom, manifestations of U.S. hegemonism.
Dedicated to a mentality of bullying and driven by a desire to dominate the
Persian Gulf, Washington wanted to keep Iran weak and vulnerable. It was
U.S. "interference" in the Persian Gulf and U.S. bullying of Iran, which created the problem. As Hong Kong's pro-PRC paper *Wen wei bao* commented
in April 1995, during the 1980s U.S. military forces sank several Iranian warships and shot down several Iranian warplanes. These U.S. moves "prompted
Iran to strengthen its strategic defense strength. Therefore, if Iran is currently
developing nuclear weapons as the United States has said, it probably is out
of consideration of national defense strategy. At least from now on, the United
States will have to think three times when making decisions to launch military raids on Iran."[5] Keeping Iran in a condition of military impotence might
be desirable from the standpoint of U.S. hegemonism, but there was no need

for those who despised hegemonism to embrace this goal. United States hegemonist wishes should not dictate the limit of China's relations with various developing countries, especially ones of substantial size and importance, which happened to have conflicts with the United States. The belief otherwise was the essence of u.s. hegemonist mentality. If the world bowed to American wishes, then the United States would truly achieve its dream of global hegemony. China felt no compunction to go along with such schemes.

In spite of these antihegemonist principles, Beijing would compromise when necessary to protect its relation with the United States. But it would try to do this in ways that did not destroy its political influence in Tehran. Cooperation with Iran in nuclear energy and missile development were ways of building Chinese influence with a major regional state. Simultaneously, China could earn substantial foreign currency via these cooperation efforts, cash that could be used to foster China's own development.

Chinese policy was a continual pulling and tugging between these antihegemonist principles and desire for influence in Tehran on the one hand, and the imperative of avoiding alienating of the United States, on the other. Antihegemonist logic dominated Chinese policy until about 1996–97 when China acceded to key u.s. demands and suspended nuclear and cruise missile cooperation with Iran. Stated simply, the clash between the United States and China over Sino-Iranian cooperation involved a clash of Chinese and u.s. national interests. The result would be two decades of bargaining.

SINO-AMERICAN CONFLICT OVER
SINO-IRANIAN COOPERATION: THE REAGAN PERIOD

The Reagan administration (inaugurated in January 1981) early on saw China's desire for access to u.s. nuclear power technology as an opportunity for engaging Beijing in a dialogue about nuclear nonproliferation. As noted earlier, China's nuclear industry circa 1978 was quite large, but entirely for military purposes. There was great opportunity if China's large nuclear industry could be used to produce fuel to generate electricity. Washington was happy to find foreign markets for u.s. nuclear technology but wanted to ensure that technology transferred to China would not cascade to aspiring nuclear weapons states.

Preliminary talks began in Beijing in fall 1981. Five rounds of talks between July 1983 and April 1984 led to the text of an agreement on nuclear cooperation providing for sale of u.s. nuclear power technology to China. In each round of the talks, the u.s. side made clear that shared nonproliferation norms were essential for transfer of u.s. civilian nuclear technology to China. Early in the negotiations China indicated willingness to join the IAEA, which it did in January 1984. Upon joining the IAEA, China indicated to the United States that it would implement IAEA safeguards to prevent inappropriate nuclear exports to non-nuclear weapons states under the NPT. In addition China pledged it would also make sure its nuclear exports were used only for peaceful purposes. On the basis of this progress, an agreement on nuclear cooperation was initialed during President Ronald Reagan's April 1984 visit to China. Shortly afterward U.S. intelligence received reports of the China-Iran nuclear cooperation agreement signed in June 1985, along with reports that China had indicated to Iran that it was willing to provide what the United States felt was sensitive nuclear technology. This intelligence generated strong pressure on the administration from Congress. Congressional critics charged that China was selling nuclear technology to a wide range of developing countries (which, as shown in a previous chapter, was indeed the case) and charged that the administration was suppressing evidence of China's proliferation activity.[6] As a result of mounting U.S. concerns, when the nuclear cooperation agreement was approved by Congress in December 1985, it contained an additional requirement for presidential certification of China's nonproliferation behavior before it could be implemented. This presidential certification was not forthcoming until January 1998, and making certification possible constituted a major U.S. mechanism of leverage during the intervening twelve years of bargaining.

In mid 1986 U.S. intelligence learned of an Iranian decision to buy Silkworm missiles from China. At this juncture the "tanker war" between Iran and Iraq was escalating and the United States was edging toward military action against Iran to end attacks on neutral oil commerce in the Gulf. The United States cited Iran's acquisition of Silkworm missiles as a major reason for the reflagging of Kuwaiti ships. Reagan administration officials began mobilizing pressure on China by informing the media of U.S. "concerns" about China's Silkworm sales. "We obviously are displeased that the Chinese are selling these kinds of weapons," presidential national security advisor Frank Carlucci announced.[7] Chinese representatives officially denied sale of arms to Iran, but unofficially argued that those sales were justified to secure Iranian support for the anti-Soviet struggle in Afghanistan. United States diplomats rejected this argument on grounds that the Afghan struggle did not require antiship missiles.[8]

Secretary of State George Schultz pressed the issue during a March 1987 visit to Beijing. Chinese leaders again denied selling arms to Iran. The U.S. position was weakened by the recent revelation of substantial U.S. arms sales to Iran—a development that became a domestic scandal known as "Iran-gate." Chinese representatives questioned whether the United States could credibly ask others not to sell weapons to Iran after secretly doing so itself.

China's repeated denials in the face of solid evidence frustrated U.S. representatives. "The Chinese say they are not doing it [selling arms to Iran]," Carlucci said in June 1987, "but they [the Silkworms] are coming from China."[9] When a Silkworm struck a U.S.-reflagged tanker in October 1987, U.S. ambassador in Beijing Winston Lord delivered a protest. The United States responded to Chinese denials of Silkworm sales by presenting U.S. intelligence photographs of ships loading the Silkworms at Chinese ports and unloading at Iranian facilities. This evidence left Chinese representatives unmoved. China continued to insist it was not supplying weapons to Iran. This blatant lying by the Chinese began to erode earlier goodwill toward China that had previously suffused the U.S. government.[10]

In October 1987 Washington upped the pressure by levying the first of what would become a long string of sanctions over China's assistance to Iran's military modernization programs. This was also the first U.S. sanction against China since the normalization of U.S.-PRC ties in January 1979. Under the October 1987 sanction, the United States suspended a planned elimination of licensing requirements for a wide range of high-technology U.S. exports to China. Beijing had been pressing for such a move for a number of years.[11] Table 8.1 lists this and subsequent U.S. sanctions against China over its cooperation with Iran and Pakistan.

The true significance of these sanctions as an instrument of leverage against Beijing was not in the amount of economic damage they inflicted, but in their serving as indicators of the direction of the evolution of Sino-U.S. relations. The intensification of U.S.-PRC conflict represented by these sanctions threatened to lead to the unraveling of the broader relationship. When implementing the modest October 1987 sanctions, Washington hinted at possible broader costs of China's cruise missile sales to Iran by raising the possibility that U.S. military forces might launch preemptive air strikes against Silkworm sites in Iran. United States congresspeople and senators spoke even more ominously of the consequences were U.S. ships to be attacked by Chinese Silkworms.

For five months Beijing refused to budge. Late in 1987 U.S. intelligence found evidence China was preparing to transfer to Iran an even more sophisticated antiship missile, the C-801.[12] Washington tried to persuade Beijing that Silkworm sales to Iran were contrary to China's own interests because Iran might use them to close the Strait of Hormuz, severely disrupting the global economy. China rejected such a scenario as unlikely. Iran was likely to try to close the Strait of Hormuz only if Iran's own oil shipments via the Gulf were cut, Chinese representatives replied.[13]

In March 1988, after Tehran rejected Beijing's advice to avoid direct

TABLE 8.1

U.S. Sanctions against China for Cooperation with Iran or Pakistan

Date	Chinese action	Sanction
Oct. 22, 1987	Silkworm sales to Iran	Liberalization technology transfers temporarily suspended
June 25, 1991	M-11 missiles and/or components to Pakistan	2 PRC firms barred import MTCR items & purchase computers
Aug. 24, 1993	M-11 technology sales to Pakistan	9 PRC firms and Aerospace Ministry barred 2 yrs MTCR item import for
Feb. 27, 1996	5000 ring magnets to Pakistan	Threat suspension U.S. Export-Import Bank financing China deals
May 21, 1997	Chemicals and/or chemical equipment to Iran	7 PRC entities banned U.S. market 1 yr
June 14, 2001	Chemicals and chemical technology to Iran	1 PRC firm banned U.S. market 2 yrs
Sept. 1, 2001	Missile components to Pakistan	1 PRC firm banned purchase MTCR controlled items, 2 yrs
Jan. 16, 2002	Chemicals and chemical technology to Iran	2 PRC firms and 1 citizen banned U.S. market 2 yrs
May 9, 2002	Missile technology to Iran	7 PRC firms and 1 citizen banned U.S. market 2 yrs or 1 yr
July 9, 2002	Cruise missile and chemical technology to Iran	8 PRC and 1 Indian firm banned U.S. market 2 yrs
May 23, 2003	Special steel and missile technology to Iran	NORINCO; 2-yr ban from U.S. market
June 26, 2003	Missile technology to Iran	??, 2-yr ban U.S. market
July 3, 2003	Chemicals and chemical equipment to Iran	5 Chinese and 1 North Korean company; indefinite ban from U.S.
July 30, 2003	Missile technology transfers to Iran	One China company; indefinite ban from U.S. market
Sept. 19, 2003	Missile technology transfers to Iran	NORINCO; 2-yr ban from U.S. market; 3rd ban in 1 yr.
Apr. 2004	Missile components and technology to Iran	5 PRC firms banned U.S. market 2 yrs

SOURCES: "Chinese Proliferation Cases," 1997 Congressional Hearings, Special Weapons, Subcommittee on International Security, Proliferation, and Federal Services, U.S. Senate, 10 April 1997; "U.S. Arms Control/ Nonproliferation Sanctions against China," NTI, http://wwwnti.org/db/china/sanclist.htm; "CRS Report on Chinese Illegal Transfer of Weapons of Mass Destruction and Missiles, "memorandum prepared by Congressional Research Service in response to Speaker of the House Newt Gingrich, available at Indian Embassy Web site, http://www.indianembassy.org/pic/congress/crs-ncwt.htm; and Shirley A. Kan, *China and Proliferation of Weapons of Mass Destruction and Missiles: Policy Issues*, Report RL 31555 (Washington, DC: Congressional Research Service, updated August 8, 2003).

confrontation with the United States and as Iran and the United States were moving toward a clash in the Gulf, Beijing agreed to end Silkworm sales to Iran and to prevent the diversion of Silkworms to Iran via other countries such as North Korea.[14] Foreign Minister Wu Xueqian carried China's concessions to Washington. Following a meeting with Wu, Reagan announced the lifting of sanctions imposed the previous October.[15] Washington hoped that Beijing's pledge to end Silkworm sales would be expanded to include a cutoff of all weapons sales to Iran in line with the effort then under way to compel Tehran to accept Security Council Resolution 598.[16] Beijing declined. Carlucci pressed again during a September 1988 visit to Beijing. To his counterpart, Defense Minister Qin Jiwei, Carlucci recognized that China was a sovereign country that had a right to sell arms overseas. (Carlucci became secretary of defense in November 1987.) "But missiles fit a special category," Carlucci said. Qin did not respond. Qin told reporters that China's arms sales were far less than those of the United States or the Soviet Union.[17]

Beijing's March 1988 agreement to end Silkworm sales was the first instance of what would become a pattern: the granting of an apparent concession to the United States that, while enthusiastically welcomed by negotiators on the u.s. side, would turn out to be much less than initially met the eye. China's agreement to end sales of Silkworms was greatly reduced in value by the subsequent transfer to Iran of machinery to manufacture those weapons indigenously. It was also reduced in value by China's sale shortly afterward of a different and far more advanced class of antiship cruise missile—the C-801 and C-802. In 1990 u.s. intelligence determined that China was selling C-802s to Iran, along with machinery to manufacture those potent weapons.[18] Technically China stood by its agreement. After March 1988 China no longer sold Silkworms to Iran. But this Chinese chicanery further eroded u.s. goodwill.

THE GEORGE H. W. BUSH ADMINISTRATION

Conflict over China's nuclear cooperation with Iran intensified during 1991. In October u.s. intelligence determined that Iran was attempting to develop nuclear weapons and that China's nuclear cooperation with Iran was assisting Iran in this effort.[19] This determination made China's nuclear cooperation with Iran a focus of u.s. policy attention. Another factor producing the shift in u.s. policy was the discovery by u.n. inspectors after the 1991 Gulf War of the scope of *Iraq's* covert nuclear weapons program. United Nations inspectors uncovered in Iraq an extensive and advanced nuclear weapons program. Iraq's success in concealing its nuclear weapons program for years from

IAEA inspectors highlighted weaknesses in the IAEA/NPT safeguards regime. Iraq, like Iran, had been a long-standing signatory of the NPT, and its nuclear facilities had been inspected and certified by the IAEA. Yet IAEA inspectors had not detected evidence of Iraq's covert nuclear weapons program. Might not the same be happening with Iran? U.S. analysts began to wonder. The United States also began detecting evidence that Iran had intensified its nuclear weapons program. President Rafsanjani was reported to have authorized expenditure of $100 million to acquire enriched uranium and technology needed to produce weapons grade enriched uranium. Moreover, Rafsanjani was attempting to woo back to Iran scientists involved in the shah's nuclear programs. Western intelligence agencies had also thwarted numerous Iranian efforts to purchase sensitive technology around the world, especially in Western Europe.[20] The attempted purchase of a heavy-water production plant from Argentina also suggested to U.S. analysts an effort to produce plutonium. The United States' suspicions were further heightened by comments by Iranian leaders about Israel's possession of nuclear weapons requiring Islamic countries to likewise possess such weapons.[21]

Washington's objective was to persuade *all countries*, not merely China, to suspend nuclear cooperation with Iran. Germany, Argentina, India, France, and especially Russia were all targets of U.S. lobbying regarding ending nuclear cooperation with Iran. But China was Iran's most important partner in the nuclear area from 1985 to 1997. It was only after China bowed out under U.S. pressure in 1997 that Russia stepped in to become Iran's leading nuclear partner. This meant that by late 1991 ending Chinese nuclear cooperation with Iran was high on the U.S. agenda. The assistant secretary of state for East Asia and the Pacific, Richard Solomon, told a closed U.S. Senate hearing that China had sold nuclear-related technologies to Iran despite "statements they have repeatedly made to us, both publicly and privately, that they will not support or encourage nuclear proliferation." "While the Chinese may not be selling finished weapons [to Iran], they may be transferring certain technologies or information," Solomon said. These actions were "unacceptable," and U.S. concerns had been passed on to Beijing.[22] According to another administration official in March 1992: "We're trying to tell the Chinese that in this case you've got to go beyond the letter of the law."[23] China should halt *all* nuclear cooperation with Iran, even cooperation that might technically be legal under the NPT, according to Washington. It would take five years to secure China's agreement to this demand.

Under mounting pressure from the United States, China sought to reassure Washington. A counselor of the PRC embassy in Washington stressed that "China is a responsible member of the international community and does not advocate or encourage proliferation. Nor does it help other countries develop nuclear weapons."[24] The next month Beijing announced that China would sign the NPT—which it did in March 1993. As noted in an earlier chapter, in November 1991 Beijing also began to acknowledge and discuss publicly its nuclear cooperation with Iran. The same month China officially declared it would report to the IAEA any export of nuclear materials of at least one effective kilogram to non-nuclear weapons states.[25] Apparently in the fall of 1991 decisions were made in Beijing to be more open about China's international nuclear cooperation, including cooperation with Iran.

Once it stopped denying nuclear cooperation with Iran, Beijing insisted that such cooperation was fully in accord with the NPT. Under the NPT, a key incentive for states to renounce possession of nuclear weapons was the promise that, having done so, under the treaty they could cooperate with nuclear weapons states in the peaceful use of nuclear energy. The NPT regime recognized that all states, including non-nuclear weapons states, had the right to master nuclear energy with its many peaceful uses: power generation, medical treatment and research, and scientific research. Nuclear science was a key area of scientific advance, and the purpose of the NPT regime was not, Beijing insisted, to exclude non-nuclear weapons states from that important scientific field. "To promote the peaceful use of nuclear energy is important to the implementation" of the NPT, Qian Qichen told the United Nations in April 1995, and "should be taken as seriously as other stipulations" of that treaty. "The rights of many developing countries to have a peaceful use of nuclear energy should be guaranteed. The fight against nuclear proliferation should not obstruct the peaceful use of nuclear energy."[26] Once non-nuclear weapons states pledged by signing the NPT to abstain from the manufacture or possession of nuclear weapons, and once IAEA inspection authorities certified this to be the case, those non-nuclear weapons states and nuclear weapons states could cooperate freely in the nuclear field. Only activity directly related to weapons production was prohibited by the NPT, Beijing argued. All other activity, including that related to all stages of the fuel cycle, was permissible as long as it was reported to the IAEA and certified by IAEA inspectors not to be related to weapons research, development, or production. Chinese-Iranian nuclear cooperation fell within these parameters, Beijing argued.

Washington did not dispute that China's nuclear cooperation fell within the letter of NPT and IAEA provisions. Rather, the United States argued that there was strong and convincing evidence that some countries, such as Iran and Pakistan, were attempting to develop nuclear weapons and that, under such conditions, *any* nuclear cooperation with those countries, even that permitted under the NPT, could facilitate weapons development efforts. The purpose of the NPT was to prevent the spread of nuclear weapons, U.S. representatives argued, not to serve as a cover for covert weapons programs. China should recognize this and cooperate with the United States to prevent the spread of nuclear weapons, thereby upholding the nonproliferation regime, rather than subverting it by providing nuclear knowledge, materials, and technologies to countries that solid evidence indicated were bent on acquisition of nuclear weapons.

Beijing initially rejected the U.S. demand. In essence, Beijing argued, Washington was demanding that determinations by U.S. intelligence agencies substitute for decisions made by the IAEA and its board of governors (which included China by 1984). The nonproliferation regime had set up multilateral institutions to ascertain whether non-nuclear weapons states were complying with their obligations under the NPT. Those institutions had inspected Iran and concluded that Iran was in full compliance with its NPT obligations. Now, U.S. intelligence agencies had reached contrary determinations, and Washington was insisting that China and other states act on the basis of those determinations. Simply stated, Washington was demanding that it, not the IAEA, should run the global nonproliferation regime. This was a manifestation of U.S. arrogance and hegemonism, in the Chinese view.

The first serious engagement between Beijing and the Bush administration over Sino-Iranian relations came during a visit by Secretary of State James Baker to Beijing in November 1991. As noted in an earlier chapter, there was by then evidence that Beijing was preparing to transfer 600-kilometer-range M-9 and 280-kilometer-range M-11 missiles to Iran and that Beijing had actually shipped M-11 components to Pakistan, resulting in U.S. sanctions in June. Baker's visit was the first by a cabinet-level U.S. official since the Beijing massacre of June 1989. As such, Baker's visit was highly symbolic of Beijing's reentry into international society. President Bush, facing a reelection contest in November 1992, invested a lot of political capital in Baker's China visit. Bush's willingness to "coddle the butchers of Beijing" (as Democratic vice presidential candidate Al Gore would later style Bush's behavior) was coming under mounting criticism in the United States. Baker pointed this out to Foreign Minister Qian Qichen during their talks, and called on China to make some concessions that Bush could use to demonstrate that his policy of "engagement" with China was working. During three days of extremely tough talks in Beijing, Baker pressed for China to agree to suspend all nuclear and Category I missile cooperation with Iran. Qian initially rejected any Chinese concessions, but ultimately made some modest concessions in the area of missile technology sales. Qian told Baker that if the United States would cancel the sanctions imposed in June over China's M-11 technology transfers to Pakistan, China would "respect the principles and guidelines" of the MTCR.[27] This pledge was not put in writing. United States officials nonetheless interpreted Qian's statement as a promise of an end to Chinese missile sales to Pakistan, Iran, and Syria. In Baker's account: "The Chinese side kept trying to arrange loopholes. They insisted on striking specific references to Syria, Pakistan, and Iran, and also objected to language saying China 'will observe' the MTCR guidelines, demanding that it be changed to 'intends to observe.'"[28]

On the issue of nuclear cooperation with Iran, China refused to budge.[29] An MFA spokesman explained that while China greatly valued and wanted to improve relations with the United States, it would not do this on Washington's terms. Premier Li Peng explained it as a matter of sovereignty: "The Chinese nation, with a history of more that 5,000 years, has a strong sense of national dignity. For more than 100 years we the Chinese people suffered very much from foreign aggression and humiliation, so we cherish so much our independence and sovereignty."[30]

Following the November 1991 Baker-Qian talks, U.S. negotiators tried to flesh out the specific content of Qian oral pledge to comply with MTCR "guidelines and parameters." In response to U.S. insistence, Qian sent Baker a letter on February 1, 1992, confirming his earlier verbal promise to abide by MTCR guidelines and parameters. Following receipt of this letter, the United States lifted the sanctions imposed in June 1991.[31] As with the 1988 Silkworm agreement, the November 1991 / February 1992 pledge to follow MTCR guidelines and parameters turned out to be far less valuable than initially met the American eye. It soon became apparent that China felt the agreement limited only the range and payloads of actual missiles sold and did not apply to the transfer of missile-production technologies.[32] United States negotiators maintained that this interpretation rendered Qian's pledge meaningless, but this claim was rejected by the Chinese side.

The documents outlining the MTCR included three components: the guidelines and parameters, and two annexes including lists of controlled goods. The guidelines and parameters banned export of ground-to-ground missiles capable of delivering a warhead of at least five hundred kilograms (the approximate minimal weight of a nuclear weapon) to a distance of three hundred kilometers—so-called Category I missiles. Annex I included a list of banned items that went into Category I missiles: guidance equipment, engines, reentry systems, and so on. Items in Annex I faced a "strong presumption of denial" of export approval and were to be exported only on rare occasions. Annex II listed dual-use but possibly "missile-related technology and items" that were to be controlled on a case-by-case basis by an export licensing system. Beijing's 1991–92 pledge, it turned out, appertained only to the guidelines and parameters and, apparently, Annex I. After considerable u.s. pressure, China stated in the mid-1990s that its commitment "did not include the MTCR Annex," according to the u.s. State Department.[33] This meant that China would continue to sell Iran dual-use items and technology and manufacturing equipment listed on Annex II. Chinese engineers would continue to assist Iranian non-Category I missile development efforts. As late as 2002, a CIA report to Congress stated that China "has not recognized the [MTCR's] key technology annex."[34]

ENTANGLEMENT—LINKAGE WITH TAIWAN

China's cooperation with Iran became entangled with u.s. relations with Taiwan on September 2, 1992, when President Bush announced the sale of 150 F-16 fighters to Taiwan. Beijing's response linked the F-16 sale to the Iran issue. Five days after Bush's announcement, Xinhua reported that an Iranian military delegation had arrived in Beijing to discuss arms purchases. It did not say when the team had arrived. Xinhua also quoted Vice Foreign Minister Liu Huaqiu as warning that unless Washington suspended the F-16 sale, China would find it difficult to participate in the u s -initiated, u.n.-sponsored talks among the Permanent Five members of the Security Council on Middle East arms sales.[35] China had participated in the first round of those talks in Paris in 1991. Several days after the United States announced the F-16 sale, and after it was apparent that Chinese protests would not halt it, Qian Qichen announced that because of the F-16 sale to Taiwan, China would not participate in the u.n. Middle East arms control talks. Qian explained that the u.s. F-16 sale violated the 1982 u.s.-prc arms sales communiqué, thereby demonstrating a lack of good faith. Without good faith there could be no arms control. Therefore, China found it difficult to participate in the Perm Five arms talks. As to when China might be able to participate, that "is a matter open for discussion," Qian said.[36]

Shortly after the announcement of the F-16 sale, reports began emerging that China was transferring thirty complete M-11 missiles to Pakistan in violation of both Qian's verbal pledge of November 1991 and his letter of February 1992.[37] Later reports confirmed those transfers.[38] China apparently never transferred whole missiles violating MTCR guidelines and parameters to Iran, unlike Pakistan. Chinese transfers to *Iran* of concern to the United States involved transfers of missile components and production technologies.[39] Regarding the whole-missile transfers to Pakistan, the stated range of the M-11 was 280 kilometers, while the Category I threshold was three hundred kilometers. Thus, Beijing insisted, the M-11 was not a Category I missile. Washington insisted, however, that since the M-11 was designed to deliver an eight hundred-kilogram payload, the missile could easily achieve a range of three hundred kilometers if the weight of the warhead was reduced, there being an inherent trade-off between weight and range. Beijing rejected this, and would for several years. From Beijing's perspective, u.s. F-16 sales to Taiwan violated the August 1982 joint communiqué dealing with u.s. arms sales to Taiwan. Washington, of course, pointed to certain elliptical phrases in that communiqué to justify its action, but Beijing found that completely unacceptable. Now, Beijing was saying, two can play at violating vague agreements, thereby trampling on the interests of the other side.

Beijing also played the Iran nuclear card against Washington. On September 10, 1992, eight days after Bush's F-16 announcement, Iran and China publicly signed an agreement on nuclear cooperation providing for sale of several nuclear power plants. This deal had been developing since Khamenei's 1989 visit to Beijing and should not be considered primarily as a reaction to the F16 sale. Still, the timing underlined the point that China had ways of injuring u.s. policy interests, just as the United States injured China's interests vis-à-vis Taiwan. Then, curiously, on September 23, thirteen days after agreeing to sell multiple power plants to Iran and three weeks after Bush's F-16 sale announcement, China's minister of electrical power, Liu Xuecheng, announced that China was canceling "for technical reasons" an agreement signed in 1991 to provide Iran with a 27-megawatt research reactor. Throughout 1992 the United States had lobbied Beijing to shelve the sale of that reactor. u.s. officials believed this smaller reactor posed a greater proliferation danger than the larger 300-megawatt reactors. The larger reactors contained key components produced in Western countries, which Washington was confident it could persuade not to proceed with the sales, while the 27-megawatt reactor was entirely Chinese made and thus more likely to be delivered and become operational.[40]

The relation between Beijing's September 10 agreement to sell multiple, large reactors and the September 23 cancellation of the sale of a smaller reactor is perplexing. If Beijing was trying to punish Washington for the F-16 sale, why cancel the nuclear reactor sale just at that juncture? Why move to reduce pressure on Washington just as China wished to express anger over the F-16 sale decision? Why not wait several months, allowing the Americans to stew a while longer under nuclear pressure? Virtually nothing is known about the processes within China's ruling elite through which these decisions were made. Several alternate explanations are plausible. Decisions involving sale or non-sale of nuclear reactors to Iran would be reviewed at the highest levels. It thus seems likely that the decision to cancel the reactor sale was part of an effort by Qian Qichen to navigate U.S.-PRC relations away from a possible ship-wreck. There was strong and mounting pressure in Congress to link Most Favored Nation (MFN) status to human rights. Bush was resisting that pres-sure, but he faced strong competition in the upcoming presidential election (scheduled for November 1992) from a rival condemning his "weak" China policy. Taiwan issues were generating tension, which was unavoidable since Taiwan was a core interest for Beijing. But there was a danger that Sino-American relations might become too tense. Cancellation of the reactor sale would moderate the level of tension in the relation and might help Bush defeat his "anti-China" opponent.

It is possible that the September 23 cancellation of the 27-megawatt reactor deal with Iran was one of the "mistakes" committed by Qian Qichen during this period. In mid-June 1996 before an enlarged Politburo meeting, Qian Qichen reportedly made a "self-criticism" for his inadequately firm response to U.S. moves toward Taiwan over the previous several years.[41] Cancellation of the reactor sale to Iran so shortly after the announcement of the U.S. F-16 sale to Taiwan might have been one of the moves for which Qian Qichen was criticized by hard-liners.

China's missile assistance to Pakistan and sale of nuclear power plants to Iran were not merely ways of punishing the United States. But that *was* one aspect of Beijing's calculations. Moving forward with both at the end of 1992 was a response to U.S. upgrading of relations with Taiwan. Beijing was demon-strating to Washington that it had ways of injuring U.S. interests if Washing-ton chose to injure China's interests regarding Taiwan. China's transfer of advanced antiship missiles also resumed in fall 1993. United States recon-naissance satellites photographed Chinese ships loading C-802s, and then unloading them in Iranian ports. These were not Category I missiles.

Over the next several years Chinese representatives periodically reasserted the Iran-Taiwan linkage. During his October 1994 negotiations with Secretary of State Warren Christopher, for instance, Qian Qichen rebutted the U.S. assertion that sale of M-11 components to Pakistan violated China's com-mitment to the MTCR guidelines and parameters, and raised China's con-tention that the F-16 sale to Taiwan had violated the 1982 communiqué.[42]

The Iran-Taiwan linkage was also prominent during the 1995–96 U.S.-PRC confrontation over Taiwan. On May 22, 1995, the U.S. government announced the issue of a visa for Taiwan president Lee Teng-hui to visit the United States. That visit transpired in June with far higher political profile than the U.S. government had expected.[43] Lee Teng-hui's visit, along with other U.S. moves to marginally upgrade relations with Taiwan, precipitated an extremely strong reaction from Beijing. Beginning in July and continuing through March 1996, Beijing unfolded a series of escalating military threats against Taiwan that would trigger the first military confrontation between the United States and China in twenty years. In this context, Beijing again asserted the Iran-Taiwan linkage. Several weeks after Washington granted a visa to Lee, Beijing cancelled scheduled meetings at which the United States had intended to present its concerns about Chinese technology transfers to Iran. Vice Foreign Minister Liu Huaqiu said late in 1995 that a halt to u.s. F-16 sales to Taiwan was necessary for progress on proliferation: "We believe that as a first step [toward renewal of proliferation talks] the United States should halt the sale of F-16s to Taiwan. This will help China and the United States cooperate in halting missile proliferation."[44] When u.s.-prc talks about Chinese missile sales to Iran and Pakistan finally resumed in late 1996, Beijing stressed the recent u.s. sale of man-portable Stinger antiaircraft missiles to Taiwan as a violation of the 1982 communiqué.[45]

Even after Beijing's suspension of nuclear cooperation and C-801/C-802 cruise missile sales in 1997, Beijing continued the theme of Iran-Taiwan linkage. During Clinton's 1998 visit to China, Beijing proposed and the United States considered but rejected a u.s. pledge to deny missile defense to Taiwan in exchange for a Chinese pledge to halt missile cooperation with Iran. During u.s.-prc arms control negotiations in February 2002, a Chinese official told the Associated Press that the United States could not accuse China of violating its commitments toward Iran while itself selling large amounts of arms to Taiwan. United States arms sales to Taiwan were also a type of proliferation, the official said.[46]

THE WILLIAM CLINTON ADMINISTRATION

Persuading China to suspend nuclear and missile cooperation with Iran and Pakistan remained a key u.s. objective during the Clinton administration (inaugurated in January 1993). The Clinton administration determined that China was shipping either missiles and/or missile technology to *Pakistan*— actions that many in the administration felt to be in violation of Qian Qichen's November 1991 and February 1992 promises to Baker to comply with mtcr guidelines and parameters. The issue was pursued during meetings between Christopher and Qian in Singapore in July 1993 and yet again by Undersecretary of State Lynn Davis in Beijing the same month.[47] Davis told her Chinese interlocutors that China had a choice between confession of forbidden missile transfers to Pakistan or u.s. sanctions. In response, the Chinese refused to discuss what they might or might not have shipped to Pakistan. Moreover, they informed Davis, China was willing to discuss u.s. concerns about Chinese "proliferation" only if the United States agreed to discuss Chinese concerns about u.s. "proliferation" to Taiwan.[48] As u.s. pressure on Beijing mounted, Iranian deputy foreign minister Alaeddin Broujerdi expressed confidence that China would stand firm: "Large countries such as the PRC and Russia will not succumb to [u.s.] pressure; they know Iran will use nuclear energy only for peaceful purposes. They obviously anticipated such pressure and despite the propaganda and creation of such a bad atmosphere [by the United States] when they signed agreements with us."[49]

Beijing rebutted u.s. contentions about Iran having nuclear weapons programs by asserting that the United States was upholding a double standard to China's and Iran's disadvantage. The fact that both China and Iran were signatories of the NPT guaranteed that nuclear technology exported by China would not be converted to military purposes, Vice Premier Li Lanqing said in July 1993. The United States and other Western states sold nuclear technologies around the world. Why should China be denied that right? "We should set one standard or criterion and apply it to all world states without discrimination," Li insisted.[50] "If the United States is entitled to export nuclear energy for peaceful purposes, China too is entitled to do so." The United States responded that mere signature of the NPT and IAEA inspections were not an adequate safeguard against covert nuclear weapons programs. This had been the case with Iraq prior to 1991. Solid evidence indicated, Washington argued, that Iran was pursuing, not merely civilian use of nuclear energy, but nuclear weapons.

In August 1993 the Clinton administration imposed sanctions on nine Chinese entities for transfer of Category I M-11 technology to *Pakistan*. Nine Chinese firms were barred for two years from importing MTCR-related items. This penalty was not particularly severe, but it was the first of only two times that Clinton would impose sanctions. Vice Foreign Minister Liu Huaqiu, who came to Washington to discuss the matter, did not admit the transfer, but argued that the M-11 did not fall within the MTCR guidelines and parameters since its range was only 280 kilometers. Moreover, the United States was in no position to impose sanctions when it was selling advanced fighters to Taiwan. The recent u.s. sanctions might cause China to reconsider its commitment to respect MTCR guidelines, Liu said.[51]

Clinton raised the issue with Jiang Zemin when the two met at the Asia-Pacific Economic Cooperation (APEC) summit in November 1993. Clinton indicated the United States would moderate the recent sanctions if China agreed to talks about China's adherence to the MTCR. Jiang replied that any such talks must address U.S. fighter aircraft sales to Taiwan. Late in 1993 Clinton agreed to talks including both the MTCR and F-16 sales to Taiwan.[52] This was a very important U.S. concession: Clinton was implicitly accepting a linkage between United States–Taiwan and PRC-Iran ties. Beijing's Iran card seemed to be working. Simultaneously Clinton diluted the August sanctions by approving PRC launch of three U.S. satellites. Further talks in January 1994 between Liu Huaqiu and Lynn Davis, and in March between Qian Qichen and Warren Christopher, were without result.

In May 1994 the macroclimate of negotiations changed with Clinton's decision to delink China's MFN status and human rights status. While there was no direct connection between MFN and Iranian issues, the U.S. threat to revoke China's MFN status had placed China under considerable pressure. In such a situation, it was dangerous, both domestically and in terms of negotiating credibility, for China to make concessions on Iran. Once that threat was removed, Chinese negotiators no longer faced possible charges of weakness if they made concessions under duress. There were also good reasons for Beijing to respond positively to Clinton's very important steps regarding MFN. One can only wonder what the outcome would have been if Clinton had decided to make China's military cooperation with Iran, rather than human rights in China, the quid pro quo for MFN. Human rights touched on the CCP's control over Chinese society. Cooperation with Iran was a significantly less important matter for Beijing.

In October 1994 Beijing took a significant step toward cooperation with the United States over missile proliferation by agreeing to a joint statement on the issue in exchange for Washington's lifting of the August 1993 sanctions. In the joint statement China reaffirmed its 1991–92 pledge not to export Category I missiles. This was the third time Beijing sold this concession to Washington. The joint statement also indicated China's acceptance of the U.S. position on the "inherent capability" of missile systems "regardless of its demonstrated or preadvertised combination of range and payload." This brought China's M-11 within Category I. The joint statement did not, however, restrict China's export of dual-use items covered by Annex II of the MTCR—the export of which had triggered the August 1993 sanctions. In this regard the joint statement stated merely that the United States "encouraged China to undertake negotiations on a binding agreement whereby China would adhere to current MTCR Guidelines *and Annex.*"[53]

While the agreements of 1991–94 banned Chinese exports of Category I missiles, the flow of components for missile guidance systems and computerized machine tools for missile production continued. United States officials were divided about whether these transfers constituted a violation of China's several agreements.[54] Apparently it was about this time Beijing clarified that its adherence to the MTCR was merely to the parameters and guidelines and not to Annex II.

Talks on China's assistance to Iran's nuclear programs paralleled negotiations over missiles. In March 1995 Christopher and Qian talked about Iran during a two-hour meeting at the United Nations. The two sides differed sharply. Qian rejected Christopher's call for China to cancel the sale of 300-megawatt reactors and other nuclear technology to Iran. China's nuclear cooperation with developing countries was carried out under the eyes of the IAEA and fully in compliance with international treaties, Qian insisted. The United States had no need to worry. The two sides agreed to continue discussions of the issue. The next month Vice Foreign Minister Liu Huaqiu visited Washington and was given a briefing on secret U.S. intelligence concerning Iran's nuclear weapons programs. Apparently this intelligence included information that Iran had purchased enriched uranium from Kazakhstan and other former Soviet republics, had smuggled in nuclear weapons technology, and had imported from Europe major equipment for nuclear weapons manufacture. According to a report in Hong Kong's pro-PRC paper Wen wei bao, China was not impressed by the U.S. intelligence.[55] The United States apparently received additional intelligence in mid 1995 when an Iranian general who had been in charge of Iran's military relations with Russia defected. The general took with him a sheath of top-secret documents on Iranian-Russian nuclear cooperation. These documents subsequently figured in Clinton's presentations to Russian president Boris Yeltsin and were reportedly instrumental in persuading Yeltsin to cancel a sale of gas centrifuges to Iran.[56] Presumably the same information was presented to China.

When talks between Qian and Christopher on the Iran nuclear issue resumed in September 1995, it became apparent that Chinese policy had moved considerably closer to the United States. After having resisted for three years U.S. pressure over the sale of 300-megawatt reactors to Iran, Qian Qichen informed Christopher that China had decided to "suspend" the sale because of technical disagreements with Iran. Following Qian's statement, an unidentified "senior official" of the State Department (who Robert Suettinger concludes was "probably Winston Lord") informed the press that China had "cancelled" its reactor deal with Iran. While the U.S. official stated that China had made the decision unilaterally, his formulation suggested that China's move was a goodwill gesture toward the United States.[57] These public comments highlighting Qian's concessions to the United States increased the foreign minister's vulnerability to criticism from CCP hard-liners for not being tough enough in dealing with the United States. To minimize political vulnerability due to U.S. lack of diplomatic discipline, two days after the State Department official's comments Qian told the press that the agreement with Iran had not been cancelled but only "suspended for the time being."[58] Moreover, this decision had been made unilaterally by China and not because of U.S. pressure. The next day an MFA spokesman reiterated that China's agreement on nuclear cooperation with Iran was still in effect and that China intended to proceed with such cooperation under IAEA safeguards and consistent with the NPT.[59] Yet in spite of anger at perceived U.S. efforts to embarrass China, Beijing held by its promise to suspend the reactor sale. This small episode may also have served as a useful learning experience for the United States. Two years later, when China made far more substantial concessions regarding Iran on both nuclear and cruise missile issues, Washington handled the matter much more adeptly—in a low-key fashion designed to avoid embarrassing China and China's advocates of cooperation with the United States.

Again the question, why in the midst of a campaign to punish Washington for its moves toward Taiwan did Beijing agree to shelve a major component of Sino-Iranian nuclear cooperation, in this case the 300-megawatt reactor sale to Iran? In August 1995 China had begun unfolding an impressive campaign of military intimidation of Taiwan. As in 1992, why weaken China's effort to punish Washington over Taiwan by backing away, at just that juncture, from nuclear cooperation with Iran? Why not wait until China's punitive campaign had run its course, and then make concessions over Iran? Certainly China's creative diplomats could have found a way of simply suspending action on the reactor sales to Iran for several months. Again it seems probable that the decision to drop the nuclear reactor deal with Iran was the result of a high-level decision and was part of an effort by Qian to keep that issue from overloading Sino-U.S. relations. Beijing was moving ahead to force a crisis over Taiwan and did not want to add fuel to the anticipated confrontation. Qian, and behind him Jiang Zemin and Deng Xiaoping (who did not die until 1997), did not want a breakdown in Sino-U.S. relations; they did not want the increasing tension in U.S.-Iranian relations to become linked to and perhaps multiply tension in Sino-U.S. relations necessitated by clashing interests on Taiwan. When the chips were down, the Iran card was simply too dangerous to play in the Taiwan game.

Late in 1995 events again pushed nonproliferation to the fore when U.S. intelligence learned that a PRC company had sold five thousand ring magnets to Pakistan's Abdul Qadir Khan Laboratories—Pakistan's main nuclear weapons research center, which operated outside of IAEA safeguards. The CIA concluded that the ring magnets were for use in a centrifuge-based uranium enrichment program. In response to China's sale of ring magnets to Pakistan, Washington in February threatened strong sanctions: the U.S. Export-Import Bank would not finance business involving China. This was the first truly severe U.S. sanction threatened over Pakistan and Iran. If applied, this measure would have shut down billions of dollars of trade.[60] In January 1996 Iran test-fired a Chinese-supplied C-802 from aboard a ship in the Persian Gulf.

Tehran urged Beijing to stand firm and resist U.S. pressure. Commenting in early 1996 on Beijing's reported rejection of U.S. demands to halt nuclear cooperation with Iran, the Voice of the Islamic Republic radio station reported that "informed political sources" believed that Beijing's rejection of Washington's recent demands was an indication that Beijing "would not allow growing Sino-Iranian relations to be marred by Washington's propaganda campaign and pressure tactics."[61] Beijing *may* have offered Tehran increased cooperation in the dual-use chemical area as a way of compensating for reductions of assistance in the nuclear area. In any case, in November 1996 the United States levied its first sanctions for Chinese sale to Iran of chemical warfare agent precursors. Three more sets of sanctions over dual use chemical sales would transpire through 2003.

The trauma of military confrontation in the Taiwan Strait in early 1996 impelled Beijing and Washington toward a renewed effort at engagement. The shift in U.S. policy was especially important. Shortly after PLA exercises in the Taiwan Strait in March 1996, national security advisor Anthony Lake and his deputy, Samuel Berger, presided over a review of China policy. That review ended in the conclusion that human rights issues had to be downgraded in the U.S. agenda toward China, and convergent strategic interests stressed. In the nonproliferation area, for instance, "It was in China's interest as well as the world's that China not only play by the rules but also help devise those rules," according to a later account by Lake.[62] The shift in U.S. policy was also predicated on a frank recognition of China's ability to injure U.S. interests. China could, for example, continue to "sell weapons systems to Iran that threaten U.S. naval forces," according to another participant in the 1996 rethinking of U.S. China policy.[63] As part of the mid-1996 U.S. reappraisal of China policy, Washington set four goals on arms control. China was to be induced to give up all nuclear cooperation with Iran, even cooperation permitted under international law. China was to agree to suspend contracts to sell Iran cruise missiles that posed an "over the horizon" threat to Persian Gulf shipping. China was to be persuaded to draft and enforce controls on exports of dual-use nuclear items. And, finally, China was to be persuaded to join the Zangger Committee, an international group monitoring nuclear technology exports. All four of these objectives would be achieved within six years.

In line with this approach of focusing on areas of convergent strategic interests with China, rather than on the areas of disagreement, u.s. negotiators began stressing that as a major oil importing country China had an interest in stability in the Persian Gulf. Anything that threatened to disrupt the steady flow of oil was adverse to China's interests. Wars or attacks on oil tankers transiting the Persian Gulf would force up the price of oil and possibly create oil shortages. Iran and Iraq were major sources of instability in the region, and China should cooperate with the United States to minimize the ability of those states to make war or challenge the uninterrupted, free flow of oil from the Persian Gulf, u.s. officials argued. When Defense Secretary William Perry hosted his prc counterpart Chi Haotian at a dinner in December 1996 in Washington, he pressed this argument. Since China was increasingly dependent on foreign oil, particularly oil from the Persian Gulf, Perry said, anything that increased instability in the Gulf area or that "makes Iran more confident of its military ability" could eventually backfire on China. Perry also argued that even legal Chinese arms sales to Iran threatened u.s. interests in the Gulf area.[64] Chi promised to "consider the point" made by Perry.[65] Secretary of Defense William Cohen (who replaced Perry in December 1996) advanced the same arguments during his January 1998 visit to Beijing.

From the standpoint of a Chinese antihegemonist perspective, these arguments were tantamount to an invitation for China to become a junior partner of the United States in exploiting and dominating the countries of the Persian Gulf region. Since Ji Pengfei's 1973 visit to Tehran, China had called for the countries of the Persian Gulf region to themselves provide security for the region, and condemned the "interference" of outside "big powers" in the Gulf. Acceptance of American arguments about the need for China and the United States to work together to ensure the security of the Persian Gulf, limiting Iran's military capabilities in the process, would constitute a paradigm shift in Chinese thinking. Beijing was not yet willing to go this far.

With the threat of suspension of u.s. Export-Import Bank financing pending, Deputy Assistant Secretary of State Robert Einhorn in March, and Secretary of State Warren Christopher in April 1996, traveled to Beijing to discuss u.s. proliferation concerns. Einhorn presented a draft statement pledging China not to provide support of any kind to unsafeguarded nuclear facilities anywhere in the world. The Chinese side rejected the proposal. Christopher and Qian Qichen discussed the issue further in April. Qian began toughly: "China's nonproliferation export is China's policy. We have no need to discuss it with the u.s. government."[66] By the end of the meeting, however, Qian signaled a willingness to resolve the issue. If the United States would promise not to levy sanctions for the ring magnet sale, China would unilaterally issue a statement foreswearing future cooperation with unsafeguarded nuclear facilities.[67] The United States agreed and a deal was struck. On May 10 the State Department announced that sanctions were being waived in view of China's pledge to forgo further cooperation with unsafeguarded nuclear facilities. The next day Xinhua news agency issued a terse statement reporting an MFA spokesman's answer to "a question raised by a reporter on the decision of the u.s. government not to impose sanctions on China." The operative phase of China's answer read: "China will not provide assistance to unsafeguarded nuclear facilities. China stands for the strengthening of the international nuclear nonproliferation regime, including the strengthening of safeguards and export control measures."[68] Following this "unilateral statement," China began consulting privately with the United States about establishment of an export control system.[69]

China's May 1996 statement appertained to China's nuclear cooperation with Pakistan, not Iran. Iran, unlike Pakistan, was a signatory of the NPT and permitted IAEA inspections. China's nuclear cooperation with Iran was with IAEA-safeguarded facilities and was thus unaffected by Qian's pledge. Still, the agreement pointed toward a basic decision to seek greater cooperate with the United States on nuclear nonproliferation.

By mid-1996 intense negotiations began over the format for a visit by Jiang Zemin to the United States. Early on in those negotiations the two sides agreed on an effort to revive the 1985 agreement on nuclear cooperation and make that agreement one of the "deliverables" to be formalized at the summit. Negotiations then focused on conditions for permitting this. China's missile and nuclear cooperation with Iran was a major focus. Assistant Secretary of State Jeff Bader described the u.s. position on Chinese technology transfers to Iran:

> We have expressed [to China] our strong concerns about China's inadequate controls on the export of materials and technology that can be used in missile development and chemical and biological warfare, about shipments to Iran by Chinese companies of dual-use chemicals that could be used in a weapons program, and about its arms sales to Iran and Pakistan. At every level, including at the very top, we stress the importance we place on nonproliferation and urge China to accept and abide by international nonproliferation agreements and norms. Where we disagree, we express our concerns frankly. We will continue

a series of intensive discussions at the expert level to make satisfactory progress in these areas. If we determine there are violations of our laws, we will not hesitate to take appropriate action against those responsible, as we have done in the past.[70]

In November 1996 the first of a series of vice ministerial-level regular "global security dialogues" was held between Lynn Davis and Vice Foreign Minister Li Zhaoxing. Meetings were also held in Beijing between Arms Control and Disarmament Agency director John Holum and Li Zhaoxing. At the experts level, u.s. interagency teams met as frequently as three or four times a year for detailed discussions on nonproliferation issues with their Chinese counterparts.[71] Two key foci of u.s. concern were China's supply of antiship cruise missiles to Iran (under way since 1993) and China's supply of a uranium hexafluoride plant to Iran (agreed to in 1994). Holum returned from the talks in November 1996 "encouraged" by a "new willingness" of China to control the export of "sensitive technologies."[72] After these intensive talks China quietly informed the United States that it was canceling the "hex plant" sale agreement.[73]

As United States–China talks progressed, Beijing tried to reassure Tehran. At the end of 1996 an MFA spokesman told the Iranian media that, contrary to reports, China would not stop military cooperation with Iran as Washington was demanding. "China will never come to terms with one country over a third one," the spokesman said.[74]

Further sanctions against two Chinese companies in May 1997 for helping Iran make chemical weapons cast a shadow over Jiang's u.s. visit, tentatively projected for that fall. These sanctions were announced only after the cases had been made known to the Chinese government, but no remedial steps were taken by Beijing.[75] Making public information about Chinese technology transfers to Iran and Pakistan was one way the u.s. pressured Beijing to resolve the issue.

Einhorn and National Security Council senior director for arms control and nonproliferation Gary Samore traveled to Beijing for talks with Qian Qichen and foreign ministry counselor He Yafei in mid-1997. Einhorn agreed with a Chinese request that details of the talks about China's nuclear cooperation with Iran be kept secret and not released to the press.[76] Qian agreed to the implementation of export controls for nuclear-related items and to China's membership in the Zangger Committee, which China joined in November 1997. Qian also agreed to end sales of C-801 and C-802 cruise missiles to Iran. The u.s. side reportedly pressed to know whether the Chinese pledge applied to production technology and were told by Qian that it did.[77] Apparently this was a verbal commitment only. The most difficult issue was Washington's insistence on an end to all nuclear cooperation with Iran, even cooperation that was technically within the requirements of the NPT-IAEA regime.[78] In fact, Qian's major concern during these fall 1997 negotiations seems to have been, not departing from multilateral agreements, but not publicizing any agreement with the United States regarding Iran. Negotiations between Einhorn, Samore, and He Yafei over the issue were still under way the night before Jiang Zemin's scheduled arrival in the United States. Eventually agreement was reached on the text of a confidential letter to be sent by Qian Qichen to Secretary of State Madeleine Albright committing China to forgo any and all future nuclear cooperation with Iran. Qian also committed China to halt cruise missile sales to Iran—an agreement that reportedly included production technologies for such missiles.[79] He Yafei sought and secured assurances that Clinton would not embarrass Jiang by speaking in front of him about China's relations with Iran.[80] During the run-up to Jiang's visit, the White House announced that "Secretary Albright has raised in all her meetings with the Chinese foreign minister our deep concerns about the sale of conventional weapons and cruise missiles to Iran." Regarding the Chinese response to these U.S. "concerns," the White House spokesman had "no comment."[81]

A second letter between Qian and Albright dealt with nuclear issues and committed China not to supply a heavy-water modulated reactor, a uranium conversion facility (the hex plant), or reactors for producing power—all items agreed to or discussed by China and Iran in the 1990s. China also agreed to undertake no new nuclear cooperation with Iran after the completion of two low-proliferation-risk projects currently under way.[82] On the basis of these Chinese guarantees, the United States agreed to implement the long-stalled 1985 Nuclear Cooperation Agreement, and the joint statement signed during Jiang's October 1997 visit so stipulated. In January 1998 Clinton certified to Congress that "the People's Republic of China has provided clear and unequivocal assurances to the United States that it is not assisting and will not assist any non-nuclear weapon state, either directly or indirectly, in acquiring nuclear explosive devices or the material and components for such devices."[83]

As Jiang's 1997 visit to the United States approached, Tehran warned Beijing not to submit to U.S. pressure. If China gave in to U.S. pressure, "It would lose Iran's trust," an Iran foreign ministry spokesman said. Therefore, Iran expected China to "remain a trustworthy ally at the time of crisis."[84] China's interest in maintaining comity in Sino-American relations outweighed its interests in Tehran.

United States officials were surprised by the speed and completeness of China's 1996–97 break with earlier policy. First of all, the link with Taiwan was dropped. China also shifted direction on both nuclear and missile issues with considerable speed—and at considerable cost to its relations with Iran.[85] Shortly after the 1997 Jiang-Clinton summit an incident occurred that satisfied Washington that China was serious about implementing the recent nuclear agreement. United States intelligence learned from telephone intercepts that a Chinese company was negotiating to sell to an Iranian entity $100 million worth of anhydrous hydrogen fluoride—a chemical used to extract pluto-nium from spent reactor fuel. United States diplomats confronted Chinese officials with the intelligence, and China reacted swiftly and halted the deal.[86]

Through the first half of 2001, CIA semiannual reports to Congress cer-tified that China appeared to be complying with its October 1997 agreement to suspend nuclear cooperation with Iran.[87] Caveats began appearing in CIA reports to Congress starting in the second half of 2000. "We are aware of some interactions between Chinese and Iranian entities that have raised questions about [China's] 'no new nuclear cooperation' pledge," said that report. The U.S. government was "seeking to address these questions with appropriate Chinese authorities." Starting with the report for the second half of 2001, the certification of China's compliance with the 1997 agreement disappeared from CIA reports, while expressions of "concern" that China might be violating the 1997 agreement continued.

The U.S.-PRC Nuclear Cooperation Agreement (NCA) came into effect on March 11, 1998, but the United States chose not to implement it—that is, not actually to issue licenses permitting export of U.S. nuclear technology to China as per the agreement. Not until February 2005 would the Nuclear Regulatory Commission issue the first licenses for major U.S. nuclear tech-nology sales to China.[88] In 1998 Washington demanded from Beijing guar-antees that any nuclear technology sold to China would not be transferred to third parties. Beijing declined to give such assurances because they might constrain China's future export of indigenous nuclear technology similar to technology imported from the United States (i.e., reverse engineered from U.S. technology). With this dispute outstanding, the Nuclear Regulatory Commission simply refused to issue licenses to U.S. companies for export of nuclear technology to China under the NCA.[89] It is possible that Wash-ington's ongoing "concern" about clandestine Sino-Iranian nuclear cooper-ation was a factor producing the nonimplementation of the long-delayed 1985 nuclear cooperation agreement.

Meanwhile, negotiations continued over Chinese assistance to Iran's ballistic missile programs. During a January 1998 visit to Beijing, Defense Secretary Cohen pressed for a Chinese pledge to stop selling *all* missiles to Iran.[90] Chi Haotian was willing to reiterate earlier pledges regarding Category I missiles and C-801/C-802 missiles. Some reports assert that Chi also pledged that China would not assist Iran in upgrading its existing inventory of anti-ship missiles.[91]

Early in 1998 the Clinton administration shifted course on China and the MTCR as part of the effort to expand strategic engagement with China. Previously Washington was not enthusiastic about having China inside the MTCR, but sought merely to secure China's adherence to the rules of that regime. Early in 1998 U.S. policy changed. China's entry into the MTCR was now sought, with an offer of expanded cooperation in satellite launches extended as an additional incentive for China to take that step.[92] Chinese membership in the MTCR would require acceptance of the crucial Annex II. Clinton in March 1998 offered China restoration of cooperation on commercial space ventures in return for an end to *all* PRC assistance to Iranian ballistic missile programs and for its joining the MTCR. Jiang replied, in June, that China would "actively consider" joining the MTCR. Beijing was in no hurry to join, however. Asked about Jiang's commitment to Clinton, China's top arms control negotiator Sha Zukang pointed out that Jiang's commitment did not include the word "soon."[93] It would take Washington five years to reach its goal of Chinese entry into the MTCR. China applied to join the MTCR in September 2003. Beijing's reluctance to join the MTCR was partly a function of the limits that membership would impose on its cooperation with Iran. CIA biannual reports to Congress reported a steady flow of Chinese assistance and materials to Iranian ballistic missile programs.

By mid-2000 the Clinton administration tried to find a way around Chinese reluctance to join the MTCR and began pushing for China to adopt its own export control laws covering missile technology. Beijing indicated its general acceptance of this approach, and negotiations centered on how detailed and explicit Chinese laws would be. On November 21, 2000, during the interregnum between George W. Bush's presidential election victory and his inauguration, Beijing issued a statement on missile proliferation addressing a number of U.S. concerns. The statement said China "has *no intention to assist, in any way, any country in the development of ballistic missiles*" with Category I capabilities.[94] The U.S. State Department "welcomed" the Chinese statement and deemed it "a clear [Chinese] policy commitment not to assist, in any way, other countries'" Category I missile programs.[95] Actually, the Chinese wording was more equivocal. "Has no intention" is considerably weaker than the "will not export" used in the 1994 U.S.-PRC joint statement. Intentions can easily change, while the phrase "will not export" is categorical. Beijing also pledged in the November 2000 statement to "further improve and reinforce its export control system by publishing a comprehensive export control list of missile-related items including dual use items." This statement was qualified by the declaration that China's forthcoming export control system would be based on China's "own missile nonproliferation policy."[96] In other words, China would tighten its control of missile-related exports, but would make its own export licensing decisions. If the controlling Chinese agency granted licenses, controlled items would be exported. The U.S. quid pro quo was agreement to begin processing of licenses for Chinese launches of U.S. commercial satellites. The United States also waived imposition of sanctions for past Chinese assistance to Iranian or Pakistani missile programs.

INTENSIFICATION OF U.S. SANCTIONS:
THE GEORGE W. BUSH ADMINISTRATION

President George W. Bush (inaugurated in January 2001) shifted policy toward China's missile, chemical, and nuclear cooperation with Iran and Pakistan. The Clinton administration had been reluctant to impose and actually implement sanctions against Chinese firms dealing with Iran. Between mid-1994 and mid-1998 there were eighteen instances of reported Chinese transfers of banned items to Pakistan or Iran that were not sanctioned by the Clinton administration.[97] Clinton's team had insisted on a high level of proof that the Chinese government knew of particular transfers, or that Chinese transfers were "destabilizing." These were provisions of various U.S. laws providing the basis for presidential actions, but, as congressional critics charged at the time, these provisions could have been interpreted in a far less lenient way. In any case, Bush was far more willing than Clinton to resort to sanctions. Clinton imposed sanctions on China twice during his eight years in office, while Bush imposed sanctions ten times in his first two years.[98] Bush's sanctions also typically imposed far heavier economic penalties than Clinton's. Clinton-era sanctions were largely symbolic (except for the threatened suspension of Export-Import Bank financing in 1996), involving Chinese firms with little business in the United States. Bush sanctions targeted major Chinese firms heavily involved in U.S. markets—such as the North China Industries Corporation (NORINCO). Bush sanctions also threatened serious injury to the overall Sino-U.S. economic relation. One provision of the

September 2003 sanctions, for example, threatened to block as much as $12 billion in Chinese exports to the United States. Bush was also willing to repeatedly sanction Chinese companies for repeated violations.[99] Bush's approach also differed from Clinton's by attempting to compartmentalize nonproliferation disagreements while stressing cooperation with China in other areas. Clinton had treated nonproliferation disagreements with China in a high-profile way as part of an effort to mobilize public opprobrium against Chinese actions. This threat to China's international image combined with a readiness to waive sanctions was seen under Clinton as the way to end China's proliferation. The Bush team reversed the emphasis, being quite willing to actually impose sanctions, while publicly playing down proliferation disagreements and stressing cooperation with China on issues such as terrorism and North Korea.

Several factors underlay this new approach. First of all, the Bush and Clinton teams had different views of China's proliferation. Clinton and his officials had tended to stress China's steady if erratic and still incomplete progress toward embrace of nonproliferation. They believed that China had come a long way. Bush and his team stressed the continuation of Chinese proliferation in spite of repeated agreements. Clinton's team felt the cup half-full, while Bush's concluded it was half-empty. Bush's people also felt that Clinton's team had a naïve approach to world affairs, including China, and had often been taken in by Chinese deception. Ending Chinese assistance to Iranian missile and chemical programs required consistent and severe penalties, the Bush team believed. This point of view was expressed by a U.S. embassy spokesman shortly after the levying of severe sanctions against NORINCO in May 2003: "While [the United States] will continue to work with China to expand its areas of common interest, [we] will not paper over our differences. When necessary, we will take action in response to the proliferation activities of Chinese entities."[100]

Another factor behind the new Bush approach was heightened concern with terrorism following the September 11, 2001, attacks. One paramount American fear was that future terrorist attacks would employ chemical, biological, or, especially, nuclear weapons. In the view of the Bush administration, Iran was linked to various terrorist groups—Lebanon's Hezbollah, for example. September 11 had another sort of effect as well. According to U.S. officials, the flow of Chinese ballistic missile technology to Iran and Pakistan increased after the October 2001 Anglo-American intervention in Afghanistan. Those officials surmised that Beijing calculated that, with U.S. forces fighting in Afghanistan, Washington would be less willing to punish China for such transfers.[101] Still another factor was the u.s. estimate of the inadequate nature of China's missile technology export control system established as a result of the November 2000 agreement with the United States.

In August 2002 China issued its first systematic regulations controlling the export of missiles and missile-related technologies. This publication came while Undersecretary of State Richard Armitage was in Beijing to discuss missile proliferation, and just before a planned meeting between Bush and Jiang Zemin at Bush's Crawford, Texas, ranch—a meeting at which Bush too was expected to press proliferation concerns. China's new export control system was modeled after the mtcr and explicitly designed to control Category I missiles. Following the mtcr model, it was divided into three parts, a preamble and two lists of items to be controlled. The first list corresponded to mtcr Annex I and listed major subsystems that go into Category I missiles. The second list corresponded to mtcr Annex II and listed dual-use "missile-related items and technologies" that might or might not be used to make Category I missiles. In October China issued regulations and registration and licensing procedures both for biological and chemical agents, technologies, and equipment.

A "wait and see" attitude prevailed in Washington following the November 2000 statement and the August 2002 promulgation of China's export control guidelines. But as instances of Chinese support to Iran's missile program continued even after the seemingly definitive August 2002 regulations, Washington decided to up the pressure.[102] In the first instance, the prc system established in 2002 provided for licensing of exports, not the outright prohibition of exports or certain types of goods or to certain countries. While no listed item could be exported without a license, any item could be exported with a license. As director general of the mfa Arms Control and Disarmament Department Liu Jieyi explained when the new system was promulgated: "The mtcr itself is a control regime, not a prohibition regime. No item contained in the mtcr is prohibited. So China is simply doing something that all other countries are doing, taking fully into consideration the risk of proliferation in the relevant field."[103] The United States had pushed for the outright banning of certain types of exports to certain countries through such elliptical formulations as "countries of concern" or "high proliferation risks." Beijing had rejected this approach. China's new licensing system was also predicated on the good faith of the foreign party acquiring Chinese missile-related items and technologies. Chinese firms applying for licenses to export controlled items were required under the new system to include guarantees from the foreign "receiving party" attesting to the nonmilitary end use and end user of the desired items, along with a pledge from the "receiving party" not to transfer the item to any third party without the consent of the Chinese government. But what if the foreign recipient was willing to lie in these statements regarding end use? What if deception and ruse were part of the foreign state's missile development strategy?

Determinations under China's new export licensing system were, of course, made by Chinese officials on the basis of China's own rules. While this could not have been otherwise, the consequence was a fairly lax approval process. After announcing its new export control regulations, Beijing pointedly stated that China's implementation of the new regulations would be based on its own understanding of which countries posed proliferation risks.[104] Strangely, the regulations did not explicitly require that China's licensing authorities make a determination of proliferation risk when considering a license application. Instead, those authorities were merely to examine the application, including certificates of end use and end user along with documents of guarantee from the foreign recipient, and "make a decision of approval or denial within 45 working days." While an opening section of the regulations did state that the purpose of the licensing system is "to prevent the proliferation of missiles that can be used to deliver weapons of mass destruction," licensing authorities were not specifically charged with making a determination about proliferation risk when approving or denying applications. Their function, under the wording of the regulations, was to make sure the application was in proper order. The entire export control system was also limited to items and technology that could be used for missiles capable of delivering five hundred kilograms a distance of three hundred kilometers. Items and technologies relevant to missiles below that threshold were not controlled. The potent FL-7 antiship missile that Iran and China began jointly developing circa 1999, for example, was well below the range limit of the new control system. Finally, China's control lists omitted a significant number of items on MTCR annexes, meaning that those items could still be exported freely.[105] The Chinese list omitted, for example, high-acceleration gyros and accelerometers that could be used as fuses in reentry vehicles, global positioning systems that can be used to improve missile accuracy, or maraging steel used for rocket motors. Some of these omitted items would be the target of further U.S. sanctions. Interestingly, about this time North Korea entered the picture in terms of helping modernize Iran's C-802 cruise missiles.[106]

In October 2002, barely a month after the promulgation of China's new licensing system, U.S. agencies determined that the giant Chinese firm NORINCO was providing specialty steel to an Iranian missile-manufacturing company. When informed of the matter, Beijing denied that the transaction had occurred. In response, in May 2003, Washington imposed the most severe sanctions to date: NORINCO, one of China's largest manufacturers, was banned for two years from conducting any business in the United States.[107] The severity of the sanctions reflected Washington's dissatisfaction with China's unwillingness to halt assistance to Iran's missile program. According to a U.S. official involved in arms control negotiations with China, "We've given them names of those serial proliferators and said 'you ought to look into this' and they've come back to us basically and said: 'We've investigated and no problem here.'"[108] China's new regulations were apparently being implemented, and China was fulfilling its obligations undertaken to the United States, but Chinese technology and components apparently continued to support Iran's missile development programs.

Parallel with continued "leakage" under China's export control system, low-level Chinese cooperation with Iran's nuclear programs seems also to have resumed. CIA director George Tenet told Congress in February 2003 that Chinese "firms" (i.e., not government) "may be backing away" from Beijing's 1997 pledge to forgo new nuclear cooperation with Iran. The next month Tenet reported "some interactions" that "may run counter" to the 1997 pledge.[109]

During their meeting on the sidelines of the G-8 summit at Evian, France, on June 1, 2003, President Bush raised with President Hu Jintao the issue of Chinese assistance to Iran's strategic programs. Iran's pursuit of nuclear weapons represented a grave threat that China and the United States should work together to address, Bush told Hu. Hu did not pick up on Bush's comment.[110] Beijing objected strenuously to Washington's growing resort to sanctions. "We express our strong opposition to the U.S. manner of constantly implementing sanctions on others based on their own domestic law," said an MFA spokesman.[111]

IRAN AND CHINA'S CHOICE
OF COOPERATION WITH THE UNITED STATES

The broad pattern of twenty years of Sino-American bargaining over Iran has been incremental Chinese subordination of Sino-Iranian cooperation to Sino-American comity. When the potential loss to China became great enough, China disengaged from Silkworm and then more advanced antiship missile, Category I ballistic missile, and nuclear cooperation with Iran, though it did this in a fashion intended to minimize loss of face and influence in Tehran. Bluntly stated, China seems to have decided not to confront the

United States in the Middle East over Iran. Beijing was determined, however, to give up no more than was absolutely necessary and to find other ways of being useful to Tehran. Beijing has balanced continuing strategic cooperation with Iran with maintaining comity in Sino-American relations.

China's decision to suspend nuclear cooperation with Iran says much about China's diplomatic strategies. From 1991 through 1996 the United States demanded China end all nuclear cooperation with both Pakistan and Iran. In the end, Beijing satisfied u.s. demands regarding only Iran. Then, Beijing rejected u.s. demands to end nuclear cooperation with *Pakistan*, while it acceded to this demand in the case of Iran. This was in spite of the fact that Iran was an NPT signatory in good standing with the IAEA, while Pakistan was not. Toward Pakistan, Beijing agreed in May 1996 only to terminate cooperation with *unsafeguarded* facilities. Toward Iran, Beijing agreed in October 1997 to abstain completely from any new nuclear cooperation with Iran. Given the intrinsic fungibility of nuclear knowledge and skills and the weaknesses of the IAEA inspection regime, China's cooperation with Pakistan's IAEA-safeguarded facilities assisted to some degree Pakistan's nuclear weapons programs. In effect, while Beijing agreed to cease supporting a possible Iranian nuclear weapons effort, it insisted on continuing to support Pakistan's nuclear effort against India. The fundamental difference between the two cases seems to have been that Pakistan's nuclear weapons were directed primarily against India, while Iran's hypothetical nuclear weapons targeted the United States and u.s. ally Israel. Stated simply, Beijing was willing to support Pakistan's nuclear challenge to India, but not Iran's nuclear challenge to the United States. This suggests that Pakistan plays a geopolitical role in Chinese strategy not played by Iran. Very probably, Beijing views a strong, even nuclear-armed, Pakistan as crucial to maintaining a balance of power that constrains an India potentially hostile to China. Iran apparently plays no comparable strategic role in Chinese strategy. China's nuclear and missile cooperation with Iran seems to have been much more opportunistic—a way of earning foreign currency and punishing the United States for Taiwan transgressions, while accumulating political capital in Tehran.

China's 1996–97 decisions to suspend nuclear, Category I, and antiship cruise missile cooperation with Iran were a function of calculations about China's relations with the United States. The mainstream of China's leaders were dismayed by the downward spiral of u.s. PRC relations after June 1989. They understood that the remarkable success of China's post-1978 development effort was predicated to a substantial degree on u.s. goodwill. Conversely, collapse of u.s.-PRC comity could deliver a devastating blow to

China's development drive. Moreover, the United States exercised immense influence over a range of other objectives highly valued by Beijing—from unification with Taiwan, to securing status as a well-respected and leading member of the community of nations. Thus, most of China's leaders sought comity with Washington via compromise. Such compromise could not come at the expense of core values. There could be no compromise on such matters as upholding the Chinese Communist Party's absolute control over Chinese society or promoting the "return" of Taiwan to the motherland. On other noncore matters compromise was possible—once China's negotiators drove the best bargain possible. China's nuclear cooperation with Iran apparently fell into the latter category.

There is little question that China's leaders loathed u.s. policy toward the Persian Gulf and Iran. They deemed the United States an arrogant hegemonist bully bent on dominating this energy-rich region via subordination of Iran and Iraq. But the question before China's leaders was whether China should stand with, support, and encourage the world's antihegemonist forces. Such a stance might move the world toward multipolarity, a condition that China's leaders ardently desired. It also comported with principles of global justice, or so China's leaders felt. And some among China's leaders believed that the United States was already pursuing covert efforts to partition and weaken China. Given this, support for other stalwart anti-u.s. forces in the world made sense. These arguments for standing up against u.s. hegemonist bullying were emotionally very satisfying to many in China. But from a practical point of view, from the perspective of China's development, China's leaders had to ask themselves how long the United States could be expected to view benevolently a China that supported or led opposition to it or that aligned itself with Iran and/or Iraq. However, cooperating with Washington on such matters as global nuclear nonproliferation could help stabilize Sino-u.s. relations. Expanded cooperation with the United States on nonproliferation would also open access for China to u.s. advanced nuclear power technology, a development that would both raise China's general technological level and help address its growing energy needs. If China could actually forge a "strategic partnership" with the United States, China's power might wax over the first several decades of the twenty-first century under the benevolent patronage of u.s. hegemony.

Israeli lobbying was another factor nudging Beijing away from Tehran. Israel opened a military technology supply relation with China in the 1980s and gradually expanded that into a political relationship leading to full diplomatic relations in 1992. As relations improved, Tel Aviv consistently urged Beijing not to support the missile and nuclear programs of Middle East states hostile to

Israel, including those of Iran. Israeli lobbying dovetailed with the American. It is also possible that Beijing saw its ties with Iran endangering its valuable, and u.s.-endorsed (at least until the 2000s), military technology relation with Israel.

China's self-identity goes some distance toward explaining Beijing's 1996–97 choice to move away from Iran. There are several competing voices in the discourse on China's contemporary national identity. While the role of champion of the Third World is still attractive to many Chinese, so too is the competing image of China as an esteemed and front-ranking state among the leading nations of the world. A central component of China's modern political culture, and a component to which the ccp must appeal, is a craving for international respect. Contemporary Chinese ardently desire that China be seen by the world community as a strong, modern, progressive, civilized nation—as a nation worthy of respect. Regarding nuclear nonproliferation, there was growing awareness in China during the 1980s and 1990s that nonproliferation principles were genuinely global norms, even though u.s. hegemony might exploit them for its own purposes. Given this, if China aligned with rebels against those nuclear proliferation norms—with countries like Iran, Pakistan, and North Korea—it would not expect to win the international respect it desired. Rather, it might itself win reputation as a "rogue nation."

Finally, China's decision to draw away from Iran was predicated on recognition that China's interests were best served by having fewer rather than more nuclear weapons states in the world. China enjoyed exclusive privileges and rights as one of only five nuclear weapons states specified by the npt. It was not in China's interest to see its special nuclear status diluted by proliferation of nuclear weapons.

But parallel to China's incremental disengagement from the iri was tenacious Chinese resistance to u.s. demands for such disengagement. China's representatives were adept at crafting loopholes in agreements with the United States over Iran: agreeing to end Silkworm sales only to sell technology and manufacturing machinery to make those missiles, and then selling a far superior class of antiship missile, the C-801/C-802; agreeing repeatedly to mtcr guidelines and parameters but excluding Annex II; insisting on a distinction between a 280-kilometer-range, 800-kilogram missile and a 300-kilometer-range, 500 kilogram missile; and implementing an export control system and then continuing to license export of sensitive items. Beijing clearly valued cooperation and friendly ties with Tehran and was loath to sacrifice those entirely on the altar of Sino-American comity. Protracted resistance to u.s. pressure provided sufficient time for Chinese cooperation with Iran in various areas to contribute substantially to Iran's indigenous, self-reliant capabilities. Beijing consistently avoided commitments restricting China's ability to sell technology and capital goods to Iran. And when Beijing capitulated to U.S. pressure in one area, it found other areas in which to be useful to Tehran. In short, Chinese policy balanced between Washington and Tehran.

9 / The Sino-Iranian Energy-Economic Relationship

Iran's 1979 revolution had a profound impact on Sino-Iranian economic relations. It is impossible to compare Sino-Iranian trade before and after the revolution and infer that increases were due to the change of Iranian regime because there was a profoundly important exogenous variable: China's post 1978 opening to the world and the consequent explosive growth of China's exports to *all* countries. In one way, however, it is clear that Iran's revolution had a deep impact—it led to the exit from Iran of several of Iran's traditional major trading partners, especially the United States and Britain. Their departure created opportunities for China. Figure 9.1 shows that in 1978 the United States accounted for 21 percent of Iran's imports, but by 1991 had fallen to 3 percent, and by 2003 to zero. The United Kingdom's share declined from 8 percent in 1978 to virtually zero in 1991, before rising to 3 percent in 2003. China's share of Iran's imports grew from 1 percent in 1978 to 2 percent by 1991 and to 8 percent by 2003. Those figures do not include arms sales or Chinese goods smuggled into Iran from the United Arab Emirates. If SIPRI estimates for PRC arms sales to Iran in 2003 are added, plus another estimated 12 percent of the value of registered trade for Chinese goods smuggled into Iran from Dubayy, China's share of Iranian imports for 2003 rises to 9.5 percent. China has shoehorned itself into the lucrative Iranian market.

Sino-Iranian trade has grown steadily and rapidly, as shown by table 9.1. Average annual growth in two-way trade between 1990 and 2001 was 55 per-

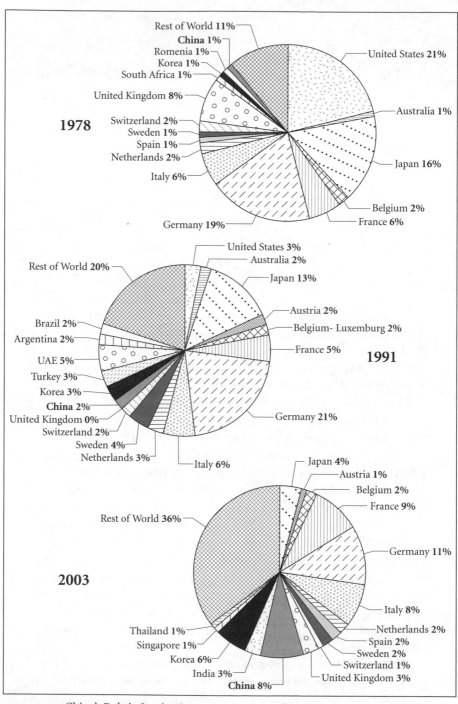

FIGURE 9.1: China's Role in Iranian Imports, 1978, 1991, 2003
SOURCE: International Monetary Fund, *Direction of Trade Statistics Yearbook*

cent. Excluding the outlying postwar year 1990, when trade rose nearly three times, the annual growth rate is still a healthy 33 percent. Iran ran a chronic deficit in trade with China until the 2000s, when large Chinese oil purchases gave Iran a large and apparently continuing surplus. China has provided a stable customer for Iran's major export, petroleum. The fact that this customer was unlikely to capitulate to Western demands for economic sanctions against Iran was also important to Tehran.

The IRI has continually faced strong economic pressures. The combination of war with Iraq and revolutionary turmoil, nationalizations, and emigration produced a precipitous economic decline during the 1980s. Religious and nationalist fervor mitigated popular discontent with that decline, but the end of the war with Iraq in August 1988 and the death of Khomeini in June 1989 unleashed that discontent. By 1989 Iran's leaders, or at least the more pragmatic among them, believed that rapid and substantial improvement in economic conditions was essential to the health of Iran's Islamic revolution—essentially the same conclusion reached by Deng Xiaoping a decade earlier about the fate of China's CCP-led revolution. Thus, in 1989, Tehran launched a major effort to rehabilitate and reconstruct Iran's economy: the First Five Year Economic, Social, and Cultural Development Plan (1989–93). China would be a major partner in Iran's postwar development.

A serious problem for China's efforts to expand cooperation with Iran has been that the technological level of Chinese capital goods (machinery, equipment, and embedded technology used in manufacturing, mining, and transportation sectors) was often inferior to that of Western countries. Iranian managers sometimes (perhaps even typically) preferred more advanced Western technology. In the 2004 view of one Chinese diplomat with extensive experience in the Middle East, Iranian preference for Western technology sometimes bordered on irrational "superstition." Iranians sometimes simply believed without inquiry that Western goods were superior to Chinese, even when this was not the case. Moreover, in purchasing Chinese goods Iranian businessmen often demanded very low prices because they assumed Chinese goods would be of low quality, but the low prices they demanded meant that those prices could be met only by lowering quality. When negotiating to buy Western goods, however, Iranian agents expected to pay high prices and therefore received higher quality. This situation had changed somewhat as Chinese technology won a degree of acceptance via assistance in developing Tehran's subway and Iran's mining and metallurgy, according to the Chinese diplomat. Still, in June 2003 PRC ambassador to Iran Liu Zhentang twice complained (on two consecutive days) to Iranian officials that some people in Iran's foreign contact bidding process acted with prejudice against China and in a "pro-Western"

TABLE 9.1
Iran-China Trade, 1974–2003

		(US $ millions)			
Year	Iran exports	Iran imports	Total trade	Percentage increase in two-way trade	Iran balance
1974	0	111	111	0	-111
1975	0	53	53	-52	-53
1976	0	93	93	75	-93
1977	0	134	134	44	-134
1978	0	174	174	30	-174
1979	29	40	69	-60	-11
1980	53	133	186	170	-80
1981	2	179	181	-3	-177
1982	81	45	126	-30	36
1983	0	294	294	133	-294
1984	0	170	170	-42	-170
1985	7	48	55	-68	-41
1986	0	26	26	-53	-26
1987	4	53	57	119	-49
1988	16	36	52	-9	-20
1989	43	48	91	75	-5
1990	39	321	360	296	-282
1991	19	322	341	-5	-303
1992	155	335	490	44	-180
1993	329	326	655	34	3
1994	223	147	370	-44	76
1995	216	232	448	21	-16
1996	74	242	316	-29	-168
1997	543	395	938	197	148
1998	508	655	1163	24	-147
1999	771	613	1384	19	158
2000	1612	785	2397	73	827
2001	2204	978	3182	33	1226
2002	2133	960	3093	-3	1173
2003	3007	2547	5554	80	460

SOURCE: *Direction of Trade Statistics* (Washington, DC International Monetary Fund, 1975–2004).

manner. Liu deeply rejected and "did not understand" this behavior and asked that his views be conveyed to the appropriate officials.[1]

However, the lower technological level of China 's capital goods also held certain advantages for Iran. They were easier for Iranian personnel to master, thereby lessening the need for large numbers of expensive Western specialists associated with import of more advanced Western technology. Chinese experts, who often accompanied equipment to assist with setup, also cost a lot less than Western specialists. According to one top manager at Iran's Petro Pars oil company, a European petroleum engineer could cost the company $30,000 a month, while a Chinese engineer at the same skill level cost $500 a month. China was also quite willing to transfer to Iran advanced Western technology only recently acquired by China itself. This assisted Iran's efforts at indigenous industrialization.

Chinese capital goods also had advantages for Iran in terms of job creation—a major objective for IRI leaders. One of the characteristics of Iran's development is a relatively high level of urbanization and relatively low reliance on the agricultural sector. This placed a premium on job creation in industry. From this perspective, reliance on somewhat simpler, labor-intensive capital equipment made sense—although enterprise managers might well have different views of this matter. Western sanctions also prevented Iranian access to a wide range of Western capital goods, or made them available only with lots of "strings" over things like end-use inspections. Moreover, Tehran never knew when U.S. pressure would lead Western nations to suspend or restrict cooperation with Iran. China, however, was willing to take Iran on its own terms. Unlike the Western countries, Beijing did not "interfere in the internal affairs of Iran" because of scruples over the nature of Iran's Islamic regime or nuclear, chemical, or advanced conventional weapons program. Finally, Chinese capital goods were typically cheaper than European or Japanese goods. An informal survey by this author of a dozen industrial tool shops in Tehran, Esfahan, and Shiraz during November 2004 found Chinese compressors, motors, drill presses, lathes, pumps, and electrical switches competing with European, South Korean, and Indian products. According to the shopkeepers, the main attraction of the Chinese products was their substantially lower prices.

EVOLUTION OF THE ECONOMIC RELATIONSHIP

During the 1980s, the Sino-Iranian economic relation was a top-down process driven by the two governments. Iran's Islamic revolution had transferred large swaths of the economy to Islamic foundations that functioned as loosely regulated state-owned enterprises. Moreover, the war with Iraq intensified the need for centralized control and allocation of resources. Throughout the 1990s and into the new millennium Iran's economy remained very much state dominated. China was moving the opposite direction, toward a market economy. During the 1980s the central trade monopolies of the Maoist era were abolished and the economy increasingly organized on a market basis. But Chinese firms were quite familiar with operating under conditions of government control. Under these conditions, officials of the two governments would meet and agree on projects and then nominate companies from their respective countries to execute the agreements. In 1985 these meetings were regularized and institutionalized in the Joint Committee for Trade, Science, and Technology Cooperation. During the 1980s this Joint Committee was the motor of the economic relationship. In the Joint Committee, vice premiers of the two governments plus representatives of the ministries would discuss possible areas of cooperation. Once agreement was reached, the two sides would select and introduce particular firms, which then negotiated forms of mutually beneficial cooperation. Under the Joint Committee were three subcommittees: commerce and oil, the economy and industry, and science and technology.[2]

By the 1990s China's economy was becoming highly marketized, with representatives of independent and entrepreneurial enterprises roaming the world in search of profitable deals. Iran remained very much of a state-run economy. Yet marketization of China's economy, plus the expansion of direct contacts between Chinese and Iranian companies, progressively reduced the role of the Joint Committee. Increasingly Chinese enterprises would ferret out deals with Iranian entities independent of the Joint Committee. Deals and contracts would increasingly be initiated and decided on by enterprises prior to Joint Committee meetings, and those deals were then retroactively bundled into the committee's announcements. Increasingly the Joint Committee became a venue for working out problems that arose in the course of commercial interactions—a role that was especially important given the weak commercial codes and civil judicial institutions of the IRI. Large projects with substantial financial underwriting from the Chinese government were still handled by the Joint Committee.

PRC-IRI economic cooperation began in 1982 when China agreed to send thirty senior water conservancy experts to help design a large dam in southern Iran and to dispatch twenty-six fishing boats and more than eight hundred workers to the Persian Gulf to enhance Iran's fishing industry. These two projects proved quite satisfactory from the Iranian point of view.[3] In 1984 Chinese firms began undertaking construction contracts in Iran. By the end of the Iran-Iraq war, twelve such projects with a total value of $25 million had been signed.[4] The largest of these projects was the construction of three fish-canning factories worth $20 million. China also agreed to transfer to Iran technology for pisciculture and shrimp breeding.[5] There was also continued cooperation in small hydropower projects and fishing, with Iran purchasing thirty-six Chinese trawlers, eighteen of which were manufactured in Iran.[6] Between 1984 and November 1989 Chinese firms had signed nineteen contracts totaling $66.74 million in thermo- and hydroelectricity generation projects, atomic energy, dam design, nonferrous metals, geology and mining, light industries, and fisheries.

The end of the Iran-Iraq war led to further increased economic cooperation. In mid-August 1988, shortly after Iran's formal acceptance of Security Council Resolution 598, Vice Foreign Minister Qi Huaiyuan visited Iran to say that China attached "special importance to its ties with Iran" and was ready to cooperate with Iran in postwar construction.[7] The next month Iranian deputy premier Hamid Mirzadeh led to Beijing a delegation including representatives from the ministries of commerce, finance, foreign affairs, mines and metals, industries, construction, agriculture, fisheries, and education. Iran hoped that China would offer cooperation in Iran's postwar reconstruction and attached "great importance" to the current Joint Commission meeting, Mirzadeh said. Third World countries should increase their unity, Mirzadeh advised. Iran wanted to "utilize global technology" while safeguarding its culture and values.[8] Vice Premier Tian Jiyun told Mirzadeh that China was "willing to give a hand" with Iran's reconstruction.[9] Premier Li Peng gently indicated to Mirzadeh that Iran should not expect large amounts of Chinese concessionary assistance. China was willing to assist Iran's reconstruction effort "so far as it is able" and "on the basis of equality and mutual benefit," Li told Mirzadeh.[10] Since Iran was rich in resources, it would rehabilitate its national economy and rebuild its country by relying on its own efforts, Li continued. The 1989 session of the Joint Committee agreed to more than double trade from the 1988 level. Two-way trade was pegged at $600 million.[11]

China's minister of light industry, Zheng Xianlin, led an eighteen-member Chinese economic delegation to Tehran in October 1988 to introduce Iranian businesses to Chinese automobiles, electrical utensils, tobacco products, paper manufacturing machinery, and construction materials. Zheng's Iranian counterpart, industries minister Gholamreza Shafei, indicated that Iran was prepared to cooperate in paper manufacturing, tobacco products, detergent powder, and utensils. Shafei also urged China to buy a variety of Iranian "non-oil products."[12] This plea to buy non-oil products pointed toward a perennial problem in Sino-Iranian relations. Iran simply had little that China needed other than oil and raw materials, while Iran had a strong demand for Chinese manufactured products. Immediately after the Chinese light industry delegation left Tehran, another led by the deputy minister of machine building and electronics industry, Zhao Mingsheng, arrived in Tehran to explore possibilities for industrial and technical cooperation.[13] Zhao visited eighteen factories in Tabriz, Esfahan, and Arak, and became familiar with Iran's "industrial output and technology."[14] The general manager of China National Petroleum Corporation (CNPC), Wang Tao, was also in Tehran about the same time to discuss the petroleum side of Sino-Iranian cooperation.

During talks in Beijing at the end of 1988 Foreign Minister Ali Akbar Velayati returned to the issue of China's role in Iran's postwar reconstruction effort.[15] "We very much welcome China's earnest and wide-ranging participation in Iran's postwar reconstruction," Velayati told premier Zhao Ziyang. The latter welcomed expanded Sino-Iranian cooperation and suggested that China had certain strengths in technology, labor, and machinery. China was quite willing to expand cooperation "on the original basis," Zhao told Velayati.[16] This too was probably a hint that Beijing was not prepared to extend large concessionary assistance to Iran. Velayati conveyed to Zhao a letter from Rafsanjani placing Chinese support for Iran's postwar reconstruction in a geopolitical context: "Bilateral cooperation between Iran and China is indisputably useful to maintaining regional peace, Asian peace, and stability and security, and even useful for upholding world peace. It is our hope that cooperation between Iran and China will become a model for cooperation between nonaligned and Third World nations."[17] In plain words, Velayati was saying that, given Iran's strategic importance, Beijing should be prepared to underwrite financially Sino-Iranian economic cooperation.

Early in 1989 PRC Foreign Minister Qian Qichen gave a token of China's good intentions to Velayati when the two met on the fringes of the Chemical Weapons Conference in Paris in January. China was prepared to increase its purchases of Iranian oil and to construct a paper plant in Iran, Qian said.[18] This established the pattern of China's cooperation with Iran's postwar reconstruction: China would supply industrial equipment, technology, and engineering services in exchange for Iranian oil. The paper plant was probably an aid project, a token of China's goodwill and commitment to Iran's postwar reconstruction.

An authoritative and high-level statement of China's willingness to participate in Iran's postwar reconstruction efforts was conveyed by Vice Premier

Tian Jiyun during a five-day March 1989 visit to Tehran. China viewed relations with Iran as "strategic," Tian said, and was prepared to cooperate with Iran in postwar reconstruction.[19] President Khamenei told Tian: "We prefer to cooperate with those countries of which Iranian people have no unpleasant memories," that is, with non-Western countries.[20]

The economic relationship was put on a more solid commercial basis in January 1990 when the two sides shifted bilateral trade and economic cooperation from a running credit-ledger with a quarterly reckoning (a system established in 1973) to a cash payment basis. China also began extending credits to support expanded cooperation. In January 1993 the Bank of China signed an agreement with Iran's Sepah Bank providing a US$50 million credit to support exports by Iran's state-owned enterprises. This was the first formal loan by China to Iran and seems to have been tied to the award of the Tehran metro project to the China International Trust and Investment Company (CITIC)— a matter discussed below. In any case, the loan was extended ten months after CITIC won a second round of bidding for the metro project and while negotiations were under way about the terms of cooperation. The month after the loan was announced CITIC signed a contract to supply equipment and technology sets for eleven cement factories, each with a daily output of seven hundred tons of cement, to be used in building the Tehran metro and with a total contract value of $110 million.[21]

In July 1993 China extended two more loans, one of $150 million for the Tehran metro project and another of $120 million to refurbish and build ten cement factories.[22] Chinese construction of a 300-megawatt nuclear power plant and Iranian construction of a refinery in China to handle Iran's high-sulfur crude oil were also part of the July 1993 package of deals—although both elements of that deal would collapse. Securing Iranian investment in constructing refineries capable of handling high-sulfur Iranian oil was a long-standing Chinese objective. Linking of China's construction of a nuclear power plant and Iran's investment in Chinese refineries suggests a quid pro quo. Later in 1997, when China pulled out of the nuclear power plant deal, Iran apparently responded by withdrawing from the plan to invest in the refinery in China. In the late 1990s, China itself financed construction of high-sulfur-capable refineries in China.[23] Toward the end of 1995 Xinhua announced that $1.08 billion worth of cooperation contracts had been signed between Iran and China in 1995.[24]

Long-term prospects for expanded Sino-Iranian cooperation are good. In October 2003 the head of Tehran province told Ambassador Liu Zhentang that Iran hoped to strengthen cooperation with China over the coming twenty years. Iran planned to increase its annual growth rate to 8.6 percent during the Fifth Five Year Plan (2009–13), the Iranian official said, thereby establishing Iran as the leading economy in the region. Liu Zhentang responded by requesting detailed information about Iranian proposals for expanded cooperation. As of mid-2004, forty-one Chinese firms maintained representative offices in Iran.[25] Under way were forty to fifty joint projects with a total value of about $1 billion.[26]

THE CAPITAL GOODS FLOW

The crux of the PRC-IRI economic partnership has been China's export of large quantities of capital goods, engineering services, and munitions to Iran in exchange for Iranian oil, minerals, and base metals. This has been an important exchange, highly beneficial to both parties. It grew in importance during the 1990s as China's need for imported petroleum and raw materials increased. The exchange with Iran has permitted China to meet a large and growing portion of its spiraling energy requirements via cooperation with a geopolitically important country that could be expected to reject U.S. demands for sanctions against China. At the same time, China found a major market for its high-value-added, high-technology capital goods and services. Moving up the value-added ladder instead of remaining a mere exporter of cheap, labor-intensive goods has been a high-ranking Chinese objective. Finding markets for Chinese capital goods, especially capital goods upgraded by incorporation of recent acquisition of Western technologies, is a major way of accomplishing that objective.

Figure 9.2 illustrates the composition of Chinese trade with Iran in 2003. Machinery, electrical appliances, vehicles, aircraft, and instruments accounted for 47 percent of China's exports to Iran. Chemical products, plastic and rubber goods, and textiles accounted for another 28 percent. Together these manufactured goods made up three-quarters of China's exports to Iran. Crude oil made up 80 percent of China's imports from Iran. Minerals and base metals constituted another 14 percent of imports. The major items in this category are shown in table 9.2. Oil and minerals together made up 94 percent of China's imports from Iran. The significance of China's trade with Iran in this regard is indicated by comparing the value of China's petroleum imports from Iran with the value of its export of capital goods to Iran. In 2003 China imported $2.6 billion in oil from Iran and sold Iran $1.1 billion worth of civilian machines, electrical equipment and appliances, vehicles, aircraft, and instruments. In other words, China was able to cover 42 percent of the value of its oil imports plus a significant portion of its strategic mineral imports

Exports

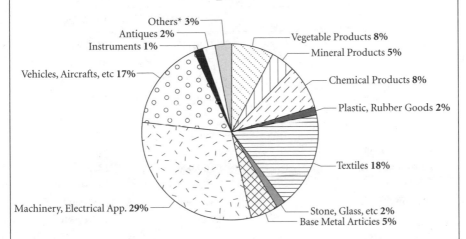

Others* **3%**
Antiques **2%**
Instruments **1%**
Vehicles, Aircrafts, etc **17%**
Machinery, Electrical App. **29%**

Vegetable Products **8%**
Mineral Products **5%**
Chemical Products **8%**
Plastic, Rubber Goods **2%**
Textiles **18%**
Stone, Glass, etc **2%**
Base Metal Articles **5%**

"Others" Animal Products, Fats and Oils, Foodstuff and Beverages, Leather and Skin Products, Wood, Cork, etc, Umbrellus, etc, Precious Medals etc, Arms and Weapons, Miscellaneous Manufactured Items

Imports

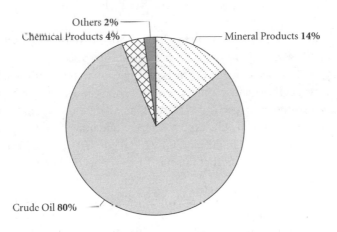

Others **2%**
Chemical Products **4%**
Mineral Products **14%**
Crude Oil **80%**

"Others" Animal Products, Vegetable Products, Foodstuff and Beverages, Plastic and Rubber Goods, Leather and Skin Products, Wood, Cork, etc, Textiles, Shoes, Umbrellus, etc, Stone, Glass, etc, Precious Medals etc, Base Metal Articles, Machinery and Electrical App, Vehicles, Aircrafts etc, Instruments, Miscellaneous Manufactured Items, Antiques

FIGURE 9.2: Composition of China's Trade with Iran, 2003
SOURCE: *Zhongguo haiguan nianjian (China customs yearbook)*, Beijing 2003

TABLE 9.2

China's Major Mineral and Base Metal Imports from Iran, 2003

	US$ value	Thousand kilograms
Stone	36,159,345	188,939,241
Sulphur	32,866,034	381,539,137
Copper ore	32,378,499	68,099,030
Copper, copper alloys, items, and scrap	19,043,309	13,226,381
Zinc ore	21,002,924	131,287,273
Rolled iron and steel	15,526,765	55,878,973
Chromium ore	8,860,024	113,892,059
Lead ore	5,592,474	22,310,463
Iron ore	4,878,609	137,445,071
Aluminum, alloys and items	2,245,757	1,845,346
Aluminum ore	57,920	347,870

SOURCE: *Zhonghua renmin gongheguo haiguan tongji nianjian, 2003* [People's Republic of China Customs Statistical Yearbook, 2003] (Beijing: Zhongguo haiguan, 2003).

from Iran by export of high-value-added and relatively high-technology capital goods.

Machinery exports are useful to China's efforts to reform its machine tools industry. Reforming China's heavy industrial enterprises has been one of the banes of China's reformers. It was typically China's light industry that was able to attract foreign investment, produce goods in demand on global markets, and prosper from post-1978 reform. China's capital goods industry found reform much more difficult. Exports to Iran (and other countries) addressed this difficulty. Iran's high demand for capital goods, combined with its ability to pay with oil, meant that this hard-pressed sector of China's economy was better able to move into the mainstream of the global economy.

Table 9.3 lists Sino-Iranian economic cooperation projects. In terms of specific areas of cooperation, repair of war-damaged facilities was a key focus during the early postwar period. During his March 1989 visit, Tian Jiyun told his counterpart, Hamid Mirzadeh, that China was prepared to help with the reconstruction of war-damaged oil refineries and offshore oil platforms and with the dredging of waterways silted in from wartime disuse.[27] Housing construction was another early area of cooperation. Demand for housing was high in postwar Iran because of high internal migration during the war, combined with wartime destruction of housing. Chinese prefabrication techniques

TABLE 9.3

China's Major Economic Projects in Iran, 1988–2004

Year	Type of project	Location	Value	Details
1988	Design, engineering, & manufacturing of equipment for refineries, power stations, & ports			letter of understanding
1988	manufacture of 18 fishing trawlers			technology transferred from China
1988	3 canned-fish factories			total daily output = 70 tons
1988	dam & hydropower plant	Kharke, Khuzistan		technical services for 2nd phase construction
1988	cement & metal jetties			technology transferred from China
1989	housing construction			technology & engineering services from China
1989	dam and hydropower plant	Ahvaz province		
1989	power plants, sugar, paper, machine tools, engineering machinery manufacture			MOU re technology transfer
1989	joint design & manufacture two 300 MW steam power generators			MOU re between machine building ministries
1989	Manufacting sugar refinery equipment & crane trucks	Kerman province		
1989	paper factory			50 tons daily output; use of cotton stems?
1989	geology and mining cooperation; zinc smelter	Bafq		MOU re cooperation
1989	ion beam implantation equipment		$210 thousand	SW Physics Institute
1989	reconstruction damaged oil fields			
1989	four 125 MW power plants	Gilan province		
1991	coal exploration	Tabas	$2.6 million	China National Overseas Engineering Company China provide engineering plans & all equipment

TABLE 9.3 (continued)

Year	Type of project	Location	Value	Details
1991	zinc smelter	Yazd		
1991	mining equipment & engineering services			MOU re technology transfer
1991	copper mill and cement factories	Khatoonabad?		copper mill = 200 K ton annual output
1991	joint design, engineering & manufacturing of machinery for oil, gas, petrochemicals, electrical power generation, diesel motors & maritime uses			MOU between heavy industry ministries re establishment of joint companies
circa 1991	launch of space satellite			radio & TV broadcasting & reconnaissance
circa 1992	manufacturing of graphite electrodes & fire resistant materials			
circa 1992	malamine powder factory	Urumiyeh		
circa 1992	zinc factory	Qeshm Free Trade Area		10,000 tons / yr. Output
1993	11 cement plants	$110 million		complete technology sets; CITIC, CMEIX Co.
1993	four 22K ton cargo ships purchased			
1993	nuclear power plant			300 MW; later suspended
1992	metro subway and rail system	Tehran, Karaj	$1.5 billion?	CITIC, NORINCO,
1993	fisheries, bees, animal husbandry			MOU re cooperation
1993	copper mine	Khatoonabad	$60 millon	Foreign Engineering & Construction Co.
circa 1993–95	railway	Mashhad-Tedzhen		connect Turkmen & Iran rails for first time
1995	cement plants, glass factory			MOU re railway cooperation
1995	325 mw thermal power plant	Arak, Markazi prov.		
1995	six 2,500 ton ships purchased		$150 million	

Date	Project	Location	Amount	Notes
1995	subway system	Tehran	$573 million	CITIC, National Technology Import & Export Co.
circa 1995	sugar cane production		$240 million	transfer of Chinese production methods
circa 1995	four 32.6MW thermal power plants			Sichuan Dongfang Copr.
circa 1995	ferro-alloy production	Kahnuj		
1996	two thermal & hydropower plants	128 km sw Tehran		325 & 10 MW; irrigates 123 K hectacres
1996	copper mine	Songon, Abar, E. Azerbaijan	$350 million	joint venture
1996	medical instruments & pharmaceuticals production			MOU re
1996	22.6 K ton multi-purpose ship delivered by PRC			
1996	325 MS thermal power plant	Zarand	$30 million	Shanghai Electricity Corp.
late 1990s	coke plant			120 k tons / year output
circa 1998	gold deposits, joint exploitation	Neishabour		CMIEX co.
circa 1998	floating glass factory	Bandar-Abbas		MOU signed
circa 1998	iron smelting plant [sic]	Meybod, Yazad prov.		
1998	zinc & copper cooperation			
1998	complete set oil exploration equipment			Sinopec Shengli Oil co.
1999	alkaline battery production equipment			
1999	railway construction	Tehran-Karaj		41 km westward extension Tehran metro; NORINCO
1999	five VLCC			2000 = $370 million exporters credit supports
1997–2000	manufacture of 31 ships			
2000	steel mill rennovation	Assadabad	$3.2 million	CMIEX co.
2000	railway construction	Tehran	$500 million	expansion of subway system; NORINCO
2000	gold mining	Neishabour		China Geology Exploration Organization
2000	cigarette production equipment & tech			
2000	renovation 3 oil refineries	Tehran, Rey, Tabriz		Sinopec Engineering Construction co.

TABLE 9.3 (continued)

Year	Type of project	Location	Value	Details
2000	drill 19 wells oil & gas wells	southern Iran	$85 million	Sinopec, CNPC; expand production of existing fields
2000	sodium carbonate / bicarbonate factory	Khuzestan	Rials 90 billion	200 K tons / year. Deal signed May 1992
2001	oil loading & mixing facility	Neka	$150 million	Sinopec; CROS project
2001–2004	construction of 16 " pipeline	Neka-Rey		Sinopec; engineering consulting role?
2001	dam and hydropower plant	Seimarreh, Ilam prov.		
2001	railway equipment manufacturing	Tehran-Hashtgerd	$100 million	manufacturing equipment transferred to Iran
2001	dam and hydropower plant	Takestan	$143 million	National Water Resources & Hydropower Company
2001	complex ethylene plant rennovation	Bandar Imam		
2001 output	aluminium smelter	Arak, Markazi prov.	$200 million	Ministry Nonferrous Metals; 110 K ton/ yr =
2001	exploratory drilling for oil	Ardestan	$13 million	Sinopec
2003	automobile factory	Mashhad		Shanghai Auto Industry Corp.
2003	automobile and truck factory	Esfahan		First Auto Works
2003	railway construction	Esfahan–Shiraz		MOU signed
2004	natural gas condensing refinery	Bandar Abbas		Sinopec
2004	dam and powerplant	Ahvaz		600 MW & 185 K hectacres irrigation
2004	oil field development	Yadavaran	$75mil.—1 billion	
2004	highway & tunnel construction	Tehran-Chalus		under Elbruz Mts to Caspian coast

Sources: *Tehran Times*, *Renmin ribao*, and *Xinhua*.

in housing construction were useful in Iran's efforts to meet the postwar demand. Iran's minister of housing and urban development, Serajeddin Kazeruni, visited Beijing in 1989 to call for Chinese assistance in urban planning, design, management, and technical service and labor. Vice Premier Yao Yilin told Kazeruni that China was prepared to assist Iran in these areas, and at the end of Kazeruni's stay a contract on cooperation in manufacture of construction materials, housing construction, as well as joint "research" in construction techniques was signed.[28]

Mining and metallurgy were also important areas of cooperation. The shah's government had carried out an extensive survey of Iran's mineral resources and found considerable deposits, but revolution and war interrupted exploitation. Once the war ended and the First Five Year Plan launched, mining development became a major thrust of Iran's development effort. Mining played a key role, being recognized, according to an official Iranian account, as "one of the main routes to achieving economic independence."[29] China was Iran's major partner in the mining area. China's mining industry was quite strong, having received extensive Soviet technological assistance in the 1950s and further Japanese and Western investment starting in the 1970s. Throughout the period of China's planned economy the demand for metals was high, leading to heavy investment in China's mining sector.

A Chinese geological delegation headed by the vice minister of geology and mineral resources, Zhang Wenju, visited Iran in September 1989 to conclude a memorandum of understanding on cooperation in geology and mining. Under the agreement, the two countries agreed to undertake joint projects in seismotectonics, paleomagnetism, stratigraphy, oceanography, engineering geology, and ore dressing—scientific fields useful in prospecting and mining—and to establish a noble metals laboratory in Iran.[30] Iran also expressed a desire to purchase mining and geology machinery, equipment, instruments, and tools. Iran's mines and metals minister visited Beijing in November 1991 for talks on cooperation in copper, zinc, lead, aluminum, manganese, and gold mining. The Iranian minister visited Chinese mines and mills and discussed the possibility of "making use of Chinese experiences" in zinc production technology.[31] The two sides agreed to cooperate in setting up a zinc smelter at Bafq.[32]

China assisted Iran in exploiting its rich deposits of nonferrous metals. The Chinese mineral resources delegation of September 1989 visited the Sarcheshmeh copper complex in Kerman province, then the second largest open-pit copper mine in the world.[33] Sarcheshmeh's output would triple during the First Five Year Plan.[34] In November 1991 the two sides agreed to construct a copper factory with an annual capacity of two hundred thousand tons and a cement factory with a daily output of one thousand tons.[35] Cement is an essential material in mine construction. Two years later China's non-ferrous metal ministry won a $60 million contract from the Iranian ministry of mines and metals to build a copper mill at Khatoonabad, Kerman province. The Chinese firm was to design the plant, provide manufacturing technology and equipment, and train Iranian technicians and engineers. The mill was to utilize the latest flash smelting technology, which China itself had acquired only several years earlier. When finished in forty-eight months, the plant would turn out eighty thousand tons of copper a year, increasing Iran's production of that commodity by 40 percent.[36] (It is unclear whether this factory was different from the one agreed to in November 1991, or if it is the same project with a scaled-down production goal.) In mid-1996 Chinese and Iranian firms agreed on a joint investment of $350 million to mine copper in the East Azerbaijan province of Iran.[37] The copper deposits there were estimated to be among the richest in the world.[38]

In October 1998 Beijing and Tehran signed a memorandum of understanding to expand cooperation in zinc and copper mining and the transfer of technology in nonferrous metals. Officials reviewed cooperation at the Khatoonabad copper complex and at the Bafq zinc smelter and decided to expedite work at both sites by dispatching more Chinese experts.[39] Two years later the two countries agreed to exploit jointly rich gold deposits at Neishabour, in northeast Iran. China's Geology and Mineral Exploration Organization was to transfer technology and set up a laboratory via a joint venture for production of gold bullion.[40] In mid-2001 a unit of China's non-ferrous metal ministry won a $200 million contract for the construction of a 110,000-ton per year aluminum smelter in Arak. The Chinese firm would provide technology and key equipment, including transformers and compressors, for the project, although some of this equipment was to be purchased from European suppliers. The new plant would replace an older one built by the U.S. Reynolds corporation in the 1970s.[41]

Coal mining was another important area of cooperation. In May 1991 the China National Overseas Engineering Corporation began exploratory drilling for coal in Iran's Tabas region. In November another agreement stipulated that China would provide $2.6 million in engineering services and equipment for Iran's coal mines.[42] In 1992 Iran's vice minister for mines and metals visited China to survey coal-mining machinery and production techniques. Iran also asked China to help Iran establish a coal-mine design and research institute under the National Iranian Steel Company.[43]

Ferrous metals were a less important area of cooperation. In 2000 an

Iranian steel firm contracted with a Chinese firm to purchase $3.2 million in technology to renovate a steel mill in Assadabad. The Chinese firm had earlier signed an accord with an Iranian iron smelting company in Meybod, Yazd province.[44] By early 1999 nineteen large Chinese-assisted projects under way in Iran included the zinc smelter at Bafq, a ferro-alloy plant at Bandar Abbas, the copper mine and mill at Khatoonabad, five cement factories, and a floating glass production line.[45]

China supplied a considerable amount of manufacturing equipment, enabling Iran to establish a number of new factories and to manufacture machinery and equipment indigenously for those factories. The earliest Chinese assistance in this area regarded munitions production during the war. Unfortunately little is known about this cooperation. During the postwar period, during an August 1989 visit, IRI deputy minister of heavy industry, Mohsen Alizadeh, visited a Chinese center for research in the manufacture of machine tools. The result was a memorandum of understanding regarding the transfer of Chinese technology in power station equipment, sugar- and papermaking machinery, and machine tools and engineering machinery manufacturing equipment. The Chinese machine-tool-building research center was also to cooperate with Iranian machine-building factories at Arak and Tabriz.[46] The two countries were also to manufacture jointly two 300-megawatt thermal power plants. A paper factory (apparently the one pledged by Qian Qichen in January 1989) was to be built with a daily capacity of fifty tons. Machinery for sugar refining plants and crane trucks with up to twenty tons capacity were to be manufactured with Chinese assistance.[47]

In December 1991 China's ministry of machine building and electronics and Iran's ministry of heavy industries signed a memorandum of understanding establishing joint industrial design and engineering companies to set up industrial production lines. The two sides were to cooperate in manufacturing equipment for oil, gas, petrochemical, electrical, and maritime industries and in building heavy diesel motors and electrical motors.[48] Several years later an Iranian firm contracted to purchase an alkaline battery factory from China.[49] China's Export-Import Bank provided a credit of $8.5 million to Iran's Industry and Mines Bank in January 2000 to produce sodium carbonate for use in glass manufacture. Iran then imported $8 million worth of sodium carbonate from China, but once the new factory went into production Iran would be self-sufficient in this chemical.[50] During the same year, the Iranian Tobacco Company purchased a cigarette factory from China.[51] In mid-2001 a major Iranian petrochemical company announced that it was purchasing Chinese technology to revamp its production units, including a complex ethylene plant in Bandar Imam.[52]

Cooperation expanded to automobile manufacture in 2003 when China's two major auto manufacturers undertook separately to establish factories in Iran. The Shanghai Automobile Industry Corporation (SAIC) undertook to build an automobile factory in Mashhad, reportedly the first automobile factory approved by the Iranian government in twenty years. First-phase production at the Mashhad plant targeted thirty thousand sedans per year. SAIC was to provide technology, design assistance, auto parts, and marketing support to the Iranian partner.[53] SAIC had acquired modern automobile design and manufacturing technology from General Motors of the United States and Volkswagen of Germany in the 1990s. In May of the same year, China's First Auto Works (FAW), of Jilin province, signed a contract with Iran's SAM Motor Company to set up a factory in Esfahan, with a projected output of one thousand trucks and fifty thousand sedans per year. FAW was to set up and test operate the production lines.[54]

Automobile manufacturing was an example of China's transfer to Iran of advanced manufacturing technologies only recently acquired by China itself. Another example came in 1989 when the Southwest Physics Institute of Chengdu signed an agreement to provide ion beam implantation equipment, used to enhance the hardness and durability of metals, and to train Iranian technicians in the use of this equipment. China itself had acquired ion implantation technology only in the early 1980s, but by 1989 it was exporting that technology to Iran.[55]

Dam construction, hydro- and thermoelectricity production, and irrigation were other areas of Sino-Iranian economic cooperation. China was historically highly adept at irrigation, and during its 1950s partnership with the Soviet Union gained strong competence in dam construction and the manufacture of heavy electrical power generation machinery. During his 1989 visit to Tehran, Tian Jiyun indicated that China was prepared help Iran build four 125-megawatt power plants in Gilan province. Late the same year an Iranian energy ministry delegation toured China to investigate cooperation in the area of water conservancy construction. The result was the identification of several additional cooperative projects.[56] Early in 1995 a Chinese electrical machinery manufacturer won a contract to export four 325-megawatt thermoelectrical power generators with a total value of $2.6 million to Iran for use in the Arak power plant. The company would also provide technical services for the Arak plant, which was scheduled to go into operation in 2000.[57] Two other China-assisted power plants with a value of $8 million were finished in 1996.[58] One was a 10-megawatt hydropower and 123,000-hectare irrigation complex located 128 kilometers southwest of Tehran.[59] The other 1996 project was a 325-megawatt thermal-power-generating facility with "ancillary service items" supplied by China. The Shanghai Electricity Corporation manufactured the generating equipment and was responsible for design of the project, technological services for construction, installation, and test running of the facility. Once in operation it was Iran's largest power plant.[60] Early in 2001 Iran's energy ministry reached an agreement with a Chinese firm for the construction of a dam and power plant at Seimarreh, Ilam province.[61] In August 2001 the China National Water Resources and Hydropower Engineering Corporation began work on a dam and power station at Takestan, 150 kilometers west of Tehran. The total value of the contract was $143 million and included main dam, spillways, diversion tunnels, and irrigation galleries. The project was designed to ease Tehran's water supply difficulties and increase the capital's electricity supply.[62]

According to China's Ministry of Commerce Web site, in mid-2004 Chinese companies were then involved in four major electrical power projects in Iran worth cumulatively $393 million and with 323-megawatt generating capacity. Chinese representatives were assisting in the design and construction of a dam in Ahvaz province to generate 600 megawatts of electricity and provide water to irrigate 185,000 hectares of land. The Web site saw great potential for further expansion in the energy sector. Iran's Fourth Five Year Plan (2004–8) called for the renovation and expansion of one-third of Iran's power plants, while the country had water-fall capacity to generate 50 million megawatts but currently produced only 2 million megawatts by hydropower. China's main competitors in power-generation projects in Iran were, the Web site said, Russia and South Korea.[63]

Agriculture was a secondary area of Sino-Iranian cooperation. During a November 1993 visit to Iran by vice minister for agriculture Zhang Yanxi, China agreed to assist Iran with the raising of bees, fish, and shrimp. Chinese specialists would assist Iran in both fresh and seawater pisciculture and in the production of fish powder that would be sold in both countries. Zhang's visit produced an agreement that the two countries would also exchange breeds of animals. Iranian officials reportedly showed great interest in China's agricultural achievements.[64] Early in 1995 a firm in Anhui province exported to Iran nearly $1 million worth of underwater electrical pumps and control equipment for use in irrigating newly established sugar cane fields—apparently to provide raw material for the new China-assisted sugar refineries.[65]

In the late 1990s China assisted Iran's modernization of its oceanic shipping fleet. According to one Iranian shipping official, Iran then owned 110 ships, 76 of which were oceangoing. A large number of those had more than twenty years service and needed replacing. Between 1997 and 2000 Chinese firms contracted to manufacture thirty-one ships for the Islamic Republic of Iran Shipping Lines (IRISL), according to that company's deputy head. Early in 1998, IRISL announced its intention to purchase twenty-seven new ships of various types at a cost of $700–$800 million. Chinese firms won contracts to build five. (South Korean firms were contracted to build six vessels.) The first of the five China-built ships, worth $25.5 million, was delivered to Bandar Abbas in April 1999. The rest were to be delivered one each every four months.[66] In mid-1999 Tehran reached agreement with Beijing on Chinese manufacture of five very large crude carriers (VLCC) of three hundred thousand tons, a type of vessel Chinese shipyards had not previously built. Iran's order allowed China "to break the monopoly of Japan and South Korea" in this area, according to *Tehran Times*. This was the "largest ever" order received by Chinese shipbuilders.[67] In March 2000 the China Export-Import Bank granted a $370 million export seller's credit and insurance to support the VLCC sale to Iran.[68] The first VLCC, built at Dalian, was delivered to Iran in August 2002.[69]

Transportation was still another important area of cooperation. In 1992 China's railway ministry signed with Iran a memorandum of understanding on cooperation in "establishment of new railway lines," including a 295-kilometer (183-mile) rail line linking the Iranian and Central Asian rail systems for the first time.[70] The memorandum provided for Chinese supply of technical experts, transfer of technology, and provision of railway "parts." In May 1996 the Mashhad to Tedzhen, Turkmenistan, line opened with China's railway minister Han Shubin in attendance. As a Xinhua article noted, the new link would allow China further access to the Persian Gulf through Iran and to the Mediterranean via Turkey.[71] During his visit to inaugurate the new line Han signed another memorandum of understanding with Iran's roads and transport minister.[72]

Cooperation in transportation continued into the 2000s. Iran's transportation minister Ahmad Khorram informed China's ambassador Liu Zhentang in June 2003 that Iran's leaders had decided to increase emphasis on transportation by expanding railways and controlled-access expressways. Iran hoped that Chinese companies would participate in this effort, seeking financing via the international banking market. Ambassador Liu replied that China "greatly stressed" transport cooperation with Iran and was highly competitive in this area as regarded technology transfer, financing terms, and post-sale service.[73] In November Khorram visited China to brief officials about Iran's plans to expand its transportation infrastructure and to invite Chinese firms to bid on railway, expressway, harbor, and airport projects. A memorandum of understanding was signed on the construction of a railway from Esfahan to Shiraz. In Beijing vice premier and former Shanghai mayor Huang Ju explained to Khorram the role of transportation infrastructure in economic development, and promised that the Chinese government would continue to encourage Chinese firms to participate in transportation construction projects in Iran.[74] Khorram invited Chinese firms to tender bids for the manufacture of six hundred railway passenger wagons, five thousand freight wagons, a number of ships, construction of five thousand kilometers of expressway plus construction of six thousand kilometers of railway, seven international airports, and three large trade ports. One of the ports was Chabahar, which was to be transformed into a "mega port." Khorram said that during his talks in Beijing the two sides "reached agreement" on investment of $3–$4 billion in Iran over a three-year period.[75] As of late 2004 Chinese firms were working on construction of a new road between Tehran and Chalus on the Caspian shore. When completed the new roadway will include many bridges and tunnels under the Elburz Mountains to the north of Tehran and will reduce the drive time between Chalus and Tehran from four and a half to one and a quarter hours. This expansion will make possible work commutes and strengthen Iran's role in the emerging Caspian regional economy.[76]

The sale of Chinese labor and engineering services to Iran is reflected in statistics on China's international economic cooperation presented in table 9.4. These numbers express the total annual value of contracts including contracted projects, design services, and labor cooperation. Hong Kong and Singapore consistently top the list. The large economies of Japan and the United States are also perennials. More interesting for the purposes here is a small cohort of developing countries that routinely appear in the list: Pakistan, Myanmar, Bangladesh, and Iran. These friendly, independent-minded developing countries are China's favored Third World partners.

In sum, large swaths of Iran's economy have been built using Chinese designs, technology, and machinery. Iranian technicians and engineers are being trained in China or by Chinese experts. They are becoming familiar with the strengths and weaknesses of Chinese capital goods and technology, in comparison with European and Japanese (though not with u.s.) goods. Chinese enterprises earn profits via this cooperation, while China earns foreign currency and expands high-value-added exports. China does all this while meeting a substantial portion of its demand for imported energy. At the most general level, Chinese strategists hope that via this cooperation will emerge a robust, deep-rooted, and stable partnership with Iran similar to the one Beijing enjoys with Pakistan.

TABLE 9.4

China's Foreign Economic Cooperation, 1998–2002

(total value, US$ millions; top 10 partners ranked in cardinal order)

	2002		2001		2000		1999		1998	
1	Hong Kong	2313	Hong Kong	1883	Hong Kong	2250	Hong Kong	2192	Hong Kong	2017
2	Singapore	1086	Singapore	1180	Singapore	1208	Singapore	1019	Singapore	925
3	USA	707	Japan	488	Japan	397	Sudan	743	Sudan	636
4	Japan	594	Pakistan	425	Iran	368	USA	323	Myanmar	523
5	Sudan	440	USA	399	USA	351	Pakistan	308	Pakistan	372
6	Bangladesh	412	Bangladesh	352	Pakistan	329	Japan	288	Japan	332
7	Iran	383	Sudan	303	Bangladesh	231	Macau	249	USA	306
8	Pakistan	357	Myanmar	257	Macau	221	Kuwait	216	Thailand	278
9	Myanmar	300	South Korea	227	South Korea	216	Iran	206	Macau	266
10	Kazakhstan	243	Iran	215	Myanmar	187	Myanmar	198	Saudia Arabia	231
11	South Korea	211	Kazakhstan	210	Taiwan	123	South Korea	167	Bangladesh	223
12	Germany	207	Macau	202	Sudan	119	Bangladesh	155	Iran	179

SOURCE: *Zhongguo tongji nianjian* [China Statistical Yearbook] (Beijing: National Bureau of Statistics of China, 2000, 2001, 2003). (Statistical yearbooks prior to 1998 did not break amounts down by partner countries.)

THE TEHRAN METRO PROJECT

The flagship of Sino Iranian economic cooperation during the 1990s was the Tehran subway, or metro. Work on a subway system in Tehran was begun under the shah, but was shelved once the war with Iraq began. Completed portions of the tunnel were used as bomb shelters during that war. Once peace was restored and during Yang Shangkun's visit to Iran in October 1991, President Rafsanjani invited Chinese companies to participate in bidding for work on the system (then projected to be ninety-six kilometers when completed). This was a prestige project that would make Iran the first country in the Middle East and only the twentieth in the world to operate a subway system.[77]

The Tehran Urban and Suburban Railway Company (TUSRC) was the Iranian authority responsible for the metro project, and Asghar Ebrahimi, who served for twelve years as chairman and managing director, was TUSRC's point man for the project. China was not among the initial set of bidders on the Tehran metro tender. Bids received from Western firms were evaluated by TUSRC and found to be extremely expensive—"inflated" by high Western salaries and advanced technology. TUSRC negotiators also sensed that European representatives felt they held a dominant bargaining position and, because of this, were not willing to reduce price demands significantly. At this point TUSRC turned to China. China was interested, but had not built a subway since the 1970s, and then with technology supplied by the Soviet Union in the 1950s. By 1990s' standards, Chinese subway technology was antiquated. Various possibilities were discussed, with Ebrahimi traveling to China more than thirty times in this regard. After visiting the Changchun railway car and Shenyang locomotive manufacturing factories and inspecting Beijing's subway system, Ebrahimi concluded that China indeed had the ability to undertake the project and at prices well below what European firms demanded, but also at a far lower technological level. Chinese wagons, for example, were very heavy and the locomotive electrical motors were completely antiquated. In the course of discussions, the two sides recognized a common interest in acquiring advanced Western subway technology and explored modes of cooperating in this regard.[78]

On the basis of tenders submitted by Western companies in the first round of bidding, four areas were identified in which acquisition of Western technology was especially critical: braking, signaling, ventilation, and manufacturing workshops. China could acquire Western technology in these areas, use it to modernize its own manufacturing base, use these updated facilities to produce modern components for the Tehran metro, and later transfer this modern technology to Iran. The two sides would share the cost of this joint acquisition of technology. Working out this complex arrangement took a year longer than would have cooperation with a Western firm, TUSRC determined, but the cost would be far less—one-forth of the European price—while Iran could modernize its manufacturing base. On a comparable segment of the project, Siemens' bid had been about $3.2 billion, while CITIC's came in at $848 million. The European asking price per passenger wagon was $2.2 million, while the Chinese price was $430,000. China's government was also willing to underwrite substantially the metro project. All together China would provide about $2 billion in soft loans to support the metro. TUSRC sensed that China had made a top-level decision to support the metro as a way of entering and expanding Middle Eastern markets. China had a very strong foreign currency reserve and capital inflow positions. It also placed high priority on modernizing its industrial manufacturing base. TUSRC concluded that China was willing to accept a low return on the metro project as a way of modernizing its own industry, creating jobs, and expanding exports to Iran and the Middle East.

Bids from a second solicitation were opened in 1992 and CITIC won the contract. CITIC was to serve as general contractor for the project, as well as to provide an initially projected $360 million worth of equipment for construction of the first forty-nine kilometers of the system. Award of the project to CITIC apparently encountered considerable suspicion in Tehran as to whether China had the technology to build a high-quality subway.[79] Apparently some people in Iran feared that a technologically inferior partner was being foisted on them for political reasons. Other bidders for the project had been Siemens of Germany, a South Korean consortium including Daewoo and Hyundai, and Swedish, French, Italian, and Japanese firms, as well as Iran's own Industrial Development and Renovation Organization.[80] The China-Iran metro contract stipulated that Iran would provide 25 percent of project content and China would supply 75 percent, of which 25 percent was to be produced by newly imported Western technology. As part of the contract, Iran helped pay the cost of China's acquisition of this new technology.[81] By the time the project was nearing completion, 76 percent of the machinery and electrical equipment used in the project was "Made in China" and, according to CITIC's Web site, had won recognition by Iranian experts as reliable and durable. This good reputation won by Chinese-made machines and electrical equipment laid a basis for further Sino-Iranian cooperation in railway development.[82]

In March and May 1995 contracts valued at $573 million were signed between TUSRC and CITIC, the China National Technology Import and

Export Corporation, and NORINCO. CITIC would supply generators for high-voltage power production, equipment for distribution of low-voltage power throughout the system, signaling equipment, cars, and locomotives. The initial contract also included supply of five cement production plants, each producing seven hundred tons of cement a day, and intended to provide adequate supplies of this vital construction material in an otherwise high-demand Iranian market. In April 1994 the Bank of China agreed to extend a $50 million buyer's credit to support construction of five cement plants— with equipment being transferred from China. This was the first buyer's credit extended by the Bank of China to Iran.[83]

In May 1995 CITIC set up its International Cooperation Company, CITIC ICC, with Rmb 150 million registered capital (US $18.3 million) to act as its agent in executing the Tehran metro project. CITIC ICC had overall responsibility for surveying, designing, manufacturing or purchasing equipment and technology, assembly, and testing. CITIC recruited fourteen Chinese banks to participate in a syndicated loan agreement supporting the Tehran subway project with a $270 million buyer's credit.[84] In mid-1996 China's Changchun Passenger Car Company received a $138 million contract to supply 217 coaches for the subway over a period of twenty-five months.[85] Design work and preparation for construction began in 1997. Active construction began in 1998.[86] By May 1997 fifty-four tramcars and two power-generating cars produced in Changchun and shipped via Dalian port were under way to Tehran for the project.[87] By April 1998 another twenty-four double-decker shuttle buses and six locomotives were dispatched from Shanghai.[88] CITIC ICC subcontracted NORINCO to construct an above-ground electrified rail line forty-one kilometers westward from the end station of the Tehran metro to Karaj city. This line was test run by NORINCO in February 1999.[89]

The first section of the metro line was inaugurated in February 2000 with President Khatami and Foreign Minister Tang Jiaxuan in attendance. Additional sections of the system were opened in August 2000, August 2001, March and October 2002, and March 2003. Keeping on schedule required that the Chinese firms "overcome all kinds of difficulties," according to a report in Renmin ribao.[90] By mid-2004 the first two phases (with a total length of fifty-two kilometers) were 80 percent complete.

As work on the first stage of the Tehran subway neared completion, China undertook to assist the next stage. During President Khatami's June 2000 visit to Beijing, China agreed to finance and provide equipment for a $500 million extension of the Tehran subway. In October a Chinese firm contracted for $3.4 million to transfer railway locomotive and wagon manufacturing technology to Iran. The Chinese firm was to provide Iran with all the equipment necessary to produce wagons and locomotives for use in the next phase of expansion of the metro system.[91] The upgraded manufacturing capabilities acquired by China in the first phase were now being transferred to Iran. The Chinese firm was to "invest" $100 million in the project, with repayment guaranteed by the Central Bank of Iran.[92] In January 2001 a Chinese company agreed to build a twenty-five-kilometer spur westward from Tehran to Hashtgerd and Mehrshahr. NORINCO won a giant $836 million contract with TUSRC in May 2004 to engineer, equip, and build yet another nineteen kilometers of the Tehran metro line. As part of the arrangement, NORINCO and TUSRC formed a $12 million joint venture to produce rail wagons and locomotive engines and parts in China. NORINCO was to supply $527 million worth of machines and electric equipment for the new rail line.[93]

Beijing extended substantial financial support to make the Tehran metro project a success. Work on the project was initially scheduled to begin in 1994, but was delayed for several years because of lack of funding by the Iranian government. Once work on the project was under way in 1999, NORINCO's project manager in Iran, Han Lizhong, told the *Tehran Times* that China had invested $1.5 billion to finance the project.[94]

In the estimate of CITIC ICC, Iranian officials were satisfied with the quality and pace of work, and this was reflected in Iran's decision to negotiate the westward extension of the line in April 2004. Completion of the entire system was projected for the end of 2006. The Tehran metro project was the largest mechanical-electrical project undertaken abroad by Chinese companies. According to China's vice minister of trade, its successful completion demonstrated the ability and strength of Chinese companies and their ability to meet international standards in carrying out large, overseas engineering projects. This gave "a large stage" for Chinese companies to "go abroad" (*zuo-chu guomen*) and develop international markets. Iran's minister of interior speaking at an opening ceremony in March 2003 termed the Tehran metro a model for Iranian-Chinese cooperation in other areas.[95] Two distinctive characteristics of the Tehran metro model were large-scale Chinese financial support and joint acquisition of advanced technologies.

THE OIL SUPPLY RELATIONSHIP

During the 1990s deteriorating Sino-American relations combined with growing Chinese dependence on imported oil caused China's leaders to become increasingly concerned about China's energy security. Two major concerns were that the United States might use its influence to restrict China's oil imports in the event of a confrontation over Taiwan or that events abroad might lead to major price fluctuations that could hurt China's economy. Various means were devised to address these concerns. China's MFA advocated cultivation of close relations with major oil producing states. China's major oil firms favored expanded international operations, seeing that as vital to realization of the global competitive position to which they aspired.[96] Both prescriptions pointed toward cooperation with Iran. Iran too was concerned with energy security—of exports in Iran's case. Tehran feared Western sanctions choking Iranian oil exports. Iran's oil minister Bijan Namdar Zanganeh alluded to China and Iran's mutual energy security cooperation in 2004 when the two countries signed huge, record-breaking, multidecade contracts for natural gas purchase. Iran and China both needed security, Zanganeh said, Iran for supply and China for demand. Given Iran's large energy resources and China's large energy needs, Zanganeh explained, Iran "can be considered a reliable source for China's energy needs."

The growth of China's oil imports from Iran is illustrated by table 9.5. The largest leaps in this process came in 1988–89 (at the end of the Iran-Iraq war) when imports increased 25.6 times, in 1994–95 when they grew 12.5 times, and again between 1999 and 2001 when the value of oil imports jumped 2.7 times. A major part of the Iranian capital goods imports discussed in the previous section was paid for by these increases in oil exports to China, averaging 45 percent a year during the eight years between 1995 and 2003.

By the beginning of the twenty-first century Iran was consistently one of China's largest suppliers of crude oil, as is illustrated by table 9.6, listing China's twenty leading oil suppliers in 2001 and 2003. While all of this petroleum was delivered by sea and therefore vulnerable to potential disruptions of those sea-lanes, both Beijing and Tehran at least had the comfort of knowing that their major energy partner would resist American political pressure to close China's oil spigot. This would strengthen somewhat the position of either in the event of confrontation with the United States.

China's interest in expanded energy cooperation with Iran goes back to Li Peng's and Yang Shangkun's 1991 visits, when both Chinese leaders broached China's interest in participating in the development of Iran's petroleum resources.[97] By that point China's looming energy supply problem was becoming apparent. In 1993 China became a net importer of petroleum, and it was increasingly clear that China would need to import ever more petroleum if its skyrocket-like growth was not to be hobbled. China preferred not to remain a mere purchaser of Iranian oil, but to become involved in Iranian oil development projects as a way of both locking in Iranian oil sales and further expanding Chinese capital goods exports to Iran. One obstacle was Iranian concern for the relatively low technological level of China's oil industry. China

TABLE 9.5

China's Crude Oil Imports from Iran, 1983–2003

Year	Metric tons	US $
1983	0	
1984	0	
1985	0	
1986	0	
1987	0	
1988	9,987	1,637,790
1989	266,215	34,500,619
1990	301,240	39,534,000
1991	55,000	7,641,000
1992	114,990	15,574,000
1993	67,860	9,513,000
1994	69,119	8,715,000
1995	931,105	121,317,000
1996	2,311,105	337,072,000
1997	2,756,718	418,409,000
1998	3,619,989	414,915,000
1999	3,949,291	519,838,000
2000	7,000,465	1,464,018,000
2001	10,847,008	2,068,760,522
2002	10,629,865	1,901,986,000
2003	12,393,834	2,635,085,866

SOURCE: *Zhonghua renmin gongheguo haiguan tongji nianjian*
[People's Republic of China Customs Statistical Yearbook] (Beijing:
Zhongguo haiguan, 1983–2004).

attempted to ease these concerns by stressing the recent technological
advances of China's oil industry achieved via cooperation with international
firms. For instance, in May 1995 CNPC president Wang Tao visited Iran to
participate in a five-day conference on world petroleum. In talks with petroleum minister Gholamreza Aqazadeh, Wang expressed interest not only in
increasing oil purchases from Iran but in cooperating in prospecting for oil,
drilling wells, and supplying production equipment. Concerning the quality
of Chinese equipment, Wang assured Aqazadeh that, through "reform and
opening up," the technological level of China's petroleum industry had greatly
improved and was in demand in various parts of the world.[98] Aqazadeh continued the discussions in May 1997 in Beijing during talks with Li Peng and

TABLE 9.6

China's Major Crude Oil Suppliers, 2001 and 2003

(U.S. $; top 20 suppliers)

	2001			2003	
1	**Iran**	2,068,760,522	Saudi Arabia	3,231,949,613
2	Saudi Arabia	1,629,285,592	**Iran**	2,635,085,866
3	Oman	1,599,736,283	Angola	2,205,664,993
4	Sudan	936,548,774	Oman	1,978,256,687
5	Angola	721,464,446	Yeman	1,520,734,722
6	Indonesia	515,612,703	Sudan	1,416,098,196
7	Yeman	449,697,386	Russia	1,101,198,013
8	Russia	327,106,404	Indonesia	732,544,942
9	Kuwait	267,834,264	Malaysia	499,413,909
10	Oatar	256,636,952	Brunei	312,246,990
11	Malaysia	205,856,051	Kazakhstan	217,066,079
12	Norway	173,210,959	Norway	210,245,330
13	Nigeria	161,478,273	UAE	194,043,452
14	Brunei	146,511,491	Kuwait	186,365,024
15	UAE	136,908,642	Oatar	140,353,338
16	UK	103,110,843	Venezuela	78,172,611
17	Kazakhstan	96,862,877	UK	43,470,122
18	Iraq	73,006,341	Algeria	33,353,377
19	Libya	52,025,323	Libya	28,004,853
20	Venezuela	10,280,333	Nigeria	27,228,036

SOURCE: *Zhonghua renmin gongheguo* haiguan tongji nianjian [People's Rebublic of China Customs Statistics Yearbook], 2001 and 2003 (Beijing: Zhongguo haiguan, June 2002 and May 2003).

CNPC general manager Zhou Yongkang. Regarding the technological level of China's petroleum industry, Li Peng assured Aqazadeh that, after years of effort, China's petroleum industry had applied advanced technology and now manufactured up-to-date equipment. China also had experience using advanced equipment in oil prospecting and development, Li informed Aqazadeh.[99] During the visit, CNPC and an Iranian entity signed a general agreement on joint prospecting and exploration for oil and gas. Li Peng lauded the agreement and its promise of expanded energy cooperation between the two countries.

In 1998 Sinopec subsidiary Shengli Oil Company transferred to Iran a com-

plete set of China-made oil-field equipment up to 1990s' international standards.[100] (Sinopec is China's second-largest oil company.) This transfer
allowed Iran to assess the caliber of China's latest oil-field exploration technology. Chinese analysts were hopeful regarding expanded oil cooperation.
According to a 1998 CNPC survey, Iran had abundant oil and natural gas
resources that it could exchange for Chinese goods and services. Western companies' participation in Iranian energy development had been disrupted by
Iran's 1979 revolution and by the Iran-Iraq war, the report said, and those
Western companies therefore lacked *guanxi* (connections) for cooperation
with Iran. China, however, had long experience of cooperation with Iran (and
implicitly lots of *guanxi*). Finally, even though Iran was still strongly anti-
American, Tehran was attempting to improve relations and expand economic
cooperation with Europe and Japan. Indeed, the Western oil giants were
already "one step ahead of China."[101] Between the lines one could discern this
message: because Western firms were already violating U.S. efforts to prevent foreign participation in Iranian petroleum development, Washington
could not blame Chinese participation too strongly.

Beijing was careful not to allow its companies to take the lead in oil cooperation with Iran less they become targets of U.S. sanctions. In August 1996
President Clinton had signed into law the Iran-Libya Sanctions Act (ILSA)
requiring imposition of "two or more" of a long list of stiff penalties against
any foreign "person" that was found to have invested $20 million or more in
oil and gas development in Iran.[102] Although President Clinton chose not
to enforce ILSA, largely because the United States' European allies objected
to what they saw as its "extraterritorial" nature, Chinese firms might offer
Washington a more attractive target than European firms because of the
intense anti-China animus in the Congress during the late 1990s. Once
European firms led the way, however, it might be safe for Chinese firms to
follow. Sinopec's 2000 annual report noted in its "chronology of major international events" that in October 1999 Dutch Royal Shell had signed a deal
worth $850 million for rehabilitation of Iranian oil fields damaged in the Iran-
Iraq war.[103]

An important juncture in Sino-Iranian energy cooperation came in June
2000 when president Khatami informed Beijing and Tokyo, during his visits
to those capitals, that Iran had decided to award *Japanese* firms preferential
rights in the development of a huge, recently discovered oil field at Azadegan,
in southwestern Iran. The Azadegan field, discovered by Iran in 1999, strad-
dled the Iraq-Iran border west of Ahwaz and was estimated to contain 26 billion barrels of oil, making it one of the richest undeveloped oil fields in the
world. There was a glaring disjuncture between this Iranian decision in favor

of Japan and the Chinese decision, also announced during Khatami's June 2000 visit to China and Japan, to provide a half-billion-dollar credit supporting the Tehran subway project. Beijing's generous support to Tehran was matched by Tehran's decision in favor of Tokyo. Could this have been Iranian payback, at least in part, for Beijing's 1997 accession to u.s. pressure over nuclear cooperation with Iran? However, Beijing may have felt the Azadegan project was simply too large and high profile and, if undertaken by China, was likely to subject China to strong u.s. pressure.

But Beijing did not lose out entirely; it soon won China's first direct involvement in exploitation of Iranian petroleum resources, in August 2000, when cnpc won from nioc a two-year, $85 million contract to drill nineteen wells at existing natural gas fields in southern Iran. cnpc was to provide technology and equipment to increase output in the fields to 860 million cubic meters per day.[104] A further contract between nioc and Sinopec involved exploration for oil and gas in the Kashan-Ardestan bloc, 205 kilometers south of Tehran in Esfahan province. Chinese engineers would conduct an initial forty days of geological study followed by the drilling of two exploratory wells over the course of a three-to-four-year exploration period.[105] Sinopec would finance the entire cost of the project as long as exploration efforts did not produce major results. Drilling operations began in early 2003. By May 2004 the exploratory wells had yet to yield positive results, although both sides professed continued optimism.[106] In January 2001 Sinopec and nioc signed yet another agreement, this one for $13 million to explore for oil in Zavareh, Kashan province. By 2002 cnpc had five seismology crews operating in Iran—the largest number of any of the twelve countries hosting cnpc exploration crews, as is indicated by table 9.7. China had wedged its way into Iran's upstream petroleum operations.

Japanese equivocation and Chinese stalwartness during the Azadegan negotiations may have demonstrated to Tehran China's greater reliability. After Tehran announced during Khatami's 2000 Far East trip its decision to award the $2.8 billion Azadegan project to Japan, Tokyo agreed to provide a $3 billion credit supporting the project over a period of three years. Complex and difficult negotiations ensued, lasting nearly four years and reaching a successful conclusion only in February 2004. There were numerous difficulties. The geological structure of the Azadegan region was very complex and costs of development correspondingly high. Political problems also arose. Washington warned Tokyo that the Iran-Libya Sanctions Act imposed sanctions on non-u.s. companies that invested more than $20 million in Iran's oil and gas sector. Iran's nuclear program also deeply troubled Tokyo. A combination of political, financial, and technical factors caused Japan to hesitate. Iran

TABLE 9.7

Overseas Geophysical Exploration Activity of CNPC, 2002

Country	Seismology crews	2D data acquired km	3D data acquired square km
Iran	5	2,295	633
Sudan	4	2,921	296
Pakistan	4	1,336	491
Libya	2	1,069	470
Yemen	2	839	–
Kazakhstan	1	615	–
Peru	1	294	–
Indonesia	4	1,019	409
Nigeria	3	–	1,381
Venezuela	3	377	218
Mexico	2	–	28
Russia	1	–	54

SOURCE: CNPC Web site, (accessed, July 1, 2004). http://www.cnpc.com/cn/english/inter/overseas.htm.

had specified the end of June 2003 as the deadline for an agreement to be reached, and when that threshold was crossed without result, Tehran notified Tokyo (in September) that its preferential rights over the Azadegan field had been terminated. Tehran also sent an "official letter" to Tokyo setting a December 15, 2003, deadline for the Japanese consortium to announce whether they intended to participate in the project. Shortly after that deadline passed, the Japanese consortium announced its withdrawal from the Azadegan project.[107]

While this tough bargaining between Tokyo and Tehran was under way, Tehran raised the ante by putting some additional third-country bargaining chips on the table. One was China. On July 6, 2003, shortly after the expiration of the initial deadline, a team from Sinopec flew to Tehran for talks. "Because the deadline for completion of talks [with Japan] expired at the end of June," Iranian oil minister Aqazadeh told the media, "we may sign a contract with other countries interested in doing the development work here."[108] Sinopec head Mou Shuling told Aqazadeh that Sinopec was more willing than ever to develop jointly giant oil and gas projects with Iran.[109] These comments led the Islamic Republic News Agency to announce that "China [was] Iran's new partner in developing Azadegan . . . After Japan waived the opportunity . . . China announced it would take up the project."[110] The deputy head of NIOC flew to China for talks with CNPC and Sinopec. It was announced that the talks would continue at the ministerial level. Playing the China card gained leverage for Tehran.

United States pressure was one factor causing Tokyo to hesitate. Similar pressure was put on Beijing but without effect. According to a Sinopec official, in January 2004 the U.S. embassy in Beijing contacted the firm with a request that it withdraw from bidding in the Azadegan project. "Sinopec is paying no attention to the U.S. request," according to the official, and "will do its utmost to carry on its bidding" for the project.[111] Only in December 2003 after Iran signed an Additional Protocol with the IAEA bringing its nuclear programs under fuller international supervision did the Japanese consortium decide to move ahead with the project. On February 18, 2004, the Japanese consortium and the NIOC signed agreements providing for Japanese assistance in the development of the Azadegan field. As Iran's ambassador to Japan Ali Majedi told an Iranian reporter shortly after Tokyo and Tehran signed the Azadegan contract: "It seems that if Iran would not have signed the Additional Protocol [with the IAEA], the contract [with Japan] may not have been concluded."[112] Tokyo also insisted on including in the Azadegan contract an escape clause that would allow Japan to suspend cooperation if Iran and the IAEA reached confrontation over Iran's nuclear programs.[113] Clearly China, although its technology might be less advanced than Japan's, was the more reliable partner for Iran.

After awarding Azadegan to Japan, Tehran drew China into Iran's energy development through a major package of deals announced in 2004. In March China's Zhuhai Zhenrong corporation signed an agreement to purchase 2.5 million metric tons of liquefied natural gas (LNG) per year worth $20 billion over a period of twenty-five years, beginning in 2008. This was reportedly the world's largest natural gas purchase up to that point.[114] One of its advantages from the Iranian point of view was that it guaranteed a stable demand for this product. An even larger deal came in October when Sinopec agreed with NIOC to purchase 250 million tons of LNG over a period of thirty years at a value of $70–$100 billion. The two sides also agreed to construct a gas-condensing refinery at Bandar Abbas to produce LNG for the contract. Sinopec was also to invest in development of new oil fields at Yadavaran, taking the leading role in that development, in exchange for the right to purchase 150,000 barrels per day of crude from the fields at market prices once the fields were operational. Sinopec was to cooperate with a "credible" international oil contractor who could supply advanced technologies to develop the Yadavaran field.[115] China had finally become a major partner in Iranian oil and gas production. Iran's ambassador to China, Fereydun Verdinezhad, explained the political significance of the linked LNG purchase and Yadavaran development deals: "Iran and China in the east and west of Asia chose each other as long-term part-ners . . . the importance of this agreement is mostly its situational aspects and effects, especially since it was signed under conditions when the government of China says [it ignores] the rules and regulations imposed by certain coun-tries, such as the D'Amato law [of the United States] embargoing . . . Iran." Iran needed stable markets for its huge gas resources, and China needed a sta-ble energy supply, the ambassador explained.[116]

Chinese support for Tehran on the IAEA nuclear issue paralleled the con-clusion of the LNG purchase and Yadavaran deals. As discussed in the earlier chapter on nuclear cooperation, Foreign Minister Li Zhaoxing supported Iran at the IAEA by countering U.S. efforts to take the nuclear issue to the Security Council.[117] Japan's insistence on the escape clause suggested that Tokyo would go along with U.S.-inspired sanctions should it come to that. Beijing's words, and the underlying mutual energy security relation of Tehran and Beijing, suggested China would *not* go along with U.S. moves. This was the main reason oil minister Zanganeh said that while "Japan is our number one energy importer due to historical reasons . . . we would like to give prefer-ences to China."[118]

CHINA AND IRAN'S CROS PROJECT

A significant dimension of Chinese support for IRI oil development efforts was help in advancing Tehran's Caspian Republics Oil Swap (CROS) project— a major effort by the IRI to play a role in development of Caspian Sea energy resources. With the 1990s' opening of the Caspian Sea littoral with its immensely rich oil and gas resources, Iran hoped to become the major cor-ridor for movement of those resources to world markets. This would gener-ate substantial revenues and increase Iran's strategic leverage. A statement by the IRI embassy in Poland stated very well Iran's view of the situation:

> Situated between the Caspian Sea and the Persian Gulf, Iran serves as the most economical outlet for the export of the ample hydrocarbon resources of Iran's newly emerging though landlocked northern neighbors Kazakhstan, Azer-baijan, and Turkmenistan. . . . To the south [of those nations] Iran has the longest coastline along the Persian Gulf and controls half of its body of water providing access to global markets. . . . As such, the positioning of Iran as the only geographic landmass bridging the gap between two of the globes most important oil regions has highlighted its critical role in the adequate develop-ment of these nations' hydrocarbon resources. In light of the above, coopera-

tion with Iran for the export of oil and gas through the utilization of Iranian territory would seem to be the most viable option for the development of the hydrocarbon resources of these nations and the full utilization of the market potential of the region.[119]

In the mid-1990s Iran developed a three-stage plan to realize its ambition of serving as the transit corridor for Caspian energy. The first stage involved using existing Iranian oil production facilities in the south to supply agents of Central Asian republics at Persian Gulf ports an amount and quality of oil equivalent to the quality and quantities of Central Asian oil delivered to Iran's Caspian ports of Neka or Anzali. Because Iran's major population and industrial centers, and therefore its fuel demands and its petroleum refiner-ies, were in the north, while its major petroleum-producing centers were in the south of the country, Caspian crude delivered in the north could thus be refined and distributed in Iran's north. This meant that Iranian crude pro-duced in the south no longer had to be shipped north for refining but could be swapped at Persian Gulf ports for Caspian oil delivered to Iran's Caspian ports. Caspian crude would not need to be shipped south to the Gulf, and southern Iranian crude would no longer need to be shipped north, thereby producing considerable cost savings. At least in theory.

Stage two of Tehran's CROS project involved strengthening Iran's infra-structure to move Caspian crude oil. The Iranian Caspian port of Neka was designated as the main entrepôt for Caspian oil under the CROS plan, but since it could not handle the fairly large tankers typically carrying Caspian crude, it needed expansion and modernization. The flow over an existing small-gauge pipeline used to deliver fuel from a refinery at Rey, south of Tehran, to Neka could be reversed, but the line was too small to carry the substantial volumes envisioned under the CROS plan. A new pipeline was needed. The projected third stage of Tehran's oil corridor plan was eventual construction of a pipeline directly from the eastern Caspian littoral through central Iran to the Gulf of Oman.

China played a major role in stage two of the CROS plan—modernization of Neka. Iranian authorities initially demanded that minimally qualified Ira-nian firms play leading roles in the Neka project, plus hefty subsidies by for-eign partners. NIOC, the Iranian principle for the project, played French and Chinese firms against each other. CNPC was initially involved in negotiations, but withdrew early in 2000 because of what it felt were economically nonvi-able prices being insisted on by NIOC. CNPC was also about to begin listing stock on the New York Stock Exchange and may not have wished to anger Washington at that juncture.[120] Following CNPC's withdrawal, Tehran sent a delegation to Beijing in late January 2000 to make a plea for Chinese government support for the Neka project.[121] Foreign Minister Tang Jiaxuan discussed the issue further during his February visit to Tehran. Tang told his hosts that "China attaches paramount importance" to economic and oil cooperation with Iran.[122] A year later Sinopec signed a $150 million contract for the engineering, design, construction of, and purchase of equipment for, an oil-unloading terminal at Neka, plus the upgrading of two Iranian refineries at Rey and Tabriz to handle high-paraffin Caspian crude oil. The Neka terminal was to include large storage facilities plus measuring and mixing capabilities—these being necessary to insure uniform quality and quantity of oil at the two ends of the CROS system.[123] Sinopec also apparently had an engineering advisory role in construction of a new sixteen-inch pipeline between Neka and a city midway to Rey. The Neka project was the largest overseas project yet undertaken by Sinopec.[124]

The opening of the Neka complex in spite of u.s. efforts to contain the IRI was a significant victory for Tehran. President Khatami outlined the significance of the Neka project system in his comments during the opening ceremony for the China-built oil terminal in April 2004:

> We have repeatedly stated that the cheapest, shortest, and most reliable way of transferring the energy resources of the Caspian Sea region to the market is through Iran, and there is no doubt about this. The arrogant and incorrect American policies are facing defeat in the world every day. We hope for the American officials to come to their senses and realize that in this world they must respect and treat all the people equally. The time for bullying, unilateralist, and imposing wills which would only serve the interests of one nation with greater capacities has passed.[125]

It is safe to assume that Sinopec was motivated by purely commercial considerations. Yet it is virtually certain that Sinopec would not have proceeded in such a sensitive venture as the Neka project without a green light from higher levels of China's government—a green light conveyed to Tehran by Tang Jiaxuan in February 2000. That higher-level go-ahead would have been based, in part, on strategic calculations regarding the utility of China's partnership with Iran balanced against the damage to China's relations with the United States likely to result from Sinopec's involvement in the Neka/CROS project. The essential calculation behind Beijing's green light to Sinopec in early 2000 was probably along the following lines: European firms had already violated Washington's taboo on cooperation with Iranian oil projects, and given that, it would be difficult for Washington to target Sinopec.

THE PATTERN OF SINO-IRANIAN ECONOMIC COOPERATION

China is beginning to play a major role in Iran's oil industry. A breakdown of foreign investment following the Yadavaran deal in 2004 is offered in table 9.8. The $750 million–$1 billion invested by Sinopec was the first major Chinese investment in Iranian energy. That amount places China considerably behind Italy, Japan, and South Korea in terms of amount invested, but is adequate to put China in the big league of foreign investors in Iranian energy.

There seems to be a psychological dimension to the robust Sino-Iranian economic relationship. Iranian negotiators reportedly find that Westerners tend to think their way of doing things is the only right way—the modern, scientific, or efficient way. They tend to look down on Iranian ways. Chinese, however, approach Iranians with a more equal mentality. They are more willing to accommodate Iranian requirements and ways of doing things. Nor does China insist on all sorts of "strings."[126] China has been less concerned than Western countries about "end use" of dual-use exports—the possibility that technologies might be diverted to military use. While the laws of Western countries subject sales of many technologies by Western firms to all sorts of postsale inspection requirements, Chinese sales do not carry such strings. Magnetic resonance imaging (MRI) technology, for example, can be used for medical diagnosis and examination of welds on structural steel components, or it can be used to examine missile castings and the internal structure of solid missile propellants. MRI technology was unavailable from the United States and could be acquired from European firms only with all sorts of inspection requirements. China, however, sold it with no strings attached.[127]

Iranian negotiators also believe that Chinese firms are more willing than Western firms to transfer full production processes to Iran. While Western firms seem to be concerned with job creation in their home countries or with protecting particular processes, Chinese firms are interested in sale of production processes. Iran has rich marble deposits, for example, and it pushed to exploit those deposits as part of its postwar emphasis on mining as a leading sector. An Italian firm with considerable experience in this area was brought in, but proved to be interested only in bulk purchase of Iranian marble, with the final dressing and finishing of the marble to be done in Italy. A Chinese firm was then brought in and proved quite willing to sell and transfer to Iran all relevant technologies so that Iran could finish the marble, adding that value to its final export.[128]

Beijing has extended large-scale financial support to underwrite the expansion of Sino-Iranian economic cooperation. Table 9.9 gives a very rough estimate of Chinese financial support for Iranian projects identified in the

TABLE 9.8

Foreign Investment in Iran's Oil and Gas Industry, 1999–2004

Year	Country	Companies	Field	Value (US$ millions)
1999	France	Elf Aquitaine/ Totalfina	Doroud	1,000
1999	France, Italy, Canada	Elf Aquitaine, Bow Valley	Balal	300
1999	UK, Netherlands	Royal Dutch Shell	Soroush & Nowruz	800
2000	Italy	ENI	South Pars 4 & 5	3,800
2000	Norway	Statoil	Salman	850
2000	Norway	Norsk Hydo	Anarn	NA
2001	UK, Netherlands	Enterprise Oil	South Pars 6, 7, 8	NA
2001	Sweden	GVA Consultants	Caspian Sea	226
2001	Italy	ENI	Darkhovin	550–1,000
2001	Japan	Ipex, Indonesium Petro, Tomen	Azadegan	2,500
2002	Canada	Sheer Energy	Masjid-e-Soleman	80
2002	South Korea	LG Engineering Group	South Pars, 9, 10	1,600
2002	Norway	Statoil	South Pars, 6, 7, 8	300
2002	South Korea	Hundai	Processing Trains	1,000
?	Spain	Cepsa, OMV	Cheshmeh-Khosh	300
2003	Japan	Japanese consortium	South Pars 6, 7, 8	1,200
2004	**China**	**Sinopec**	**Yadavaran**	**750–1,000**

SOURCES: Kenneth Katzman, "The Iran-Libya Sanctions Act (ILSA)," CRS Report for Congress, July 31, 2003. "Iran," Country Analysis Briefs, EIA, November 2003. The number for Yadavaran is from Mikkal Herberg, National Bureau of Asia Research, personal communication with author, March 30, 2005.

previous narrative. Before solid contracts for the Tehran metro project were signed by CITIC in early 1995, China provided $370 million in buyer's credits and preferred loans. In early 1999 NORINCO project manager Han Lizhong said that China had "invested" $1.5 billion in the project.[129] After Han's statement, China extended another $870 million in exporter's credits and loans to support the metro project. There was also a loan of $8.5 million to Iran's Industry and Mines Bank. Totaling these amounts gives $2.38 billion as a rough

TABLE 9.9

Estimate of China's Financial Support
for Sino-Iranian Economic Cooperation

Date	Amount	Specifics
Jan. 1993	$50 million export credit	Bank of China to Sepah Bank; Tehran metro
July 1993	$150 million preferential loan	
July 1993	$120 million	for cement factories; Tehran metro
Apr. 1994	$50 million buyer's credit*	Bank of China to Sepah Bank; for cement factories
1995–99	$1.5 billion "invested"	statement by NORINCO project manager (assume above amounts included in this sum)
Mar. 2000	$370 million exporter's credit	probably in support of Tehran metro
June 2000	$500 million loan	in support of Tehran metro
Subtotal	**$2.37 billion**	
Non-Metro		
Jan. 2000	$8.5 million loan	PRC Export-Import Bank to Iran Industry and Mines Bank
Estimate total	**$2.38 billion**	

* This could be the same "export credit" announced in January 1993.

estimate of China's support for projects with Iran. In spite of China's financial support, Chinese capital goods and technology still encounter considerable resistance from Iranian managers, who favor more sophisticated Western, Japanese, or South Korean goods.

The amount of Chinese support has been a perennial source of tension. Comments by Chinese representatives stressing "mutual benefit" and Iran's ability to be "self-reliant" with its "rich mineral resources" should be read as polite rejections of Iranian pleas for more robust Chinese financial support. The value of the Sino-Iranian economic relationship to Beijing, combined with an underlying convergence of perspective about the "unbalanced" international situation, gives Tehran a degree of leverage with Beijing. Iran's government values China's contribution to Iran's industrialization and is willing to allow China to pay for a substantial portion of its oil imports with industrial equipment and technology, thereby helping expand China's high-value capital goods exports. However, the value of this relation to Beijing, plus the requirements of "sincerity" with self-proclaimed Third Worldist principles, allows Tehran to insist that China demonstrate a degree of solidarity with Iran by subsidizing economic cooperation and rendering support on non-economic concerns such as nuclear issues before the IAEA. An important dynamic of the Sino-Iranian relation is bargaining over what level of solidarity on political issues is commensurate with various levels of Chinese financial support and types of Sino-Iranian economic cooperation.

Numerous difficulties plagued the economic relationship. Iran's negotiating style is extremely tough, according to knowledgeable Chinese former officials. Iranian representatives pressed their Chinese counterparts for the lowest possible price, often bringing in third-party competitors to push the price down a bit more. They were willing to revisit points already seemingly agreed on. The Iranian bureaucracy, with overlapping authorities, was also extremely complex and very slow-moving. Even on issues with clear political support from the very highest levels of Iran's government, it could take years to secure action by relevant Iranian agencies. Even then, agreement and action by other agencies might not be forthcoming.[130] In this regard, Chinese businessmen face the same difficulties as those of third-party countries operating in Iran.

Chinese firms also sometimes encountered arbitrary and contract-violating actions by Iranian agencies. One example involved the Haerbin Electric Engineering Company, which signed a contract with the Iranian hydroelectrical power office in March 2003 to supply equipment and construct a hydroelectric plant. On April 23, shortly after the contract was signed, the Haerbin company received a letter from the general manager of the Iranian hydropower office informing it of the cancellation of the contract on the grounds that, since all the contracts related to the project could not be concluded by the end of April, the entire project would be reopened for international bidding, and expressing the hope that the Chinese firm would participate in that rebidding. This unilateral cancellation of an already signed contract led Ambassador Liu Zhentang to seek redress with the Iranian Ministry of Foreign Affairs, Ministry of Commerce, and Planning Office. This was an important project with support from top leaders in both countries and drawing on a preferential loan extended by China, Liu said. Moreover, Liu said, Iranian actions violated the contract. The head of the international section of the Iranian Management and Planning Authority subsequently explained to Liu that the Iranian government had decided to cancel the project in order to shift funds to railway and telecommunications efforts. In good diplomatic style, Liu called for expanded bilateral cooperation.[131]

Iran was sometimes unable to pay its debts. In 1994, for instance, Iran reportedly petitioned Beijing (along with New Delhi) for a rescheduling of $2 billion in outstanding debt. Beijing (and again New Delhi) reportedly explained to Iranian leaders that future sales of military equipment depended on Iranian payment for earlier arms purchases.[132]

Another problem in the Sino-Iranian economic relation was a chronic Iranian deficit in two-way trade, at least until 1999. In that year, as noted earlier, the problem was overcome by major increases in China's petroleum purchases. But this exacerbated another chronic problem—the dominance of petroleum in China's imports from Iran. This too has been a perennial source of Iranian discontent and a constant source of efforts at redress. The inadequacy of China's non-oil imports from Iran were discussed at the third session of the Joint Committee in August 1987, and China agreed to purchase non-oil goods equivalent to 20 percent of the value of oil purchased.[133] Of course, this arrangement would limit the size of China's petroleum purchases from Iran. The underlying problem was that Iran simply produced too few non-oil goods that China needed—pistachio nuts, carpets, and nonferrous metals being among those few.[134] The issue of China's non-oil purchases was reengaged at a Joint Committee session in November 1989. Apparently a new arrangement was adopted whereby the export of Iranian non-oil goods was to match the level of Iranian purchases from China. "We hope that this arrangement will encourage our non-oil exports," said Iranian economic and finance minister Mohsen Nurbakhsh at the time.[135] Of course this arrangement could have the effect of limiting Iran's imports of Chinese capital goods and technology.

The Joint Committee tried market-based methods of increasing Chinese purchase of non-oil goods. In July 1989, for example, thirty-two Iranian companies participated in an international trade fair in Beijing, displaying an array of Iranian nonpetroleum products: carpets, handicrafts, dried fruit, medicines, textiles, metals, ceramics, and household electrical appliances. The president of Iran's Export Promotion Center explained that "for a long time Iran's major export has been petroleum, but now Iran wants to export a big variety of products including food, furniture, porcelain, handicrafts, ore, and building materials."[136] At a meeting of the Joint Commission in August 1991 Finance Minister Nurbakhsh expressed concern about the substantial surplus enjoyed by China in bilateral trade and called for China to increase imports of non-oil goods. Nurbakhsh also called (not entirely consistently) for China to increase its supply of construction materials and skilled manpower for Iran's reconstruction projects. The final agreement provided that the two sides would merely strive for balanced trade.[137]

In spite of multiple difficulties, there is a high degree of economic interdependence between Iran and China. Iranian leaders see China's technology and financial assets as able to make very major contributions to Iran's industrialization and economic development. It may well be that China is Iran's preferred partner, although there is probably a trade-off between perceived low price, flexibility, and political affinity, on the one hand, and lower technology level, on the other. China's leaders see the large-scale transfer of Chinese industrial technology and machine tools to Iran, under generous terms regarding financing and technology transfer, as laying the basis for a long-term and close, multidimensional partnership based on trust and mutual understanding. Just as China helped Iran in a very practical manner fight its war in the 1980s, so in the postwar period it is assisting Iran, in an equally practical manner, with economic development.

A broad and deep economic, industrial, and technological partnership between China and Iran has been built over the past several decades. If China's developmental trajectory over the next several decades continues to be successful, this Sino-Iranian economic partnership may become even stronger. Iran may look increasingly to China as a partner in economic development, while Beijing will be happy to expand cooperation with a powerful state in the Middle East.

10 / Patterns of Sino-Iranian Relations

PARTNER OR RIVAL?

Americans coming to Iran-China relations in the early twenty-first century will probably ask the question, Is China a partner of the United States in the maintenance of the global order, or is it a rival of the United States seeking to establish a new, alternative world order? Does China cooperate with the United States in key policy areas involving Iran and the Middle East, or does it oppose u.s. efforts in that region in tandem with the IRI? Unfortunately, there does not seem to be a simple answer. China is both a partner and a rival of the United States. At times it has cooperated with the United States in ways contrary to Iranian policy. At other times, it has cooperated with Iran in ways contrary to u.s. policy. Perhaps one-armed political scientists are no more common than one-armed economists.[1]

Beijing has cooperated with Washington in many areas. During the Iran-Iraq war, Beijing consistently urged Tehran to end the war. It urged Tehran to avoid military confrontation with the United States in 1987–88. It urged Tehran to accept Security Council Resolution 598 with its cease-fire and u.n.-sponsored peace talks. In all, Beijing played a significant role in ending the Iran-Iraq war. Beijing complied with u.s. demands in 1987 to end the sale of Silkworm antiship missiles and seems to have persuaded Tehran to desist from using already delivered Silkworms against u.s.-protected Gulf commerce. A decade later Beijing agreed to halt sale of C-801 and C-802 and other antiship missiles to Iran. It also agreed with Washington not to sell Iran Category I ballistic missiles and then accepted a somewhat broader definition of prohibited missile cooperation. Beijing supported the late 1990 u.n. effort to

compel Iraq via sanctions to withdraw from Kuwait and did not veto the crucial Security Council vote authorizing use of force in that effort. Beijing suspended nuclear cooperation with the IRI in response to U.S. demands, and
urged Tehran to cooperate with the IAEA regarding Iran's nuclear programs.
This was part of a larger Chinese embrace of the global NPT regime and a
decision to uphold that regime in tandem with the United States. Beijing also
rejected Iranian urging that China keep Israel at arm's length or that it use
its Security Council seat to oust Israel from the General Assembly and otherwise "uphold Palestinian rights." Beijing played a role in teaching the IRI
the costs of violating interstate norms about engaging foreign Muslim communities in violation of the laws of other states. Beijing also declined Tehran's
repeated invitations to form one or another type of united front against U.S.
hegemony.

But Beijing's opposition to U.S. policy in cooperation with the IRI has
been equally robust. Beijing consistently rejected and thwarted U.S. efforts
to sanction the IRI. During the Iran-Iraq war, Beijing rejected Operation
Staunch and served as Iran's major arms supplier. During the postwar period,
Beijing rejected U.S. dual containment policy and pursued economic and technological cooperation with Iran. While U.S. policy sought to contain the IRI,
Chinese policy sought expanded economic and political cooperation with the
IRI. Beijing helped Tehran circumvent U.S. efforts to deny Iran access to
advanced, militarily relevant technology and consistently supplied the IRI with
dual-use technology and machinery applicable to missile, advanced conventional weapons, and chemical warfare programs. China has been a major
partner of Iran in its military modernization efforts, including especially the
development of capabilities targeting U.S. air and naval forces. Beijing has
rejected U.S. efforts to hobble IRI energy development and assisted with the
Neka terminal in the CROS scheme, long-term LNG purchases, and joint development of the Yadavaran oil field. During the lead-ups to both the 1991 and
2003 wars against Iraq, Beijing cooperated with IRI peace diplomacy intended
to avert those U.S.-led military campaigns. Beijing has rejected, in tandem
with Tehran, the U.S. policy of U.S. military forces serving as guardian of
the Gulf and upheld, instead, the role of "littoral states" in that regard. This
implicitly assigns a major role to the IRI in contradiction to the U.S. effort
to restrict the IRI role. For twelve years, China served as the IRI's major nuclear
partner, playing a major role in development of IRI nuclear capabilities.
During 2004 Beijing opposed U.S. efforts to have the IRI nuclear issue transferred from the IAEA to the Security Council. Chinese diplomacy often
embraced antihegemony and pro-multipolarity themes in tandem with the

IRI. Beijing and Tehran supported one another in rejecting what they saw as the U.S. and Western tendency to sit in judgment on what is right and what is wrong with the non-Western world.

The United States–China–Iran relation involves elements of Sino-American cooperation at the expense of IRI policy interests and elements of Sino-American rivalry, with Beijing supporting Tehran against U.S. policy aims.

MANAGING CONTRADICTIONS IN CHINA'S RELATIONS WITH THE UNITED STATES AND THE IRI

China's cooperation with Iran has frequently come into conflict with the imperative of maintaining a broadly cooperative relation with the United States for the sake of China's development. This imperative required repeated trade-offs between China's cooperation with Iran and maintenance of Sino-American comity. China made repeated adjustments in its support for Tehran in order to placate Washington. In effect, China has decided not to oppose the United States in the Middle East.[2]

Yet Beijing has not made such adjustments easily or readily. Nor has it been willing to entirely abandon cooperation with Iran for the sake of placating Washington. Beijing has tenaciously resisted U.S. efforts to ratchet down Sino-Iranian cooperation and occasionally persisted in expanding that cooperation in spite of U.S. pressure. While agreeing to end Silkworm, C-801, and C-802 cruise missile sales to Iran, and while agreeing to forgo sales of M-9 and M-11 ballistic missiles, Beijing transferred to Iran machinery and technology allowing Iran to develop and manufacture comparable missiles indigenously. In the area of ballistic missile cooperation, Beijing crafted its agreements with the United States so as to create loopholes for it to continue cooperation with Iran in the general industrial and technological areas relevant to Iran's missile development efforts. Similarly in the area of possible chemical warfare, China has credited Iran's disclaimers of any such intentions or programs over U.S. assertions to the contrary, and continued to provide Iran with dual-use industrial facilities. China supported Tehran's CROS program and has undertaken major investments in Iranian energy development, again in spite of U.S. pressure. China occasionally subordinated Sino-Iranian cooperation to higher-priority Sino-American comity, but only when U.S. pressure became intense and only in limited ways.

China has found many ways to be helpful to Iran. China supported Iran's economic development efforts, working with it to strengthen key economic sectors like mining, power generation, manufacturing, and transportation. Beijing provided several billion dollars worth of concessionary support for Iranian development projects, including the high-profile Tehran metro project. China also provided Tehran with key, sensitive technologies unavailable from the West. China worked with Iran to accomplish the latter's efforts to develop an indigenous defense industrial base. At the political level, Beijing time and again used its U.N. position to say a few supportive words on Iran's behalf on issues ranging from Security Council debates over mandatory arms embargoes in 1987–88 to IAEA debates over Iran's nuclear programs in 2003–4. Beijing cooperated with Tehran to arm the Islamicist government of Sudan. Beijing also spoke out against George Bush's January 2002 designation of Iran as a member of "an axis of evil." Beijing supported President Khatami's call for a "dialogue among civilizations" at the United Nations, and then organized several appropriate activities once the General Assembly designated 2001 as the Year of Dialogue among Civilizations. Beijing broke dramatically with U.S. treatment of the IRI as a pariah state by conducting a high-profile, thick, and high-level series of exchanges with the IRI—a case in point being Jiang Zemin's visit to Tehran several months after Bush's "axis of evil" speech.

Beijing's management of contradictions between Sino-Iranian and Sino-U.S. cooperation seems to have worked pretty well. China has continued its military cooperation with Iran and built a broad and fairly deep relation with Iran, even while drawing deeply on U.S. inputs into China's development. Objectively speaking, Beijing seems to have gotten just about right the balance between appeasing Washington and forging a partnership with Tehran. Beijing's balancing effort sometimes produced tension in Sino-Iranian or Sino-U.S. relations, but the bottom line was that Beijing sustained U.S. support for China's development drive while simultaneously forging a partnership with the IRI. Neither Washington nor Tehran was completely happy with Beijing's policy, but neither was so unhappy that China's relation with either collapsed. Sino-American cooperation and Sino-Persian cooperation expanded in tandem even as U.S.-Iranian tensions festered. From a purely scholarly perspective, this is an impressive diplomatic accomplishment.

From Beijing's perspective, Washington's presumption of authority to regulate Sino-Iranian relations is the epitome of hegemonism. Iran and China are sovereign countries with full and rightful authority to cooperate together as they see fit. For the United States to dictate, on the basis of U.S. interests and domestic legislation, what is and is not acceptable Sino-Iranian cooperation is pure hegemonism. Beijing occasionally makes concessions to this hegemonism, but such concessions are hard for Chinese to swallow.

CHINA'S LONG-TERM, OVERARCHING GOAL

Within the context of avoiding confrontation with the United States that would undermine China's development drive, China's strategic goal regarding Iran has been to build a durable, multifaceted partnership based on mutual understanding and mutual trust and transcending regime changes in either country. Here the discussion returns to the spiritual level of value-laden beliefs used to interpret and integrate the world. Chinese and Iranians tend to share a similar deep sense of grievance and victimization with the course of modern history, which, they believe, humiliated them and their nations. Chinese tend to view Persia as a fellow great and ancient civilization brought low by Western aggression during the modern era. The trauma of modern national experience is interpreted as a passion play involving the victimization of a great, peaceful, and benevolent nation by violent, aggressive, and amoral Western and Japanese imperialists. China's nationalist project now is about ending, blotting out, and preventing the future repetition of that national degradation. Chinese tend to see in Persia a comrade in this drama of historical humiliation and renewal, justifying China's own vision of itself and requiring solidarity with kindred Iran. Iran's impressive imperial history, its role in revolutionary and anti imperialist struggles of the twentieth century, plus its strong contemporary national capabilities signify that Iran is a relatively powerful state and thus an attractive partner.

Beijing has consistently promulgated a set of ideas putting the IRI on the side of justice—that is, on China's side—in world affairs. The frame of reference has evolved, but the positioning of the IRI on the moral side of world affairs has remained constant. In the 1970s and 1980s Beijing extolled unity of the developing, Third World countries against the hegemony-seeking Soviet and American superpowers. Iran, both the Kingdom of Iran and the IRI, stood in the camp of Third World countries seeking liberation from superpower interference, domination, and exploitation. During the immediate post–Cold War period, Beijing framed world trends in terms of trends toward multipolarity and against U.S. attempts to uphold unipolar domination. By the late 1990s Beijing downplayed the theme of incipient multipolarity, but condemned U.S. unilateralism, power politics, bullying, double standards, and interference. Again Chinese commentary made clear that, in the Chinese view, Iran was a victim of all these evil behaviors. I do not believe these formulations should be dismissed as mere rhetoric. While their appeal in the United States, perhaps even in the West, is limited, this is not the case, I believe, in much of the non-Western world. In much of the world these ideas represent an attractive and persuasive appeal. The dissemination of these ideas via such mechanisms as China's foreign information apparatus is, in fact, a significant form of China's soft power.

This affinity of worldviews and mutual respect for the other's power explains the strong similarity between the Sino-Iranian ententes during the shah's rule and during the IRI period. It explains too the continuity between Chinese courtship of Iran during a period of intensely anti-Soviet Chinese policy in the 1970s and similar courtship during a period of equally intense anti-U.S. Chinese policy during the 1990s. This principle also suggests that a strong relation would exist between China and a post-IRI Iran or between a post-PRC China and Iran—perhaps even stronger than the one existing now, since U.S. opposition would presumably no longer stand frequently in the way of Sino-Iranian cooperation as it did between 1979 and 2004. China-Iran ties would presumably no longer be burdened by fears of possible Islamic revolutionary subversion in Xinjiang or by fears of tarnishing China's international reputation by overly close association with a pariah Iranian regime. Be this as it may be, Beijing will certainly be willing to accept, and will seek to cooperate with, whatever government assumes sovereign power over Iran. Beijing will strive to make the Sino-Iranian cooperative partnership a durable element of the emerging pattern of Asian international relations. Viewing the Iran-China partnership from the standpoint of brilliant and non-Western civilizations and relatively powerful nations in a world emerging from a long period of Western global domination suggests that partnership between Iran and China will become a durable element of the evolving interstate system.

The Sino-Pakistan relationship offers a model of the durable, multidimensional relationship of mutual benefit, understanding, and trust that Beijing is attempting to build with Iran. In the first instance, Pakistan's role as perennial intermediary in Sino-Iranian relations is worth noting. Pakistan's foreign minister, Zulfikar Ali Bhutto, apparently tried to arrange a stopover by Zhou Enlai in Tehran in 1965—an effort that failed.[3] In April 1971 it was Pakistan that delivered to Zhou Enlai the message that Princess Ashraf desired to visit China as Zhou's guest. Then on her way to China, Princess Ashraf stopped for two days in Pakistan and was accompanied to China by the wife of Pakistan's air force chief. When Empress Farah traveled to China in 1973, she too stopped in Pakistan, where she was received and seen off by President Bhutto.[4] After Iran's 1979 revolution, Pakistan again played a role in renormalizing Sino-Iranian relations, with Agha Shahi delivering Hua Guofeng's letter to Khomeini and counseling Iran's new Islamic rulers that China could be a reliable supplier of munitions. This consistent Pakistani record of support for Sino-Iranian cooperation was premised on Pakistan's desire to foster an international situation that constrained India. For the purpose here, the significance lies in Pakistan's recognition of Sino-Iranian ties as a significant element of the Asian structure of power.

Beijing hopes that Sino-Iranian cooperation becomes like the Sino-Pakistani entente in that it is able to transcend various regimes in Iran—or even different regimes in China, for that matter.[5] The Sino-Pakistani entente traces back to the Bandung Conference in 1955, when Pakistan was under civilian rule and was a close ally of the United States. The Sino-Pakistani entente deepened during the 1960s, when Pakistan was under military leadership and as it moved from close to estranged ally of the United States. Then throughout the 1970s and 1990s, China's entente with Pakistan continued as Pakistan alternated between civilian and military regimes and from warm engagement to estrangement with the United States. In the rhetoric of the Sino-Pakistani relation, the bond is "all-weather." With Iran, the modern cooperative relation began under the shah, but after the Islamic revolution Beijing left no stone unturned in an effort to revive that earlier partnership. Nor did China concern itself with the internal nature of Iran's regime, but sought cooperative ties with whatever government controlled Iran.

Yet another similarity between the long-standing Sino-Pakistani relation and the emerging Sino-Iranian tie is that both links have been "tested by adversity"—a phrase favored in Chinese pronouncements on Sino-Pakistani ties. In Pakistan's case, this phrase refers to China's support for Pakistan during Pakistan's various wars with India and to China's support for Pakistan's military and nuclear development in spite of opposition by India and the United States. In other words, cooperation will not be suspended in times of war or in deference to third-country pressure. Regarding Sino-Iranian ties, those links were tested by adversity when China continued its arms supply to Iran during the 1980–88 war in spite of Washington's Operation Staunch. Testing by adversity continued with China's nuclear cooperation for at least twelve years in spite of intense u.s. pressure. Ties were again tested when China found ways to circumvent u.s. opposition to China's assistance to Iran's missile development programs. By this perseverance during periods of testing by adversity Beijing demonstrated to Iran that China was a reliable partner. It was not fickle—unlike the United States, which is wont to sever military support when wars begin and need is greatest. Chinese behavior seeks to demonstrate that China is prepared to stand by its friends when the going gets tough. China is able and willing to bear some political costs for the sake of sustaining cooperation with friendly powers. In American parlance this is referred to as the credibility of a great power to its alliance partners.

Of course, this willingness to bear costs for the sake of the cooperative relationship works both ways. By persuading Tehran that China's support is valuable, Beijing hopes to persuade Tehran to stand by China, should that need arise, in times of crisis and in spite of opposition by third powers. In the context of the post–Cold War world the gravest possibility in the back of Chinese minds is probably a u.s.-prc conflict over Taiwan in which the United States attempted to sever China's oil imports. Dealing with that eventuality would be a monumental task, but cooperation by a major oil supplier like Iran would give Beijing considerably more options.

Beijing's periodic submission to u.s. pressure over Iran has weakened China's credibility in Tehran. One reason Beijing persisted in missile and chemical cooperation with Iran in spite of intense u.s. pressure was to offset blows to China's credibility occasioned by China's earlier submissions to u.s. pressure in the areas of nuclear and missile cooperation. By maintaining credibility and influence with Tehran, Beijing hedges against possible deterioration of Sino-American relations.

IRAN AND CHINA'S SOUTHWESTERN CORRIDOR TO THE SEA

Iran, along with Pakistan, plays an increasingly important role in providing western China access to the oceanic highway of the global economy. Economic and strategic factors converge here. The striking success of China's post-1978 development drive was predicated on integrating eastern China into the global economy, and that, in turn, was predicated on the many fine ports on China's east coast. Those ports offered access to the oceanic highways that carried China-manufactured goods to distant markets. Western China, locked deep in the interior of Eurasia, suffered a distinct disadvantage in this regard. Western, interior provinces, with strong support from Beijing, attempted to mitigate this disadvantage by opening transport links with their neighbors. Yunnan province in China's southwest achieved considerable success in opening or improving road, riverine, and rail links with and through Myanmar to ports (including several that were China built) on the Bay of Bengal. Myanmar's location in the southeastern foothills of the Tibetan plateau had for many centuries made it a natural transit route between southwestern China and the Bay of Bengal. Xinjiang was not so fortunate. Its traditional international trade routes were the long and tenuous lines of the various "silk roads" across Central Asia.

Beijing attempted to strengthen Xinjiang's transport links with Central Asia. In 1990 the Soviet Central Asia railway grid was finally linked to that of Xinjiang when a line was opened between Urumqi and Aqtoghay, Kazakhstan. Then in the late 1990s a rail line was pushed south along the western rim of the Tarim Basin, reaching Kashgar by 1999. As of 2005, construction of two trans-

Kyrgyzstan highways running westward from Kashgar is under way, with the intention of eventually transforming one of those routes into a rail line The China-supported construction of the rail line from Mashhad to Tedzhen, Turkmenistan, opened in 1996, as noted earlier, was also part of this effort to link Xinjiang to Iranian ports. Figure 10.1 shows these various transport routes.

China's adoption in 2000 of a program to accelerate development of its western regions made development of transportation lines to the southwest even more important. Pakistan was China's major partner in this regard. In August 2001 Premier Zhu Rongji committed China to provide $198 million to support the first phase of construction of a new seaport at Gwadar in Pakistan's Baluchistan.[6] Zhu also promised unspecified support for two subsequent phases of the project. When complete, the new Gwadar port was to have a cargo throughput capacity equivalent to Karachi, thereby nearly doubling Pakistan's maritime capacity and allowing cargoes to circumvent Karachi's extremely crowded facilities. Also in 2001, China committed $250 million to assist Pakistan in modernizing its railway system.[7] In March 2003 Beijing committed an additional $500 million to Pakistan's railway modernization, including construction of new tracks.[8] China also agreed to provide financial support for construction of a new rail line northward from Gwadar and linking up at Dalbandin with the existing east-west rail line. China also agreed to finance construction of a highway east from Gwadar along the Makran coast. Simultaneously measures were taken to expedite the flow of truck traffic along the Karakoram Highway running from Kashgar to Rawulpindi in northern Pakistan.

While China's major transportation investments in southwest Asia have been in Pakistan, Iran has played a role via several railway projects that dovetailed with China's efforts in Pakistan. The first of these Iranian projects was construction of a rail line between Kerman in southeast Iran and Zahedan on the Iran-Pakistan border. Work on this line was under way in 2002.[9] When complete, this rail line will link the Iranian and Pakistani rail systems for the first time. Work was also under way on a new rail line extending southwest from Mashhad directly across northeastern Iran to Bafq.[10] This line was to be operational by early 2005.[11] The completion of these new lines will mean that Chinese cargo moving via the Tedzhen-Mashhad link can proceed directly to seaports without having to take the long, circuitous, and crowded but previously required detour via Tehran. Once these new lines are open, Chinese cargo will also be able to move between Pakistan and Iran and via ports in either of those two countries. These new lines will add considerable redundancy to China's southwest Asia transportation system.

While the major significance of these new, Chinese southwesterly lines of

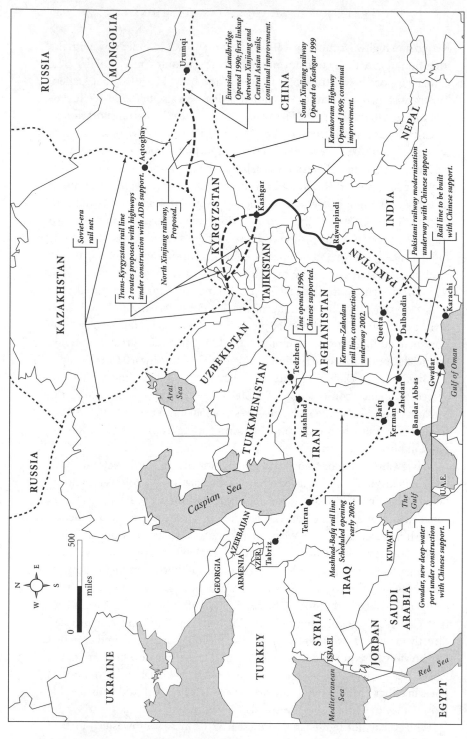

FIGURE 10.1 China's Southwest Corridor to the Sea

The following labels appear on the map:

Soviet-era rail net.

Trans-Kyrgyzstan rail line 2 routes proposed with highways under construction with ADB support.

North Xinjiang railway, Proposed.

Eurasian Landbridge Opened 1990; first linkup between Xinjiang and Central Asian rails; continual improvement.

South Xinjiang railway Opened to Kashgar 1999

Karakoram Highway Opened 1969; continual improvement.

Pakistani railway modernization underway with Chinese support.

Rail line to be built with Chinese support.

Line opened 1996, Chinese supported.

Kerman-Zahedan rail line, construction underway 2002.

Mashhad-Bafq rail line Scheduled opening early 2005.

Gwadar, new deep-water port under construction with Chinese support.

international transportation is commercial, they also have a strategic role. In the event of a u.s.-prc military confrontation that became protracted and in which the United States used its naval supremacy to blockade China's coast, China's ability to continue prosecution of the war would be influenced by its ability to import vital materials overland. In such a situation it would be extremely useful to have robust and redundant transport links via Pakistan and Iran and to have long-standing, cooperative ties "tested by adversity" with both of those countries.

A COMPLEX, SECOND-ORDER RELATIONSHIP

There have been strong elements of conflict as well as cooperation in the Sino-Iranian relationship. Beijing and Tehran, more often than not, have had divergent interests toward the superpowers. Throughout the history of post-1971 Sino-Iranian relations there has typically existed an asymmetry in interest in a closer partnership to counter one or another superpower. During the pre-1979 era, it was China that was the more ardent suitor in the Sino-Iranian relationship, with Beijing pressing Tehran to play a greater role in what Beijing saw as the emerging global united front against Soviet social imperialist expansionism. The shah was reluctant to go down that path. His aim in cooperating with China was deterring and moderating Soviet behavior, not provoking the Soviet Union. China, however, felt a dire threat of encirclement or even direct attack by the Soviet Union, and urgently wanted a global anti-Soviet coalition that would lessen Soviet pressure on China. During the post-1979 period, the situation was reversed. Tehran became the more ardent suitor and Beijing the more hesitant party. Confronted with the deterioration of relations with the United States, the European countries, and its Arab neighbors, Iran needed friends. The end of the Iraq-Iran war freed Moscow from its alliance obligations to Iraq and opened the door to Soviet-Iranian cooperation, but the dissolution of the Soviet state greatly reduced the willingness and ability of Russia to support Iran against the West. In its search for international partners during the 1990s, Tehran propounded joint Iranian-Chinese confrontation of the United States and various sorts of anti-u.s. hegemony blocs to include China, Iran, India, Pakistan, Russia, and even Japan. Beijing was not interested. Tehran responded by criticizing China's close relations with the United States in 1979, during Reagan's 1984 visit, and again when Beijing capitulated to u.s. pressure over nuclear and missile cooperation in 1997. Beijing moved to mollify Iranian criticism but did not alter the course of its underlying u.s. policy.

Beijing has been wary of overly close association with the IRI. The potential financial costs of close association with Iran may have been one Chinese consideration here. A major element of antihegemony, Third World solidarity was to be, Tehran insisted, robust Chinese financial support for development projects in Iran. A key theme of China's post-1978 foreign policy line was to avoid, with rare exceptions (one of which was the Tehran metro), such costly overseas projects that, Deng Xiaoping felt, had helped impoverish China under Mao Zedong's rule. Iran's very size meant that as an ally its demand on Chinese resources could be quite heavy.

Political factors were probably more important in explaining the distance Beijing maintained in ties with the IRI. Overly close association with the IRI could hurt China's international reputation. Deng Xiaoping strove quite effectively to shed China's revolutionary image acquired during Mao's rule. Close association with revolutionary Iran ran counter to Deng's effort to normalize China's reputation and diplomacy. After 1978 and with increasing clarity into the 1990s, China desired to be accepted as a responsible power qualified to be admitted by the international community into the ranks of the leading nations of the world. Achievement of this respectability was not facilitated by close association with Islamic revolutionary IRI or by implication in possible IRI nuclear weapons efforts. Close alignment with the IRI could also injure China's ties both with the Arab countries and with Israel.

There were also numerous smaller frictions in the Sino-Iranian relationship. The propensity of some Iranian foundations, and perhaps even the IRI government, to foster radical Islamic thought in China's Muslim communities and in Central Asian countries contiguous to China generated conflict in the PRC-IRI relation. This conflict led not to estrangement but, paradoxically, to greater emphasis on "friendship." Beijing sought to demonstrate to Tehran that cooperation with China was valuable, but that such cooperation would be impossible if Iranian "interference" in the affairs of China's Muslim communities continued. In effect, Beijing made cessation of Iranian subversion the price of Chinese friendship and cooperation. Conflict thus led to engagement and friendship, rather than to sanctions and hostility.

Tehran sometimes defaulted on payment of its bills to Beijing. Difficulties of doing business in Iran certainly tested the patience of Chinese businesspeople no less than German, South Korean, Canadian, or Norwegian. Arbitrary and unilateral Iranian changes in agreements sometimes led to Chinese protests. So to did Iranian "discrimination" against Chinese goods in favor of Western technology. Negotiations over business deals were often long and hard, with Iranian calls for Third World solidarity being met with Chinese insistence on mutual benefit.

Frictions over relative status also periodically troubled the Beijing-Tehran relationship. During the mid-1970s the shah was dismayed with Zhou Enlai's failure to visit Iran in reciprocation for the visits by the two Pahlavi princesses, a prince, the queen, and Prime Minister Amir Abbas Hoveyda. The shah suspected that Zhou's reported "illness" was diplomatic and resented Beijing's lack of attention to reciprocity in the relation. In 1989 Khamenei was offended by the initial failure to arrange a meeting with Deng Xiaoping. The Chinese side, for its part, took umbrage at Tehran's presumption in criticizing Beijing's warm reception of u.s. president Reagan in 1984. It may be that the same sense of victimization that helps bring Beijing and Tehran together makes them sensitive to perceived slights in their mutual relationship.

The Sino-Iranian relation has consistently been a second-order relationship in the sense that both parties have periodically subordinated that relationship to other objectives. As noted earlier, Iran in the 1970s insisted on subordinating its relation with China to Iran's relation with the Soviet Union. Similarly, in the 1990s Beijing insisted on subordinating its relation with Iran to China's far more important relation with the United States. Here comparison with Sino-Pakistani ties is again instructive. China shares with Pakistan a common interest in constraining India. It shares with Iran a common (though perhaps less immediate) interest in constraining the United States in the Persian Gulf. Yet China's support for nuclear and military ties with Pakistan has been far denser than similar relations with Iran. One reason for this is that the potential costs associated with supporting Iran against the United States are greater than the potential costs of supporting Pakistan against India. India is not inclined, and perhaps not able, to penalize China for nuclear and military ties with Pakistan. The United States, however, can and does penalize China for links with Iran. United States decision makers are more willing than Indian to resort to sanctions and penalties, and the United States has the ability to undermine seriously China's successful post-1978 development drive.

The Middle East generally has been an area of secondary Chinese foreign policy attention, although this may well change with China's growing energy demand. Traditionally, Beijing placed priority on relations with the major powers that had historically bedeviled or befriended China: Japan, the Soviet Union / Russia, and the United States. At a second level, China stressed ties with its contiguous neighbors that were in a position either to cooperate or abstain from cooperation with what Beijing deemed anti-China plots of Moscow or Washington: Vietnam, Korea, Burma, Thailand, and Laos. More remotely, China courted significant regional powers. Iran fell in this category. China recognized the importance of oil in the global balance of power and identified this as the factor driving "superpower" policy toward the region, and as one factor facilitating or thwarting superpower achievement of global domination. Until the 1990s, however, China had the luxury of not being highly dependent on Middle East oil.

CHINA'S RISE AND THE AMERICAN IMPERIUM

Iran and China have constructed out of their remarkable histories beliefs in their respective greatness and destiny to lead an Asia restored from the degradation that began with the Western eruption in the fifteenth century CE. For Iran, that translates into a belief in Iran's destiny to play a leading role in the Persian Gulf region. China has implicitly endorsed that Iranian ambition.

The shah secured u.s. support for realization of this vision following London's decision to withdraw from east of Suez. An authoritative Chinese endorsement can be traced back to Foreign Minister Ji Pengfei's June 1973 expression of China's "firm support" for Iran's "just position" of calling for the "joint management" of the affairs of the Persian Gulf region by Iran and "other Persian Gulf countries." Shortly after Ji's declaration, Beijing further implicitly acknowledged Iran's leading regional role by endorsing Iranian military intervention to counter "subversion" in Oman and Pakistani Baluchistan. Washington revoked its support of Iran's leading regional role after 1979, but China has continued its endorsement. This is the implicit content of China's periodically reiterated endorsement of Iran's call for the withdrawal of all foreign military forces from the Gulf and management of the security affairs of that region by the Gulf littoral countries themselves. Given the realities of power in the Gulf region, u.s. withdrawal would leave Iran de facto paramount power in the region. Twenty-seven years after Ji's declaration, the joint communiqué issued at the conclusion of President Khatami's June 2000 visit to China proclaimed the two sides "emphasized that the security and stability of the Persian Gulf should be safeguarded by the countries of the region free from outside interference."[12]

Unfortunately for both Tehran and Beijing, events have moved opposite of the direction they desired. Step-by-step throughout the post-1979 era, the United States expanded its military position in the Persian Gulf region: Jimmy Carter's 1979 announcement of u.s. assumption of direct military responsibility for Gulf security; Ronald Reagan's 1983 upgrading of Carter's Rapid Deployment Force to a full-fledged regional headquarters; expansion of Diego Garcia into a major forward support base; the pre-positioning of supplies and equipment for combat in the Gulf; construction or expansion of military-use facilities in Egypt, Kenya, Saudi Arabia, and other countries in the region; and the development of Persian Gulf war plans and training of u.s. forces to operate in a desert environment. The exercise of this newly developed U.S. military power in Lebanon, Libya, Somalia, and Iran in the 1980s, and against Iraq in 1991 and again from 1998 to 2003, began to shape events in the Gulf region. By 2003 U.S. forces were in direct occupation of Iraq, a leading Arab country, trying to foster emergence of a Western-style political system. This in a region of the world previously peripheral to the U.S. global military system prior to 1979.[13]

Beijing and Tehran are in agreement that the growth of the U.S. military position in the Persian Gulf region is a manifestation of U.S. hegemony, inspired by a desire to control the region's oil resources as a step toward realizing the dream of global domination. They also agree that the U.S. push for hegemony over the Middle East is antithetical to the interests of both countries and, of course, to fundamental principles of justice. The vision of a Persian Gulf without extraregional military forces and with regional security affairs managed by the countries of the region themselves can be taken as an alternate course of development preferred by Beijing and Tehran.

As noted in an earlier chapter, A. H. H. Abidi argues in his perceptive 1982 book that China's insistence on Gulf security affairs being managed by *all* the countries of the region after withdrawal of extraregional military forces signals Beijing's rejection of the Iranian claim to be *primus inter pares* among the Gulf countries and insistence on an Iranian status as merely *unus inter pares*.[14] Beijing would reject an Iranian attempt to dominate the Gulf and would act as a "subtle brake" on Iranian tendencies in that direction, Abidi argues. My own reading of the Sino-Iranian relationship is that Beijing would be quite comfortable with Iran playing a leading, even dominant, role in the Persian Gulf region. Chinese strategists must certainly realize that China alone will not be able to fill the vacuum created by a post–U.S.-dominated Asia. All great powers need allies, and Iran offers one of the best prospects for a genuine Chinese ally. A Chinese anchor in East Asia paired with an Iranian anchor in West Asia could well emerge as a central element of a post-unipolar, China-centered Asia circa the middle of the twenty-first century. It may well be that China is building toward that long-term objective.

A key Chinese objective is multipolarity—a world in which U.S. power is much reduced, with the United States merely one of several competing, independent, and more or less equal centers of power. In such a world, China's leaders believe, China's diplomatic situation would be much enhanced. A strong Iran dominating the Persian Gulf could be a significant pole in a multipolar system. If the U.S. global position is enhanced by increased control over Persian Gulf oil, China's position would be correspondingly diminished. Conversely, if the U.S. global position is diminished by transfer of control over Gulf oil to an independent, perhaps even anti-u.s. Iran, China's vulnerability to u.s. control over its oil supply would be correspondingly reduced. Viewed from this perspective, Beijing's long-term strategy may be to subordinate Sino-Iranian ties when necessary to Sino-American comity so as to maintain u.s. support for China's post-1978 modernization drive, while simultaneously strengthening Iran and forging a durable Sino-Iranian partnership to prepare for the post-u.s. hegemony era.

However, one can discern a grand strategic bargain between China and the United States implicit in China's diplomacy. Stated in simple terms, the deal would be this: Washington accepts that Taiwan is in China's sphere of influence and agrees not to oppose China's efforts to order China's relations with Taiwan. In exchange, Beijing accepts that Iran and the Middle East are in the u.s. sphere and agrees not to oppose u.s. efforts to reorder the Middle East. In effect, Taiwan for Iran. I do not know if this proposition has been placed before official u.s. representatives, but it does seem to be implicit in Beijing's handling of the situation. Chinese representatives have repeatedly linked u.s. arms sales to Taiwan with China's arms sales to Iran. Both are forms of proliferation and must be discussed together, Chinese representatives have said. China is willing to consider u.s. concerns over Chinese arms transfers to Iran, if the United States is willing to take seriously Chinese concerns over u.s. arms transfers to Taiwan.

Support for Iran's military development gives Beijing leverage with Washington on the issue of u.s. arms sales to Taiwan. The United States' arms sales to Taiwan have been a core issue because they run counter to Beijing's effort to engineer a gradual shift of the military balance in the Taiwan Strait in the PLA's favor and to Taipei's disadvantage, a shift that Beijing hoped would convince Taipei of the wisdom of accepting status as a special autonomous region of the PRC. Beijing views incorporation of Taiwan into the administrative system of the PRC as the final and yet unfulfilled act of China's national liberation. The United States' sale of arms to Taiwan is the main obstacle to accomplishing this, in Beijing's view. Phrased in terms of accommodation between a rising China and an incumbent American hegemon, the bargain implicit in China's diplomacy is this: China is rising and that rise is just, inevitable, and unstoppable. Taiwan *will* be incorporated into the PRC. To avoid a war with China, the United States must accept this reality. Once the United States does this, Beijing is prepared to be extremely lenient and guarantee Taiwan's continued practice of democratic politics and substantial self-rule. Beijing might also be prepared to respect u.s. interests in certain other regions of the world. United States satisfaction of China's demands on Taiwan would effectively eliminate the danger of a United States–PRC war, thereby greatly reducing China's apprehension over U.S. control of China's Middle Eastern oil supply arising from the derivative fear that the United States might cut those supplies in the event of a war over Taiwan. The prospects for long-term peaceful cooperative relations between China and the United States—the world's rising great power and the world's reigning hegemon—would be much improved. The Chinese and the American people will have much better prospects of avoiding war, possibly a nuclear war. For such an arrangement to work, there must be incentives for Washington to enter into such a bargain. From this perspective, Chinese nuclear, missile, and chemical weapons support for Iran can be seen as a way of bidding up the value of China's Iranian leverage. Of course, if Beijing were actually to enter into such an arrangement with Washington, it would be tantamount to abandoning Iran as an important, long-term partner—contrary to what has been argued throughout this book. Taiwan just might be an adequate prize for Beijing to do so.

Failing a sphere of influence arrangement between China and America, China will probably prepare for eventual confrontation with the United States over Taiwan. In such an eventuality, Iran would be an important partner. Should a United States–PRC war over Taiwan become protracted, the United States would be likely to cut off China's oil imports one way or another. The willingness of a major petroleum power like Iran to continue supplying China could be highly important under these circumstances. Overseas shipment would be precluded by control of the seas, but overland shipment via Russia, Kazakhstan, or Pakistan might be possible.

Sino-Iranian relations should not be reduced to Taiwan. They are much richer than that. While Taiwan scenarios do, I believe, enter into Beijing's calculations in the early twenty-first century, the stakes are much broader than that. At their broadest level, Sino-Iranian relations involve two ancient and proud peoples who recognize the other as a peer and a partner and are determined to cooperate in building a post–Western-dominated Asia.

CHINA'S STRATEGIC OPPORTUNISM

China's policy toward Iran has been a combination of pure opportunism and long-term strategic vision—an approach that might be called "strategic opportunism." On the one hand, opportunities for China to develop relations with Iran have been created by circumstances beyond Beijing's control. The unwillingness of Iran's traditional Western partners to continue selling arms to Iran after 1979, combined with the unwillingness of Moscow and Tehran to open military links at that juncture, created an opportunity for

Beijing during the Iran-Iraq war. United States and Western restrictions on technology transfer to Iran, likewise created opportunities for Chinese firms to edge into new Iranian markets. United States opposition to Western involvement in Iranian energy development projects later created opportunities for Chinese firms—although in this case Washington's European allies refused to follow the u.s. lead. The poor state of u.s.-Iranian, European-Iranian, and Arab-Iranian relations produced an Iranian desire for international comfort and support, and China, with its veto-backed voice in the Security Council, nuclear weapons, strong international media, and fluency in the language of civilizational solidarity, was able to offer such support. In most general terms, the Islamic revolution itself, which tore Iran away from a Western model of development and set it on a course of deliberate rejection of the Western model of society, offered an opportunity for China to provide a comradely, kindred spirit.

While Beijing seized these fortuitous opportunities to expand ties with Tehran, Chinese policy was inspired by a sense that Iran was a significant country whose friendship China would do well to cultivate. China recognizes Iran as a nation whose large area and population, educated people, rich energy resources, strategic location, and spirit of national cohesion as manifest in its ancient and modern history make it a major regional power in a strategically important region of the world. It is this combination of substantial national capabilities that Chinese leaders are alluding to when they refer to the importance of Sino-Iranian cooperation. Iran is a nation with considerable capabilities in the Middle East that can, by cooperating with Chinese policy, further China's attainment of its national interests.

At a deeper level, Chinese leaders see Iran as a nation with which China can cooperate at it rises to high stature in Asia and the world. As noted earlier, the large purpose driving Chinese foreign policy is blotting out the national humiliation inflicted on China by Western and Japanese imperialism in the century of national humiliation between 1839 and 1949, and restoring China to the exalted international status that it enjoyed (Chinese believe) for many centuries prior to that humiliation. Accomplishing this aim was the key reason why a generation of young Chinese adopted Marxism-Leninism after 1917; Communism seemed like the way to quickly make China rich, strong, and influential in the world. The same aim led a later generation of Chinese to reject Marxism-Leninism after 1978; experience had proved that this road would not make China rich, strong, and respected. Since 1978 China's leaders have through trial and error arrived at a new developmental path, but their purpose remains the same: to restore China to its rightful position of great eminence in the world, to establish China as one of the leading powers in the world and, perhaps, as the preeminent power in Asia. Given this drive to accomplish the rise of China, leaders in Beijing must ask themselves: which countries are likely, over the long run, to look with sympathy on Chinese preeminence in Asia and offer China sincere cooperative partnerships?

Japan will be ruled out. As far back as the seventh century CE, Japan refused to fit into the Chinese world order and accept a theoretical position for its ruler subordinate to China's Son of Heaven (emperor). Once Japan was unified in the sixteenth century, it began challenging China's preeminence in Asia, first by pirate raids and then by outright invasion of China's Korean tributary. Japan then turned inward with the Tokugawa shogunate and its polity of national seclusion. But as soon as Japan turned outward with the Meiji Restoration in 1867, it again challenged China—first by stripping away China's Korean tributary and Taiwan, then by establishing itself in the hated Treaty System, then via the Twenty-one Points of 1915, and finally via the Greater East Asia Co-Prosperity Sphere and an effort to turn China into a Japanese satellite. In the early twenty-first century, as China's power and status grow rapidly, Japan is again refusing to accept a subordinate position in a China-centric Asia and is demanding a moral and political position in Asia equal to that of China. Japan is far more likely to seek to balance China than to serve as its ally.

India is similarly problematic. The two countries dispute ownership of a large track of land corresponding to India's state of Arunachal Pradesh. They have been unable even to agree on the location of the line of actual control along their common border, let alone solve the boundary issue, in spite of decades of negotiations, dialogues, joint working groups, expert working groups, and confidence-building measures. China's major stake in South Asia is with Pakistan—India's perennial nemesis. It may well be that China's refusal to define the border with India is linked to an understanding with Pakistan not to eliminate India's two-front concerns. India and China disagree profoundly about the status of Tibet and the Himalayan lands of Nepal, Bhutan, and Sikkim. For several decades during the post–World War II era, China and India vied for status in the then newly independent Afro-Asian world. India watches with deep apprehension the expansion of Chinese relations with India's neighbors—Myanmar, Bangladesh, Nepal, and Pakistan. There is also the still-vivid memory of India's 1962 humiliation via defeat by China's PLA. India's smaller neighbors can be expected to welcome the growth of Chinese power as a way of escaping Indian domination. But India itself, the greatest power in the South Asian region, almost certainly will remain deeply apprehensive of the growth of Chinese power and influence. India cannot be counted among China's sincere, long-term friends.

Russia's position is more equivocal, but here too China's strategists must have doubts. Many Russians are deeply apprehensive about their long-term control of the Russian Far East, the vast and mineral-rich territory lying between Lake Baikal and the Pacific Ocean. During the 1960s and 1970s Soviet leaders convinced themselves, with not a little help from Mao Zedong, that China's aim was to recover this land "stolen" from China by Russia's czars. These fears no longer dominate Russian policy, at least at the central level, but they remain widespread especially in the Russian Far East, where a population of 7.5 million confronts a population of 112 million in just the three provinces of China's northeast. Below these Russian fears of Chinese revanchism are broader demographic trends. With one of the lowest fertility rates in the world, Russia faces a shrinking population. One recent study projected Russia's 2010 population at 142 million, a decline of 3 million from 2000, giving Russia a population smaller than Nigeria, Bangladesh, or Pakistan to populate an area twice the size of the United States.[15] A shrinking Russian population, combined with an exodus of Russians from the Russian Far East, will further exacerbate Russian apprehensions. Chinese policy since the breakup of the Soviet Union has been highly sensitive to these Russian fears and has sought at every turn to reassure Moscow and Russian public opinion. These efforts have not been without success, but Russian fears remain, rooted in cultural stereotypes and the realities of the diverging national power trajectories of Russia and China. From this perspective, Beijing will be lucky if it can persuade Russia to remain in a "nonaggression" relation with China and keep Russia from drifting toward its "European home" and possible membership in NATO. Russia, over the long term, will not be China's sincere friend but will probably try to limit and hedge the growth of Chinese power.

At a somewhat lower level in the hierarchy of national power are Australia and Indonesia. Australia is linked by language, culture, ideology and governmental form, history, and race to the United States and Europe. It is not likely to forgo those primordial bonds for a strategic partnership with a rising China. Indonesia is more promising for Beijing, but here too Indonesian resentment of the economic position enjoyed by Chinese-origin Indonesians, Indonesia's own aspirations for regional leadership, and Indonesia's emerging democratic political culture will probably mitigate against political partnership between China and Indonesia. Nor will Indonesia's growing Islamic consciousness incline Jakarta toward Beijing.

So where in Asia will Beijing find partners as China realizes its "peaceful rise"? Among the significant powers, Iran offers the most promising opportunity. As this discussion has shown, Chinese analysts find no incident of armed conflict in the long history of interaction between Chinese and Persian states, but find, rather, lots of mutually beneficial cooperation, including occasional convergence of strategic interests.

I do not mean to suggest that Chinese diplomacy has or will write off Japan, India, Russia, and others. Beijing's diplomacy has striven and will continue to strive to make these countries comfortable with China's growing power. But I suspect, at bottom, there is an understanding, perhaps implicit rather than explicit, that Iran promises to be more comfortable with great Chinese power than does any other major Asian state.

From the standpoint of thirty-five years of Sino-Iranian cooperation, the specific strategic content of that cooperation in specific periods is secondary. During the 1970s Sino-Iranian cooperation was directed primarily toward containing Soviet-Indian-Iraqi "expansionism." During the 1980s its primary content focused on the conduct and international politics of the Iran-Iraq war. During the 1990s the substance of Sino-Iranian cooperation shifted to an oil-for-capital-goods swap and countering u.s. "unipolarity" in an "unbalanced" post-Soviet world. Taking an even longer view, in ancient times Sino-Persian cooperation was directed against the Xiongnu. During the early medieval period it was directed against the Arabs. In the future it may well be directed against some other power. The specific opponent and content are transitory. It is the element of cooperation between China and Persia that endures and is fundamental. To say it another way, the Sino-Iranian relation is essentially about power and influence.

The Sino-Iranian relation partners two proud peoples who see in the other an affirmation of their own self-identity. They respect the history of the other and are aware of the long chronicle of mutually beneficial contact and, sometimes, cooperation between the two nations. They see that historic cooperation as an important element of the world order prior to the European eruption and their consequent humiliation, and are determined to cooperate in putting the world once again to right. They share a large set of values about the unjust condition of the modern world. Each respects the power, strong national consciousness, and national accomplishments of the other and sees in it an influential partner well worth cultivating. The ways in which China and Iran cooperate will vary depending on mutual interests, but the impulse toward cooperation will remain constant.

Appendix / Chronology of Iran-China Relations

ABBREVIATIONS

COSTIND	Commission for Science, Technology, and Industry for National Defense
DFM	Deputy Foreign Minister
Dir.	Director
DPM	Deputy Premier
FM	Foreign Minister
M	Minister
MD	Minister of Defense
MFA	Ministry of Foreign Affairs
MOU	Memorandum of understanding
NPC	National People's Congress
PAK	Pakistan
PM	Premier
PRC	People's Republic of China
ROC	Republic of China
SC	Standing Committee
TM	Trade Minister
VFM	Vice Foreign Minister
VM	Vice Minister
VPM	Vice Premier

MAIN SOURCES: Zhongguo waijiao (Beijing: Ministry of Foreign Affairs). *Tehran Times*, Tehran. Foreign Broadcast Information Service.

NOTE: A question mark after the day indicates uncertainty about the exact date of an event, or, after the year, about the very occurrence of the event.

Chronology of Iran–China Relations

1920–49

June 1, 1920	Republic of China (ROC)–Iran friendship treaty signed, Rome; establish diplomat relations	China's 1st treaty not conferring consular judicial power (extraterritoriality)
1933	Iran opens consulate in Shanghai	Tend to Iranian business-people in Chinese cities
1941	Iran asks Netherlands to tend to Iranian interests in China	
1944	Iran mission upgraded to embassy, Chongqing	Embassy moves to Nanjing after Japanese surrender

1949–70

1951	PRC supports Musaddiq's nationalization of oil industry	
1953	PRC media condemns coup ousting Musaddiq	Condemnation more nuanced and less harsh that Soviet condemnation
1954?	PRC ambassador to Pakistan accredited to Iran as well	
1955	PRC media condemns Iran membership in Baghdad pact	
1956	ROC (Taiwan) and Kingdom of Iran establish diplomatic relations	
May 1958	Shah visits Taiwan	

1958	PRC expresses interest commercial relations w/ Iran	
February 1963	Iran goodwill delegation to Taiwan; Majlis speaker Hikwat heads	
March 1963	Iran goodwill delegation to Taiwan; M State, S.A. Azizi heads	
Fall 1963	Iran receives offer of barter trade from China	
October 1964	Prince Gholam Reza Pahlavi visits Taiwan	
December 1964	Gen. Jiang Weiguo, commander ROC army and head of Staff College, visits Iran	Talks with shah
January 1965	Chancellor of University Tehran Ali Sheikholeslam to Taiwan	Talks with universities and re cultural exchanges
January 1965	ROC Chinese Muslim Association makes goodwill visit to Iran	
1965	PAK FM Z.A. Bhutto conveys to China Iranian solicitation of invitation visit	Invitation to Pahlavi princess issued, but visit "not realized"
1965	Iran abstains on question of China representation at United Nations	
June 1965	Premier Zhou Enlai radios best wishes while crossing Iran air space	Some sources report landing in / visit to Tehran by Zhou Enlai
September 1965	PRC threatens strike against India during India-Pakistan war	Establishes China as credible backer of Pakistan

1966	Iran permits limited trade with PRC	
1966	Iran abstains on question of China representation at United Nations	
September 1967	ROC land reform experts visit Iran to study White Revolution	
1967	Shah in media interview says would support PRC to UN w/o Taiwan expulsion	
1967	Iran abstains on question of China's representation at United Nations	
February 1968	ROC trade mission to Taiwan	
January 4, 1969	Shah at press conference in India indicates support for PRC UN entry	
January 15–29, 1969	Exhibition of Chinese paintings in Tehran, sponsored by ROC	Madame Chiang Kai-shek and Empress Farah sponsor exhibition
May 1969	Iran Minister of agriculture visits Taiwan	Agreement re technical cooperation
May 1969	Iran Foreign Minister visits Taiwan	Communiqué re cooperation
September 1969	Shah interview w/ Pakistan paper supports PRC UN entry	

1970–78

| 1970 | Iran again abstains on UN vote re PRC representation | |

January 1971	Pakistan's Z. A. Bhutto conveys to PRC interest of Pahlavi princess to visit	
April 17, 1971	Princess Ashraf (Shah's younger sister) visits PRC	
April 30– May 11, 1971	Princess Fatema (Shah's younger sister) visits PRC	
August 16, 1971	Chinese and Iranian ambassadors to Pakistan meet in Islamabad	Agreement re establishment diplomatic relations
August 17, 1971	Initiation of Iran-China diplomatic relations	
September 17– 27, 1971	Empress Farah, PM A. Hoveyda to China	10 day official visit; Zhou & Hoveyda hold talks; shah in Moscow
October 3, 1971	PRC chargé d'affaires ad interim Wang Ching-jung arrives Tehran	
October 14, 1971	Iran chargé d'affaires ad interim A. Nayernouri arrives Beijing	
October 16?, 1971	Special envoy Chang Tung joins celebration 2,500th anniversary of Iran empire	Conveys letter from Zhou Enlai. Kuo Mojou initially appointed
October 31, 1971	Iran government authorizes trade with China	
April 4, 1972	1st PRC ambassador presents credentials	Chen Hsin-jen; holds post til Oct. 1974
April 17, 1972	civil aviation agreement	Tehran-Beijing flights established
November 18, 1972	civil aviation treaty signed	
April 8, 1973	Eco M Hushang Ansari to PRC	1st trade agreement; 5 yrs; rials accepted
June 6, 1973	FM Ji Pengfei makes brief stopover in Tehran on way to London	Received at airport by Chief of Protocol
June 14–17, 1973	FM Ji Pengfei visits Iran	Shah receives PRC FM for 1st time; Ji endorses Iranian primacy in Gulf

June 30–July 10, 1973	Senate president Jaafar Sharif-Emam leads parliamentary delegation to PRC	
December 5–13?, 1973	Prince Gholam Reza Pahlavi and wife to PRC	Same plane carries 1st Iran ambassador Abbas Aram
December 1973	Iran ambassador Abbas Aram presents credentials	
November 29–December 6, 1974	TM Li Qiang to Iran	
April 3–?, 1975	VPM Li Xiannian to Iran	Talks w/ PM Hoveyda; received by Shah
May 1975	Princess Ashraf makes courtesy call on ailing Zhou Enlai	
December 15, 1975	PRC MFA & Iran embassy China sign reciprocal trademark agreement	
July 24–August 1, 1976	Princess Ashraf Pahlavi to PRC	
November 15–22, 1976	NPC chair Ulanfu and Ji Pengfei visit Iran	Stress continuity of PRC foreign policy; 25th anniversary of Pahlavi dynasty
September 16?, 1977	President of Chinese foreign affairs association Wang Bingnan to Tehran	
November 26–December 3, 1977	NPC vice chair Deng Yichao, VFM He Ying to Tehran	Surrogate for recently deceased Zhou Enlai
June 16–19, 1978	FM Huang Hua visits Iran	
August 29–31, 1978	Paramount leader Hua Guofeng to Iran, marks 8th anniversary diplomatic rel.	3 day official visit; first-ever visit by PRC paramount leader to non-Communist country

1979–2004

February 14, 1979	PRC officially recognizes revolutionary gov. of Iran	IRI proclaimed February 11; shah leaves Iran January 16

April 21, 1979	Amb. Jiao Ruoyu meets PM Medhi Barzargan	
"early 1979"?	Seyed Jaafar Khatami to PRC to investigate situation of Muslims there	
January 3–February 13, 1980	PRC Muslim Association visits Iran, Zhang Jie heads delegation to IRI	
April 8, 1980	Amb. Extraordinary & Plenipotentiary Zhuang Yan to Iran	
May 9, 1980	Hua Guofeng & FM Qotbzadeh meet Belgrade	Tito's funeral
September 22, 1980	Iraq attacks Iran, start of 8 year war	
February 9–15, 1981	Ayatollah Mohammad Khamenei to PRC	1st high-level IRI envoy to PRC; "clarify stance" re Gulf war; talks w/ Gong Dafei
May 1982	1st full IRI amb. to PRC Ali Khorram assumes post	MFA advisor He Ying briefs shortly afterward
July 16, 1982	Iran economic delegation to China, led by acting agriculture M	Sign technical and cultural agreements
December 30, 1982– Jan. 5, 1983	VM foreign economic relations and trade Jia Shi leads economic delegation to Iran	
January 27–29, 1983	MFA advisor He Ying to Iran	Exchange views; also visits Yemen, Yugoslavia
February 1983	PRC Muslim Assoc. delegation to Iran, Ma Jin heads	
April 1983	High-level Iranian military delegation secretly visits Beijing	Talks re arms purchases

September 12–13, 1983	FM Ali Akbar Velayati to Beijing	Talks with Wu Xueqian
September 14, 1983	Cultural, scientific & technology cooperation agreement signed in Beijing	
February 27–March? 1984	IRI mines & metals delegation to PRC	
October 15?, 1984	Agri. M He Kang to IRI	1st PRC minister visit since revolution
November 23–26, 1984	FM Wu Xueqian to Iran	"New start" in relations
February 26–March 5, 1985	Zhang Jingfu, state councillor, to Iran	Joint Economic, Trade, S&T Committee established
March 20, 1985	IRI special envoy Mojtaba Mir Medhi to China	Talks with Zhao Ziyang on Iran-Iraq war
June 27–July 1, 1985	Majlis speaker Hashemi Rafsanjani to China	MOU re eco. & nuclear cooperation signed; meets Deng Xiaoping
September 12–?, 1985	VM of industry A.Q. Jamshidi leads economic delegation to China	
February 18–22, 1986	FM advisor Gong Dafei to Tehran	Talks with DFM Sheikholeslam
March–April 1986	State councillor Zhang Jingfu to Iraq	Discuss, mediate Iran-Iraq war
April 1986	IRI MFA research director to PRC	
June 1986	IRI MFA Asian Dept. director to PRC	Talks re Afghan situation
July 1986	IRI VPM leads economic delegation to PRC	2nd meeting Joint Committee
July 1986	Assistant premier & chair sports organization Darghahi to China	
August 1986	IRI oil minister to PRC	Asks PRC to coop. with OPEC by reducing production

October 1986	Director general Xinhua news agency Mu Qing to Iran	
November 1986	Dep. Director National Education Committee Liu Zhongde to Iran	
November 1986	VM radio and television Xu Chonghua to Iran	
December 1986	Geng Biao leads NPC delegation to IRI	
February 7, 1987	DFM Javad Larijani to Beijing	Talks w/ Qi Huaiyuan, conveys letter to PM Zhao Ziyang
February 1987	DPM Taha Yasin Ramadan to PRC	
May 24, 1987	DFM for political affairs Hussein Sheikholeslam to PRC	Talks re Iran-Iraq war and situation in Gulf
June 1987	VM education Abuthi to PRC	
June 1987	Dir. National Sports Committee Liu Menghua to Iran	
June 14, 1987	FM Ali Akbar Velayati to Beijing	One-day visit; talks re reflagging Kuwait ships in Gulf
July–August, 1987	DFM Qi Huaiyuan to Tehran and Kuwait	Talks re UN mediation Iran-Iraq war
July 31, 1987	Commerce M Liu Yi to Iran	3rd Joint Committee meeting; 1 million tons crude sold
August 15–27, 1987	DFM Qi Huaiyuan to IRI	Talks re Persian Gulf situation
September 1987	Special envoy "Bei Sha La" (transliteration) to PRC	Convey's Rafsanjani's "oral letter" to Zhao Ziyang, talks w/ Zhao & Qi Huaiyuan
October 21–28, 1987	Superintendent Holy Shrine Eslam Va'ez Tabesi to PRC	Offers facilities in Iran for Chinese Muslim youth

December 6–12, 1987	M construction Bijan Namdan-Zanganeh to PRC	
February 4–11, 1988	Majlis vice speaker Mohammad Yazdi leads delegation to PRC	Working meeting w/ Geng Biao, conveys Rafsanjani's letter to Peng Zhen
April 1988	OPEC and non-OPEC producers meeting	
August 16–19, 1988	DFM Qi Huaiyuan to Tehran	Talks re Iran-Iraq war, Gulf situation, bilateral relations
September 19–26, 1988	DPM Hamid Mirzadeh to Beijing	Talks re aid, 4th meeting Joint Committee. Meets with Tian Jiyun
September 1988 ?	FM Velayati to Beijing	
October 16–23, 1988	M light industry Zheng Xianlin to Iran	Talks re post-war reconstruction; 8-person delegation
October 23–25, 1988	DFM Mohammad Hoseyn Lavasani to Beijing	Talks w/ Qian Qichen re Geneva talks re Iran-Iraq war
October 25– November 2, 1988	Head of China Oil Co. Wang Tao to Iran	Talks re increasing petroleum cooperation
October 31– November 8, 1988	M electrical equipment Zhao Mingsheng to IRI	Talks re increasing economic cooperation
December 2, 1988	VM foreign trade Wu Lanmulon to IRI for discussion of barter trade	6-person delegation
December 15– 17, 1988	FM Ali Akbar Velayati to Beijing	Talks w/ Zhao Ziyang, Qian Qichen. Conveys letter for Zhao
December 21, 1988	Geng Biao to Iran	5-day official visit; during Rajiv Gandhi visit to China
December 1988	IRI VM communications to PRC	Agreement re sale of satellite communications technology

January 8, 1989	FM Qian Qichen and FM Velayati meet fringe CWC meeting in Paris	
March 30–April 6, 1989	Iran M housing & urban development to China	Meets Yao Yilin & construction minister
March 3–8, 1989	VPM Tian Jiyun makes 5 day visit to Iran	Terms relations with Iran "strategic"; discusses China's role in IRI postwar construction
March 1989	Secretary PRC labor union to IRI	
March 1989	PRC Youth League delegation to IRI	
April 11, 1989	IRI M of Housing Serajeddin Kazeruni to Beijing	Sign draft agreement urban developing & housing construction
April 1989	IRI women's association delegation to PRC	
April 1989	DFM Javad Mansuri to PRC	
May 1989	DPM Hamid Mirzadeh to PRC	
May 26–31, 1989	VM culture Liu Deyou to IRI	
May 9–14, 1989	President S.A. Khamenei to China, FM Velayati accompanies	First-ever visit of Iran president to China. China agrees double oil purchases
July 10–16, 1989	PRC Religious Aff. Bureau & Muslim Assoc. official to IRI	Attend ceremony mourning Khomeini's passing
July 1989	PRC broadcasting and journalist delegation to IRI	
July 13–17, 1989	IRI industry & commerce association head to PRC	Rong Yiren meets with
July 28–31, 1989	Iran DM heavy industry, M. M. Alizadeh, to China	MOU re long-term industrial cooperation
July 27–August 7, 1989	Political advisor IRI government to PRC	Talks with head PRC gov. personnel office; convey Yang Shangkun letter

August 1989	Iran energy ministry delegation to China, acting M heads delegation	
August 14–28, 1989	IRI VM culture & higher education to PRC	
Septembert 11–21, 1989	Islamic Propagation Organ head visits China	Wang Zhen meets with and instructs re non-interference; Li Xiannian meets with
September 1989	PRC Persian studies delegation to IRI	
September 13–27, 1989	PRC VM of geology and mineral resourcs to Iran	2 week visit, MOU coop mining and geology signed
October 2–5, 1989	IRI M petroleum to PRC	
October 6–8, 1989	FM Qian Qichen to Tehran	Talks w/ Velayati re Iraq. Also visits Jordan, Egypt, Syria, Tunesia
November 1989	PRC banking and insurance association vice director to IRI	
November 26–29, 1989	M trade Zeng Tuobin to IRI	5th meeting Joint Committee; change from barter to cash basis
January 1990	Dep. director state science and technology commission Gen Jiang Hua to Tehran	Signs 10-year agree re nuclear and military cooperation with Defense Minister Torkan
April 1990	M agriculture Kalantari to PRC	Attends UN food organization conference
April 1990	Majlis forms PRC friendship group	
May 1–4, 1990	M public health Chen Minzhang to Iran	Promote cooperation between health ministries
May 6–9, 1990	NPC SC chair Wan Li leads parliamentary delegation to Tehran	Most senior PRC leader visit since 1979 revol.

August 16–19, 1990	Iran M of ports, telegraph, telephones to China	Talks re satellite communication cooperation
September 20–27, 1990	V. president Qafuri-Fard to China	W/ athletic group for Asian Games; endorses Beijing for 2000 Olympics
October 8–18, 1990	DM Ali Akbar Torkan to China with "senior military delegation"	1st visit by defense minister since 1971 relations established; letter for Yang Shangkun
October 15–24, 1990	Political advisor president, Hoseyn Musavi, to China	
December 10–20, 1990	Delegation from IRI strategic studies center visits PRC	Talks with Wu Xueqian
December 13–20, 1990	Majlis delegation visits China	
February 21, 1991	DFM and special presidential envoy Yang Fuchang to IRI	
February 1991	Sports M and Olympics committee head He Zhenliang to Iran	
March 1991	COSTIND head Ding Henggao to Iran	
June 1991 ?	FM Velayati to Beijing	
July 7–9, 1991	PM Li Peng to Iran. FM Qian Qichen talks w/ Velayati	Part of 6 Middle East country tour
July 7–11, 1991	NPC friendship deleg to Iran, He Ying, NPC SC member heads	
August 15–19?, 1991	M economics and financial affairs Mohsen Nurbakhsk to PRC	6th meeting of joint committee
Aug. 1991	PRC VM civil affairs to IRI	
August 30–September 4, 1991	PRC TV & broadcasting delegation to IRI	

September 1991	PRC MFA research center delegation to IRI	
October 1991	PLA general logistics department delegation to IRI	
October 30–November 2, 1991	President Yang Shangkun to Iran, VPM Wu Xueqian accompanies	Part of multination tour; 1st stop = Pakistan; reciprocates '89 Khamenei visit
November 10, 1991	Agriculture ministers meet at UN FAO conference in Rome	
November 12–22?, 1991?	M of construction Hou Jie to Iran	4 day visit
November 14, 1991	M of mines and metals Mohammad Hoseyn Mahlujehid to China	
November 1991	PRC MFA research center delegation to IRI	
November 17, 1991	VM foreign economic relations and trade Wang Wendong to IRI	7th joint committee meeting; group of 77 meeting
December 16–21, 1991	Majilis speaker Mehdi Karrubi to PRC	Talks w/ Qian Qichen, Wan Li
December 14, 1991	M electric equipment He Guangyuan to IRI	
1991	IRNA chief Mahlouji to PRC	Inaugurates IRNA office in China
February 1992	Secretary Xian party committee to IRI	
February 1992	IRI VM of commerce to PRC	
March 1992	IRI M of industry and mining visits PRC	
April 13–14, 1992	FM Velayati to Beijing	Talks w/ Qian Qichen re Central Asia, Afghanistan, and Bush's "new world order"
April 1992	IRI VM oil to PRC	

April 1992	IRI vice chair planning and budget organization to PRC	
May 1992	Head China women's association to IRI	
May 1992	IRI VM mining to PRC	
May 25–June 1, 1992	IRI VFM to PRC	Talks w/ Qian Qichen
May 1992	IRI VM transportation to PRC	
June 1992	IRI VM civil affairs to PRC	
July 4–6, 1992	IRI VFM "Bu Lu Jie Ni" (transliteration) to PRC	Talks w/ Yang Fuchang & Qian Qichen
September 7, 1992?	IRI army logistic chief General Alastu Tuhidi to PRC	Talks w/PLA logistics department vice chief Li Lun
September 9–12, 1992	Pres. Rafsanjani to China	Accompanied by Defense Minister Torkan, chief of general staff, & IAEO head R. Amrollahi
September 17–19, 1992	VFM Yang Fuchang to IRI	Talks with DFM Broujerdi
September 1992	Chairman joint chief of staff Iran military, major general Ali Shahbazi to PRC	
September 1992	Mayor of Esfahan city to PRC	
September 10, 1992	State councilor Song Jian and IAEO head Amrollahi sign agreement	Re peaceful uses of nuclear energy
October 26–27, 1992	IRI VFM "Bu Lu Jie Ni" (transliteration) to PRC	Talks w/ Yang Fuchang
October 27–30, 1992	PRC minister of defense Qin Jiwei to Iran	Talks w/ IRI chief of staff major general Ali Shahbazi
November 21, 1992	PRC VM public security Jiang Xianjin to IRI	Talks re combating narcotics
November 17–25, 1992	President China National Nuclear Corp Jiang Xinxiong to Tehran	Talks re sale 300 MW reactor power plant
December 1992	PRC VM railways to IRI	

January 4–11, 1993	Revolutionary Guards commander Mohsen Reza'i to China	Talks with military officials: Zhang Wannian, Qin Jiwei
February 17–19, 1993	VFM Yang Fuchang to IRI	Talks with DFM Broujerdi
February 12–21, 1993	Pres. China Nat. Nuc. Corp Jiang Xinxiong to Tehran	Talks re sale 300 MW reactor
June ? 1993	M of culture and Islamic guidance Ali Larijani to PRC	Signs cultural agreement
July 30, 1993	DFM Mohammad Javad Zarif to PRC	Talks with DFM Liu Huaqiu, VFM Yang Fuchang, & Qian Qichen
July 3–6, 1993	VPM Li Lianqing to IRI	Agreements re trade and industry cooperation, including 300 mw nuc power plants
July 1993	IRI VM of defense to PRC	
August 1993	IRI "strategic representatives group" to PRC	
August 1993	IRI naval staff college group to PRC	
August 9–12, 1993	VFM Iran to China for seminar on "Central Asia"	
September 3–8, 1993	PLA meteorological group to IRI	
October 2, 1993	FM Velayati and Qian Qichen meet sidelines of UN General Assembly meeting	
November 1993	VM agriculture Zhang Yanxi to IRI	
1993?	FM Qian Qichen to IRI	
January 1994	Commander Islamic Revol. Guards, Mohsan Reza'i, to China	Talks w/ DM Qian Jiwei & General Staff chief Zhang Wannian
March 4–6, 1994	FM Qian Qichen to IRI	Talks w/ FM Velayati

April 11–18, 1994	IRI Majilis delegation to PRC	Talks w/ NPC delegation led by Meng Liankun
June 30–July 6, 1994	IRI Islamic foundation delegation to PRC	Talks w/ foreign trade & transportation ministries
August 29–31, 1994	1st vice president Hasan Habibi to China	
October 1–10, 1994	PRC foreign trade promotion delegation to IRI	Participate in Tehran trade expo
January 23–26, 1995	Chief Justice Esmail Shushtari to China	Discuss coop in legal and justice fields
March 27–29, 1995	FM Velayati to PRC	1st stop on 4 nation tour; "important talks" w/ Li Peng
May 1–8, 1995	Vice head China People's Insurance Company to Iran	Talks re Tehran metro project
May 18, 1995	VFM "Bu Lu Jie Ni" to PRC	Talks w/ VFM Tian Zengpei
May 25–29, 1995	Vice president Hamid Mirzadeh to China	8th session joint committee
May 7, 1995	CNPC head Wang Tao to Iran	5-day oil conference
August 30–September 17, 1995	IRI vice presidential advisor on women's affairs to PRC	Participate in 4th international women's conference
October 2–9, 1995	PRC trade promotion delegation to Iran	
October 1995	Deputy minister of interior Cholam Hoseyn Bolandian to PRC	
November 6–14, 1995	PRC VM of inspection to IRI	
January 8–10, 1996	DFM Tian Zengpei to IRI	
May 6, 1996	DFM Alaeddin Broujerdi to PRC	Conference on trans-Asia r.r., talks w/ PRC vice MFA

May 1996	PRC labor union vice head to IRI	
May 19–27, 1996	Iranian womens delegation to China	
May 10–15, 1996	M railway Han Shubin to Iran	Opening of Mashhad-Tedzhen railway; MOU signed re increased railway cooperation
June 1996	PRC VM public health to IRI	
June 17–24, 1996	M energy Bijian Namdar Zanganeh to China	Discuss coop in energy and machine building
July 25–30, 1996	NPC delegation to Iran, foreign affairs committee vice head Zhu Qizhen heads	2-week goodwill visit, also to Tunesia and Libya
August 26–September 2, 1996	IRI MD Mohammad Firouzandeh to Beijing	Talks w/ PRC defense minister Chi Haotian re increasing military ties
August 29–September 5, 1996	Head IRI inspection organization to PRC	
September 13–22, 1996	M railway Han Shubin to Iran	Exchange views w/ VFM Tian Zengpei
September 16, 1996	State Council secretariat head Lo Gan meets IRI delegation	Third-country conference on solar energy
September 27, 1996	FM Qian Qichen meets w/ FM Velayati at UN in New York	
November 16, 1996	PM Li Peng talks w/ vice president Hasan Habbibi in Rome	Talks re nuclear cooperation?
November 10–20, 1996	PRC forestry delegation to IRI	
November 12–15, 1996	NPC SC chair Qiao Shi to Iran	Also visits Turkey, Jordan, Vietnam, and Laos
November 18, 1996	IRI mining delegation to PRC	
December 16–25, 1996	PRC M machine building Sun Changji to IRI	

January 3–9, 1997	PRC association for international exchange vice head to IRI	
February 17–24, 1997	VPM Li Lanqing to Iran	After visit to Israel
April 14–17, 1997	VFM Alaeddin Broujerdi to PRC	Talks w/ FM Tang Jiaxuan, Qian Qichen
April 18–25, 1997	PRC M hydrolic Zhang Chunyuan to IRI	
April 22–27, 1997	PRC M forestry to IRI	
May 3–4, 1997	VPM Li Lanqing to Iran	9th session Joint Committee, visits 5 Latin American nations
May 97	IRI afforestation chief attends conference in PRC	Talks re afforestation
May 18–26, 1997	Petroleum M Gho-lamreza Aqazadeh to China	Agreement w/CNPC re prospecting & development
June 24, 1997	PRC science and technology head Song Jian talks w/ FM Velayati at United Nations	
June 26–29, 1997	PRC VFM Ji Pengding to IRI	Talks w/ IRI VFM
August–September 1997	DM Mohammad Firouzandeh to PRC	Large arms purchase contracts
November 14, 1997	President of Iran Broadcasting to China	
December 23–29, 1997	NPC delegation to IRI, led by SC member Meng Liankun	
February 26–March 1, 1998	FM Mohsen Aminzadeh to China	Talks w/ FM Qian Qichen, VFM Tian Zengpei, and Li Lanqing
April 2–9, 1998	IRI VM energy to PRC	
May 14–17, 1998	PRC trade promotion delegation to IRI	
March 5–8, 1999	PRC trade VM Chen Xinhua leads delegation to IRI	

May 9–16, 1999	PRC VM inspection Gan Yisheng leads delegation IRI	
August 9–11, 1999	VFM Ji Pengding to IRI	
August 1999	IRI VM petroleum to PRC	Signs contract re purchase 5 VLCC
September 21, 1999	FM Tang Jiaxuan talks w/ FM Velayati at UN in New York	Agree re establishment diplomatic consultation mechanism
September 1999	Prosecutor General Morteza Moghtadai to China	Talks re judicial cooperation
November 29– December 2, 1999	Vice president Moham- mad Hashemi to China	10th session Joint Committee
January 27–29, 2000	National Iranian Oil Cor- poration head to PRC	
February 20–23, 2000	FM Tang Jiaxuan to Tehran	Agree regular pol consul- tations. 1st FM visit since 1994
February 24– March 2, 2000	IRI VM petroleum to PRC	
May 29–June 1, 2000	IRI VFM Mohsen Amin- zadeh to PRC	"political talks" w/ VFM Ji Pengding
June 22–26, 2000	Pres. Mohammad Khatami to China w/ 170 person delegation	2 MD talk, 2 FM hold talks; joint communiqué signed
July 13–16, 2000	Head IRI "inspection" organization to PRC	Memo in increased coop- eration on "inspection" signed
July 21–26, 2000	PRC vice director posts to IRI	
November 10– 16, 2000	PRC meteorological bureau deleg to IRI	Sign minutes of meeting
December 5, 2000– January 9, 2001	M Science, Technology, & Industry for National Defense Liu Jibin to IRI	

January 5–10, 2001	Vice Pres. Hu Jintao visits Tehran	5-nation tour, also Syria, Jordan, Cyprus, Uganda
February 2001	Majlis delegation led by Mohsen Mirdamadi, head foreign policy and national security committee	Week-long goodwill tour, meets Li Peng
March 1–9, 2001	IRI energy ministry delegation to PRC	Sign minutes
September 8, 2001	VFM Yang Wenchang to Iran	2nd session of "diplomatic consultation mechanism," talks re Middle East & Afghanistan
March 16–20, 2002	State Councilor Wu Yi to Iran	11th Joint Committee meeting; sign minutes
April 17–22, 2002	Pres. Jiang Zemin to Iran	1st visit by paramount leader since 1978; also visits Germany, Libya, Nigeria & Tunisia
April 2002	Framework Agreement on conducting Cooperation in the Field of Petroleum signed	
September 8, 2002	VFM Yang Wenchang to IRI	
November 3, 2002	"Special envoy" Sha Lin delivers Jiang Zemin letter to President Khatami	
December 10–14, 2002	Majlis speaker Mehdi Karrubi leads Majlis delegation to PRC	Meets with Jiang Zemin
July 18–21?, 2002	Head CCP international liaison department Dai Bingguo to IRI	At invitation of Pres. Khatami's Islamic Participation Front
2002	Head PRC Supreme People's Court to IRI	
2002	1st secretary China trade union association to IRI	

2002	Head IRI Majlis foreign policy & national security committee to PRC	
February 23, 2003	Majlis delegation led by foreign affairs committee head, Mohsen Mirdamadi to China	
April 10?, 2003	Majlis deleg led by chair economic committee Mohammad Shadi Arablu, to China	
July 8?, 2003	Sinopec head Mou Shuling to Iran	Talks re long term energy cooperation
August 2003	China National Petroleum Corporation head Ma Fucai to Iran	Talks re increased energy cooperation
August 27?, 2003	NIOC dep. Head Mehdi Husseini to PRC, talks with CNPC head Ma Fucai	Part of Kharrazi delegation; also visits Japan & India
August 24–27?, 2003	FM Kamal Kharrazi to PRC	Talks w/ Hu Jintao, Li Zhaoxing, Wu Yi re Afghan, Iraq, nuclear issue & trade
September 15?, 2003	Head Iranian news agency to China	Agree w/ Xinhua re cooperation
October 22, 2003	DFM Gholam Ali Khoshrou to China	Talks re regional & international issues
October 9?, 2003	Revolutionary Guards commander Mohammed Hejazi to China	Talks w/ PLA leaders re exchange of experience and knowledge on security issues
November 13, 2003	FM Kamal Kharrazi to PRC	Talks re nuclear issue; visits Japan too
November 27–30, 2003	M culture & islamic guidance Ahmad Masjed Jamei to China	Participate in Iran culture week in Beijing
December 4–11, 2003	Police force commander Mohammad Baqer Qalibaftoc to China	Talks w/ Ministry of Public Security officials; MOU re increased police cooperation

December 2–7, 2003	Han Qide vice chair NPC SC goodwill visit to Iran	Participate in Iran Culture Week
December 8–12, 2003	IRI M road & transport Ahmad Khorram to PRC	Solicit assistance re roads, harbors, and RR construction; inspects Shanghai infrastructure
January 8, 2004	Head Asia section PRC ministry commerce to IRI	Talks re increasing role small & medium enterprises in bilateral cooperation
February 27–March 8, 2004	VM petroleum Mohammad Hosseinian leads oil delegation to PRC	Talks re long-term energy cooperation
March 20?, 2004	Director general petrochemical development corp. Golamhossein Nejabat to PRC	Explore increased PRC investment in IRI petrochemicals; meets with Hu Jintao
April 8–11, 2004	IRI vice president Mohammad Sattaritar to PRC	12th Joint Committee meeting; head of IRI management and planning organization
May 17–18?, 2004	DFM Mohsen Aminzadeh to PRC	3rd round of political consultations
June 18?, 2004	IRI House of Parties head Hassan Ghafouri-Fard to PRC	Talks re legislative cooperation
July 2?, 2004	IRI environment head Masonmeh Ebtekar to PRC	MOU signed re environmental cooperation
July 2?, 2004	IRI DFM Gholam-Reza Ansari to PRC	Talks re Iraq and Afghanistan reconstruction
September 2–4, 2004	IRI DFM for education & research Aliereze Moayeri to Beijing	Official visit, talks re IAEA & nuclear issue
September 11?, 2004	Deputy Interior M for social & council affairs Ashraf Boroujerdi to PRC	International conference on population and development
September 11–14?, 2004	IRI M welfare & social security Mohammad Hossein Sharifzadegan to PRC	Talks re social security systems, MOU signed

September 21?, 2004	Chair IRI-PRC economic commission Asadollah Asgarowladi to PRC	Attend world industrial & commerical organization summit
September 27–28, 2004	IRI M petroleum Bijan Namdar Zanganeh to PRC	MOU re Yadavaran oil field cooperation
October 13, 2004	PRC deputy minister of agriculture Qi Jingfa to IRI	MOU re fishery and rural development; 2nd working committee meeting on agricultural coop.
October 18, 2004	IRI M culture & islamic guidance Ahmad Jamei to PRC	Annual ministerial conference of international network on cultural policy
October 22, 2004	FM Li Zhaoxing & DFM Gholam Khoshru meet on sidelines Almaty conference	Discuss IAEA/ nuclear issue; Li stresses IRI right to peaceful use nuclear energy
October 26–29, 2004	IRI M petroleum Bijan Namdar Zanganeh to PRC	MOU re Yadavaran field signed; 150 personnel for conference on energy cooperation
November 21?, 2004	Tehran province governor to PRC	Talks re Tehran-Karaj rail project
November 6–7, 2004	FM Li Zhaoxing to IRI	Supports on nuclear issue before IAEA; meets with President Khatami
November 27, 2004	PRC social science academy deputy director Wang Luolin to IRI	Signs agreement re teaching and research cooperation
November 30, 2004	DFM Gholam Ali Khoshru to PRC	Talks re IAEA & nuclear issues
December 1–4?, 2004	Head IRI space agency Hassan Shafti to PRC	Signs agreement re cooperation in satellite communications

Notes

1 / THE SPIRIT OF SINO-IRANIAN RELATIONS: CIVILIZATION AND POWER

1. Iran, "land of the Aryans," has always been known as "Iran" by its own inhabitants. The Iranians were part of the great Indo-European migration and began moving into Iran circa the second millennium BCE. Westerners came to know the land as "Pars" from Greek historians. Pars is a region of southern Iran. But Iranians also came to call themselves "Persians"—a word derived from Pars. *Iran* became the favored term in the 1920s, perhaps under the influence of the racialist philosophies popular in that era. In 1935 the government specified that *Iran* should be used as the formal name of the country, but use of *Persia* was allowed until 1949. Thus, *Iran* is the formally correct name. Since the country includes many non–Persian-speaking people (Kurds, Azeris, Arabs, and Turkomans), *Iran* offers a more inclusive appellation. Of course, by the same logic, one could not use the name *China* since many people living in China do not speak Chinese (Tibetans, Uighurs). Nor are Iran's Semitic Arabs "Aryans." This study uses Iran and Persia interchangeably as a matter of style.

2. Ann-Marie Brady, *Making the Foreign Serve China: Managing Foreigners in the People's Republic of China* (Boulder, CO: Rowman and Littlefield, 2003).

3. Jose Manuel Garcia, *The Persian Gulf: In the 16th and 17th Centuries* (Tehran: Center of Documents and Diplomatic History, Publishing House of the Foreign Ministry, 2002). Percy Sykes, *A History of Persia*, 3 vols. (London: Routledge and Kegan Paul, 1969).

4. "Premier Chou En-lai Gives Banquet in Honor of Her Royal Highness Princess Ashraf Pahlavi," Xinhua, April 14, 1971, China Mainland Press—Survey of China Mainland Press (hereafter CMP-SCMP), no. 71–17, April 26–30, 1971, 32–34.

5. "*Jen-min Jih-pao* Editorial: Greeting Establishment of Diplomatic Relations

between China and Iran," Xinhua, August 19, 1971, CMP-SCMP-71–35, August 31–September 3, 1971, 60–61.

6. "Speech by Premier Chou En-lai at Banquet in Honor of Shahbanou of Iran Farah Pahlavi," CMP-SCMP-72–39, September 25–29, 1972, 209.

7. "Chairman Hua Kuo-feng's Speech, (Excerpts)," *Peking Review* (hereafter PR), September 8, 1978, 8–9.

8. "Iran's Rafsanjani Meets PRC Leaders, Ends Tour," Xinhua, June 28, 1985, Foreign Broadcast Information Service—China (hereafter FBIS-CHI), July 1, 1985, I-1. Rafsanjani was then speaker of the Majlis, the Islamic Consultative Assembly, the IRI's parliament.

9. "Iran's Rafsanjani, Delegation Continue PRC Tour," Xinhua, June 27, 1985, FBIS-CHI, June 28, 1985, I-1.

10. "President Khamenei Accorded Warm Welcome in China," *Tehran Times* (hereafter TT), May 10, 1989.

11. "Chinese President Hails Iran's Important Role in Mid-East Peace," TT, October 28, 1991.

12. "Iran: President Khatami Stresses Implementing Agreement with China," Tehran Islamic Republic News Agency (hereafter IRNA), June 23, 2000, via Dialog, at http://wnc.dialog.com/.

13. "Xinhua Carries 'Full Text' of PRC, Iran Joint Communiqué," June 22, 2000, Dialog.

14. "Wu Yi Says Iran, PRC to Further Develop Friendship, Cooperation Ties," Xinhua, March 17, 2002, Dialog.

15. Rouhollah K. Ramazani, *Iran's Foreign Policy, 1941–1973: A Study of Foreign Policy in Modernizing Nations* (Charlottesville: University of Virginia Press, 1975), 439.

16. Rouhollah K. Ramazani, "Iran's Foreign Policy: Both North and South," *Middle East Journal* 46, no. 3 (Summer 1993): 393–412; emphasis added.

17. "Address by Ali Akbar Hashemi-Rafsanjani, President of the Islamic Republic of Iran," November 20, 1988, at Conference of Center for Persian Gulf Studies, Institute for Political and International Studies, Tehran. Translation in *Middle East Journal* 44, no. 3 (Summer 1990): 463.

18. Ibid., 465.

19. Zhu Jiejin, *Zhongguo he yilang guanxi shigao* [Draft History of China-Iran Relations] (Urumqi: Xinjiang renmin chubanshe, 1988), 2.

20. The English word *magic* comes via Greek and Medieval French from the Old Persian word *magus* (plural *Magi*). *Magi* were Zoroastrian priests, among whose several skills was sorcery.

21. Edwin G. Pulleyblank, "Chinese-Iranian Relations: Pre-Islamic Times," in *Encyclopaedia Iranica*, http://www.iranica.com/articlenavigation/alphabetical/bodya.html.

22. Liu Yingsheng and Peter Jackson, "Chinese-Iranian Relations in the Mongol

Period," and J. M. Rogers, "Chinese-Iranian Relations in the Safavid Period," both in ibid.

23. Zhu, *Zhongguo he yilang guanxi shigao*, 1.

24. Ibid., 95.

25. Sen. Abbas Massoudi, *China: A Land of Marvels* (Tehran: Iran Chap Press, 1973).

26. Ibid., 7.

27. Ibid., 76.

28. Ibid., 12. In an Islamic cultural context in which dogs are considered unclean animals on a par with pigs, this linking of dogs to Chinese would be even more degrading than in its original Confucian, Chinese, cultural context. Regarding the inaccuracy of this "no dogs or Chinese sign" story, see Robert A. Bickers and Jeffrey N. Wasserstrom, "Shanghai's 'Dogs and Chinese Not Admitted' Sign: Legend, History, and Contemporary Symbol," *China Quarterly*, no. 142 (June 1995): 444–66.

29. Massoudi, *China: A Land of Marvels*, 13.

30. Ibid., 39, 43.

31. *Iran: Time for a New Approach*, report of an independent task force sponsored by the Council on Foreign Relations (New York: Council on Foreign Relations, 2004), 72–73.

32. "Meets Li Xiannian," Xinhua, September 14, 1983, FBIS-CHI, September 15, 1983, F1.

33. Xinhua, February 21, 1986, FBIS-CHI, February 21, 1986, F2.

34. "China Praises Iran's Policy of Self-Sufficiency and Independence," *TT*, June 29, 1985.

35. Xinhua, July 7, 1991, FBIS-CHI-91–132, July 10, 1991, 11.

36. "Pakistan, Iran Ties Reviewed," *Liaowang* (overseas edition, Hong Kong), October 28, 1991, FBIS-CHI-91–211, October 29, 1991, 21.

37. Li Guofu, "Jiang's Tour to Libya, Tunisia, and Iran: Friendly Visits to Promote Cooperation," *Beijing Review* (hereafter RR), May 16, 2002, 11–13.

38. "China's President Stresses Expansion of Ties with Iran," Tehran IRNA, April 9, 2004, Dialog.

39. "USSR Covets Iran's Geophysical Position, Oil," Beijing domestic service, April 22, 1979, FBIS-CHI, April 25, 1979, I8.

40. "China Has Important Position in Iranian Foreign Policy," *TT*, February 25, 2001.

41. Xinhua, February 21, 1986, FBIS-CHI, February 21, 1986, F2.

42. Zhu, *Zhongguo he yilang guanxi shigao*, 1.

43. Denis Twitchett and Howard Wechsler, "Kao-tsung (Reign 649–683) and the Empress Wu: The Inheritor and the Usurper," in *The Cambridge History of China; Volume 3, Sui and T'ang China, 589–906; Part 1*, ed. Denis Twitchett and John K. Fairbanks (Taipei: Caves Books, 1989), 280.

44. "PRC's Yang Grants 'Exclusive' Interview," Tehran IRNA, October 26, 1991, FBIS—Near East and South Asia (hereafter NES), no. 91–209, 55–56.

45. Twitchett and Wechsler, "Kao-tsung," 280.

46. Zoroastrianism was the state religion of both the Achaemenid and Sassanian empires—for a total of about a thousand years. After the Arab conquest, Zoroastrians found refuge in China and in India (where their origin in "Pars" gave them the name Parsi) and in a few remote mountainous regions of Iran.

47. *Di san shijie shiyou duozheng* [The Third World's Oil Struggle] (Beijing: San lian shudian, 1981).

48. Ibid., 3.

49. Ibid., 6.

2 / THE PRC–KINGDOM OF IRAN RELATIONSHIP, 1971–78

1. Amin Saikal, *The Rise and Fall of the Shah* (Princeton, NJ: Princeton University Press, 1980), 137–47.

2. Said Amir Arjomand, *The Turban and the Crown: The Islamic Revolution in Iran* (New York: Oxford University Press, 1988), 118–19.

3. A good synopsis of the shah's development effort is Malise Ruthven, *Islam in the World* (New York: Oxford University Press, 1984), 335–52.

4. Ramazani, *Iran's Foreign Policy*, 373–86.

5. SAVAK stood for, in Farsi, Sazeman-e Attela'at va Amniyat-e Keshuar (Organization for Information and Security of the Country).

6. Rouhollah K. Ramazani, "Emerging Patterns of Regional Relations in Iranian Foreign Policy," *Orbis* 18, no. 4 (Winter 1975): 1043–69.

7. Regarding the role of British primacy in this region and the implications of the decision to end it, see, Michael A. Palmer, *Guardians of the Gulf: A History of America's Expanding Role in the Persian Gulf, 1832–1992* (New York: Macmillan, 1992).

8. Ramazani, *Iran's Foreign Policy*, 348.

9. Maryam Daftari, "Sino-Iran Relations and 'Encounters': Past and Present," *Iranian Journal of International Affairs* 7, no. 4 (Winter 1996): 854–76.

10. Dilip Hiro, *The Longest War: The Iran-Iraq Military Conflict* (New York: Routledge, 1991), 7–15.

11. Asadollah Alam, *The Shah and I: The Confidential Diary of Iran's Royal Court, 1969–1977* (London and New York: I. B. Tauris, 1991), 146–49.

12. Ramazani, *Iran's Foreign Policy*.

13. Franz Borkenau, *World Communism: A History of the Communist International* (Ann Arbor: University of Michigan Press, 1962), 284–95.

14. All of the quotations from *Renmin ribao* in this paragraph along with the interpretation of the moderation of these words are from Rosemary Foot, "China's

New Relationship with Iran," *Contemporary Review* 226, no. 1 (February 1, 1975): 100–104.

15. Peter Van Ness, *Revolution and Chinese Foreign Policy: Peking's Support for Wars of National Liberation* (Berkeley: University of California Press, 1971), 92.

16. "Premier Chou En-lai Gives Banquet in Honor of Her Royal Highness Princess Ashraf Pahlavi," Xinhua, April 14, 1971, CMP-SCMP-71–17, April 26–30, 1971, 32–34.

17. "Jen-min Jih-pao Editorial," August 19, 1971, CMP-SCMP-71–35, August 31–September 3, 1971, 60–61.

18. "Iranian People's New Achievements in Safeguarding Their Oil Rights," PR, August 17, 1973, 17.

19. "Rise of Third World and Decline of Hegemony," Xinhua, December 28, 19740 CMP—Survey of People's Republic of China Press (hereafter SPRCP), U.S. Consulate, Hong Kong, no. 5776–5770, January 6–10, 1975, 206–10.

20. "Third World Oil-Producing Countries' Inalienable Rights," PR, April 4, 1975, 22–23.

21. "Iranian Prime Minister Fetes Chinese Vice Premier," Xinhua, April 5, 1975, CMP-SPRCP-75–16, 135–39.

22. "Oil Producing Countries, U.S. Threat of Force Opposed," PR, January 24, 1975, 30–31.

23. Mohammad Reza Pahlavi, *The Shah's Story* (London: Michael Joseph, 1980), 135.

24. Until about 1970, concern that heavy defense spending would slow down the pace of reform and economic development led Washington to oppose large military budgets proposed by the shah. This changed once Washington endorsed Iran as Britain's successor as guardian east of Suez.

25. Ramazani, "Emerging Patterns," 1060–61.

26. *Asian Recorder*, March 12–18, 1973, 11278.

27. Ramazani, *Iran's Foreign Policy*, 434.

28. MSN Encyclopedia, http://reference.allrefer.com/country-guide-study/iran/iran154.html.

29. Yang Gongsu, "Lunsang jiushi nian" [Tumultuous Ninety Years] (Haikou: Hainan chubanshe, 1999), 282–83. Yang Gongsu served in the Chinese foreign ministry and delivered the crucial ultimatum to India at the time of the 1965 India-Pakistan war. For further discussion of Mao's 1965 decision for war with India, including documentation from the Pakistani side, see John W. Garver, *Protracted Contest: Sino-Indian Rivalry in the Twentieth Century* (Seattle: University of Washington Press, 2001), 203–4, 411 n. 97.

30. A. H. H. Abidi, *China, Iran, and the Persian Gulf* (Atlantic Highlands, NJ: Humanities Press, 1982). Rather than reinvent the wheel, this chapter draws heavily on Abidi's excellent study.

31. "Chinese Foreign Minister Honored at Tehran Dinner," Xinhua, June 14, 1973, CMP-SCMP-73–26, June 25–29, 1973, 72–75.

32. The full text of the treaty is in *Asian Recorder*, May 27– June 2, 1972, 10795–96.

33. S. M. Burke, *Pakistan's Foreign Policy: An Historical Analysis* (London: Oxford University Press, 1973), 354. Also, Ramazani, *Iran's Foreign Policy*, 326.

34. Alam, *The Shah and I*, 399.

35. Ibid., 419.

36. Yun Shuizhu, *Guoji fengyun zhong de zhongguo waijiaoguan* [Chinese Diplomats in the Midst of International Storms] (Beijing: Shijie zhishi chubanshe, 1992), 130–39.

37. Daftari, "Sino-Iran Relations and 'Encounters,'" 854–76.

38. Wang Taiping, ed., *Xin zhongguo waijiao wushi nian* [Fifty Years of New China's Diplomacy] (Beijing: Beijing chubanshe, 1999), 603. Ex–foreign minister Qian Qichen was the "advisor" for this volume. According to the same source, Bhutto, then serving as Pakistan's foreign minister, had conveyed a similar Iranian solicitation in 1965. On that occasion Beijing "issued an invitation," but the visit failed to materialize.

39. "Premier Chou En-lai Gives Banquet in Honor of Her Royal Highness Princess Ashraf Pahlavi," CMP-SCMP-71–17, April 26–30, 1971, 32–34.

40. Abidi, *China, Iran, and the Persian Gulf*, 63–69. Ramazani, *Iran's Foreign Policy*, 431.

41. "Jen-min Jih-pao Editorial: Greeting Establishment of Diplomatic Relations between China and Iran," Xinhua, August 19, 1971, CMP-SCMP-71–35, August 31–September 3, 1971, 60–61.

42. Hashim S. H. Behbehani, *China's Foreign Policy in the Arab World, 1955–1975* (London and Boston: Kegan Paul International, 1981), 164–88.

43. *Facts on File, 1975* (New York: Facts on File Inc., February 8, 1975), 65.

44. Pahlavi, *The Shah's Story*, 135.

45. Abidi, *China, Iran, and the Persian Gulf*, 107.

46. Jamshid Nabavi, "A Commentary on Relations between Iran and the People's Republic of China," *Relations Internationales, International Relations* (Centres des hautes etudes internationales de university Tehran), 2 (Winter 1974–75): 127–38.

47. "Chinese Foreign Minister Honored at Tehran Dinner," Xinhua, June 14, 1973, CMP-SCMP-73–26, June 25–29, 1973, 72–75; emphasis added.

48. Ibid.

49. Ramazani, "Emerging Patterns," 1064.

50. Abidi, *China, Iran, and the Persian Gulf*, 114–15.

51. "Chinese Foreign Minister Honored at Tehran Dinner," Xinhua, June 14, 1973, CMP-SCMP-73–26, June 25–29, 1973, 72–75.

52. Alam, *The Shah and I*, 317.

53. "President of Iranian Senate Fetes Chinese NPC Delegation," Xinhua, November 16, 1976, CMP-SPRCP-76-47, November 1976, 240; emphasis added.

54. Ibid.

55. Arjomand, *The Turban and the Crown*, 118–19. Another move by the shah to placate Islamic militants was dissolution of the ministry of women's affairs, a key focus of militant criticism.

56. Hua visited Yugoslavia and Romania, both Communist countries, before Iran. Mao Zedong visited the Soviet Union in 1950 and again in 1957. Deng Xiaoping's visit to the United States in 1979 came after Hua's Iran visit.

57. Abidi, *China, Iran, and the Persian Gulf*, 166.

58. Ibid.

59. Interview with retired PRC ambassador to Iran, Beijing, September 2004.

60. Ibid.

61. Pahlavi, *The Shah's Story*, 147.

3 / REVOLUTIONARY IRAN
AND POSTREVOLUTIONARY CHINA, 1979–88

1. Arjomand, *The Turban and the Crown*.

2. Speech of October 26, 1978, in Ayatollah Ruhollah Khomeini, *Ayatollah Khomeini, on Issues Related to the Struggle of the Muslim People of Iran, Speeches of January 1978–January 1980* (San Francisco: Consulate General of the IRI, n.d.).

3. Interview with Greek paper *Touyuma*, November 6, 1978, in ibid., 4; emphasis added.

4. "*Tehran Times* Commentary, Chinese Tanks for Saddam Paid for by Saudis," TT, February 26, 1983, 1.

5. Interview with retired PRC ambassador to IRI, Beijing, September 2004.

6. Ibid.

7. I develop this theme in John W. Garver, "China's U.S. Policies," in *China Rising: Power and Motivation in Chinese Foreign Policy*, ed. Yong Deng and Fei-ling Wang, 201–43 (Lanham, MD: Rowman and Littlefield, 2005).

8. Rouhollah K. Ramazani, *Revolutionary Iran: Challenge and Response in the Middle East* (Baltimore and London: Johns Hopkins University Press, 1986).

9. Xinhua, February 14, 1979, FBIS-CHI, February 14, 1979, A23.

10. "Iranian Prime Minister Receives PRC Ambassador," Xinhua, April 21, 1979, FBIS-CHI, April 24, 1979, I4.

11. "Peking Leader Apologizes for Official Visit to Shah," *Arab News*, July 30, 1979.

12. Interview with retired PRC ambassador to IRI, Beijing, September 2004.

13. "Chinese Foreign Ministry Official Issues Statement on Recent Developments

in Iran-U.S. Relations," Press Release no. 79/011, November 28, 1979, Embassy of the People's Republic of China, Washington, DC.

14. *"Renmin ribao* Discusses Impact of U.S.-Iranian Crisis," *Renmin ribao* (hereafter *Rmrb*), January 12, 1980, FBIS-CHI, January 16, 1980, B1.

15. Bani-Sadr in his memoir recounts how "the mullahs" charged him with "being a supporter of Mao Zedong's theory of a European, Japanese, and Third World alliance against the two superpowers. Once again, I had to clarify my position, for there was a huge difference between my philosophy and that of Mao." Relevant for the purposes here was the utility of "Maoist" as a political invective in Iran circa 1980–81. Abol Hassan Bani-Sadr, *My Turn to Speak: Iran, the Revolution and Secret Deals with the U.S.* (Washington, DC: Brassey's, 1989), 119.

16. "China Hopes U.S., Iran Solve Differences through Peaceful Consultations," April 27, 1980, Press Release no. 80/018, April 30, 1980, Embassy of the People's Republic of China, Washington, DC.

17. "PRC Official Discusses Iran Sanctions with Italian Envoy," Agenzia Nazionale Stampa Associata (hereafter ANSA), Rome, April 29, 1980, FBIS-CHI, May 1, 1980, A2. ANSA is Italy's main press agency.

18. "Ye Jianying Congratulates Bani-Sadr on Election," Xinhua, January 30, 1980, FBIS-CHI, January 31, 1980, I1.

19. "PRC Islamic Leader, Party Leave for Iran," Xinhua, January 31, 1980, FBIS-CHI, February 1, 1980, I2. "Chinese Muslims Attend Iranian Ceremony; Leaders Speak," Xinhua, February 4, 1980, FBIS-CHI, February 6, 1980, I1. "Chinese Islamic Leader Leaves Iran for Home," Xinhua, February 13, 1980, FBIS-CHI, February 14, 1980, I1.

20. Information on Zhang's biography is found at http://info.datang.net/z/z0309.htm (accessed September 2004).

21. "Hua Guofeng En Route to Yugoslavia Cables Bani-Sadr," Tehran international service, May 7, 1980, FBIS–South Asia, May 7, 1980, I13.

22. "Report of Hua Guofeng Meeting," Tehran radio, May 10, 1980, FBIS—Daily Report, South Asia, May 12, 1980, I20.

23. Rouhollah K. Ramazani, "Iran's Foreign Policy: Contending Orientations," *Middle East Journal* 43, no. 2 (Spring 1989), 202–17.

24. Ahmed Hashim, *The Crisis of the Iranian State: Domestic, Foreign and Security Policies in Post-Khomeini Iran*, Aldelphi Paper no. 296 (London: International Institute of Strategic Studies, 1995), 4.

25. This is the estimate given in Michael Clodfelter, *Warfare and Armed Conflicts: A Statistical Reference to Casualty and Other Figures, 1500–2000* (Jefferson, NC: McFarland, 2002), 653. The official Iranian figure for killed in the war is 123,000. The population figure is from World Bank, World Development Indicators.

26. *Strategic Survey, 1982–83* (London: International Institute of Strategic Studies, 1983), 79–80.

27. "Premier Zhao on Iran-Iraq Disputes," *BR*, September 29, 1980, 4.

28. "Curbing Expansion of Iran-Iraq Conflict Is Top Priority," *RMRB*, September 25, 1980, FBIS-CHI, September 26, 1980, I2.

29. "Ji Pengfei Issues Statement prior to Leaving for Oman," Xinhua, October 3, 1980, FBIS-CHI, October 6, 1980, I-1.

30. "China Sympathetic to Iran but Neutral on War," *TT*, February 18, 1991.

31. "Khamenei-Ulanfu Meeting," Xinhua, February 14, 1981, FBIS-CHI, February 18, 1981, I1.

32. "Iran's Chinese Air Force," *Middle East Defense News* (hereafter *Mednews*) 2, no. 4 (November 21, 1988): 1–2.

33. *Facts on File, 1987,* 420.

34. "Agri-Delegation off to China," *TT*, July 18, 1982.

35. "PRC Economic, Trade Delegation Visits Iran," Xinhua, December 30, 1982, FBIS-CHI, January 7, 1983, F3.

36. China was trying to improve ties with both New Delhi and Tehran in the early 1980s, and both of those capitals were deeply suspicious of Beijing's close alignment with Washington.

37. Interview with retired IRI ambassador to PRC, Tehran, November 2004.

38. Palmer, *Guardians of the Gulf,* 20–111.

39. "People's Daily Critical of Soviet Position on Iran," Xinhua, January 5, 1979, FBIS-CHI, January 8, 1979, A3.

40. "USSR Covets Iran's Geographical Position, Oil," Beijing radio, April 22, 1979, FBIS-CHI, April 25, 1979, 18.

41. "*Rmrb* Commentary on Khomeini's Warning to Soviets," FBIS-CHI, June 19, 1979, I1.

42. Interview in Tehran, November 2004. In an interesting intersection of individual and civilizational factors, Dr. Khorram was offered three choices for his new, third posting: Germany, the USSR, or China. He discussed the choice with his wife, and they decided to select China because of their interest in Chinese culture and their awareness of Chinese-Persian cultural interactions throughout history.

43. "Iran China Vow to Fight Imperialism," *TT*, February 1, 1983.

44. Interview with retired PRC ambassador to IRI, Beijing, September 2004.

45. "Velayati Confers with PRC President," *TT*, September 15, 1983.

46. "Iranian Foreign Minister's PRC Visit Continues," Xinhua, September 14, 1983, FBIS-CHI, September 15, 1983, F1.

47. "Sino-Iran Accord for Cultural, Scientific Exchanges," *TT*, September 17, 1983.

48. "Iranian Foreign Minister Arrives for Visit," Xinhua, September 11, 1983, FBIS-CHI, September 13, 1983, F1.

49. "Wu Meets Iranian Leaders," Xinhua, November 25, 1984, FBIS-CHI, November 26, 1984, I2.

50. "Sign's Joint Communiqué," Xinhua, November 26, 1984, FBIS-CHI, November 27, 1984, I1.

51. "More on Foreign Minister Wu's Visit to Iran," Xinhua, November 26, 1984, FBIS-CHI, November 27, 1984, I1; emphasis added.

52. "Briefs," Joint Publications Research Service—China: Political, Sociological, and Military Affairs (hereafter JPRS-CPS), no. 84–075, China Report, November 1, 1984, 7.

53. Tehran IRNA, November 25, 1984, JPRS-CPS-84–089, China Report, December 19, 1984, 12.

54. "Talks with Velayati Begin," Tehran IRNA, November 24, 1984, in ibid.

55. "China Threatens to Call off $1 Billion Arms Deal with Iran," *International Defense DMS Intelligence* 6, no. 31 (July 30, 1984): 1.

56. "Iran, China Talks on Cooperation," *TT*, February 28, 1985. "Iran, China Talks," *TT*, March 4, 1985.

57. "Iran Seeks Ties with Genuine Friends," *TT*, March 4, 1985.

58. "Iranian President, Zhang Jingfu Hold Talks," Xinhua, March 3, 1985, I1. "Trade, Exchange Protocols Signed with Iran," Xinhua, March 5, 1985, FBIS-CHI, March 6, 1985, I1.

59. "Iran Seeks Ties with Genuine Friends," *TT*, March 4, 1985.

60. James Clad, "Iran Woos Peking," *Far Eastern Economic Review* (hereafter *FEER*), June 13, 1985, 44–45.

61. *Deng Xiaoping nianbu, 1975–1997* [Deng Xiaoping Chronicle, 1975–1997] (Beijing: Zhongyang wenxian chubanshe, 2004), 2:1055.

62. "Zhao Ziyang Hosts Banquet," Xinhua, June 27, 1985, FBIS-CHI, June 28, 1985, I1.

63. *Zhongguo waijiao gaijian, 1987* [Overview of China's Diplomacy, 1987] (Beijing: Shijie zhishi chubanshe, 1987), 104. This is the annual diplomatic almanac published by the PRC foreign ministry.

64. "China-Iran Should Join in Favor of Oppressed," *TT*, March 2, 1985, 1, 3.

65. "Rafsanjani: Third World Can Stand against Superpowers," *TT*, August 17, 1982.

66. "China Praises Iran's Policy of Self-Sufficiency and Independence," *TT*, June 29, 1985; emphasis added.

67. "Economic Delegation Departs for Beijing 18 Sep [*sic*]," Tehran IRNA, September 18, 1988, FBIS-NES-88–192, 49. "Good War Time Relations with PRC Noted," Tehran IRNA, August 18, 1988, FBIS-NES-88–160, August 18, 1988, 50.

68. "PRC's Qi Huaiyuan Continues Talks with Official," Tehran Domestic Service, August 18, 1988, FBIS-NES-88–161, August 19, 1988, 36.

69. Interview with retired IRI ambassador to PRC, Tehran, November 2004.

70. Michael Weisskopf, "China Sells Arms to Iran via North Korea," *Washington Post* (hereafter *WP*), April 3, 1984, A17.

71. "Peking Signs Lbs 1.3 Billion Deal to Give Khomeini New Arsenal," *Times*

(London), March 27, 1985, 10. As indicated by Chinese Customs data presented in chapter 9, China did not import oil from Iran until 1988. Nor were Chinese refineries equipped to handle sulfur-heavy Iranian crude in the early 1980s. Apparently China sold its Iranian crude in Singapore during the early and mid-1980s.

72. "Iran's Chinese Air Force," *Mednews* (see above).

73. Yitzhak Shichor, "Unfolded Arms: Beijing's Recent Military Sales Offensive," *Pacific Review* 1, no. 3 (1988): 320–30, 323. "Iran, China Set to Sign Arms Purchase Agreement," *Al-Sharq al-Awsat* (London), August 29, 1996.

74. James Dorsey, "China Pledges to Sell Iran Nearly $600 Million in Arms," *Washington Times* (hereafter *WT*), June 8, 1987, 1.

75. Dilip Hiro suggests that Saddam Hussein escalated the tanker war as a way of forcing Security Council intervention to compel Iran to end the war, thus concluding a war that Hussein now feared losing. Hiro, *The Longest War*.

76. House of Representatives, *Developments in the Middle East, May 1986: Hearings before the Subcommittee on Europe and the Middle East of the Committee on Foreign Affairs*, 96th Cong., 2nd sess., May 6, 1986, answers submitted by State Department in response to congressional questions, 55.

77. "Provisional Verbatim Record of the Two Thousand Five Hundred and Forty-Sixth Meeting," June 1, 1984, U.N. Security Council, S/PV.2546.

78. Palmer, *Guardians of the Gulf*, 121

79. Xinhua, February 6, 1987, FBIS-CHI, February 9, 1987, I1

80. Ibid.

81. Ibid.

82. *Zhongguo waijiao gaijian, 1988*, 102–3. See also "Sheikholeslam in Beijing," *TT*, May 24, 1987; "Persian Gulf Too Small for Superpowers Presence," *TT*, May 23, 1987.

83. Agence France-Presse (hereafter AFP), Hong Kong, June 12, 1987, FBIS-CHI, June 15, 1987, F2.

84. *Zhongguo waijiao gaijian, 1988*, 102–3.

85. Tehran IRNA, July 10, 1987, FBIS-CHI, July 14, 1987, F1.

86. United Nations Security Council, "Speech by Chinese Representative Huang Jiahua," S/PV.2750, 5 10.

87. Interview with retired IRI ambassador to PRC, Tehran, November 2004.

88. Xinhua, July 11, 1987, FBIS-CHI, July 13, 1987, B1.

89. "Security Council Demands a Truce in Iran-Iraq War," *New York Times* (hereafter *NYT*), July 21, 1987, 1.

90. *Zhongguo waijiao gaijian, 1989*, 97.

91. Wang, *Xin zhongguo waijiao wushi nian*, 582.

92. Xinhua, August 27, 1987, FBIS-CHI-87-166, 3–4.

93. "Qi Huaiyuan Arrives in Iran to Actively Mediate for Peace," *Hsin Wan Pao* (Hong Kong), August 26, 1987, FBIS-CHI-87-166, August 27, 1987, 4–5.

94. Palmer, *Guardians of the Gulf*, 131–38.

95. Xinhua, October 21, 1987, FBIS-CHI-87–206, October 26, 1987, 3.

96. Xinhua, September 30, 1987, FBIS-CHI-87–190, October 1, 1987, 8.

97. Zhuang Hanlong, "Peace, the General Trend in the World," *Jiefangjun bao* [Liberation Army Daily], August 29, 1988, FBIS-CHI-88–169, August 31, 1988, 16–17.

98. "Foreign Ministry Urges End to Military Conflict," Xinhua, April 19, 1988, FBIS-CHI-88–075, 2.

99. *Strategic Survey, 1988–89*, 173–77.

100. "Velayati Receives Message from PRC Counterpart," Tehran IRNA, August 1, 1988, FBIS-NES-88–148, August 2, 1988, 48.

101. "Foreign Ministry Statement on Gulf, Angola," Beijing Domestic Service, August 9, 1988, FBIS-CHI-88–154, August 10, 1988, 1.

102. Xinhua, August 18, 1988, FBIS-CHI-88–161, 18.

103. Interview with retired PRC ambassador to IRI, Beijing, September 2004.

104. "Arrives in Beijing," Tehran IRNA, October 24, 1988, FBIS-CHI-88–205, October 24, 1988, 9.

105. "Meets with Li Peng," Xinhua, October 24, 1988, FBIS-CHI-88–205, October 24, 1988, 9.

106. Qian Qichen, Iranian Counterpart Hold Talks," Xinhua, December 15, 1988, FBIS-CHI-88–241, December 15, 1988, 10.

107. "Bilateral Relations Viewed," Beijing Domestic Service, December 17, 1988, FBIS-CHI-88–243, December 19, 1988, 16–17.

108. "Iranian Foreign Ministry Official Visits," Tehran IRNA, April 11, 1989, FBIS-CHI-89–068, April 11, 1989, 12.

109. Wang, *Xin zhongguo waijiao wushi nian*, 5844.

4 / POST–COLD WAR U.S. UNIPOLAR PREEMINENCE, 1989–2004

1. Hashim, *The Crisis of the Iranian State*.

2. Ayatollah Ruhollah Khomeini, *Imam's Final Discourse: The Text of the Political and Religious Testament of the Leader of the Islamic Revolution and the Founder of the Islamic Republic of Iran, Imam Khomeini* ([Tehran?]: Ministry of Guidance of Islamic Culture, [1990?]), 11.

3. Lo Ping, "Notes on the Northern Journey," *Cheng Ming*, October 10, 1989, FBIS-CHI-89–190, 3–6.

4. Richard Bernstein and Ross H. Munro, *The Coming Conflict with China* (New York: Alfred Knopf, 1997), 7, 12. Steven W. Mosher, *Hegemon: China's Plan to Dominate Asia and the World* (San Francisco: Encounter Books, 2000), 101–2. Bill Gertz, *The China Threat: How the People's Republic Targets America* (Washington, DC: Regnery Publishing, 2000), 101–8.

5. Edward Timperlake and William C. Triplett II, *Red Dragon Rising: Communist China's Military Threat to America* (Washington, DC: Regnery Publishing, 1999), 97–108.

6. Li and Qian were both born in 1928, but Li was one month senior to Qian. Qian served as second secretary at the Chinese embassy in Moscow in the 1950s when Li was studying hydroelectric engineering in Moscow. Later, as Li Peng rose to high-level positions, he assisted Qian's advance.

7. Xinhua, October 17, 1995, FBIS-CHI-95-201, 10.

8. Quoted in Yu Jianhua, "Dangdai zhong yi guanxi yu yilang dui hua zhengce dongyin" [Contemporary Sino-Iranian Relations and the Driving Factors of Iranian Policy toward China], *Xiya feizhou* [West Asia and Africa], no. 4 (1998): 43–47.

9. PRC's Wan Li Meets with Hashemi-Rafsanjani," Tehran Domestic Service, May 9, 1990, FBIS-NES-90-091, May 10, 1990, 42.

10. Quoted in Yu, "Dangdai zhong yi guanxi."

11. "Imam Calls for 'Strong' Ties with Moscow to Confront West," *TT*, February 27, 1989, 1, 3.

12. "Exchange of Messages Marks 'Turning Point' in Tehran-Moscow Ties," *TT*, February 28, 1989, 1.

13. "Tian Jiyun in Tehran for 4-Day Visit," FBIS-CHI-89-042, March 6, 1989, 10–11.

14. "Musavi Welcomes Expansion of Relations with China," *TT*, March 7, 1989, 2. "China Seeks Economic Ties with Iran," *TT*, March 5, 1989, 1.

15. "Iran, China to Improve Relations," *Arab News*, March 8, 1989.

16. "President off to China—Closer Ties in the Offing," *TT*, May 9, 1989.

17. "President Leaves Today for High-Level Talks in China," *TT*, May 8, 1989, 1, 5.

18. "Iran, China Sign Pact Covering Diversified Fields," *TT*, May 13, 1989, 1, 5.

19. "Zhao Takes up Khamenei's Invitation to Visit Iran," *TT*, May 11, 1989, 1, 15.

20. "Khamenei Arrives in China," *Arab News*, May 10, 1989.

21. "Deng, Khamenei Talk Viewed," *Rmrb*, May 12, 1989, FBIS-CHI-89-091, May 12, 1989, 14.

22. "Talks with Muslim Leaders," Tehran IRNA, May 10, 1989, and "Visits Mosque, Temple," Xinhua, May 10, 1989, both in FBIS-CHI-89-089, May 10, 1989, 10.

23. *Zhongguo waijiao gaijian, 1990,* 96.

24. "PRC's Yang Grants 'Exclusive' Interview," Tehran IRNA, October 26, 1991, FBIS-NES-91-209, October 29, 1991, 95–96.

25. "Li Peng zongli tong lafusanni zongtong huitan" [Premier Li Peng's Talks with President Rafsanjani], *Rmrb*, June 9, 1991, 1.

26. "Li Peng Supports Iranian Stand on Gulf," Tehran IRNA, August 18, 1990, FBIS-CHI-90-165, August 24, 1990, 13.

27. "Li: Gulf Crisis Should Be Resolved by Peaceful Means," *BR*, September 10–16, 1990, 7.

28. "Tehran, Beijing for Peaceful Solution to P. Gulf Crisis," *TT*, October 18, 1990, 2.

29. "China Ready to Help with Iran's 5–Year Development Plan," *TT*, October 17, 1990.

30. Qian Qichen, *Waijiao shi ji* [Ten Diplomatic Episodes] (Beiing: Shijie zhishe chubanshe, 2003), 97, 187–88.

31. Ibid.

32. Ibid.

33. "Li Peng, Iranian Envoy Discuss Iraq, Relations," Tehran IRNA, November 30, 1990, FBIS-CHI-90–232, December 3, 1990, 2.

34. "Fiendish Plot," *FEER*, January 31, 1991, 6.

35. "Yang Interviewed on Arrival in Tehran," Tehran Domestic Service, February 21, 1991, FBIS-CHI-91–036, February 21, 1991, 2.

36. Ellis Joffe, "China after the Gulf War: The Lessons Learned" (paper prepared for the Center for National Security Studies, Los Alamos National Laboratory, November 1991).

37. Xinhua, July 7, 1991, FBIS-CHI-91–132, July 10, 1991, 11.

38. Xinhua, July 8, 1991, FBIS-CHI-91–132, July 10, 1991, 12.

39. "Ayatollah Khamenei Receives Li," *TT*, July 9, 1991.

40. "Chinese President to Visit Iran Soon," *TT*, October 8, 1991.

41. "Ayatollah Khamenei Receives Li," *TT*, July 9, 1991.

42. Xinhua, September 11, 1991, FBIS-CHI-91–179, 16.

43. Xinhua, September 8, 1991, FBIS-CHI-91–174, September 9, 1991, 17–18.

44. "Yang Shangkun Interview with IRNA Reported," Xinhua, October 28, 1991, FBIS-CHI-209, October 29, 1991, 13.

45. "Coverage of Yang Shangkun's Continuing Iran Visit," Xinhua, October 31, 1991, FBIS-CHI-91–212, November 1, 1991, 20–21.

46. "Daily on Hashemi-Rafsanjani Talks," *Rmrb*, November 1, 1991, FBIS-CHI-91–215, November 6, 1991, 15.

47. "Chinese President Visits Nuclear Center in Iran," *Mednews*, November 25, 1991, LexisNexis, http://www.lexisnexis.com/.

48. "Iran Financing $300 Million in PRC Arms for Sudan," *Al-Sharq al-Awsat* (London), November 27, 1991, FBIS-NES-91–232, December 3, 1991, 11. "Iran Finances Purchase of PRC Military Aircraft," *Al-Wafd* (Cairo), December 8, 1991, FBIS-NES-91–240, December 13, 1991, 31.

49. "Sudan: Arms Deal Concluded with China, Financed by Iran," Middle East News Agency (hereafter MENA), Cairo, March 31, 1996, FBIS-NES-96–063, April 1, 1996, 22. The member of the Egyptian Islamic Jihad that assassinated Anwar Sadat in 1980 is deemed a hero by the IRI, Sadat being deemed a traitor to the Islamic

cause who abandoned struggle against the "Zionist entity" via the Camp David peace agreement.

50. Tehran Voice of the IRI, April 14, 1992, FBIS-CHI-92–074, April 16, 1992, 16.

51. Michael Dillon, *Xinjiang—China's Muslim Far Northwest* (London and New York: Routledge and Curzon, 2004), 133.

52. "Daily Previews President's Trip to China," Tehran Voice of the IRI, September 9, 1992, FBIS-NES-92–176, September 10, 1992, 37–38.

53. "New Asian Countries Group to be Studied with PRC," Tehran IRNA, December 18, 1992, FBIS-NES-92–240, December 22, 1992, 64.

54. "China to Supply Military, Nuclear Power Equipment," *Al-Sharq al-Awsat* (London), September 11, 1992, FBIS-NES-92–180, September 16, 1992, 46.

55. "Hashemi-Rafsanjani Sums up Three Nation Tour," Tehran IRNA, September 12, 1992, FBIS-NES-92–178, September 14, 1992, 47–48.

56. Major Jerry L. Mraz, "Dual Containment: U.S. Policy in the Persian Gulf and a Recommendation for the Future," research paper in partial fulfillment of graduation requirements of the Air Command Staff College, March 1997, AU/ACSC/0305/97–03.

57. The text of the act is available on the Nuclear Threat Initiative Web site, at http://www.nti.org/db/china/engdocs/iraniraq.htm.

58. Tehran IRNA, July 30, 1993, FBIS-CHI-93–146, August 2, 1993, 10.

59. Beijing China Radio International, March 6, 1994, FBIS-CHI-94–044, March 7, 1994, 11.

60. *Zhongguo waijiao gaijian*, 1995, 115.

61. "Clinton Bans U.S. Oil Pacts with Iran," WP, March 15, 1995, 1.

62. "Clinton to Order a Trade Embargo against Iran," NYT, May 1, 1995, 1.

63. "Calling Iran 'Outlaw State,' Christopher Defends U.S. Trade Ban," NYT, May 2, 1995, 6.

64. Tehran Voice of the IRI, March 26, 1995, FBIS-CHI-95–058, March 27, 1995, 15–16.

65. Tehran IRNA, March 27, 1995, FBIS-CHI-95–059, 6–7.

66. Tehran IRNA, March 28, 1995, FBIS CHI 95–060, March 29, 1995, 6–7.

67. "Economic Relations with China Viewed," TT, May 25, 1995.

68. "Plan to Counter U.S. 'Dominance,'" *Asian Recorder*, June 17–23, 1996, 25699.

69. "U.S. a Threat to the Region," *Asian Recorder*, November 12–18, 1995, 25203–4.

70. "Spokesman on 'Futile' U.S. Pressure on Iran," IRNA, Tehran, April 19, 1995, FBIS-CHI-95–078, April 24, 1995, 1.

71. *Zhongguo waijiao gaijian*, 1995, 116–17.

72. "Rejects U.S. Embargo on Iran," Xinhua, May 4, 1995, FBIS-CHI-95–086, 1.

73. Li Xuejiang, "Alone and Helpless," *Rmrb*, May 15, 1995, FBIS-CHI-098, May

22, 1995, 4–5. "Roundup: The United States Imposes Chain Sanctions," *Rmrb*, May 15, 1996, FBIS-CHI-96–101, 3–4.

74. Wang Nan, "Another Example of Failure of Sanctions," *Rmrb*, July 25, 1995, FBIS-CHI-95–156, August 14, 1995, 6–7.

75. Zhu Mengkui, "Out of Keeping with the Times," *Rmrb*, January 23, 1996, FBIS-CHI-96–021, January 31, 1996, 2.

76. Avery Goldstein, "The Diplomatic Face of China's Grand Strategy: A Rising Power's Emerging Choice," *China Quarterly* 168 (December 2001): 835–64.

77. *Tehran Norooz*, April 20, 2002, FBIS-NES, 2002–0420. Dialog.

78. *Tehran Resalat*, December 17, 2002, FBIS-NES, 2002–1227. A similar analysis is in *Tehran Hayat-e Now*, April 20, 2002, FBIS-CHI-2002–0429. Dialog.

79. *Tehran Towse'eh*, April 22, 2002, FBIS-NES-2002–0430. Dialog.

80. *Tehran Norooz*, April 20, 2002, FBIS-NES-2002–0426. Dialog.

81. Discussion with Chinese diplomat who served in the Middle East.

82. "Iran's China Agenda," *FEER*, July 6, 2000. This meeting of defense ministers is confirmed by *Zhongguo waijiao, 2001*, 123.

83. Xinhua, June 22, 2000, FBIS-CHI-2000–0622. Dialog.

84. "Chinese Minister Stresses Expansion of Ties with Iran," *TT*, January 7, 2001.

85. "Chinese Minister Meets Iranian Army Commander," *TT*, January 11, 2001.

86. "China Eager to Buy More Crude Oil from Iran," *TT*, December 10, 2000.

87. "Economy, Iran," *Middle East Economic Digest* (hereafter *MEED*), February 22, 2002, 24.

88. Tehran IRNA, May 3, 2004, "Iran's Rafsanjani Urges Expansion of Strategic Cooperation with China," BBC Monitoring Middle East, via LexisNexis.

89. "Evaluation of President's Trip to China," *Tehran Abar*, June 29, 2000, FBIS-NES-2000–0801, Dialog.

90. Tang Shiping, "Lixiang anquan huanjing yu xin shiji zhonguo da zhanlue" [Ideal Security Environment and China's Grand Strategy in the New Century], *Zhanlue yu guanli* [Strategy and Management], no. 6 (2000): 45–46.

91. "PRC FM Spokesman: China Disapproves of Term 'Axis of Evil,'" Xinhua, February 4, 2002, Dialog.

92. Tehran IRNA, April 20, 2002, FBIS-NES-2002–0420. Dialog.

93. *Wen hui bao* (Hong Kong), April 8, 2002, FBIS-CHI-2002–0408. Germany, Libya, Tunisia, and Nigeria were the other countries visited by Jiang. Dialog.

94. "Iran: Khamenei, Jiang Zemin Discuss Cooperation, Opposition to U.S., Israel," Tehran Vision of the Islamic Republic of Iran Network, April 21, 2002, FBIS-NES-2002–0421, Dialog.

95. "Iran: FM Spokesman Comments on Jiang's visit," April 22, 2002, FBIS-NES-2002–0422. Dialog.

96. Tehran IRNA, April 20, 2002, FBIS-NES-2002–0420. Dialog.

97. "AFP:PRC FM Spokesman Says China 'Hopeful' over Istanbul Meeting on Iraq Crisis," January 23, 2003, Dialog.

98. "Iran: Chinese Ambassador Says Tehran-Beijing Ties Significantly Improved," *Iran Daily*, March 10, 2003, Dialog.

99. Interviews, Beijing, September 2004.

100. "PRC: Li Guofu Predicts Iran Will Be Next U.S. Target," *Wen wei bao* (Hong Kong), March 21, 2003, Dialog.

101. Wang Jiping, Hong Yousheng, and Ji Liqiang, "Yilang he wenti yu daguo guanxi" [The Iranian Nuclear Issue and Great Power Relations], *Meiguo yanjiu* [American Studies], no. 1 (2004): 78–90. The three authors were professors at Nanjing University and the Shijiazhuang College of Military Machinery Engineering.

102. Joseph Y. S. Cheng and Zhang Wankun, "Patterns and Dynamics of China's International Strategic Behavior," *Journal of Contemporary China* 11, no. 31 (May 2002): 235–50.

103. "Xinhua Carries 'Full Text' of PRC, Iran Joint Communiqué," Xinhua, June 22, 2000, Dialog.

104. Such Sino-Russian declarations include the Joint Statement on the Multipolarization of the international order, April 23, 1997; Joint Statement on the Eve of the New Century, November 23, 1998; Joint Statement on Anti-Missile Defense, April 14, 1999; Conclusions and Comments on the Anti-Ballistic Missile Treaty, December 10, 1999; and Joint Presidential Statement on Anti-Missile Defense, July 18, 2000.

105. *Tehran Norooz*, April 20, 2002, FBIS-NES-2002–0421. Dialog.

106. *Tehran Norooz*, April 20, 2002, FBIS-NES-2002–0426. Dialog.

5 / THE XINJIANG FACTOR IN PRC-IRI RELATIONS

1. *China Statistical Yearbook, 2003* (Beijing: China Statistics Press, 2004), 48. Like many official Chinese statistics these data are disputed. Some estimates of China's Muslim population run as high as 113 million.

2. Raphael Israeli, "Muslims in China: The Incompatibility between Islam and the Chinese Order," in *Islam in China: Religion, Ethnicity, Culture, and Politics* (Boulder, CO, and New York: Lexington Books, 2002), 7–30.

3. Ahmed Rashid, *Jihad: The Rise of Militant Islam in Central Asia* (New York: Penguin Books, 2003).

4. "4 Main Waves of 'East Turkistan' Terrorism in Xinjiang since 1990s," *Liaowang*, September 30, 2000, no. 40, 10–11, Dialog. Igor Rotar, "The Growing Problem of Uigur Separatism," *China Brief: A Journal of Information and Analysis* (online newsletter) 4, no. 98 (August 15, 2004).

5. R. K. Ramazani, *Revolutionary Iran: Challenge and Response in the Middle East*

(Baltimore: Johns Hopkins University Press, 1986), 19–29; Ramazani, "Iran's Export of the Revolution: Politics, Ends, and Means," in *The Iranian Revolution: Its Global Impact*, ed. John Esposito, 40–62 (Miami: Florida International University Press, 1990).

6. Sohail Mahmood, *Islamic Fundamentalism in Pakistan, Egypt, and Iran* (Lahore, Karachi, and Islamabad, Pakistan: Vanguard Books, 1995), 152–56.

7. Cesar Adib Majul, "The Iranian Revolution and the Muslims in the Philippines," in Esposito, *The Iranian Revolution*, 263–78.

8. Rashid, *Jihad*, 102.

9. Several discussions with well-connected Chinese Middle Eastern specialists in Beijing in September 2004 touched on this point. Unfortunately, discussions of this issue were, usually, in general terms only.

10. "IPO Head in China," *TT*, September 12, 1989, 3.

11. "Li Xiannian Meets Iranian Islamic Delegation," Xinhua, September 21, 1989, FBIS-CHI-89–182, 10.

12. *Zhongguo waijiao gaijian*, 1990, 95.

13. Islam holds the Arabic language to be the authentic language of God's final divine revelation to man. Unlike Christianity, which has translated the Bible into many languages, Islam requires its believers to read its scripture in Arabic. In many cases this is a rote or formulaic knowledge of Arabic, but it still offers a basis for deeper mastery of the language.

14. Discussion with Chinese diplomat who served in Middle East.

15. Alī Akbar Omid Mehr (also transliterated Umidmīhr), *Guzārish bih mardum: khāṭirāt-i siyāsī-i yak dīplumāt-i Jumhūrī-i Islāmī* [Report to the People: Political and Diplomatic Remembrance] [in Farsi] (Sweden: Spanga, 2000), 68, 303. I hired a native Farsi speaker to read, identify, and translate China-related portions of this 346–page work.

16. Rashid, *Jihad*, 102, 105, 110, 172, 204.

17. *Facts on File*, 1992, 313, 405, 565.

18. "Urged to Help Bosnians," Tehran IRNA, February 18, 1993, FBIS-NES-93–032, February 19, 1993, 71.

19. *Facts on File*, 1992, 894; *Facts on File*, 1994, 423.

20. "Visits Xinjiang 12 May," Xinhua, May 12, 1989, FBIS-CHI-89–092, 25–26.

21. Dillon, *Xinjiang—China's Muslim Far Northwest*, 136, 185.

22. Xinhua, "Iranian President Concludes Tour of Xinjiang, Leaves for Hong Kong," June 25, 2000, Dialog. It is sometimes said that monogamous marriage is the West's major cultural gift/imposition on the non-Western world. Both the Confucian and Islamic traditions practiced polygamous marriage. Modern China now embraces monogamous marriage, while Iran continues to adhere to polygamy. It is probably

too much of a stretch, though, to see a visit to a concubine's tomb as symbolic testament to the common non-Western heritage of China and Persia.

23. AFP, Hong Kong, "AFP: Iranian President to Visit Troubled Xinjiang," "Inks Trade Pact on China Trip," June 21, 2000, Dialog.

24. Regarding the function of China's "foreign affairs system," see Brady, *Making the Foreign Serve China.*

6 / CHINA'S ASSISTANCE TO IRAN'S NUCLEAR PROGRAMS

1. "Implementation of the NPT Safeguards Agreement with the Islamic Republic of Iran," report by the Director General to the IAEA Board of Governors, original date November 10, 2003 (GOV/2003/75), derestricted November 26, 2003; and report of same name on November 15 (GOV/2004/83), derestricted November 29, 2004. Both are at http://www.iaea.org/publications/documents/board/2003/gov2003.75.pdf and 2004/gov2004.83.pdf. Annex I of the 2003 report is a "Detailed Technical Chronology" (hereafter cited as such).

2. "*Agreement for Nuclear Cooperation between the United States and China, Communication from the President of the United States,* transmitting a report relating to the approval and implementation of the agreement for nuclear cooperation between the United States and the People's Republic of China pursuant to 42 U.S.C. 2153 (d), February 3, 1998, 105th Congress, 2nd sess., House Document 105–197 (hereafter *Agreement for Nuclear Cooperation*).

3. "News Review," *Nuclear Engineering International,* December 1984, 13, via "Iran Nuclear Chronology" (created and maintained by the Nuclear Threat Initiative [NTI] and the Nonproliferation Center of the Monterey Institute for International Studies [MIIS]), available at http://www.nti.org/e_research/e1_iran_nch.html (hereafter "Iran Nuclear Chronology"). NTI and MIIS also maintain a very large database containing articles on nuclear issues, including China-Iran nuclear cooperation. This database is linked to the "Iran Nuclear Chronology" but cited below as NTI-MIIS database.

4. IAEA, "Detailed Technical Chronology."

5. *Agreement for Nuclear Cooperation,* 8. In September 1995 the Chinese ambassador to Iran said that nuclear cooperation between the two countries was carried out under an agreement "signed ten years ago." See "Iran Nuclear Chronology."

6. *Agreement for Nuclear Cooperation,* 8.

7. "Iran, Research Reactors Details—ENRC," International Atomic Energy Agency Web site, at http://www.iaea.org/.

8. "Sino-Iranian Nuclear Pact Alleged," *Nuclear Week,* May 2, 1991, 17.

9. *Nucleonics Week* 33, nos. 17–18 (1991), via "Iran Nuclear Chronology."

10. "Dimona et al.," *Economist*, March 14, 1992, 46.

11. Tehran radio, August 3, 1991. Also *Mednews*, June 8, 1992. Both via "Iran Nuclear Chronology, 1991."

12. IAEA report of November 15, 2004.

13. Raymond L. Murray, *Nuclear Energy: An Introduction to the Concepts, Systems, and Applications of Nuclear Processes* (Boston: Butterworth, 2001), 99–100.

14. "Spokesman Comments on Nuclear Assistance to Iran," Xinhua, November 4, 1991, FBIS-CHI-91–214, November 5, 1991, 19.

15. Shirley A. Kan, *Chinese Proliferation of Weapons of Mass Destruction: Background and Analysis*, Report no. 96–767F (Washington, DC: Congressional Research Service, September 13, 1996).

16. Mark Gorwitz, "Foreign Assistance to Iran's Nuclear and Missile Programs: Emphasis on Russian Assistance, Analysis and Assessment" (unpublished manuscript, October 1998), 23.

17. "Uranium Exploration with China," *Iran Brief*, May 6, 1996. "U.S. Protests Chinese Hex Plant," *Iran Brief*, July 3, 1997.

18. "Iran's Uranium Program," *Iran Brief*, June 1, 1995, 11.

19. Reza Aghazadeh, "Iran's Nuclear Policy: Peaceful, Transparent, Independent" (presentation to IAEA Headquarters, Vienna, Austria, May 6, 2003).

20. "U.S. Protests Chinese Hex Plant," *Iran Brief*, July 3, 1997.

21. Tehran radio, January 20, 1990, from "An Iranian Nuclear Chronology, 1987–1992," *Mednews* 5, nos. 17–18 (June 8, 1992), via NTI-MIIS database.

22. "Micro-nuclear Reactor Contract with Iran Signed," Xinhua, June 11, 1990, FBIS-CHI-90–113, June 12, 1990, 13.

23. Mark Hibbs, "Sensitive Iran Reactor Deal May Hinge on MFN for China," *Nucleonics Week*, October 1, 1992, 5–6, via NTI-MIIS database.

24. Douglas Frantz, "Iran Closes in on Ability to Make Atomic Bomb" *Los Angeles Times* (hereafter LAT), June 19, 2003. Also Frantz, "Iran Says It Received 1,800 Kg of Uranium from China," Deutsche Presse-Agentur, June 10, 2003, via LexisNexis.

25. IAEA, "Detailed Technical Chronology."

26. "PRC to Supply Nuclear Technology," *Sawt al-Kuwait* (London), July 11, 1991, 1–4, JPRS—Transnational Nuclear Development (hereafter TND), no. 91–0012, August 8, 1991, 19–20.

27. "Nuclear Facilities," *Mednews*, June 8, 1992, from "Iran Nuclear Chronology."

28. Bill Gertz, "Chinese Build Reactor for Iranian Program," WT, October 16, 1991, A3.

29. "Iran Insists Nuclear Supplies Aren't for Arms," *San Francisco Chronicle*, November 1, 1991, A12.

30. "Spokesman Comments on Nuclear Assistance to Iran," Xinhua, November 4, 1991, FBIS-CHI-214, November 5, 1991, 19.

31. "Agreements on Nuclear Cooperation Ratified," Tehran IRNA, April 13, 1993, FBIS-NES-93-070, April 14, 1993, 49.

32. *Nuclear News*, October 1992, 17–18. Elaine Sciolino, "China Will Build A-Plant for Iran," NYT, September 11, 1992, A6.

33. "The China-Iran Nuclear Cloud," *Mednews* 4, no. 20 (July 22, 1991): 1–2.

34. "Iranian Ambassador on Hashemi-Rafsanjani Visit," FBIS-CHI-92–184, September 22, 1992, 14.

35. Hibbs, "Sensitive Iran Reactor Deal May Hinge on MFN for China," 5–6.

36. "Signs Nuclear Power Station Accord," FBIS-CHI-93–033, February 22, 1992, 9.

37. "Rafsanjani on Nuclear Cooperation," Xinhua, February 17, 1993, FBIS-CHI-93–033, February 22, 1993, 8.

38. Steven Murfson, "Chinese Nuclear Officials See No Reason to Change Plans to Sell Reactor to Iran," WP, May 18, 1995, A22.

39. Murray, *Nuclear Energy*, 174–79.

40. "Technology Transfer (China/Iran)," *S&T Perspective* 5 (June 30, 1995): 6, from "Iran Nuclear Chronology."

41. "'Transfer' of Nuclear Device to Iran Cited," Zhongguo tongxunshe (China news agency), April 21, 1995, FBIS-CHI-95–078, April 24, 1995, 8–9.

42. "Russia, China, Iran, and India Agree to Fusion R&D Cooperation," *Nucleonics Week*, February 21, 1996, 15, via Nuclear Threat Initiative, Center for Nonproliferation Studies, China-Iran Missile Abstracts database, http://www.nti.org/e_research/e7 data bases.html (hereafter "NTI-CNS missile database").

43. Murray, *Nuclear Energy*, 107–9. Discussion with Noland Hertel, nuclear physicist at Georgia Institute of Technology, Atlanta, December 2004.

44. Leonard S. Spector, *Going Nuclear* (Cambridge, MA: Ballinger Publishing Company 1989), 46–48.

45. Charles Ferguson and Jack Boureston, "IAEA Puts Iranian Laser-Enrichment Technology in the Spotlight," *Jane's Intelligence Review* 6, no. 7 (July 2004): 38–41.

46. IAEA Report of November 15, 2004.

47. Interview with nuclear physicist / analyst at Institute for Defense Studies and Analysis, New Delhi, January 2005.

48. Mark Hibbs, "German-U.S. Nerves Frayed," *NuclearFuel*, March 14, 1994.

49. IAEA Report of November 15, 2004.

50. "Iran May Be Using Lasers to Harvest Fuel for Nukes," *Oakland Tribune*, September 11, 2003, http://www.oaklandtribune.com/.

51. "Iran Laser Program Shocks Experts," *Tri-Valley Herald*, November 12, 2003, http://www.trivalleyherald.com/.

52. "Iran's IR-40 Reactor: A Preliminary Assessment," Firstwatch International, November 2003, http://www.firstwatchint.org/.

53. Frantz, "Iran Closes in on Ability."

54. Ibid.

55. Herbert Krosney, *Deadly Business, Legal Deals and Outlaw Weapons: The Arming of Iran and Iraq, 1975 to the Present* (New York: Four Walls Eight Windows, 1993), 268–69.

56. Hibbs, "German-u.s. Nerves Frayed."

57. "Uranium Exploration with China," *Iran Brief*, May 6, 1996.

58. IAEA, "Detailed Technical Chronology." The IAEA's placing of supply of the UCF in the "mid-1990s" fits with reports during that time about China's involvement in the supply and construction of a UCF. China itself later reported the supply of a UCF to Iran. Finally, the IAEA "Detailed Technical Chronology" indicates that the "foreign supplier" terminated its contract for the UCF in 1997. This date too fits with China's 1997 cancellation, under u.s. pressure, of nuclear cooperation with Iran.

59. IAEA, "Detailed Technical Chronology." The specific attribution to China is inferred in accord with the previous note.

60. Bill Gertz, "Iran Gets China's Help on Nuclear Arms," *WT*, April 17, 1995.

61. "Iran Told IAEA It Will Build Chinese UF6 Plant at Isfahan," *NuclearFuel*, vol. 21, no. 26 (December 16, 1996).

62. "u.s. Protests Chinese Hexplant," *Iran Brief*, July 3, 1997.

63. IAEA, "Detailed Technical Chronology."

64. Mark Hibbs, "u.s. in 1983 Stopped IAEA from Helping Iran Make UF6," *NuclearFuel* 28, no. 16 (August 4, 2003): 12.

65. Aghazadeh, "Iran's Nuclear Policy."

66. Mark Hibbs, "Iran, China Said to Disagree Only on Site Selection for New PWR," *Nucleonics Week*, October 5, 1995, 1, 8–9. Also, "Nuclear Plans with China near Collapse," *Al-Sharq al-Awsat* (London), May 21, 1995. Both via "Iran Nuclear Chronology."

67. "Chinese Diplomat Interviewed on Nuclear Assistance," *Tehran Resalat* (Tehran), September 12, 1995, FBIS-NES-95-187, September 27, 1995, 52–53.

68. "Foreign Ministry Holds Regular News Conference on Nuclear Cooperation with Iran," Tehran IRNA, January 9, 1996.

69. "Iran's Chinese Shopping List," *Iran Brief*, October 1, 1996, 4–5.

70. Barton Gellman, "Reappraisal Led to New China Policy," *WP*, June 22, 1998.

71. "AFP: Spokesman Calls for Nuclear Accord," AFP, Hong Kong, October 21, 1997, NTI-MIIS.

72. "Iran Admits Chinese Link Severed," *Nuclear Engineering International*, January 31, 1998, via "Iran Nuclear Chronology."

73. Gorwitz, *Foreign Assistance to Iran*, 29.

74. Timperlake and Triplett, *Red Dragon Rising*.

75. *Facts on File, 2003*, 421–22, 531.

76. "China Diplomat Interviewed on Nuclear Assistance" (see above).

77. "Kharrazi Says China Opposes Referring Iran's Nuclear Case to UNSC," Tehran IRNA, November 6, 2004, Dialog.

78. "Iran: Chinese Envoy Upbeat on Economic Ties; Supports Right to Nuclear Energy," Tehran IRNA, August 5, 2004, Dialog.

79. "RRC [sic] Envoy to UN Zhang Yan Urges Peaceful Resolution of Iranian Nuclear Issue," Xinhua, September 19, 2004, Dialog.

80. "PRC Envoy to UN Calls for Solving DPRK, Iran Issues through Dialogue," Zhongguo wang (China Internet), Beijing, November 3, 2004, Dialog.

81. "IRNA: China Says IAEA 'Only Proper Forum' to Resolve Iranian Nuclear Case," Tehran IRNA, September 16, 2004, Dialog.

82. "Kharrazi Says China Opposes Referring Iran's Nuclear Case to UNSC" (see above).

83. "RMRB Urges Dialogue on Dealing with Iran Nuclear Issue," September 22, 2004, Dialog.

84. "Chinese FMN Says Referring Iran Nuclear Case to UN Would Complicate Standoff," Tehran IRNA, November 6, 2004, Dialog.

85. "Daily Wants China to Stop Iran Dossier Going to UN Security Council," Aftab-e Yazd, November 7, 2004, Dialog.

86. "Iran Sends 'Secret Envoy' to PRC for Support at IAEA," Sankei Shimbun, March 11, 2005, Dialog.

87. "Iran, China Discuss Expansion of Mutual, Regional Cooperation," Tehran IRNA, November 6, 2004, Dialog.

7 / CHINA AND IRAN'S MILITARY DEVELOPMENT EFFORTS

1. Zezid Sayigh, "Arms Production in Pakistan and Iran: The Limits of Self-Reliance," in Military Capacity and the Risk of War: China, India, Pakistan, and Iran, ed. Eric Arnett, 176–94 (London: Oxford University Press, 1999).

2. Lu Ning, The Dynamics of Foreign Policy Decisionmaking in China (Boulder, CO: Westview Press, 2000), 122, 136–37, 155.

3. Hiro, The Longest War, 112, 122, 172–75, 194.

4. Yitzhak Shichor, "Mountains out of Molehills: Arms Transfers in Sino–Middle East Relations," Middle East Review of International Affairs 4, no. 3 (September 2000).

5. Xinhua, April 19, 1983, FBIS-CHI, April 19, 1983, A1.

6. Ta Kung Pao, June 5, 1986, FBIS-CHI, June 5, 1986, W1.

7. "Yao Yilin Denies Arms, Missiles Sale to Iran," Manama Wakh (Al Sariqah), November 17, 1985, FBIS-NES, November 18, 1985, C4.

8. Hong Kong AFP, April 7, 1987, FBIS-CHI, April 8, 1987, I1.

9. "Ghali Cites PRC Denial of Arms to Iran," MENA (Cairo), November 9, 1987, FBIS-NES-87–217, November 10, 1987, 28.

10. *Facts on File, 1988*, 172.

11. Shichor, "Unfolded Arms," 320–30.

12. Xinhua, July 29, 1987, FBIS-CHI, July 29, 1987, F2.

13. News Conference, June 22, 1983, *Department of State Bulletin*, August 1983, 8.

14. Stephen R. Shalom, "The United States and the Iran-Iraq War," http://www.zmag.org/zmag/articles/ShalomIranIraq.html.

15. Anthony H. Cordesman, *Iranian Arms Transfers: The Facts* (Washington, DC: Center for Strategic and International Studies, October 2000). Kenneth Katzman, *Iran: Arms and Weapons of Mass Destruction Suppliers*, report to Congress, RL 30551 (Washington, DC: Congressional Research Service, January 3, 2003).

16. Tehran domestic radio, January 21, 1990, FBIS-NES-90–010, January 25, 1990, 48.

17. "Yang Shangkun Meets Iranian Defense Minister," Xinhua, October 16, 1990, FBIS-CHI-90–200, October 16, 1990, 13.

18. "Ding Henggao Leads Defense Delegation to Iran," Xinhua, March 11, 1991, FBIS-CHI-91–048, March 12, 1991, 17.

19. "Missile Production with PRC Discussed," *Al Ittihad* (Abu Dhabi), September 18, 1989, FBIS-NES-89–181, September 20, 1989, 56.

20. Sayigh, "Arms Production in Pakistan and Iran."

21. "China Arms for Iran," *Asian Defense Journal*, June 1984, 104.

22. "China (People's Republic)" *Milavnews*, February 1991.

23. "Beijing Reportedly Buys Iraqi MiGs from Iran," Tokyo Kyodo, January 8, 1993, FBIS-CHI-93–005, January 8, 1993, 9.

24. Tan Han, "Meiguo junkong zhengce de yanbian" [Evolution of U.S. Arms Control Policy], *Guoji wenti yanjiu* [International Studies], no. 4 (October 13, 1993): 18–22, 48.

25. Bu Ran, "Missiles: Proliferation and Control," *BR* 34, no. 48 (December 2–8, 1991): 14.

26. Hua Di, "China's Case: Ballistic Missile Proliferation," in *The International Missile Bazaar: The New Suppliers Network*, ed. William Potter and Harlan Jenks, 173–77 (San Francisco: Westview Press, 1994).

27. Robert E. Mullins, "The Dynamics of Chinese Missile Proliferation," *Pacific Review* 8, no. 1 (1995): 137–57. John Wilson Lewis and Hua Di, "China's Ballistic Missile Programs," *International Security* 17, no. 2 (Fall 1992): 5–40.

28. Chinese participant in a track two dialogue on proliferation, in Evan S. Medeiros, *3rd U.S.-China Conference on Arms Control, Disarmament and Nonproliferation, U.S.-China Arms Control and Nonproliferation Cooperation: Progress and Prospects*, conference report, Center for Nonproliferation Studies (Monterey, CA: Monterey Institute of International Studies, September 2000), 17.

29. Tan, "Meiguo junkong zhengce de yanbian."

30. Saideh Lotfian, "Threat Perception and Military Planning in Iran: Credible Scenarios of Conflict and Opportunities for Confidence Building," in Arnett, *Military Capacity and the Risk of War*, 199–200.

31. Statement of Dr. Seth Carus, research analyst, Center for Naval Analysis, "Consequences of China's Military Sales to Iran," Hearing before the Committee on International Relations, House of Representatives, 104th Congress, 2nd sess., September 12, 1996, 4.

32. "Iran's Chinese Hy-2 Missiles and Iraq's French Exocets," *International Defense Review*, June 1987, 715.

33. Carus, "Consequences of China's Military Sales to Iran," 5, 31.

34. "Tehran Upgrades Chinese Missile," IAEA *Daily Press Review*, January 12, 2000. "China's Missile Exports and Assistance to the Middle East," Monterey Institute of International Studies, http://cns.miis.edu/iiop/. Hereafter cited as "NTI-MIIS missile database."

35. Katzman, *Iran: Arms and Weapons of Mass Destruction Suppliers*, 15.

36. "Cohen Says Iran Is Testing a Cruise Missile," NYT, June 18, 1997. Paul Mann, "China Alleged Top Trafficker in Mass Destruction Weapons," *Aviation Week and Space Technology*, August 4, 1997, 42.

37. Shirley A. Kan, *China and Proliferation of Weapons of Mass Destruction and Missiles: Policy Issues*, Report no. RL 31555 (Washington, DC: Congressional Research Service, updated August 8, 2003), 12.

38. *Jane's Strategic Weapons Systems*, ed. by Duncan Lennox (Surrey, UK: Jane's Information Group, 2004), 65–67.

39. "Iran Adds New Threat with Cruise Missile Test," *Jane's Defence Weekly*, February 7, 1996, 14. *Jane's Fighting Ships, 2003–2004*, ed. Stephen Saunders (Surrey, UK: Jane's Information Group, 2004), 339.

40. *Jane's Naval Weapons Systems*, ed. E. R. Hooton (Surrey, UK: Jane's Information Group, 2001), 298–99.

41. "China, Iran Share Missile Know-How," *Jane's Defence Weekly*, December 4, 2002, 15.

42. "Iran, China Set to Sign Arms Purchase Agreement," *Al-Sharq al-Awsat* (London), April 29, 1996, Dialog.

43. "China Agrees to Deal with Iran on Missiles," WT, August 19, 1999, 1. Cordesman, *Iranian Arms Transfers*, 8. Katzman, *Iran: Arms and Weapons of Mass Destruction Suppliers*, 16.

44. *Jane's Fighting Ships, 2003–2004*, 341.

45. *Jane's Underwater Warfare Systems, 2004–05*, ed. Anthony J. Watts (Surrey, UK: Jane's Information Group, 2004), 331. This volume states, "Reports indicate [these mines] may be in service with Iranian forces." Carus noted in his 1996 testimony to the U.S. Senate that Iran was trying to acquire this mine from China.

46. Christopher Chant, *Air Defense Systems and Weapons: World AAA and SAM Systems in the 1990s* (London: Brassey's Defense Publishers, 1989), 3.

47. *Jane's Land-based Air Defence, 2004–05*, ed. James C. O'Halloran (Surrey, UK: Jane's Information Group, 2004), 15, 138.

48. "China Steps up Air-Defense Work in Iran's Borders." *WT*, October 18, 2001. Also, Statement by Gary Milhollin, Subcommittee on Near East and South Asian Affairs, Committee on Foreign Relations, U.S. Senate, May 6, 1997.

49. SIPRI, "Ballistic Missile Programs in the Third World," in SIPRI *Yearbook: World Armaments and Disarmament, 1989* (Oxford and New York: Oxford University Press, 1989), 297–98.

50. Seth Carus and James Bermudez, "Iran's Growing Missile Forces," *Jane's Defence Weekly* 10, no. 3 (July 23, 1988): 126–31.

51. Kan, *China and Proliferation*, 16. Also, "Proliferation Briefing," *Mednews*, December 21, 1992, 5.

52. Duncan Lennox, "Iran's Ballistic Missile Projects: Uncovering the Evidence," *Jane's Intelligence Review*, June 1998, 24.

53. Korean Central News Agency, October 25–26 1983, "Iranian Prime Minister's Visit to North Korea," BBC Summary of World Broadcasts, October 29, 1983, in NTI "Iran Profile, Missile Chronology, 1960s–1984," http://www.nti.org/e_research/ profiles/Iran/missile/1788.html.

54. Cordesman, *Iranian Arms Transfers*, 20.

55. Joseph S. Bermudez, *A History of Ballistic Missile Development in the DPRK*, Occasional Paper no. 2 (Monterey, CA: Monterey Institute of International Studies, Center for Nonproliferation Studies, November 1999), 10–13.

56. Carus and Bermudez, "Iran's Growing Missile Forces," 130.

57. Sayigh, "Arm's Production in Pakistan and Iran," 187.

58. "Proliferation Briefing," *Mednews*, December 21, 1992, 5.

59. "Iran Seeking Solid Rocket Fuel," *Iran Brief*, January 9, 1995, 8. "China Backs off from Iran—Maybe," *Iran Brief*, November 11, 1997, 1, 2.

60. Michael Eisenstadt, *Chinese Military Assistance to Iran: An Overview*, testimony before the House of Representatives Committee on International Relations, Congress of the United States, September 12, 1996, 37–40. Also, "Iran's Chinese Shopping List," *Iran Brief*, October 1, 1996.

61. "The Tondar-68 and Iran-700 Programme," *Jane's Intelligence Review*, April 1992, 151. "Iranian SSMS in Production," *Aerospace/Defense Markets and Technology*, April 1991, 156, NTI-MIIS missile database.

62. "Proliferation Briefing," *Mednews*, December 21, 1992, 5. Mullins, "The Dynamics of Chinese Missile Proliferation," 137–57. Lewis and Hua, "China's Ballistic Missile Programs," 5–40.

63. Shichor, "Mountains out of Molehills."

64. "Sino-Iran Arms Link," *Daily Telegraph*, September 10, 1992, NTI-CNS missile database.

65. One source says "a" M-11 was transferred circa 1992. See "Iran's Ongoing Arms-Buying Binge," *WT*, June 4, 1992, G3, NTI-CNS missile database.

66. "Iran/China in Secret Missile Project," *Flight International*, May 23, 1993, 16, NTI-CNS missile database.

67. "DPRK and PRC Co-operation in the Iranian Missile Programme," *Jane's Intelligence Review*, April 1992, 151.

68. Elaine Sciolino, "C.I.A. Report Says Chinese Sent Iran Arms Components," *NYT*, June 22, 1995, 1, 6.

69. "Special Report: The Zelzal Missile Program," *Iran Brief*, September 9, 1996, 1–2.

70. "Iran Has Acquired Chinese Missile—IISS," Reuters, October 12, 1994. "Sneaking in the Scuds," *Newsweek*, June 22, 1992, 42–46. Both from NTI-MIIS missile database.

71. "Iran's Chinese Shopping List," *Iran Brief*, October 1, 1996. "N-Tech Sold to Iran," *Asian Recorder*, December 23–31, 1996, 26128.

72. James Bruce, "Iran and China in $4.5 Billion Partnership," *Jane's Defence Weekly*, September 11, 1996, 3.

73. Mann, "China Alleged Top Trafficker in Mass Destruction Weapons," 42.

74. "China Joins Forces with Iran on Short-Range Missile," *WT*, June 17, 1997, A3. "China, Iran Align to Develop Short-Range Missiles: Report," *Times of India*, June 18, 1997, 14.

75. "China Aids Syria and Iran in Long Range Missile Development," *Middle East Newsletter*, June 4, 2000, NTI-CNS missile database.

76. "China Still Shipping Arms Despite Pledge," *WT*, April 15, 1999, NTI-MIIS missile database.

77. *Jane's Strategic Weapons Systems*, 100–101.

78. "U.S. Protests China Arms Move," *WT*, December 7, 1998, NTI MIIS missile database.

79. Kan, *China and Proliferation*, 9–10.

80. Central Intelligence Agency, "Unclassified Report to Congress on Acquisition of Technology Relating to Weapons of Mass Destruction and Advanced Conventional Munitions," July 1–December 31, 2003, www.cia.gov/cia/reports/index.html.

81. "Iran Enhances Existing Weaponry by Optimizing Shahab-3 Ballistic Missile," *Jane's M&R*, February 2004, 8.

82. "News in Brief," *Jane's Defence Weekly*, January 7, 1989, 8.

83. "Five Nations to Help Iran with Satellites," *Defense News*, August 10–16, 1998, NTI-CNS missile database.

84. Eric Croddy, "China's Role in the Chemical and Biological Disarmament Regimes, *Nonproliferation Review* 9, no. 1 (Spring 2002): 16–47.

85. Pan Zhenqiang, ed., *Guoji Caijun yu Junbei Kongzhi* [International Disarmament and Arms Control] (Beijing: National Defense University Press, 1996), 167; cited in ibid, 32.

86. Cordesman, *Iranian Arms Transfers*, 29.

87. Katzman, *Iran: Arms and Weapons of Mass Destruction Suppliers*, 2.

88. Regarding the enduring memory of the Yinhe incident in China's foreign policy circles, see David M. Lampton, *Same Bed, Different Dreams: Managing U.S.-China Relations, 1989–2000* (Berkeley: University of California Press, 2001), 77–78.

89. Nayan Chanda, "Drifting Apart," FEER 156, no. 34 (August 26, 1993), 10–11.

90. Regarding the Yin He incident, see Patrick Tyler, *A Great Wall, Six Presidents and China: An Investigative History* (New York: A Century Foundation Book, 1999), 396–400.

91. Foreign Ministry Statement, *Rmrb*, September 5, 1993, FBIS-CHI-93–171, September 7, 1993, 2–3.

92. Ibid.

93. Ibid.

94. "Foreign Ministry Holds Regular News Conference," Xinhua and AFP, July 18, 1995, FBIS-CHI-95–137, July 18, 1995, 1.

95. R. Jeffery Smith, "Chinese Exports Fuel Iran Effort on Poison Gas," *International Herald Tribune* (hereafter *IHT*), March 9–10, 1996.

96. "Iran Denies U.S. Charges on Chemical Weapons," Xinhua, November 12, 1995, FBIS-CHI-95–218, November 13, 1995, 2.

97. "China: Paper Cites CIA Report on Weapons to Iran," *Kongping Kuo Jih Pao* (Hong Kong), September 15, 1997, FBIS-CHI-97–262.

98. "Nerve Gas Produced with China's Help," *Asian Recorder*, July 2–8, 1998, 27397. "Britain Reports China Helping Iran to Make 'Advanced' Nerve Gas," *China Reform Monitor*, no. 78 (June 1, 1998): 1.

99. CIA, "Unclassified Report to Congress" (see note 80 above).

100. "Spokesman Denies Missile Technology Sale to Iran," Xinhua, February 13, 1992, FBIS-CHI-92–030, 1.

101. AFP, Hong Kong, July 18, 1995, FBIS-CHI-95–137, July 18, 1995, 1.

102. "Spokesman Refutes U.S. Allegations over Missiles," *China Daily*, November 24, 2000, 1l.

103. "AFP:PRC Foreign Ministry 'Statement' on U.S. Sanctions on Weapons Trade with Iran," January 25, 2002, Dialog.

104. James Bruce, "China's $4.5 Billion Deal with Iran Cools as Funds Fail," *Jane's Defence Weekly* 26, no. 11 (August 6, 1997): 14.

105. Discussions in Beijing, September 2004. This observation was made in the context of Sino-Iranian trade generally, not exclusively military trade, but logic suggests that the same principle would operate in military and civilian sectors.

8 / CHINA-IRAN COOPERATION AND THE UNITED STATES

1. U.S. Senate, Foreign Affairs Committee, *Hearing on the Subcommittee on Near East and South Asian Affairs*, April 19, 1997, quoted in Barry Rubin, "China's Middle East Strategy," in *China and the Middle East: The Quest for Influence*, ed. P. R. Kumaraswamy (New Delhi: Sage Publications, 1999), 114.

2. *China: Arms Control and Disarmament*, Information Office of the State Council of the PRC, November 1995, *BR*, November 27–December 3, 1995, 13 (hereafter Arms Control White Paper).

3. Ibid., 18.

4. Ibid., 13.

5. "'Special Article' on Qian-Christopher Talks," *Wen wei bao* (Hong Kong), April 19, 1995, FBIS-CHI-95–086, May 4, 1995.

6. Patrick Tyler, "China Said to Offer Iran U.S. Nuclear Technology," *IHT*, October 24, 1985, 1, 2. "China, Iran Playing Nuclear Footsie," *U.S. News and World Report*, November 4, 1985, 9.

7. Nayan Chanda, "Technology Cocooned," *FEER*, November 5, 1987, 34.

8. "China Is Iran's Chief Source of Weapons, U.S. Officials Say," *IHT*, August 27, 1986. "Sales Complaints," *Aviation Week and Space Technology*, September 1, 1986, 35.

9. *Facts on File, 1987*, 145, 420.

10. James Mann, *About Face: A History of America's Curious Relation with China, from Nixon to Clinton* (New York: Alfred Knopf, 1999), 168.

11. "China, Despite Denials, Is Reported Arming Iran," *IHT*, October 29, 1987. "U.S. Retaliates against Chinese for Sales to Iran," *Wall Street Journal* (hereafter *WSJ*), October 22, 1987, A35.

12. "U.S. Says China May Be Sending Iran More and Perhaps Deadlier Missiles," *IHT*, December 25–26, 1987.

13. Lu, *The Dynamics of Foreign Policy*, 155 n. 13.

14. R. Bates Gill, "Two Steps Forward, One Step Back: The Dynamics of Chinese Nonproliferation and Arms Control Policy-Making in an Era of Reform," in *The Making of Chinese Foreign and Security Policy in the Era of Reform*, ed. David M. Lampton (Stanford, CA: Stanford University Press, 2001), 268.

15. "Gulf over Arms Sales," *FEER*, February 25, 1988, 13. "U.S. Suspects China Will Widen Arms Sales to Iran," *NYT*, March 13, 1988, 11.

16. "U.S. Concerned Beijing May Sell Jets to Iran," *IHT*, March 14, 1988.

17. "U.S. Alarmed at China's Middle East Arms Sales," *Independent*, September 7, 1988.

18. "Tracking Arms: A Study in Smoke," *WP*, April 3, 1999, 3.

19. "Iran Nuclear Chronology, 1991." Jeffrey Smith, "Officials Say Iran Is Seeking Nuclear Weapons Capability," *WP*, October 30, 1991, A1.

20. "An Iranian Bomb," *WP*, January 12, 1992, C7. "U.S., Investigating Chinese Nuclear Assistance to Iran," *LAT*, October 31, 1991, A4.

21. For example, comments by Deputy President Ayatollah Mohajerani in mid-1991, quoted in "A 15 Year Ambition," *Mednews*, June 8, 1992.

22. Jeffrey Smith, "China-Iran Nuclear Tie Long Known," *WP*, October 31, 1991, A1. Douglas Frantz, "U.S. Investigating Chinese Nuclear Assistance to Iran," *LAT*, October 31, 1991, A4.

23. "Iran Determined to Get A-Bomb, U.S. Believes," *LAT*, March 17, 1992, 1.

24. Chen Guoqing, letter to the editor, *WP*, July 2, 1991.

25. Arms Control White Paper, 18.

26. "Qian Qichen Speaks on Nuclear Export Policy," Zhongguo xinwenshe, April 19, 1995, *FBIS-CHI-95-076*, April 20, 1995, 2–3.

27. Qian, *Waijiao shi ji*, 190.

28. James Baker, *The Politics of Diplomacy: Revolution, War and Peace, 1989–1992* (New York: Putnam's Sons, 1995), 594.

29. Robert L. Suettinger, *Beyond Tiananmen: The Politics of U.S.-China Relations, 1989–2000* (Washington, DC: Brookings Institution Press, 2003), 130–31. Thomas Friedman, "Baker's China Trip Fails to Produce Pledge on Rights," *NYT*, November 18, 1991, 1, 4.

30. "Baker Fails to Win Any Commitments in Talks in Beijing," *NYT*, November 17, 1991, 1.

31. Gerald Seib, "Bush Lifts Sanctions against China in Expectation of End of Missile Sales," *WSJ*, February 24, 1992.

32. Suettinger, *Beyond Tiananmen*, 133.

33. U.S. Department of State, *Adherence to and Compliance with Arms Control and Nonproliferation Agreements and Commitments* (Washington, DC: U.S. Department of State, [2003]), 40.

34. "Unclassified Report to Congress on the Acquisition of Technology relating to Weapons of Mass Destruction and Advanced Conventional Munitions, January 1 through June 30, 2002," http://www.cia.gov/cia/reports/721_reports/jan_jun2002.html.

35. "Chinese Ire at U.S. Could Prompt More Arms Sales to Iran," *Defense News*, September 14–20, 1992, 19.

36. "PRC to Boycott UN Arms Talks," *Qol Yisra'el* (Jerusalem), September 16, 1992, *FBIS-NES-181*, September 17, 1992, 22.

37. Bill Gertz, "U.S., China Clash over Missile Deal," *WT*, October 4, 1994, A8. Barbara Starr, "U.S. Links Chinese Ties to Missile Exports," *Jane's Defence Weekly* 22, no. 15 (October 15, 1994): 5.

38. "The Secret Missile Deal," *Time*, June 30, 1997, 29.

39. "Boucher Supports China's Commitment Not to Aid Others' Nuclear Pro-

grams," see answers to question, November 22, 2000, http://usembassy.state.gov/posts/pk1/wwwh00112203.html (accessed December 2, 2004).

40. Steve Coll, "u.s. Halted Nuclear Bid by Iran," wp, November 17, 1992, 1, 30.

41. Willy Wo-lap Lam, *The Era of Jiang Zemin* (Singapore: Prentice Hall, 1999), 173–74.

42. Gertz, "u.s., China Clash over Missile Deal," A8.

43. See Warren Christopher, *Chances of a Lifetime* (New York: Scribner, 2001), 243–44.

44. Quoted in Lampton, *Same Bed, Different Dreams*, 172.

45. Reuters, Beijing, "China Says Taiwan Key Issue at u.s. Arms Talks," November 5, 1996, nti-cns database.

46. Kan, *China and Proliferation*, 20.

47. Steven Holmes, "u.s. Determines China Violated Pact on Missiles," nyt, August 25, 1993, 1, 6.

48. Tyler, *A Great Wall, Six Presidents and China*, 396.

49. "Official on Afghanistan, Nuclear Program," *Abrar* (Tehran), April 15, 1993, fbis-nes-93–800, April 28, 1993, 72.

50. "prc's Li Lanqing Defends Nuclear Project in Iran," *Al-Hayah* (London), fbis-nes-93–133, July 14, 1993, 14

51. Bingham Kennedy Jr., "Curbing Chinese Missile Sales: From Imposing to Negotiating China's Adherence to the mtcr," *Journal of Northeast Asian Studies* 15, no. 4 (Spring 1996): 57–68.

52. Ibid., 63.

53. "Joint United States—People's Republic of China Statement on Missile Proliferation," October 4, 1994; emphasis added. Available at the nti-miis Web site database, at http://www.nti.org/db/china/engdocs/mtcrusch.htm.

54. Sciolino, "c.i.a. Report Says Chinese Sent Iran Arms Components," 1, 6.

55. "'Special Article' on Qian-Christopher Talks," *Wen wei bao* (Hong Kong), April 19, 1995, fbis-chi-95–086, May 4, 1995, 6–7.

56. "Iranian General Defects," *Jerusalem Post*, June 21, 1995, 5.

57. Suettinger, *Beyond Tiananmen*, 240.

58. Christopher Wren, "Mixed Signals over Status of Iran Deal," nyt, September 30, 1995, A4.

59. "Iran Nuclear Chronology, 1995."

60. Barton Gellman, "Reappraisal Led to New China Policy," wp, June 22, 1998, 1.

61. "Iran: u.s. Attempts to Block Chinese Nuclear Cooperation Viewed," Tehran Voice of the iri, March 25, 1996, fbis-nes-96–039, March 26, 1996, 63.

62. Gellman, "Reappraisal," 1.

63. Ibid.

64. "News Briefing, Office of Assistant Secretary of Defense (Public Affairs)," no

date but regarding December 1996 visit by China's defense minister, http://www
.defenselink.mil/news/Dec1996/x121096_x1209bkg.html.

65. "China, u.s. Agree on Defense Contracts, Disagree on Iran," *Times of India*,
December 11, 1996, 12.

66. Ibid.

67. Suettinger, *Beyond Tiananmen*, 269–70.

68. "China's May 11, 1996 Pledge Not to Provide Assistance to Unsafeguarded
Nuclear Facilities," Monterey Institute of International Studies, http://cns.miis.edu/
iiop/cnsdata.

69. Suettinger, *Beyond Tiananmen*, 270, 317.

70. "Text: Bader on Sino-American Relations, u.s. Policy Options," April 23, 1997,
http://www.pnl.gov/china/bader.htm.

71. *Proliferation: Chinese Case Studies*, statement of Robert J. Einhorn, Deputy
Assistant Secretary of State for Nonproliferation, Bureau of Political-Military Affairs,
Department of States, before the Subcommittee on International Security, Proliferation
and Federal Services, of the Committee on Governmental Affairs, u.s. Senate, April
10, 1997, http://www.fas.org/spp/starwars/congress/1997_h/s970410e.htm.

72. "Chinese to Deliver Hexplant, despite Assurances," *Iran Brief*, January 6, 1997.

73. "Iran Nuclear Chronology, 1996."

74. "China Has Not Halted Military Cooperation with Iran," *Kayhan International*
(Tehran), December 25, 1996, 1.

75. Steven Myers, "u.s., Asserting Iran Link, Bars 2 Chinese Firms," *NYT*, May 23,
1997, 1.

76. Mark Hibbs, "China Agrees to End Nuclear Trade with Iran When Two Projects
Completed," *NuclearFuel*, no. 3 (1997): 3–4.

77. Suettinger, *Beyond Tiananmen*, 318. Gellman, "Reappraisal."

78. Evan S. Medeiros, "Rebuilding Bilateral Consensus: Assessing u.s.-China Arms
Control and Nonproliferation Achievements," *Nonproliferation Review* 8, no. 1 (Spring
2001): 134.

79. "China's Missile Exports and Assistance to Iran," NTI-CNS Fact Sheet, on NTI-
MIIS database, at http://www.nti.org/db/china/miranpos.htm.

80. Gellman, "Reappraisal."

81. Gill, "Two Steps Forward," 269.

82. Hibbs, "China Agrees to End Nuclear Trade," 3–4.

83. "1985 u.s.-China Nuclear Cooperation Agreement (NCA)," on NTI-MIIS database.

84. Reuters, October 22, 1997, NTI-MIIS database.

85. Joseph Fitchett, "A New China Embraces Nuclear Nonproliferation," *IHT*,
December 11, 1997, 1.

86. Barton Gellman and John Pomfret, "u.s. Actions Stymied China Sale to Iran," *wp*, March 13, 1998, A10.

87. See semiannual "Unclassified Report to Congress on the Acquisition of Technology Relating to Weapons of Mass Destruction and Advanced Conventional Munitions," by Nonproliferation Center, Director of Central Intelligence. Most reports are available at http://www.cia.gov/cia/reports/.

88. "nrc Issues Licenses Allowing Westinghouse to Export Nuclear Reactor Equipment and Fuel to China," nrc News, no. 05–037, February 25, 2005, http://www.nrc.gov.org/. Confirmation that this was the first significant sale to China was given by Kevin Burke, Senior International Relations Officer, Nuclear Regulatory Commission. Personal communication with the author, March 7, 2005.

89. "1985 u.s.-China Nuclear Cooperation Agreement (nca)," on nti-cns database.

90. "Cohen to Urge Iran Missile Sale Halt," *Financial Times*, January 19, 1998, 4.

91. "China's Missile Exports and Assistance to Iran," nti-miis database.

92. Lampton, *Same Bed, Different Dreams*, 174–75.

93. Jim Mann, "u.s. Takes New Tack on China Arms Exports," *lat*, October 5, 2000, 1.

94. "People's Republic of China Foreign Ministry Spokesperson's Statement," November 21, 2000, nti-miis database; emphasis added.

95. "Statement by Acting Assistant Secretary Richard Boucher," November 21, 2000, nti-cns database.

96. "People's Republic of China Foreign Ministry Spokesperson's Statement," November 21, 2000, nti-cns database.

97. "China and India's Ballistic Missiles, Nuclear Warheads and Nuclear Tests," on the Web site of the Indian Embassy, http://www.indianembassy.org/pic/congress/crs-newt.htm.

98. "Arms Control and Nonproliferation Sanctions against China," nti-miis database.

99. Phillip C. Saunders and Stephanie C. Lieggi, "What's behind u.s. Nonproliferation Sanctions against Norinco?" May 30, 2003, Center for Nonproliferation Studies, Monterey Institute of International Studies, http://cns.miis.edu.

100. afx News, Beijing, May 23, 2003, LexisNexis.

101. Amid Afghan War, China Sells Missiles to M.E.," Middle East Newsline, 3, no. 415 (October 31, 2001), http://www.menewsline.com/stories/2001/november/11_01_1.html.

102. Saunders and Lieggi, "What's behind u.s. Nonproliferation Sanctions?"

103. "Briefing by Mr. Liu Jieyi, Director General of Arms Control and Disarmament Dept., mfa, on the Promulgation of Regulations on Export Control of Missile and

Missile-related Items and Technologies and the Control List," August 27, 2002, NTI-CNS database.

104. Saunders and Lieggi, "What's behind U.S. Nonproliferation Sanctions?"

105. Phillip C. Saunders, "Preliminary Analysis of Chinese Missile Technology Export Control List, Preliminary Conclusions," September 6, 2002, Center for Nonproliferation Studies, Monterey Institute of International Studies.

106. Michael Evans, "Tehran Upgrades Chinese Missile" *Times* (London), January 11, 2000.

107. Bill Gertz, "U.S. Sanctions China Firm for Sale of Missile Steel to Iran," WT, May 26–June 1, 2003, 22.

108. Susan Lawrence, "U.S.—China Relations," FEER, November 6, 2003, 32.

109. Kan, *China and Proliferation*, 9.

110. "Transcript: Bush, China's Hu Jintao Discuss North Korea, SARS, Taiwan," June 1, 2003, U.S. Embassy, Tel Aviv, http://telaviv.usembassy.gov/publish/press/2003/june/060202.html (accessed May 24, 2004).

111. "AFP:PRC FM Spokesman Expresses 'Strong Opposition' to U.S. Sanctions over Missiles," September 21, 2003, Dialog.

9 / THE SINO-IRANIAN ENERGY-ECONOMIC RELATIONSHIP

1. PRC Ministry of Commerce Web site (hereafter Shangwubu Web site), at http://www.mofcom.gov.cn/ (accessed September 2004).

2. "Vice President Cited on Relations with China," TT, May 25, 1995.

3. *Zhongguo waijiao gaijian, 1988*, 104.

4. Shangwubu Web site.

5. "Construction Jihad Minister Returns from PRC," Tehran Domestic Service, December 15, 1987, FBIS-NES-87-240, 63.

6. *Zhongguo waijiao gaijian, 1988*, 104. "Fisheries to Purchase 36 Trawlers from PRC," Tehran IRNA, August 18, 1987, FBIS-NES-87, August 18, 1987, 55.

7. "PRC Deputy Foreign Minister Arrives 15 August," Tehran IRNA, FBIS-NES-88–158, August 16, 1988, 54.

8. "Iran Economic Delegation in China," TT, September 20, 1988.

9. "Tian Jiyun Meets Iranian Vice Premier," Xinhua, September 19, 1988, FBIS-CHI-88–182, 18. "Iran's Mirzadeh Continues Visit," Tehran IRNA, September 20, 1988, FBIS-CHI-88–183, 18.

10. "Confers with Li Peng," Xinhua, September 22, 1988, FBIS-CHI-88–184, 25.

11. *Zhongguo waijiao gaijian, 1989*, 98.

12. "Sino-Iran Ties Growth Discussed," TT, October 19, 1988.

13. "Discusses Machine Exports," Tehran IRNA, November 1, 1988, FBIS-NES-88–212, November 2, 1988, 66.

14. "Industrial Cooperation Planned," Tehran IRNA, November 6, 1988, FBIS-NES-88–216, November 8, 1988, 66.

15. *Zhongguo waijiao gaijian, 1989*, 98.

16. "Bilateral Relations Viewed," Beijing radio, December 17, 1988, FBIS-CHI-88–243, 16.

17. *Zhongguo waijiao gaijian, 1989*, 98.

18. "Iran Turns East: A Chronology of Iranian Relations with the Eastern Bloc and China," January–June 1989," *MEED*, July 10, 1989, 3.

19. "China Seeks Economic Ties with Iran," *TT*, March 5, 1989, 1.

20. "Musavi Welcomes Expansion of Relations with China," *TT*, March 7, 1989.

21. An Baojun, "Yilang jingji xiankuang ji zhong, yi maoyi guanxi" [Iran's Current Economic Situation and Sino-Iranian Trade Relations], *Xiya feizhou* [West Asia and Africa], no. 4 (1995): 66–68.

22. *Shijie chanyou guo, zhongdong dichu* [Oil Producing Countries of the World, Middle East Region], ed. Wu Yaowen (Beijing: Foreign Affairs Office, Information Research Center, China National Petroleum Corporation, August 1998), 51.

23. Interview with retired PRC ambassador to IRI, Beijing, September 2004.

24. "PRC: Growing Economic Cooperation with Iran Detailed," Xinhua, November 11, 1995, Dialog.

25. Shangwubu Web site.

26. Interview with Chinese diplomat with extensive Middle East experience.

27. "China Seeks Economic Ties with Iran," *TT*, March 5, 1989, 1.

28. "PRC Ready to Aid with Iran Construction," Xinhua, March 31, 1989, FBIS-CHI-89–062, April 3, 1989, 15. "Iran-China Sign Construction Pact," *TT*, April 8, 1989.

29. Saeed Laylaz, *The Era of Construction: A Narration of Eight Years of Construction during the Presidency of Hashemi Rafsanjani* (Tehran: Nashr-e Kelid, 1997), 3:334.

30. Noble metals are those such as silver, gold, and platinum that do not oxidize in air. Copper, aluminum, and mercury are sometimes included in this category.

31. "Iranian Minister Begins Talks on Mineral Ties," Tehran Voice of the IRI, November 15, 1991, FBIS-CHI-91–224, 16.

32. "Coal Mining Agreement Signed with Iran," Tokyo Kyodo, November 4, 1991, FBIS-CHI-91–219, 15.

33. "Mining, Geology Agreement Signed with Iran," Xinhua, September 27, 1989, FBIS-CHI-89–187, 15.

34. Laylaz, *The Era of Construction*, 3:344.

35. "Economic Cooperation Memo Signed with PRC," Tehran Voice of the IRI, November 21, 1991, FBIS-NES-91–226, November 22, 1991, 56.

36. "Company to Build 'Modern Copper Mill' for Iran," Xinhua, November 24, 1993, FBIS-CHI-93–228, 9.

37. "PRC: Iran to Jointly Invest in Copper Mines," Xinhua, July 10, 1996, FBIS-CHI-96–140, 57.

38. "Iran: Minister on Accord with PRC to Exploit Songon Copper Mines," Tehran IRNA, July 10, 1996, FBIS-NES-96–134, July 11, 1996, 44.

39. "Iran, China Ink MoU on Mining," TT, October 14, 1998. "Iran, China Discuss Mineral Cooperation," TT, October 12, 1998.

40. "Iran, China to Cooperate in Mining Sector," TT, November 1, 2000.

41. "Chinese Firm Wins Aluminum Project," Middle Eastern Economic Developments, November 2001, from IranExpert, http://www.iranexpert.com/.

42. "Coal Mining Agreement Signed with Iran," Tokyo Kyodo, November 4, 1991, FBIS-CHI-91–219, 15.

43. "Iran Seeks Joint Project in Coal Industry," China Daily, June 3, 1992, FBIS-CHI-92–108, 6.

44. "Iranian Steel Company to Buy Technology from China," TT, August 20, 2001.

45. "Iran-China Joint Economic Commission to Meet this Year," TT, January 24, 1999. "Iran-China Biannual Trade Down by 14.5%," TT, August 15, 1999.

46. "Signs Memorandum on Cooperation," Xinhua, July 31, 1989, FBIS-CHI-89–146, 10. "Iranian Heavy Industries Official Visits," Tehran IRNA, July 22, 1989, FBIS-CHI-89–140, July 24, 1989, 11.

47. "Industrial Ties with PRC to Top $500 million," Tehran IRNA, August 2, 1989, FBIS-NES-89–150, August 7, 1989, 56.

48. "Industry Minister, PRC Counterpart Comment," Tehran Voice of the IRI, December 14, 1991, FBIS-NES-91–241, December 16, 1991, 81.

49. "Iran to Produce Alkaline Watch Batteries," TT, July 27, 1999.

50. "Medium-Term Financial Provision Contract Signed between Iran and China," TT, January 22, 2000.

51. "Iran and China to Establish Cigarette Factory," TT, November 25, 2000.

52. "China Imports $30 Mn Petrochemicals from Iran," TT, July 23, 2001.

53. "China to Build Auto Plant in Iran," Xinhua, February 20, 2003, Dialog.

54. Shangwubu Web site.

55. "Sichuan Institute Signs Export Accord with Iran," Xinhua, April 19, 1989, FBIS-CHI-89–074, 8.

56. "Iranian Energy Ministry Delegation Visits," August 5, 1989, FBIS-CHI-89-155, 6.

57. "Further on Pact to Export Power Equipment to Iran," Hong Kong Standard, March 13, 1995, FBIS-CHI-95–050, 6–7. The article gave the value of the contract in billions. I assume that was an error. The value must have been millions.

58. Shangwubu Web site.

59. "PRC: Iran's Rafsanjani Cuts Ribbon for PRC-Built Power Plant," Xinhua, April 23, 1996, Dialog.

60. "China: Shanghai to Export Power Equipment to Iran, Azerbaijan," Zhongguo xinwen she, March 22, 1997, Dialog.

61. "Iranian Economic Delegation in China to Talk on Energy," *TT*, March 8, 2001.

62. "PRC Company Begins Construction of Water Conservancy Project in Iran," Xinhua, August 30, 2001, Dialog.

63. Shangwubu Web site.

64. "Beijing, Tehran to Begin Agricultural Cooperation," Xinhua, November 8, 1993, FBIS-CHI-93–218, 21–22.

65. "Anhui Exports Electrical Equipment to Iran," Xinhua, February 16, 1995, FBIS-CHI-95–034, 11.

66. "Iran to Buy 27 Multi-Purpose Ships," *TT*, January 11, 1998. "Iran Takes Delivery of Chinese-Built Container Ship," *TT*, August 30, 2000. "Iran-Lorestan Ship Delivered to Iran," *TT*, April 14, 1999.

67. "Iran an Important Trading Partner of China," *TT*, August 25, 1999. "Chinese Firm Hopes to Challenge Japan and Korea with Iranian Supertankers," *TT*, August 19, 2000.

68. "China Eximbank Supports Export of Oil Tankers," Xinhua, March 17, 2000, Dialog. "China Begins Manufacturing Five 300,000–Ton Crude Oil Carriers for Iran," Xinhua, August 18, 2000, Dialog.

69. "First VLCC Oil Tanker Produced in China Delivered to Iranian Owner," Xinhua, August 31, 2002, Dialog.

70. "Agreement on Railway Cooperation with China Signed," Tehran Voice of the IRI, December 20, 1992, FBIS-NES-92–245, December 21, 1992.

71. "Leaders Arrive in Iran to Inaugurate Trans-Asian Railway," Xinhua, May 13, 1996, FBIS-CHI-96–093, May 13 1996, 14.

72. "Minister Signs Railways Cooperation Agreement with Iran," Xinhua, May 16, 1996, FBIS-CHI-96–015, May 30, 1996, 9.

73. Shangwubu Web site.

74. "PRC's Huang Ju Meets Iranian Minister, Comments on Construction Projects," Xinhua, November 10, 2003, Dialog.

75. "Iran Roads Minister Calls China Visit Successful," Tehran IRNA, November 12, 2003, and "Iran: Minister Says China to Fund Major Part of $10 Billion Investment in Roads," Tehran IRNA, November 12, 2003, Dialog.

76. Interview, Tehran, November 2004.

77. "China-Made Subway Fulfills Iranian Dream," Xinhuanet, June 15, 2004, Iran Defence News, http://www.iranexpert.com/2004/subway13june.htm.

78. Interview, Tehran, November 2004.

79. "China-Made Subway Fulfills Iranian Dream," Xinhuanet, June 15, 2004.

80. "Massive Metroline Deal Inked with Iran," Iran Defence News, May 17, 2004, http://www.iranexpert.com/2004/metro17may.htm.

81. Interview, Tehran, November 2004.

82. CITIC International Cooperation Company Web site, http://www.citicicc.com .cn/ (hereafter CITIC Web site).

83. "Government Loans Iran $50 Million for Cement Plants," Xinhua, April 15, 1994, FBIS-CHI-94–071, 22.

84. "PRC: Banking Consortium Finances Tehran Subway Project," Xinhua, July 25, 1996, FBIS-CHI-96–145, 44–45. "Iran: Press Criticized for Mistakes in Report on PRC Loan," Hamshahri, Tehran, FBIS-NES-96–152, August 6, 1996, 78. Dialog.

85. "PRC: Changchun Plant Wins Iran Subway Carriage Contract," Xinhua, August 26, 1996, Dialog.

86. CITIC Web site.

87. "China: Changchun to Export Passenger Trains to Iran," Xinhua, May 30, 1997, Dialog.

88. "China: Ships with Railroad Equipment Leave for Iran," Xinhua, April 16, 1998, Dialog.

89. "Major Events in Iran-China Relations during 1999," http://octopus.cdut.edu .cn/slr/travel/1/intro-5.htm.

90. "Iran New Subway Section Constructed by China Open to Traffic," *Rmrb*, March 19, 2002, online version, http://english.peopledaily.com.cn/.

91. "China to Build Subway Worth $100 Million in Iran," TT, May 5, 2001.

92. "Chinese Company to Invest $100 million in Iran's Subway Project," TT, February 26, 2001.

93. "Massive Metro Line Deals Inked with Iran," *People's Daily* online [*Renmin wang*], May 17, 2004, http://english.peopledaily.com.cn/.

94. "Chinese Delegation Visits Tehran-Karaj Subway," TT, February 9, 1999.

95. CITIC Web site.

96. Erica S. Downs, "The Chinese Energy Security Debate," *China Quarterly*, no. 177, (March 2004): 21–41.

97. Interview, Beijing, September 2004.

98. "Petroleum Chief Views Cooperation with Iran," Xinhua, May 11, 1995, FBIS-CHI-95–092, May 12, 1995, 10–11.

99. "China: Premier Li Peng Meets Iranian Petroleum Minister," Xinhua, May 26, 1997, Dialog.

100. An Weihua, "Zhongguo yu zhongdong de nengyuan hezuo" [China's Energy Cooperation in the Middle East], *Xiya feizhou* [West Asia and Africa], no. 1 (2001): 12–16.

101. *Shijie chanyou guo, zhongdong dichu*, 51.

102. The text of the act as passed by the House of Representatives in June is available at http://www.fas.org/irp/congress/1996_cr/h9606186.htm. Background on the law is available at *Facts on File, 1996*, 444, 449–50.

103. *Xiangmu kexing yanjiu jexu jingji, sanshu yu shuzhu, 2000* [Research on the Economic and Technological Feasibility of Projects, 2000] (Beijing: Sinopec, jingji jishu yanjiu yuan, 2000), 5–6.

104. "China National Petroleum Corporation Wins 1st Gas Drilling Contract in Iran," Xinhua, August 20, 2000, Dialog.

105. "Iran, China Launch Oil, Gas Exploration Project in Esfahan Province," Tehran Voice of the IRI, December 5, 2001, via IranExpert.

106. "Iran: Official Says Drilling in Isfahan Likely to Reach 'Huge' Gas, Oil Reserves," Tehran IRNA, May 20, 2004, Dialog.

107. "Iran Reviewing Japan's Request to Extend Deadline to Bid on Azadegan Oil Field," Tehran IRNA, December 17, 2003, Dialog. "Daily: Minister Says Iran Cancels Japan's Preferential Rights on Azadegan Oil Field," Tehran IRNA, September 20, 2003, Dialog.

108. "China Studying Desirability of Investing in Large Gas, Oil Project in Iran," Moscow Interfax, July 11, 2003, Dialog.

109. "China Willing to Invest in Iranian Oil, Gas Projects," Tehran IRNA, July 6, 2003. Dialog.

110. "Iran: IRNA Carries 'Economic News Digest' Feature, 16 July," Tehran IRNA, July 16, 2003, Dialog.

111. John C. K. Daly, "The Dragon's Drive for Caspian Oil," *China Brief* (Jamestown Foundation) 4, no. 20 (May 13, 2004); online at brdcst@jamestown.org/.

112. "Iran Envoy to Japan Interviewed on Signing of Azadegan Oil Field Contract," Tehran, Iran, February 25, 2004, Dialog.

113. Matt Pottinger, "China and Iran near Agreement on Huge Oil Pact," WSJ, November 1, 2004.

114. "Oil Importer Lands LNG Contract with Iran," March 16, 2004; "Report: China, Iran Sign US$20 Billion Gas Deal," March 19, 2004. Both at http://english.peopledaily.com.cn/.

115. "Zhongguo wang: China, Iran Sign Biggest Oil, Gas Deal," Zhongguo wang (China Internet), Beijing, October 31, 2004, Dialog. "Chinese Foreign Minister to Visit Iran 6 Nov after Brief Stay in UAE," Tehran IRNA, November 5, 2004, Dialog. "China to Cooperate with Iran in Oil, Gas Sectors," Tehran IRNA, December 27, 2004, Dialog.

116. "Iran: Iran's Ambassador to China Says Iran, China to Have Long-Term Cooperation," *Tehran Sharq*, December 21, 2004, Dialog.

117. "Chinese Foreign Minister to Visit Iran 6 Nov after Brief Stay in UAE," Tehran IRNA, November 5, 2004, Dialog.

118. "AFP Cites Business Weekly: Iran Wants to Give Preference to PRC for Oil, Gas Imports," AFP, Hong Kong, November 6, 2004, Dialog.

119. "Geo-economic Factors of Oil and Gas," Iranian Embassy in Poland, http://www.iranemb.warsaw.pl/chap3V.htm.

120. Fereidun Fesharaki and Mehdi Varzi, "Investment Opportunities Starting to Open up in Iran's Petroleum Sector," *Oil and Gas Journal* 98, no. 7 (February 14, 2000), accessed via Proquest, http://proquest.umi.com/. "China CNPC, Iran Oil Min Fail to Agree on Pipeline Finance," *Dow Jones Energy Service*, February 15, 2000, accessed via Factiva, http://www.factiva.com/.

121. "Tehran Presses Beijing on Neka-Tehran Bid," *Harts Asian Petroleum News* 4, no. 4 (January 31, 2000), Factiva.

122. "Iran, China Discuss Caspian Oil Cooperation, Exports, IRNA," Dow Jones Energy Service, February 22, 2000, Factiva.

123. "Iran Finishes the First Stage of Neka-Tehran Pipeline," Azer-Press, November 21, 2000, Factiva. Another source says the new Neka terminal had 260,000 cubic meters of crude oil storage capacity. "Sinopec Completes Renovation of Iranian Oil Refinery," Interfax China Business News, December 5, 2003, Factiva.

124. "China's Oil Giant Sinopec to Explore Oil in Iran," TT, January 14, 2001. Hooman Peimani, "Russia Turns to Iran for Oil Exports," *Asia Times* online, February 11, 2003, http://www.atimes.com/. "SIIRTEC to Revamp Sulfur Units for Iranian Refineries," TT, June 11, 2001.

125. "Iran: Report Discusses Inauguration of Neka Oil Project" [in Persian], *Tehran Sharq*, May 1, 2004, Dialog.

126. Interviews, Tehran, November 2004.

127. Ibid.

128. Ibid.

129. A Xinhua report of November 1996 also said that "the Bank of China system" had provided $1.5 billion in loans to support the export of Chinese machinery and technology to Iran. "PRC: Growing Economic Cooperation with Iran Detailed," Xinhua, November 11, 1996, Dialog.

130. Interview in Beijing with former PRC ambassador to IRI, September 2004.

131. Shangwubu Web site.

132. "PRC, India Reject Tehran Call for Anti-U.S. Alliance," *Al-Sharq al-Awsat* (London), March 7, 1994, FBIS-NES-94–046, March 9, 1994, 43.

133. "Talks Termed Successful," Tehran IRNA, August 5, 1987, FBIS-NES-87, 54.

134. Interview with retired high-ranking Chinese diplomat, Beijing, September 2004.

135. "PRC Trade Minister Signs Memorandum, Departs," Tehran Domestic Service, November 29, 1989, FBIS-NES-89–229, November 30, 1989, 47.

136. "China Daily on Growing Trade with Iran," FBIS-CHI-89-136, July 18, 1989, 11.

137. "Economic, Trade Talks with Iran Held in Beijing," Tehran IRNA, August 15, 1991, FBIS-CHI-91–159, 8. "Iran-China Building Relations on Common Grounds," TT, October 30, 1991.

10 / PATTERNS OF SINO-PERSIAN RELATIONS

1. United States president Harry Truman once lamented he could not find a "one-armed economist" after noting that his economic advisors always gave him policy advice in the form of "on the one hand" and "on the other hand"—a habit that Truman did not find conducive to easy policy decisions.

2. This formulation was used by several Chinese interlocutors during interviews in Beijing in September 2004.

3. Several sources report that Zhou actually stopped in Tehran in June 1965. Authoritative Chinese chronologies of Zhou Enlai and of Sino-Iranian relations, however, mention no such stopover.

4. Abidi, *China, Iran, and the Persian Gulf*, 104.

5. In terms of changes in China's regime, the Sino-Pakistani bond survived the profound transition between Mao Zedong and Deng Xiaoping. Other of China's alliances, for example, those with North Vietnam and Albania, did not.

6. "China Assisted Gwadar Port to Be Completed in Three Years," *Karachi Business Recorder*, September 16, 2002, Dialog.

7. Nadeem Malik, "China Pledges us$1 Bn Honeypot for Pakistan," *Asia Times online*, May 15, 2001, http://www.atimes.com/china/CD15Ad05.html.

8. "Finance Advisor Speaks on Jamali's China Visit," *Nation* (Islamabad), March 24, 2003, Dialog.

9. Information indicated on "General Map of Iran," 1:1,600,000 scale, Gitashenasi Geographical and Cartographic Institute, Tehran, April 2002.

10. Ibid.

11. "Mashhad-Bafq Railroad Operational by March," *Iran Daily*, October 23, 2004, 3.

12. "Comparison—Sino-Iranian Joint Communiqué," Xinhua, June 22, 2000, Dialog.

13. Andrew J. Bacevich, "The Real World War IV," *Wilson Quarterly* 29, no. 1 (Winter 2005): 36–61.

14. Abidi, *China, Iran, and the Persian Gulf*, 115.

15. Julie DaVanzo and Clifford Grammich, *Dire Demographics: Population Trends in the Russian Federation* (Santa Monica, CA: RAND, 2001).

Bibliography

ENGLISH-LANGUAGE SOURCES

Abidi, A. H. H. *China, Iran, and the Persian Gulf.* Atlantic Highlands, NJ: Humanities Press, 1982.

Aghazadeh, Reza. "Iran's Nuclear Policy: Peaceful, Transparent, Independent." Presentation to IAEA Headquarters, Vienna, Austria, May 6, 2003.

Agreement for Nuclear Cooperation between the United States and China, Communication from the President of the United States. Transmitting a report relating to the approval and implementation of the agreement for nuclear cooperation between the United States and the People's Republic of China pursuant to 42 U.S.C. 2153 (d). 105th Cong., 2nd sess., February 3, 1998. H. Doc. 105–197.

Ahrari, Ehsan. "Iran, China, and Russia: The Emerging Anti-U.S. Nexus?" *Security Dialogue* 32, no. 4 (December 2001): 453–66.

Alam, Asadollah. *The Shah and I: The Confidential Diary of Iran's Royal Court, 1969–1977.* London and New York: I. B. Tauris, 1991.

Alam, Shah. "The Changing Paradigm of Iranian Foreign Policy under Khatami." *Strategic Analysis* 24, no. 9 (December 2000).

Albright, David, and Cory Hinderstein. "The Centrifuge Connection." *Bulletin of the Atomic Scientists* 60, no. 2 (March–April 2004).

———. "The Iranian Gas Centrifuge Uranium Enrichment Plant at Natanz: Drawing from Commercial Satellite Images." Institute for Science and International Security, Washington, DC, March 14, 2003. http://www.isis.org/publications/iran/natanz03_02.html.

Ali, Salamat. "Courting the Imams." *Far Eastern Economic Review* 154, no. 40 (October 3, 1991): 29.

Arjomand, Said Amir. *The Turban and the Crown: The Islamic Revolution in Iran.* New York: Oxford University Press, 1988.

"Arms Control and Disarmament." Information Office of the State Council of the PRC. *Beijing Review* 38, no. 48 (November 27–December 3, 1995): 10–25.

Asian Recorder. New Delhi.

Awanohara, Susumu. "Unguided Missile." *Far Eastern Economic Review* 151, no. 14 (April 4, 1991): 13–14.

Azar, Edward E. "Soviet and Chinese Roles in the Middle East." *Problems of Communism* 28 (May–June 1979): 18–29.

Bacevich, Andrew J. "The Real World War IV." *Wilson Quarterly* 29, no. 1 (Winter 2005): 36–61.

Bader, Jeffrey. Statement of Jeffrey Bader, Deputy Assistant Secretary of State for East Asian and Pacific Affairs, Hearing before the Subcommittee on Asia and the Pacific, Committee on International Relations, House of Representatives. 105th Cong., 1st sess., April 23, 1997. http://wwwfas.org/spp/starwars/congress/1997_h/hfa44150_0.htm.

Baker, James. *The Politics of Diplomacy: Revolution, War and Peace, 1989–1992.* New York: Putnam's Sons, 1995.

"Ballistic Missile Shadow Lengthens." *Jane's IDR Extra* 2, no. 2 (February 1997): 1–7.

Balouji, Heidar Ali. "Iran's 'Nuclear Choice' Examined." *Financial Times* Global News Wire, October 1, 2003. http://lexisnexis.com/ (accessed April 2004).

Bani-Sadr, Abol Hassan. *My Turn to Speak: Iran, the Revolution and Secret Deals with the U.S.* Washington, DC: Brassey's, 1989.

Baum, Richard. *Burying Mao: Chinese Politics in the Age of Deng Xiaoping.* Princeton, NJ: Princeton University Press, 1994.

Beckwith, Christopher I. *The Tibetan Empire in Central Asia: A History of the Struggle for Great Power among Tibetans, Turks, Arabs, and Chinese during the Early Middle Ages.* Princeton, NJ: Princeton University Press, 1987.

Behbehani, Hashim S. H. *China's Foreign Policy in the Arab World, 1955–1975.* London and Boston: Kegan Paul International, 1981.

Beijing Review. Beijing.

Bermudez, Joseph S., Jr. *A History of Ballistic Missile Development in the DPRK.* Occasional Paper no. 2. Monterey, CA: Monterey Institute of International Studies, Center for Nonproliferation Studies, November 1999.

Bernstein, Richard, and Ross H. Munro. *The Coming Conflict with China.* New York: Alfred Knopf, 1997.

Bitzinger, Richard A. "Arms to Go: Chinese Arms Sales to the Third World." *International Security* 17, no. 2 (Fall 1992): 84–111.

Borkenau, Franz. *World Communism: A History of the Communist International.* Ann Arbor: University of Michigan Press, 1962.

Brady, Ann-Marie. *Making the Foreign Serve China: Managing Foreigners in the People's Republic of China*. Boulder, CO: Rowman and Littlefield, 2003.

Bruce, James. "China's $4.5 Billion Deal with Iran Cools as Funds Fail." *Jane's Defence Weekly* 26, no. 11 (August 6, 1997): 14.

Burke, S. M. *Pakistan's Foreign Policy: An Historical Analysis*. London: Oxford University Press, 1973.

Calabrese, John. "Peaceful or Dangerous Collaborators? China's Relations with the Gulf Countries." *Pacific Affairs* 65, no. 4 (Winter 1992–93): 471–85.

Carus, Seth, and James Bermudez. "Iran's Growing Missile Forces." *Jane's Defence Weekly* 10, no. 3 (July 23, 1988): 126–31.

Center for Nonproliferation Studies, Monterey Institute of International Studies. "China's Missile Exports and Assistance to Iran." http://cnsinfo.miis.edu/db/china/miranpos.htm.

Central Intelligence Agency. "Unclassified Report to Congress on Acquisition of Technology relating to Weapons of Mass Destruction and Advanced Conventional Munitions." Issued semiannually by the Director of Central Intelligence. Available at http://www.cia.gov/cia/reports/index.html.

Chanda, Nayan. "Drifting Apart." *Far Eastern Economic Review* 156, no. 34 (August 26, 1993): 10–11.

———. "Technology Cocooned." *Far Eastern Economic Review* 138, no. 45 (November 5, 1987): 34.

Chant, Christopher. *Air Defense Systems and Weapons: World AAA and SAM Systems in the 1990s*. London: Brassey's, 1989.

Cheng, Joseph Y. S., and Zhang Wankun. "Patterns and Dynamics of China's International Strategic Behavior." *Journal of Contemporary China* 11, no. 31 (May 2002): 235–50.

Cheung, Tai Ming. "Missile Refrain." *Far Eastern Economic Review* 152, no. 26 (June 27, 1991): 12–13.

———. "Strategic Triangle." *Far Eastern Economic Review* 154, no. 46 (November 14, 1991): 11–12.

"China Arms for Iran." *Asian Defense Journal*, June 1984, 104.

"China Backs off from Iran—Maybe." *Iran Brief*, November 11, 1997.

"The China-Iran Nuclear Cloud." *Middle East Defense News* 4, no. 20 (July 22, 1991).

"China Threatens to Call off $1 Billion Arms Deal with Iran." *International Defense DMS Intelligence* 6, no. 31 (July 30, 1984): 1.

China's Non-Proliferation Policy and Measures. Beijing: Information Office of the State Council of the PRC, December 2003.

"Chinese Shipments Violate Controls." *Jane's Defence Weekly* 23, no. 26 (July 1, 1995): 3.

"Chinese to Deliver Hexplant, despite Assurances." *Iran Brief*, January 6, 1997.

Christopher, Warren. *Chances of a Lifetime*. New York: Scribner, 2001.

Clad, James. "Iran Woos Peking." *Far Eastern Economic Review* 128, no. 23 (June 13, 1985): 44–45.

Clements, Walter. *The Arms Race and Sino-Soviet Relations*. Stanford, CA: Hoover Institution, 1988.

Clodfelter, Michael. *Warfare and Armed Conflicts: A Statistical Reference to Casualty and Other Figures, 1500–2000*. Jefferson, NC: McFarland, 2002.

Cordesman, Anthony H. *Iran and Iraq: The Threat from the Northern Gulf*. Boulder, CO: Westview Press, 1994.

———. "Iran and Nuclear Weapons." Unpublished manuscript. February 7, 2000.

———. *Iranian Arms Transfers: The Facts*. Washington, DC: Center for Strategic and International Studies, 2000.

Cordiere, Henri. *Cathay and the Way Thither, Being a Collection of Medieval Notices of China*. 2 vols. London: Hakluyt Society, 1913 and 1915.

Croddy, Eric. "China's Role in the Chemical and Biological Disarmament Regimes." *Nonproliferation Review* 9, no. 1 (Spring 2002): 16–47.

Daftari, Maryam. "The Main Commonalities in the Islamic Culture of the Muslims of Iran and the Hui Nationality of China." *China Report* (New Delhi) 35, no. 4 (1999): 457–66.

———. "Sino-Iran Relations and 'Encounters': Past and Present." *Iranian Journal of International Affairs* 7, no. 4 (Winter 1996): 854–76.

Daly, John C. K. "The Dragon's Drive for Caspian Oil." *China Brief* (Jamestown Foundation) 4, no. 20 (May 13, 2004). Online at brdcst@jamestown.org/.

Dillon, Michael. *Xinjiang—China's Muslim Far Northwest*. London and New York: Routledge and Curzon, 2004.

Downs, Erica S. "The Chinese Energy Security Debate." *China Quarterly*, no. 177 (March 2004): 21–41.

"DPRK and PRC Co-operation in the Iranian Missile Programme." *Jane's Intelligence Review*, April 1992, 151.

"Economy, Iran." *Middle East Economic Digest* 46, no. 8 (February 22, 2002): 24.

Ehteshami, Anoushiravan. "Iran's National Strategy: Striving for Regional Parity or Supremacy?" *International Defence Review* 4 (1994): 29–37.

Eikenberry, Karl W. *Explaining and Influencing Chinese Arms Transfers*. NcNair Paper no. 36. Washington, DC: National Defense University, Institute for National Strategic Studies, February 1995.

Einhorn, Robert. "China and Non-Proliferation." *In the National Interest*, April 2, 2003. http://www.inthenationalinterest.com/articles/.

———. *Proliferation: Chinese Case Studies*. Statement of Robert J. Einhorn, Deputy Assistant Secretary of State for Nonproliferation, Bureau of Political-Military

Affairs, Department of State, before the Subcommittee on International Security, Proliferation, and Federal Services, of the Committee on Governmental Affairs, U.S. Senate, April 10, 1997. http://www.fas.ort/spp/starwars/congress/1997/s970410e.htm.

Eisenstadt, Michael. *Chinese Military Assistance to Iran: An Overview*. Testimony before the House of Representatives Committee on International Relations, Congress of the United States, September 12, 1996, 37–40.

Entessar, Nadar. "The People's Republic of China and Iran: An Overview of Their Relationship." *Asia Quarterly* (Brussels) 1 (1978): 79–88.

Etemad, Akbar, "Iran." In *A European Non-Proliferation Policy, Prospects and Problems*. Edited by Harald Muller, 203–27. Oxford: Clarendon Press, 1987.

"Ever More Perilous Isolation." *Economist* 363, no. 8274 (May 25, 2002): 44–45.

Facts on File. New York: Facts on File Inc.

Fairbank, John K., and Edwin O. Reischauer. *East Asia: The Modern Transformation*. Boston: Houghton Mifflin, 1965.

Ferguson, Charles D., and Jack Boureston. "IAEA Puts Iranian Laser-Enrichment Technology in the Spotlight." *Jane's Intelligence Review* 6, no. 7 (July 2004): 38–41.

Fesharaki, Fereidun, and Mehdi Varzi. "Investment Opportunities Starting to Open up in Iran's Petroleum Sector." *Oil and Gas Journal* 98, no. 7 (February 14, 2000).

"Five Nations to Help Iran with Satellites." *Defense News*, August 10–16, 1998.

Foot, Rosemary. "China's New Relationship with Iran." *Contemporary Review* 226, no. 1 (February 1, 1975): 100–104.

Ford Foundation. *The United Nations and the Iran-Iraq War*. New York: Ford Foundation, August 1987.

Frantz, Douglas. "Iran Closes in on Ability to Make Atomic Bomb." *Los Angeles Times*, June 19, 2003.

———. "Iran Says It Received 1,800 Kg of Uranium from China." Deutsche Presse-Agentur, June 10, 2003.

Garcia, Jose Manuel. *The Persian Gulf: In the 16th and 17th Centuries*. Tehran: Center of Documents and Diplomatic History, Publishing House of the Foreign Ministry, 2002.

Garver, John W. "The China-India-U.S. Triangle: Strategic Relations in the Post–Cold War Era." *NBR Analysis* 13, no. 5 (October 2002): 5–56.

———. "China's U.S. Policies." In *China Rising: Power and Motivation in Chinese Foreign Policy*. Edited by Yong Deng and Fei-ling Wang, 201–43. Lanham, MD: Rowman and Littlefield, 2005.

———. *Protracted Contest: Sino-Indian Rivalry in the Twentieth Century*. Seattle: University of Washington Press, 2001.

Gertz, Bill. *The China Threat: How the People's Republic Targets America*. Washington, DC: Regnery Publishing, 2000.

Gibb, H. A. R. *The Arab Conquests in Central Asia*. London: Royal Asiatic Society, 1923.

Gilinsky, Victor. "Iran's 'Legal' Paths to the Bomb." In *Checking Iran's Nuclear Ambitions*. Edited by Henry Sokolski and Patrick Clawson, 23–38. Carlisle Barracks, PA: Strategic Studies Institute, U.S. Army War College, 2004.

Gilks, Anne, and Gerald Segal. *China and the Arms Trade*. New York: St. Martin's Press, 1985.

Gill, R. Bates. *The Challenge of Chinese Arms Proliferation: U.S. Policy for the 1990s*. Carlisle Barracks, PA: Strategic Studies Institute, U.S. Army War College, 1993.

———. "Chinese Arms Exports to Iran." In *China and the Middle East: The Quest for Influence*. Edited by P. R. Kumaraswamy, 117–41. New Delhi: Sage Publications, 1999.

———. *Chinese Arms Transfers: Purposes, Patterns, and Prospects in the New World Order*. Westport, CT: Greenwood Publishing, 1992.

———. "The Impact of Economic Reform upon Chinese Defense Production." Paper presented to the sixth annual PLA conference, Coolfont, WV, June 9–11, 1995.

———. "Two Steps Forward, One Step Back: The Dynamics of Chinese Nonproliferation and Arms Control Policy-Making in an Era of Reform." In *The Making of Chinese Foreign and Security Policy in the Era of Reform*. Edited by David M. Lampton, 257–88. Stanford, CA: Stanford University Press, 2001.

Goldstein, Avery. "The Diplomatic Face of China's Grand Strategy: A Rising Power's Emerging Choice." *China Quarterly* 168 (December 2001): 835–64.

Gorwitz, Mark. "Foreign Assistance to Iran's Nuclear and Missile Programs: Emphasis on Russian Assistance, Analysis and Assessment." Unpublished manuscript, October 1998.

Grimmett, Richard F. *Trends in Conventional Arms Transfers to the Third World by Major Supplier, 1980–1987*. Report no. 88–352. Washington, DC: Congressional Research Service, May 9, 1988.

Harris, Lillian Craig. "The Gulf Crisis and China's Middle East Dilemma." *Pacific Review* 4, no. 2 (1991): 116–25.

Hashim, Ahmed. *The Crisis of the Iranian State: Domestic, Foreign and Security Policies in Post-Khomeini Iran*. Aldelphi Paper no. 296. London: International Institute of Strategic Studies, 1995.

Hewson, Robert. "China, Iran Share Missile Know-How." *Jane's Defence Weekly* 38, no. 23 (December 4, 2002): 15.

———. "China-Iraq Ties: Military Assistance for Oil." Headquarters of

USCINCPAC, Virtual Information Center, February 23, 2001. http://www.petrelresources.com.Iraq_html.html (accessed April 2004).

Hibbs, Mark. "China Agrees to End Nuclear Trade with Iran When Two Projects Completed." *NuclearFuel*, no. 3 (1997): 3–4.

———. "China Has Far to Go before U.S. Will Certify, Agencies Now Say." *Nucleonics Week* 37, no. 50 (December 12, 1996).

———. "German-U.S. Nerves Frayed." *NuclearFuel*, March 14, 1994.

———. "Sensitive Iran Reactor Deal May Hinge on MFN for China." *Nucleonics Week*, October 1, 1992, 5–6.

———. "U.S. in 1983 Stopped IAEA from Helping Iran Make UF6." *NuclearFuel* 28, no. 16 (August 4, 2003): 12.

Hickey, Dennis Van Vranken. "New Directions in China's Arms for Export Policy: An Analysis of China's Military Ties with Iran." *Asian Affairs: An American Review* 17, no. 1 (Spring 1990): 15–29.

Hiebert, Murray, and Nayan Chanda. "Dangerous Liaisons." *Far Eastern Economic Review* 163, no. 29 (July 20, 2000):16–16.

Hiro, Dilip. *The Longest War: The Iran-Iraq Military Conflict*. New York: Routledge, 1991.

Hua Di. "China's Case: Ballistic Missile Proliferation." In *The International Missile Bazaar: The New Suppliers Network*. Edited by William Potter and Harlan Jenks, 173–77. San Francisco: Westview Press, 1994.

Huntington, Samuel P. *Political Order in Changing Societies*. New Haven, CT: Yale University Press, 1968.

Huo, Hwei-ling. "Patterns of Behavior in China's Foreign Policy: The Gulf Crisis and Beyond." *Asian Survey* 32, no. 3 (March 1992): 263–76.

International Atomic Energy Agency. "Implementation of the NPT Safeguards Agreement with the Islamic Republic of Iran." Report by the Director General to the IAEA Board of Governors, original date November 10, 2003 (GOV/2003/75), derestricted November 26, 2003.

———. "Implementation of the NPT Safeguards Agreement with the Islamic Republic of Iran." November 15, 2004 (GOV/2004/83), derestricted November 29, 2004. http://iaea.org/publications/documents/board/2003/gov2003.75.pdf and 2004/gov2004.83.pdf.

"Iran." *Jane's Intelligence Review*, December 1992, 560–61.

"Iran: Chinese Arms Deal Claimed; Missiles." *Defense and Foreign Affairs Daily* (Washington, DC) 14, no. 60 (April 1, 1985): 1.

Iran: Time for a New Approach. Report of an independent task force sponsored by the Council on Foreign Relations. New York: Council on Foreign Relations, 2004.

"Iran/China in Secret Missile Project." *Flight International* 4370, no. 143 (May 19–25, 1993): 16.

"Iranian ssms in Production." *Aerospace/Defense Markets and Technology*, April 1991, 156.

"Iran's Chinese Air Force." *Middle East Defense News* 2, no. 4 (November 21, 1988): 1–2.

"Iran's Chinese Shopping List." *Iran Brief*, October 1, 1996.

"Iran Seeking Solid Rocket Fuel." *Iran Brief*, January 9, 1995.

"Iran's Nuclear Program, Enriching." *Economist* 368, no. 8332 (July 12, 2003): 42.

"Iran's Nuclear Program, Fissionable" *Economist* 367, no. 8328 (June 14, 2003): 24.

"Iran's Uranium Program." *Iran Brief*, June 1, 1995.

"Iran Told IAEA It Will Build Chinese UF6 Plant at Isfahan." *NuclearFuel* 21, no. 26 (December 16, 1996).

"Iran Turns East: A Chronology of Iranian Relations with the Eastern Bloc and China, January–June 1989." *Middle East Defense News*, July 10, 1989, 3–5.

Israeli, Raphael. "China's Muslims." In *The World's Religions*. Edited by Stewart Sutherland et al., 408–24. London and New York: Routledge, 1988.

———. *Islam in China: Religion, Ethnicity, Culture, and Politics*. Boulder, CO, and New York: Lexington Books, 2002.

———. "Medieval Muslim Travelers to China." *Journal of Muslim Minority Affairs* 20, no. 2 (2000): 313–21.

Jacobs, Gordon, and Tim McCarthy. "China's Missile Sales—Few Changes for the Future." *Jane's Intelligence Review* 4, no. 12 (December 1992): 559–63.

Jane's Fighting Ships, 2003–2004. Edited by Stephen Saunders. Surrey, UK: Jane's Information Group, 2004.

Jane's Land-based Air Defense, 2004–2005. Edited by James C. O'Halloran. Surrey, UK: Jane's Information Group, 2004.

Jane's Naval Weapons Systems. Edited by E. R. Hooton. Surrey, UK: Jane's Information Group, 2001.

Jane's Strategic Weapons Systems. Edited by Duncan Lennox. Surrey, UK: Jane's Information Group, 2004.

Jane's Underwater Warfare Systems, 2004–2005. Edited by Anthony J. Watts. Surrey, UK: Jane's Information Group, 2004.

Joffe, Ellis. "China after the Gulf War: The Lessons Learned." Paper prepared for the Center for National Security Studies, Los Alamos National Laboratory, November 1991.

Kan, Shirley A. *China and Proliferation of Weapons of Mass Destruction and Missiles: Policy Issues*. Report no. RL 31555. Washington, DC: Congressional Research Service, updated August 8, 2003.

———. *China's Compliance with International Arms Control Agreements*. Report to Congress, no. 97–850F. Washington, DC: Congressional Research Service, updated January 16, 1998.

————. *Chinese Proliferation of Weapons of Mass Destruction: Background and Analysis*. Report, no. 96–767F. Washington, DC: Congressional Research Service, September 13, 1996.

Karniol, Robert. "Iran and China in $4.5 Billion Partnership." *Jane's Defence Weekly* 28, no. 5 (September 11, 1996): 3.

Katzman, Kenneth. *Iran: Arms and Technology Acquisitions*. Report to Congress, no. RL 30551. Washington, DC: Congressional Research Service, updated January 26, 2001.

————. *Iran: Arms and Weapons of Mass Destruction Suppliers*. Report to Congress, no. RL 30551. Washington, DC: Congressional Research Service, January 3, 2003.

————. *Iran: Military Relations with China*. Report to Congress, no. 96–572F. Washington, DC: Congressional Research Service, updated June 26, 1996.

Keesing's Contemporary Archives. London.

Kennedy, Bingham, Jr. "Curbing Chinese Missile Sales: From Imposing to Negotiating China's Adherence to the MTCR." *Journal of Northeast Asian Studies* 15, no. 4 (Spring 1996): 57–68.

Khomeini, Ayatollah Ruhollah. *Ayatollah Khomeini: On Issues related to the Struggle of the Muslim People of Iran; Speeches of January 1978–January 1980*. San Francisco: Consulate General of the IRI, n.d.

————. *A Clarification of Questions: An Unabridged Translation of Resaleh Towzih al-Masael*. Translated by J. Borujerdi. Boulder, CO, and London: Westview Press, 1984.

————. *Imam's Final Discourse: The Text of the Political and Religious Testament of the Leader of the Islamic Revolution and the Founder of the Islamic Republic of Iran, Imam Khomeini*. [Tehran?]: Ministry of Guidance of Islamic Culture, [1990?].

————. *Islamic Government*. Translations on Near East and North Africa, no. 1897, JPRS-72663. Arlington, VA: U.S. Joint Publications Research Services, January 19, 1979.

————. *Selected Messages and Speeches of Imam Khomeini (from Oct. 1980 to Jan. 1982)*. N.p.: Ministry of Islamic Guidance, March 1982.

Khorram, Ali. "Joint Cooperation between China, India, and Iran." *Iranian Journal of International Affairs* 7, no. 1 (Spring 1995): 197–200.

Kibaroglu, Mustafa. "Is Iran Going Nuclear?" *Foreign Policy* 20, nos. 3–4 (1996): 35–55.

Kitfield, James. "China's Long March." *National Journal* 30 (April 25, 1998): 926–29.

Koch, Andrew, and Jeanette Wolf. "Iran's Nuclear Procurement Program: How Close to the Bomb?" *Nonproliferation Review* 5, no. 1 (Fall 1997):123–35.

Krosney, Herbert. *Deadly Business, Legal Deals and Outlaw Weapons: The Arming of Iran and Iraq, 1975 to the Present*. New York: Four Walls Eight Windows, 1993.

Lam, Willy Wo-lap. *The Era of Jiang Zemin*. Singapore: Prentice Hall, 1999.

Lampton, David M. *Same Bed, Different Dreams: Managing U.S.-China Relations, 1989–2000*. Berkeley: University of California Press, 2001.

Lawrence, Susan. "Non-Proliferation: China's Perspective." *Far Eastern Economic Review* 163, no. 29 (July 20, 2000): 18.

———. "Ties That Bind." *Far Eastern Economic Review* 166, no. 22 (June 5, 2003): 26.

Laylaz, Saeed. *The Era of Construction: A Narration of Eight Years of Construction during the Presidency of Hashemi Rafsanjani*. 3 vols. Tehran: Nashr-e Kelid, 1997.

Lee, Deng-ker. "Peking's Middle East Policy in the Post–Cold War Era." *Issues and Studies* 30, no. 8 (August 1994): 69–94.

Lee, Julian. "FSU Oil Exports through Iran Set to Increase." *Oil and Gas Journal*, April 7, 2003, 68–70.

Lee, Wei-chin. "The Birth of a Salesman: China as an Arms Supplier." *Journal of Northeast Asian Studies* 6, no. 4 (Winter 1987–88): 32–46.

Lennox, Duncan. "Iran's Ballistic Missile Projects: Uncovering the Evidence." *Jane's Intelligence Review* 10, no. 6 (June 1998): 24.

Lewis, John W., and Di Hua. "China's Ballistic Missile Programs." *International Security* 17, no. 2 (Fall 1992): 5–40.

Lewis, John W., and Xue Litai. *China Builds the Bomb*. Stanford, CA: Stanford University Press, 1988.

Liu Yingsheng, and Peter Jackson. "Chinese-Iranian Relations in the Mongol Period." Encyclopaedia Iranica. http://www.iranica.com/articlenavigation/alphabetical/body.html.

Lotfian, Saideh. "Threat Perception and Military Planning in Iran: Credible Scenarios of Conflict and Opportunities for Confidence Building." In *Military Capacity and the Risk of War*. Edited by Eric Arnett, 195–215. London: Oxford University Press, 1999.

Lu Ning. *The Dynamics of Foreign Policy Decisionmaking in China*. Boulder, CO: Westview Press, 2000.

Mahmood, Sohail. *Islamic Fundamentalism in Pakistan, Egypt, and Iran*. Lahore, Karachi, and Islamabad, Pakistan: Vanguard Books, 1995.

Majul, Cesar Adib. "The Iranian Revolution and the Muslims in the Philippines." In *The Iranian Revolution: Its Global Impact*. Edited by John Esposito, 263–78. Miami: Florida International University Press, 1990.

Maleki, Abbas. "The Islamic Republic of Iran's Foreign Policy: The View from Iran." *Iranian Journal of International Affairs* 7 (Winter 1996): 744–919.

Malik, Mohan. "China and the Nuclear Non-Proliferation Regime." *Contemporary Southeast Asia* 22, no. 3 (December 2000): 445–78.

———. "China Plays 'The Proliferation Card.'" *Jane's Intelligence Review* 12, no. 7 (July 2000): 34–36.

———. "Nuclear Proliferation in Asia: The China Factor." *Australian Journal of International Affairs* 53, no. 1 (1999): 31–41.

Mann, James. *About Face: A History of America's Curious Relation with China, from Nixon to Clinton*. New York: Alfred Knopf, 1999.

Mann, Paul. "China Alleged Top Trafficker in Mass Destruction Weapons." *Aviation Week and Space Technology* 147, no. 5 (August 4, 1997): 42.

Massoudi, Sen. Abbas. *China: A Land of Marvels*. Tehran: Iran Chap Press, 1973.

McDougall, Walter A. *Let the Sea Make a Noise: A History of the North Pacific from Magellan to MacArthur*. New York: Basic Books, 1993.

Medeiros, Evan S. "Rebuilding Bilateral Consensus: Assessing U.S.-China Arms Control and Nonproliferation Achievements." *Nonproliferation Review* 8, no. 1 (Spring 2001): 131–40.

———. *3rd U.S.-China Conference on Arms Control, Disarmament and Nonproliferation, U.S.-China Arms Control and Nonproliferation Cooperation: Progress and Prospects*. Conference Report, Center for Nonproliferation Studies. Monterey, CA: Monterey Institute of International Studies, September 2000.

"Merchants of Death." *Newsweek* 118, no. 21 (November 18, 1991): 38–39.

Mosher, Steven W. *Hegemon: China's Plan to Dominate Asia and the World*. San Francisco: Encounter Books, 2000.

Mraz, Major Jerry L. "Dual Containment: U.S. Policy in the Persian Gulf and a Recommendation for the Future." Research paper in partial fulfillment of graduation requirements of the Air Command Staff College, March 1997, AU/ACSC/0305/97–03.

Mullins, Robert E. "The Dynamics of Chinese Missile Proliferation." *Pacific Review* 8, no. 1 (1995): 137–57.

Murray, Raymond L. *Nuclear Energy. An Introduction to the Concepts, Systems, and Applications of Nuclear Processes*. Boston: Butterworth, 2001.

Nabavi, Jamshid. "A Commentary on Relations between Iran and the People's Republic of China." *Relations Internationales, International Relations* (Centers des hautes etudes internationales de university Tehran) 2 (Winter 1974–75): 127–38.

"News in Brief." *Jane's Defence Weekly* 11, no. 1 (January 7, 1989): 8.

New York Times. New York.

Nuclear Regulatory Commission. "NRC Issues Licenses Allowing Westinghouse to Export Nuclear Reactor Equipment and Fuel to China." NRC News, no. 05–037, February 25, 2005. http://www.nrc.gov.org/.

Nuclear Threat Initiative. "China's Missile Exports and Assistance to Iran." http://www.nti.org/db/china/miranpos.htm.

————. "China's Nuclear Exports and Assistance to Iran." http://www.nti.org/db/
    china/niranpos.htm.
Nuclear Threat Initiative and Center for Nonproliferation Studies, Monterey
    Institute of International Studies. "Iran Nuclear Chronology." http://www.nti
    .org/e_research/e1_iran/nch.html.
Oehler, Gordon. Testimony to Hearing of Senate Foreign Relations Committee on
    Proliferation of Chinese Missiles, June 11, 1998. http://www.lexisnexis.com/.
Pahlavi, Mohammad Reza. *The Shah's Story*. London: Michael Joseph, 1980.
Palmer, Michael A. *Guardians of the Gulf: A History of America's Expanding Role in
    the Persian Gulf, 1832–1992*. New York: Macmillan, 1992.
Peking Review. Beijing, 1979–2004.
"Proliferation Briefing: China." *Middle East Defense News*, December 1992, 3.
The Proliferation Primer. A Majority Report of the Subcommittee on International
    Security, Proliferation, and Federal Services, Committee on Governmental
    Affairs, U.S. Senate, January 1998.
Pulleyblank, Edwin G. "Chinese-Iranian Relations, Pre-Islamic Times." In Ency-
    clopaedia Iranica. http://www.iranica.com/articlenavigation/alphabetical/
    body.html.
Rafsanjani, Ali Akbar Hashemi. "Address by Ali Akbar Hashemi-Rafsanjani, Presi-
    dent of the Islamic Republic of Iran." Conference of Center for Persian Gulf
    Studies, Institute for Political and International Studies, Tehran, Iran, Novem-
    ber 20, 1988. Translated in *Middle East Journal* 44, no. 3 (Summer 1990): 459–66.
Ramazani, Rouhollah K. "Emerging Patterns of Regional Relations in Iranian
    Foreign Policy." *Orbis* 18, no. 4 (Winter 1975): 1043–69.
————. "Iran's Export of the Revolution: Politics, Ends, and Means." In *The
    Iranian Revolution: Its Global Impact*. Edited by John Esposito, 40–62. Miami:
    Florida International University Press, 1990.
————. "Iran's Foreign Policy: Both North and South." *Middle East Journal* 46,
    no. 3 (Summer 1993): 393–412.
————. "Iran's Foreign Policy: Contending Orientations." *Middle East Journal* 43,
    no. 2 (Spring 1989): 202–17.
————. *Iran's Foreign Policy, 1941–1973: A Study of Foreign Policy in Modernizing
    Nations*. Charlottesville: University of Virginia Press, 1975.
————. *Revolutionary Iran: Challenge and Response in the Middle East*. Baltimore
    and London: Johns Hopkins University Press, 1986.
Rashid, Ahmed. "China Forced to Expand Role in Central Asia." *Central Asia—
    Caucasus Analyst*, July 19, 2000. http://icas.org/english/enlibrary/libr_26
    _7_00_l.htm.
————. *Jihad: The Rise of Militant Islam in Central Asia*. New York: Penguin
    Books, 2003.

Rashid, Ahmed, and Lorien Holland. "Sifting Sands." *Far Eastern Economic Review* 163, no. 9 (March 2, 2000): 26–27.

Rogers, J. M. "Chinese-Iranian Relations in the Safavid Period." Encyclopaedia Iranica. http://www.iranica.com/articlenavigation/alphabetical/body.html.

Roshandel, Jalil. "Iran." In *Nuclear Weapons after the Comprehensive Test Ban: Implications for Modernization and Proliferation*. Edited by Eric Arnett, 55–61. London: Oxford University Press, 1996.

Rotar, Igor. "The Growing Problem of Uigur Separatism." *China Brief* 4, no. 98 (August 15, 2004).

Roth, Stanley. Testimony of Stanley O. Roth Assistant Secretary of State for East Asia and Political Affairs, Senate Foreign Relations Committee, May 14, 1998. http://usinfo.state.gov/regional/ea/uschina/roth514.htm.

Rubin, Barry. "China's Middle East Strategy." In *China and the Middle East: The Quest for Influence*. Edited by P. R. Kumaraswamy, 108–16. New Delhi: Sage Publications, 1999.

"Russia, China, Iran, and India Agree to Fusion R&D Cooperation." *Nucleonics Week*, February 21, 1996, 15.

Ruthven, Malise. *Islam in the World*. New York: Oxford University Press, 1984.

Rynhold, Jonathan. "China's Cautious New Pragmatism in the Middle East." *Survival* 38 (Autumn 1996): 102–16.

Saikal, Amin. *The Rise and Fall of the Shah*. Princeton, NJ: Princeton University Press, 1980.

"Sales Complaints." *Aviation Week and Space Technology* 125, no. 9 (September 1, 1986): 35.

Saunders, Phillip C. "Preliminary Analysis of Chinese Missile Technology Export Control List." Center for Nonproliferation Studies, Monterey Institute of International Studies, September 6, 2002. http://cns.miis.edu/.

Saunders, Phillip C., and Stephanie C. Lieggl. "What's behind U.S. Nonproliferation Sanctions against Norinco?" Center for Nonproliferation Studies, Monterey Institute of International Studies, May 30, 2003. http://cns.miis.edu/.

Sayigh, Zezid. "Arms Production in Pakistan and Iran: The Limits of Self-Reliance." In *Military Capacity and the Risk of War: China, India, Pakistan, and Iran*. Edited by Eric Arnett, 176–94. London: Oxford University Press, 1999.

"The Secret Missile Deal." *Time* 149, no. 29 (June 30, 1997): 29.

Shahi, Agha. *Pakistan's Security and Foreign Policy*. Lahore, Pakistan: Progressive Publishers, 1988.

Shalom, Stephen R. "The United States and the Iran-Iraq War." http://www.zmag.org/zmag/articles/ShalomIranIraq.html.

Shichor, Yitzhak. *East Wind over Arabia: Origins and Implications of the Sino-Saudi*

Missile Deal. Institute of East Asian Studies, Research Monograph no. 35.
Berkeley: University of California, Berkeley, 1989.

———. "The Middle East." In *Chinese Defence Policy.* Edited by Gerald Segal and
William T. Tow, 263–78. London: Macmillan, 1984.

———. "Mountains out of Molehills: Arms Transfers in Sino–Middle East Relations." *Middle East Review of International Affairs* 4, no. 3 (September 2000).

———. "Unfolded Arms: Beijing's Recent Military Sales Offensive." *Pacific Review*
1, no. 3 (1988): 320–30.

———. "The Year of the Silkworms: China's Arms Transactions, 1987." In scps
Yearbook on PLA Affairs, 153–79. Kaohsiung: Sun Yat-sen Center for China
Policy Studies, 1988.

Shultz, George. *Turmoil and Triumph.* New York: Scribner's, 1993.

Sick, Gary. "Trial by Error: Reflections on the Iran-Iraq War." *Middle East Journal*
43, no. 2 (Spring 1989): 230–45.

"Sino-Iranian Nuclear Pact Alleged." *Nuclear Week*, May 2, 1991, 17.

Sokolski, Henry. "Faking It and Making It." *National Interest* 51 (Spring 1998):
67–80.

"Special Report: The Zelzal Missile Program." *Iran Brief*, September 9, 1996.

Spector, Leonard S. *Going Nuclear.* Cambridge, MA: Ballinger Publishing
Company, 1989.

———. "Iran's Secret Quest for the Bomb." *Yale Global*, May 16, 2003. http://
yaleglobal.yale.edu/.

———. Testimony of Leonard S. Spector, Jing-dong Yuan, and Phillip C.
Saunders. Hearing on China's Proliferation Policies and Practices, U.S.-China
Economic and Security Review Commission. July 24, 2003. http://www.cns
.miis.edu/research/congress/testim/testisp.htm.

Starr, Barbara. "Iran Adds New Threat with Cruise Missile Test." *Jane's Defence
Weekly* 25, no. 6 (February 7, 1996): 14.

———. "U.S. Links Chinese Ties to Missile Exports." *Jane's Defence Weekly* 22, no.
15 (October 15, 1994): 6.

Stockholm International Peace Research Institute (sipri). *The Arms Trade with
the Third World.* New York: Holmes and Meier, 1975.

———. *sipri Yearbook: World Armaments and Disarmament.* New York and
Oxford: Oxford University Press. Annual.

Strategic Survey. London: International Institute of International Studies. Annual.

Suettinger, Robert L. *Beyond Tiananmen: The Politics of U.S.-China Relations, 1989–
2000.* Washington, DC: Brookings Institution Press, 2003.

Sykes, Percy. *A History of Persia.* 3 vols. London: Routledge and Kegan Paul, 1969.

"Tehran-Moscow-Beijing Axis against the West." *Iran Report* 4, no. 33 (September
3, 2001).

Tehran Times. Daily newspaper published in Tehran. U.S. Library of Congress has microfilm archive. Recent issues available at http://www.tehrantimes.com/archives/.

"Tehran Upgrades Chinese Missile." *IAEA Daily Press Review*, January 12, 2000.

Timperlake, Edward, and William C. Triplett II. *Red Dragon Rising: Communist China's Military Threat to America*. Washington, DC: Regnery Publishing, 1999.

Tonchev, Plamen. "China and Iran: A New Tandem in World Energy Security." *Iranian Journal of International Affairs* 10, no. 4 (Winter 1998–99): 483–99.

"The Tondar-68 and Iran-700 Programme." *Jane's Intelligence Review*, April 1992, 151.

Twitchett, Denis, and Howard Wechsler. "Kao-tsung (Reign 649–683) and the Empress Wu: The Inheritor and the Usurper." In *The Cambridge History of China; Volume 3: Sui and T'ang China, 589–906; Part 1*. Edited by Denis Twitchett and John K. Fairbank, 242–89. Taipei: Caves Books, 1989.

Tyler, Patrick. *A Great Wall, Six Presidents and China: An Investigative History*. New York: A Century Foundation Book, 1999.

"Uranium Exploration with China." *Iran Brief*, May 6, 1996.

U.S. Congress. House of Representatives. *Consequences of China's Military Sales to Iran*. Hearings before the Committee on International Relations. 104th Cong., 2nd sess., September 12, 1996.

————. *Developments in the Middle East, May 1986*. Hearings before the Subcommittee on Europe and the Middle East of the Committee on Foreign Affairs. 96th Cong., 2nd sess., May 6, 1986.

————. *Sino-American Relations and U.S. Policy Options*. Hearings before the Asia and Pacific Subcommittee of the Committee on International Relations. 105th Cong., 1st sess., April 23, 1997.

U.S. Congress. Senate. *The Arming of Iran: Who Is Responsible?* Hearings before the Subcommittee on Near Eastern and South Asian Affairs. 105th Cong., 1st sess., May 6, 1997.

————. *Iran's Ballistic Missile and Weapons of Mass Destruction Programs*. Hearings before the Subcommittee on International Security, Proliferation, and Federal Services of the Committee on Governmental Affairs. 106th Cong., 2nd sess., September 21, 2000.

————. *Proliferation: Chinese Case Studies*. Hearing before the Subcommittee on International Security, Proliferation, and Federal Services of the Committee on Governmental Affairs. 105th Cong., 1st sess., April 10, 1997.

U.S. Department of State. *Adherence to and Compliance with Arms Control and Nonproliferation Agreements and Commitments, Prepared by the U.S. Department of State*. Washington, DC: U.S. Department of State, [2003].

"U.S. Protests Chinese Hex Plant." *Iran Brief*, July 3, 1997.

Van Ness, Peter. *Revolution and Chinese Foreign Policy: Peking's Support for Wars of National Liberation*. Berkeley: University of California Press, 1971.

Wallerstein, Mitchel B. "China and Proliferation: A Path Not Taken." *Survival* 38, no. 3 (1996): 58–66.

Washington Post. District of Columbia.

Washington Times. District of Columbia.

"Weapons Bazaar." *U.S. News and World Report* 121, no. 23 (December 9, 1996): 27–38.

Weapons of Mass Destruction: The Cases of Iran, Syria, and Libya. Los Angeles and Paris: Middle East Defense News / Simon Wiesenthal Center, August 1992.

Woon, Eden Y. "Chinese Arms Sales and U.S. China Military Relations." *Asian Survey* 29, no. 6 (June 1989): 601–18.

Xia, Liping. "A Study of Non-Proliferation of Nuclear Weapons in the Asia-Pacific Region." Unpublished manuscript. Institute for Strategic Studies, PLA National Defense University, China, March 1994.

CHINESE-LANGUAGE SOURCES

An Baojun. "Yilang jingji xiankuang ji zhong, yi maoyi guanxi" [Iran's Current Economic Situation and Sino-Iranian Trade Relations]. *Xiya feizhou* [West Asia and Africa], no. 4 (1995): 66–68.

An Weihua. "Zhongguo yu zhongdong de nengyuan hezuo" [China's Energy Cooperation in the Middle East]. *Xiya feizhou*, no. 1 (2001): 12–16.

Chen Shuangqing. "Zai anquan yu lili zhijian qiu pingheng—haiwan zhanzheng hou de haiwan guojia guanxi" [Searching for Balance between Security and Interest—Relations among the Gulf Nations since the Gulf War]. *Xiandai guoji guanxi* [Contemporary International Relations] 11 (1996): 30–33.

Chen Zhaohua, Wang Fei. "Yilang 'he wenti' yu meiguo dui yi zhengce" [Iran's 'Nuclear Problem' and American Policy toward Iran]. *Xiandai guoji guanxi*, no. 1 (2004): 21–25.

Deng Xiaoping nianbu, 1975–1997 [Deng Xiaoping Chronicle, 1975–1997]. 2 vols. Beijing: Zhongyang wenxian chubanshe, 2004.

Di san shijie shiyou duozheng [The Third World's Oil Struggle]. Beijing: San lian shudian, 1981.

Dong Fangshao. "9.11 zhi hou meiguo baquan xia de zhongdong" [The Middle East under U.S. Hegemonism after 9.11]. *Xiya feizhou*, no. 6 (2002): 4–9.

Dong Manyuan. "Haiwan zhanzheng hou de zhongdong dichu anquan wenti tan-tao" [Investigation of Middle East Regional Security since the (1991) Gulf War]. *Xiya feizhou*, no. 6 (1991): 1–4.

Fan Hongda. "Geming hou de yaojin: yilang waijiao fenxi" [Postrevolutionary Great Leap: Analysis of Iran's Diplomacy]. *Zhongdong yanjiu* [Middle East Studies] 2 (2002): 35–40.

———. "Meiguo yilang guanxi dongxiang" [The Tendency of U.S.-Iran Relations]. *Xiya feizhou*, no. 1 (2002): 11–13.

Fu Mengzi. "Bushi 'dao sa' yitu ji yinxiang" [Bush's Intention of 'Ousting Saddam' and Its Influence]. *Xiandai guoji guanxi* 10 (2002): 46–54.

Gao Zugui. "Bushi zhengfu dui yilang zhengce fenxi" [Analysis of the Bush Government's Policy toward Iran]. *Xiya feizhou*, no. 3 (2004): 45–51.

Hao Zhengeng. "Yilang he elousi: Zai zhong ya de jiezhuxing lianmeng" [Iran and Russia: Alliance of Mutual Use in Central Asia]. *Xiya feizhou*, no. 6 (2001): 29–32.

Hu Ling. "Mei yi guanxi xianzhuang ji zuoxiang" [The Current Status and Trend in U.S.-Iran Relations]. *Xiya feizhou*, no. 4 (2001): 17–22.

Li Li. "Cong 'shuang zhong ezhi' zhengce shousuo kan meiguo yu yilang guanxi" [U.S.-Iran Relations from the Perspective of Setbacks in the Policy of "Dual Containment"]. *Xiandai guoji guanxi* 10 (1997): 19–21.

Qian Qichen. *Waijiao shi ji* [Ten Diplomatic Episodes]. Beijing: Shijie zhishe chubanshe, 2003.

Shijie chanyou guo, zhongdong dichu [Oil Producing Countries of the World, Middle East Region]. Edited by Wu Yaowen. Beijing: Foreign Affairs Office, Information Research Center, China National Petroleum Corporation, August 1998.

Tang Baocai. "Fangwen liang yi zaji" [Miscellaneous Recollections of a Visit to Iraq and Iran]. *Xiya feizhou*, no. 2 (2001): 68–70.

———. "Lengzhan hou daguo haiwan zhengce bijiao" [Comparison of the Gulf Policies of the Major Powers since the End of the Cold War]. *Xiya feizhou*, no. 4 (2001): 10–16.

Tang Shiping. "Lixiang anquan huanjing yu xin shiji zhongguo da zhanlue" [Ideal Security Environment and China's Grand Strategy in the New Century]. *Zhanlue yu guanli* [Strategy and Management], no. 6 (2000): 45–46.

Tan Han. "Meiguo junkong zhengce de yanbian" [Evolution of U.S. Arms Control Policy]. *Guoji wenti yanjiu* [International Studies], no. 4 (October 13, 1993): 18–22, 48.

Wang Feng. "Bushi zhengfu dui yilang de zhengce yu yilang de huiying" [The Bush Government's Policy toward Iran and Iran's Response]. *Xiya feizhou*, no. 1 (2003): 23–27.

———. "Liang yi zhanzheng hou yilang neiwai zhengce tiaozheng shuping" [Description of Iran's Internal and Foreign Policy Adjustments since the End of the Iran-Iraq War]. *Xiya feizhou*, no. 4 (1996): 34–39.

———. "Yilang he wenti jiqi zuoshi" [The Iranian Nuclear Issue and Its Direction of Development]. *Xiya feizhou*, no. 1 (2004): 35–41.

Wang Jiping, Hong Yousheng, and Ji Liqiang. "Yilang he wenti yu daguo guanxi" [The Iranian Nuclear Issue and Great Power Relations]. *Meiguo yanjiu* [American Studies], no. 1 (2004): 78–90.

Wang Taiping, ed. *Xin zhongguo waijiao wushi nian* [Fifty Years of New China's Diplomacy]. Beijing: Beijing chubanshe, 1999.

Wu Chengyi. "Lengzhan hou de meiguo zhongdong zhanlue jiqi yinxiang" [U.S. Strategy in the Middle East since the End of the Cold War and Its Influence]. *Xiandai guoji guanxi* 5 (1998): 15–19.

Wu Qiang and Qian Xuemei. "Zhongguo yu zhongdong de nengyuan hezuo" [China's Energy Cooperation with the Middle East]. *Zhanlue yu guanli* 2 (1999): 49–51.

Xiangmu kexing yanjiu jixu jingji, sanshu yu shuzhu, 2000 [Research on the Economic and Technological Feasibility of Projects, 2000]. Beijing: Sinopec, jingji jishu yanjiu yuan, 2000.

Xue Muhong et al. *Dang dai zhongguo waijiao* [Contemporary China's Diplomacy]. Beijing: Zhongguo shehui kexue yuan, 1987.

Yang Xingli. "Jiushi niandai yilang de dui wai zhanlue" [Iran's Foreign Strategy in the 1990s]. *Xiya feizhou*, no. 4 (1996): 28–31.

Yi Shui. "Yilang xuezhe zai xiya feizhou suo jieshao yilang" [Iranian Scholars Introduce Iran to the Institute of West Asia and Africa Studies]. *Xiya feizhou*, no. 5 (2000): 60.

Yu Jianhua. "Dangdai zhong yi guanxi yu yilang dui hua zhengce dongyin" [Contemporary Sino-Iranian Relations and the Driving Factors of Iranian Policy toward China]. *Xiya feizhou*, no. 4 (1998): 43–47.

Yun Shuizhu. *Guoji fengyun zhong de zhongguo waijiaoguan* [Chinese Diplomats in the Midst of International Storms]. Beijing: Shijie zhishi chubanshe, 1992.

Zhang Yang. "Shilun meiguo dui yilang de he zhengce" [Preliminary Investigation of U.S. Policy toward Iranian Nuclear Issue]. *Xiya feizhou*, no. 2 (1999): 35–39.

Zhang Yonghong. "Meiguo dui yilang de zhengce mianlin zhongda tiaozheng" [U.S. Policy toward Iran Is Facing Major Adjustments]. *Guoji wenti yanjiu* 3 (1998): 12–15.

Zhang Zhenguo. "Yilang junzhuzhi wei shemo zhongzhi yu baliewei wangqiao" [Why Did Iran's Monarchy End with the Pahlavi Dynasty?] *Xiya feizhou*, no. 4 (1992): 15–16.

Zhonghua renmin gongheguo haiguan tongji nianjian [People's Republic of China Customs Statistical Yearbook]. Published annually. Beijing: Zhongguo haiguan [China's Customs Service].

Zhongguo waijiao gaijian [Overview of Chinese Diplomacy]. Annual volumes 1987–

95. Renamed *Zhongguo waijiao* [China's Diplomacy] in 1996, annual volumes 1996–2004. Compiled by Ministry of Foreign Relations, PRC. Beijing: Shijie zhishi chubanshe.

Zhu Jiejin. *Zhongguo he yilang guanxi shigao* [Draft History of China-Iran Relations]. Urumqi: Xinjiang renmin chubanshe, 1988.

Index